B2

D0574377

The Dictionary of
Indoor Plants
in colour

The Dictionary of
Indoor Plants
in colour

———❦———

Roy Hay, F. R. McQuown, G. and K. Beckett

Photographs supplied by

Ernest Crowson and Harry Smith

Published in collaboration with The Royal Horticultural Society

EBURY PRESS AND MICHAEL JOSEPH LIMITED, LONDON

First published in Great Britain by

Ebury Press
Chestergate House, Vauxhall Bridge Road
London SW1V 1HF and
Michael Joseph Limited
52 Bedford Square, London WC1
1974

This book was designed and produced by
Rainbird Reference Books Limited
Marble Arch House, 44 Edgware Road
London W2, England

House Editor: Curigwen Lewis
Designer: Judith Allan

Printed by
Jolly and Barber Ltd
Rugby, Warwickshire, England

ISBN 0 7181 1274 1

Contents

General Introduction

Since early in the nineteenth century growing plants in the home has been very popular in Europe and America. At one time no drawing room was complete without its potted palm, and the aspidistra was lovingly cultivated by rich and poor alike.

The Victorian era was the hey day of the conservatory, the glass extension to the house usually, but not always, heated by a coke fired boiler.

The conservatory languished between and after the wars as fuel costs and wages rose. But now thousands of home extensions with mainly glass walls are being erected, and many of them are being used to grow a wide variety of plants as well as providing extra living space.

Many of these extensions are heated and it is always wise to consider, when deciding on a central heating system, whether in a year or two a home extension will be a possibility, and if so, to install a boiler large enough to permit extension of the system to warm the home enlargement.

It is easy enough in a dwelling house to provide some form of soil warming by electricity which, as is explained later considerably reduces heating costs. It provides a really warm root temperature for plants while the air temperature can be kept much lower. Of course, if the extension is to be used as an extra sitting room in winter, temperatures of around 70 °F. will be required, and this will affect the range of plants that may be grown. For some it will be just right; for others too high for comfort.

But even without a glass walled home extension many foliage and flowering plants are grown successfully indoors on windowsills and in 'jardinières', self watering troughs, and other containers. The old copper jam pans and coal buckets, so suitable for old houses, have now almost disappeared from the antique shops and, when they do appear, are very expensive. One day no doubt some enterprising firm will produce copperized facsimile containers moulded from the originals. Some reproductions have been made, and very convincing they are.

The modern plastic containers are very suitable for modern homes, but look out of place in period houses or old cottages.

In general, plants look better if several are grouped together in an attractive container than if they are stood about singly on windowsills or suspended in imitation bird cages.

The possession of a conservatory or a heated greenhouse greatly widens the possibilities of maintaining a succession of charming plants in the home. There are, of course, many plants that may be grown happily for a number of years in a living room. There are many more that may be brought indoors from a greenhouse to give pleasure for a few weeks, or even months, but which need to go back to the more congenial conditions – for them – of the greenhouse to convalesce as it were.

With a greenhouse it is possible to have a supply of flowering plants to take into the home, and thus provide colour every day of the year. As the prices of cut flowers and potted plants are unlikely to go down, the production of one's own supply of plants is obviously worth while.

PROPAGATION

House plants and greenhouse plants may be increased in various ways – by seed, by cuttings, by air layering and, in some cases, by division. Seed sowing is dealt with later.

Cuttings

Cuttings may be of semi-hard wood – half ripened shoots, as of azaleas, but most house and greenhouse plants are propagated by soft cuttings – young shoots some 2–4 in. long. Some plants may be propagated by leaf cuttings – *Streptocarpus, Begonia rex* and its varieties, and *Saintpaulia* or African Violets.

Semi-woody and soft cuttings as of pelargoniums, hydrangeas and the like, are made from the tips of shoots usually 2–4 in. long, and are cut cleanly across just beneath a node or leaf joint, usually about four nodes or joints from the top of the shoot. The bottom pair of leaves

Left to right: stem tip cuttings of a hydrangea,
a zonal pelargonium, and jasmine, with the bottom pairs
of leaves removed ready for potting.

The same cuttings inserted in pots of rooting medium.

is usually removed, and it is helpful to rapid rooting to dip the base of the cutting into a so-called 'hormone type' rooting powder. Some of these contain a fungicide which helps to prevent rotting of the cutting.

The cuttings may be inserted in a peat-based seed sowing or cutting compost, or in a mixture of half and half by bulk of peat and coarse sand. Some cuttings root well in three parts peat to one part of coarse sand. It must be emphasized, however, that the sand must be really coarse – some merchants call it grit. The ordinary soft yellow builders sand is not good for rooting cuttings.

The cuttings may be inserted around the rim of a large pot, or in a box filled with the rooting medium, and kept in a temperature of 55–65°F. Some plants need higher temperatures and can really only be rooted successfully in a warmed propagating case. In the home they may be placed in a flower pot and then covered, after thoroughly moistening the rooting compost, with a plastic bag. Many cuttings root well in this way. Cuttings may also be rooted in peat pots or Jiffy 7's.

Some plants, such as ivies and the busy lizzies, or varieties of *Impatiens*, will root if short cuttings are placed in a jar so that an inch or so of the base is in water. When the roots have formed, transfer the cuttings to pots filled with a suitable potting compost.

A few plants, mainly gloxinias, *Streptocarpus*, *Saintpaulia* and *Begonia rex* and its varieties, may be propagated by means of leaf cuttings. Leaves of gloxinias, *Streptocarpus* and *Saintpaulia* are inserted in a cutting compost with an inch or so of stem beneath the compost. The leaves of the *Begonia* and *Streptocarpus* may be cut into squares or sections and inserted vertically in the compost. Alternatively, they may be laid flat on a box of compost, and the veins cut with a razor blade at a distance of 2 in. or so between the cuts. The leaves are pegged down with pieces of bent wire, or weighted with stones to keep the cut sur-

Left to right: a Jiffy 7; a Jiffy 7 after soaking in water; a hydrangea cutting inserted in a Jiffy 7.

Left: leaf cuttings ready for propagation
top: a *Begonia* leaf;
left centre: sections of *Streptocarpus* leaf, and a
Saintpaulia leaf;
bottom left: squares cut from a *Begonia* leaf.

Below, left to right: the *Begonia* leaf, with veins cut, laid
on the surface of the compost and pegged down with pieces
of bent wire; the squares of *Begonia* leaf laid on the
surface of the compost; sections of *Streptocarpus* leaf
inserted vertically; *Saintpaulia* leaves with stems inserted
in the rooting medium.

faces in contact with the soil which must be kept moist at all times. Small plants will appear at the points where the veins are cut. A high temperature – 65–75°F. is necessary, and the cuttings should be kept covered with glass or plastic.

The greatest modern aid to propagation has been the mist technique. When you take a cutting it becomes a slowly dying piece of vegetation, and it is a race between the cutting putting on roots and dying. Thus we resort to all the tricks of keeping it closely confined and shaded to prevent undue evaporation of water from the foliage and ultimate shrivelling. We deprive it of sunlight to a large extent. It may or may not root.

Mist propagation is a technique whereby a cutting is rooted in full sunshine with full ventilation, and it does not wilt because the leaves are kept constantly and automatically covered with a layer of moisture.

An electrically operated soil warmed bench is constructed as described later, and a rod type thermostat is inserted in the sand base to keep the soil temperature at about 70–75°F. Then nozzles which emit a fine mist spray over the cuttings are set above the bench, and these are connected to a solenoid valve set in the main supply of water. This in turn is connected to an 'electronic leaf', a device which will switch on the solenoid when the cuttings need a further moistening of their leaf surfaces.

It has been found that even with mist propagation it hastens rooting if many types of cutting are dipped in a solution of water-borne plastic anti-desiccant, which is used to prevent needle drop of Christmas trees or undue shrivelling of ivy, holly and other evergreens used for Christmas decorations.

The cuttings are dipped in the solution, allowed to dry, and then placed under mist. After 24 hours the mist is turned off and the cuttings sprayed with the solution. After they have dried the mist is turned on again. Not only is rooting hastened, but a larger percentage of cuttings make roots.

Seed Sowing and Transplanting
Many greenhouse and house plants may be raised from seed – *Asparagus, Begonia, Bougainvillea, Browallia,* various

bromeliads, *Clivia, Coleus, Ficus, Grevillea, Lantana, Monstera, Primula, Saintpaulia* and *Streptocarpus* among them.

Most of these plants need a fairly high temperature for successful germination, between 70–80°F., and a steady humid atmosphere. It is not easy to raise these plants from seed in a living room because, while the temperature may normally be kept at 70°F., it is difficult to give the germinating seedlings sufficient humidity in the atmosphere. This can easily be overcome by placing them in a propagating case consisting of a plastic tray with a crystal clear plastic cover. These are available in various sizes from 8 in. by 6 in. to 22 in. by 11 in. In Britain and countries where the houses are not always centrally heated, electrically heated propagating cases are usually available.

Where only a few plants are required, as for growing in the home, it is probably easier to transplant the seedlings singly into small peat pots or, even easier still, into Jiffy 7's. These are exceedingly useful. A Jiffy 7 is a circular block of peat impregnated with fertilizer and compressed to $\frac{1}{4}$ in. thick. It is $1\frac{3}{4}$ in. diameter and is encased in an envelope of plastic net. When placed in water the Jiffy 7 swells in a few minutes to become a small 'container' $1\frac{1}{2}$ in. high.

Seedlings may be transplanted into Jiffy 7's singly, and they can be used to root cuttings. Large seeds, as of asparagus, may be sown in Jiffy 7's. The roots of the seedlings or cuttings grow through the plastic net, and the young plant is planted into a suitably sized pot – $3\frac{1}{2}$–$4\frac{1}{2}$ in. diameter – when it is well rooted in the Jiffy 7. There is no need to remove the plastic net – the roots will grow through it.

Or, of course, one may transplant seedlings into wooden or plastic seed trays filled with a suitable compost. If they are transplanted into a seed tray they will probably need potting rather sooner than if they are put into a Jiffy 7 because the latter has a larger bulk per plant of enriched peat than would normally be found in a seed tray.

As a rule it is wise to transplant seedlings when they are large enough to handle. Some seeds, such as some cacti, are rather erratic as they germinate over quite a long period. The seedlings are removed carefully one by one as they become large enough. Cultivation and propagation of succulents, including cacti, are described in more detail later.

Air Layering

This is a system of propagating such plants as *Ficus* or *Cordyline* which may eventually grow too tall for the living room or the greenhouse. It is very simple.

You remove a narrow strip of bark, say $\frac{1}{4}$ in. wide, from the stem about 2 ft from the top of the shoot and just below a joint or node. Alternatively, make an upward cut $1\frac{1}{2}$ in. deep in the stem. Treat this wound with a 'hormone' type rooting compound, and keep the cut surfaces apart with a twist of moss. Then wrap some damp sphagnum moss round the stem, starting about 3 in. below the cut and continuing 1–2 in. above it. Either slip a plastic tube over the shoot and fill it with the moss, or wrap plastic round the moss and tie it securely at the top and bottom. In about 10 weeks roots should be visible coming through the moss, and the stem may be severed below the roots and potted. March and April are good months to practise air layering.

CULTIVATION

Potting

As soon as seedlings are large enough to handle, or cuttings have made good roots, they should be moved into pots. It is a great mistake to 'overpot' – that is, to put seedlings or cuttings in a pot larger than necessary, as too large a volume of soil may become too wet and become sour.

If, as explained earlier, Jiffy 7's are used, seedlings and cuttings are quite happy in them for months and there is little risk of them rotting through over-wet root conditions.

If new clay pots are used, soak them in water for an hour or so before filling with potting compost. Place one or two pieces of broken pot, 'crocks', over the drainage hole.

Most people now use the peat or bark fibre based composts for seed sowing, cutting rooting, and for potting. Some British firms still offer composts to the John Innes formula which is a mixture of sterilized loam, sand and peat. But good loam is increasingly difficult to find, and more and more growers are turning to loamless composts. As the peat composts have been developed after much research, there are mixes that are suitable for a very wide range of plants.

One may pot plants fairly firmly when using loam-based composts, firming with the fingers, but peat-based composts should be only lightly firmed and watered to settle the compost as explained later. Always leave about $\frac{1}{2}$ in. – more in large pots – between the top of the compost and the rim of the pot, to allow for watering. Peat composts should never be allowed to dry out.

Repotting

When you buy a potted plant it is reasonable to assume that it will not need repotting or, as the old gardeners say 'potting on' – moving into a larger pot – for at least a year. Some plants, notably hippeastrums, cyclamen and *Primula obconica*, are happy in the same pot for several years.

But if you think a plant looks a bit starved, knock it out

of its pot. Hold your fingers over the surface of the ball of soil, invert the pot, and tap the rim against the edge of a bench. The ball of soil will come cleanly out of the pot. It will probably be found that the ball of soil is wrapped round with a solid wall of roots. If so, it needs moving into a larger pot.

If it is in, say, a $3\frac{1}{2}$ in. pot, move it into a $4\frac{1}{2}$–5 in. pot. If in a $4\frac{1}{2}$–5 in. pot, move into a 6 or 7 in. pot. The best time to repot most plants is in the spring.

If the plant was originally in a clay pot with a drainage hole in the bottom there will have been one or more pieces of broken pot – 'crocks' – covering the hole. Remove these, and if you are repotting into a clay pot use these crocks, with maybe another one or two, to cover the hole of the new pot. If, however, you are repotting into a plastic pot this 'crocking' is unnecessary as the many small drainage holes in a plastic pot do not need any crocks to prevent the compost from washing out.

Always scrub used clay or plastic pots before using again, and soak new clay pots in water for an hour or so before use.

When moving a plant to a larger pot scrape off some of the soil on top of the ball of roots if this is covered with green algal growth. Partly fill the new pot with compost, place the plant on this and work more into the space between the ball of soil and the pot wall. Cover the ball of soil with compost so that it is finally about $\frac{1}{2}$–1 in. below the level of the pot to allow for watering. Firm loam based composts with the fingers, but only lightly peat or fibre based composts. Allow them to settle by watering them. If they are too firm they may become waterlogged and plants may rot.

Staking
Fortunately the great majority of house plants do not need much in the way of support. But some do need staking – fuchsias for example, and bulbs such as hyacinths, daffodils and tulips.

One of the problems presented by the light peat-based composts is that it is difficult to stake large plants because the stakes move about in the soft compost. This problem has now been overcome by an ingenious wire clip which is hooked onto the edge of the pot, and which grips the stake inserted in the middle of the pot and keeps it erect.

Various climbing plants, such as ivies, *Plumbago*, *Cissus* and the like, need support and there are various types of trellis available. Or one can easily make a framework of canes, either as a kind of wigwam or in a trellis shape, adding more canes as the plants grow.

Plants in the Home
Some people have the so-called 'green fingers' or 'green thumb' and can grow indoor plants to perfection. Others, to be brutal, are plant killers. First, it must be admitted that there are easy, not so easy, and difficult indoor plants. Some growers identify these categories by attaching differently coloured labels.

The reasons why different plants are easy or difficult to grow are, in the main, concerned with maintenance of a congenial temperature, and an acceptable humidity in the atmosphere. Some plants, too, are tolerant of wide fluctuations in temperature and humidity, and also of hit and miss watering.

Ideally, for most house plants a steady temperature of about 70°F. is desirable. This, however, may not suit all plants – cyclamen do best in a temperature not exceeding 60°F. They will be quite happy in even lower temperatures.

The provision of enough moisture in the air in a living room is not all that easy, but for certain plants – *Saintpaulia*, or African Violets – it can be done.

As a general rule house plants are happiest if they are planted six or eight or more in a jardinière, a self watering trough, a large ceramic bowl, an old copper jam pan or coal bucket. In such containers the pots may be embedded in peat which is always kept moist, and the moisture evaporating from the wet peat creates a nice humid 'microclimate' around the plants. Further, when plants are growing in a container with their foliage touching each other's, this forms a kind of canopy and traps the moisture rising from the damp peat. Plants grown thus are always happier than when they are strung out singly on a windowsill or hung in a fake bird cage from a wall or ceiling.

One can, of course, create good growing conditions for house plants without going to the expense of buying deep containers. There are available shallow plastic trays of various shapes and sizes. These may be filled with shingle, small pebbles or coarse sand, and kept always full of water. The pots are just embedded in the shingle, and the plants will draw up what water they need if they are in plastic pots. If they are in clay pots, it is necessary to remove the 'crock' or piece of broken pot from the bottom of the ball of soil and replace it with a glass wool wick. But not only will the plant water itself as it were – the water in the tray will evaporate into the air and provide a congenial atmosphere.

It is of the utmost importance to keep the foliage of house plants free from dust. Dust can be a killer, and even if it is not fatal it can harm the plants and impair their performance.

With large-leaved plants such as *Ficus*, *Sansevieria*, aspidistra and the like, sponge the leaves with tepid water, ideally once a week, but certainly twice a month. Foliage plants with many small leaves have to be dipped in a basin or sink of tepid water. Put your fingers across the top of the ball of soil to keep it in place, then invert the pot and immerse the foliage in the water drawing it back and forth several times.

Bulbs Indoors

Many types of bulbous or cormous plants may be grown successfully indoors, and while most of them are not successful if they are grown in pots or bowls a second year in a living room, some such as hippeastrums, nerines, sprekelias, and vallotas may be grown in pots indoors for years.

The most popular bulbs for growing in pots or bowls indoors are hyacinths, tulips, and daffodils, although many of the small bulbs – crocuses, muscari, winter aconites, snowdrops, and bulbous irises may be grown indoors. The small bulbs are best left outdoors until the flower buds are showing, and then brought indoors. If grown entirely in over-warm conditions the leaves may grow excessively long and the flower buds may fail to develop.

Daffodil and tulip bulbs that have been 'precooled' are obtainable, and these may be had in bloom well in time for Christmas. The bulbs, after being lifted at the bulb farm, are kept in a cool chamber for some weeks, and this hastens growth when they are finally planted in their pots or bowls. Incidentally, precooled bulbs planted outdoors will flower earlier than untreated bulbs.

Hyacinths on the other hand are given heat treatment by the grower, and if planted in their bowls in September will flower for Christmas.

Supplies of these specially treated bulbs are always limited, and it is wise to order them by the middle of the summer for delivery in early autumn.

Immediately on arrival they should, in the case of tulips and daffodils, be placed in as cool a place as possible and the bags opened at the top. Then with the minimum of delay they should be planted in their containers and placed outside in a shaded spot where they may be plunged in the soil so that the top of the pot or bowl is about 6 in. below ground. Naturally mark the spot so that you can find them again easily. Alternatively they may be placed on a level surface, again shaded from hot sun, and covered with 6–8 in. of peat, straw or well weathered clinker. Straw is not always satisfactory as slugs may work their way through the layer to the bulbs, and they are very partial to tulips. They find peat and clinker less comfortable.

If the weather should turn hot when the bulbs have been placed in their plunge bed, turn on a sprinkler to wet the covering material and by so doing obtain the benefit for the bulbs of the cooling effect of the evaporation of water.

After about eight weeks the bulbs should be examined, and if the shoot of the hyacinth is well clear of the bulb, they may be brought indoors. If the bud of the tulip bulb is clear of the neck of the bulb – this is usually when about 2 in. of growth has been made, they too may be brought into warmth. It is possible to feel with the finger and thumb the slight swelling in the tulip shoot which indicates that the flower bud is clear of the bulb.

Daffodils may be brought into warmth when they have made about 2 in. of growth, as with tulips, usually about eight weeks after planting.

Bulbs grow well in proprietary peat-based potting compost. Tulips and daffodils, but not hyacinths, may be planted in a double layer in a large pot. Thus, a really imposing show is obtained. Tulips can be planted in more than two layers in a large pot, if a small-bulbed variety is used.

When planting in peat-based or 'bulb fibre' compost, make sure it is moist – when a handful is squeezed it just exudes a little moisture, no more. Place one or two pieces of crock or broken pot over the drainage hole of a clay pot before putting in the compost. This is not necessary with plastic pots as they have a number of small drainage holes, and the compost is not likely to be washed through or clog them.

When actually planting the bulbs just place them on the compost, do not press them down, and then cover.

If you are using rather special glazed bowls, wrap them in a sheet of newspaper after planting the bulbs and before plunging the bowls outside. The bulbs will push easily through the damp paper.

Watering bulbs in the home needs to be done carefully. They should be inspected every day. Today most people grow bulbs in peat-based composts. As explained earlier, these should never be allowed to dry out. If bulbs are grown in bowls with no drainage holes, it is desirable after watering the compost to let it stand for an hour and then gently tip the bowl on to one side to allow any surplus water to run out. Naturally you hold one hand with outspread fingers over the compost to keep it and the bulbs from falling out of the bowl.

In an 8 in. pot, half filled with compost, 5 double nosed daffodil bulbs may be placed. These are just covered with compost, and 6 more bulbs may be placed on top and covered with compost so that their noses are just visible above the compost surface, which should be $\frac{1}{2}$ in. below the rim of the pot. With a daffodil variety like 'Golden Harvest', which often produces three flowers from a double nosed bulb, one can usually have 30 blooms or more in one pot.

Hyacinths may be grown in special glass hyacinth jars. A piece of charcoal is dropped into the jar which is filled almost to the top with water – preferably rain water. The hyacinth bulb is then placed on top of the jar so that its base almost, but not quite, touches the water.

Feeding

All potted plants need feeding and the makers of liquid or soluble fertilizers usually give adequate instructions about the strength of the feed and the frequency of application. Generally plants take a rest in the winter and need only a minimum of water, and virtually no feeding.

But as the days begin to lengthen they will begin to grow again and need more water and some feeding. Generally it is better to apply a liquid feed to potted plants twice as often as the makers suggest but at half the recommended strength. Never, however, apply liquid fertilizer to dry soil – moisten it first.

Watering

More house plants are killed by overwatering than by being kept too dry. A plant will usually tell you it needs water by wilting slightly, but it should not be allowed to reach this stage. Potted plants may be kept watered by standing them on trays of gravel or coarse sand, but if they have to be watered by pouring water onto the soil in the pot, they need to be inspected almost every day. It would be nice if one could give precise directions for watering, but there are too many variable factors. Much depends on the heat of the room, and on the size of the plant, and the quantity and size of the leaves.

One can learn fairly quickly to know when a plant needs water. Some people can tell by lifting the pot – if it is light it needs water, if it feels heavy it does not; or by tapping a clay pot one can judge from the sound whether it needs water – a hollow sound indicates the compost is dry, a dull heavy sound that it is wet.

Many plants nowadays are grown in peat based composts, and once these are allowed to dry out they are not easy to wet again. One can stand them in a sink or a bucket up to the pot rim in tepid water; or water the compost from the top, and then after a couple of hours water it again.

With some plants, notably cyclamen, it is not desirable to allow water to fall on the plant itself – on the exposed corm – as this may cause rotting of the flowers. Similarly water should not be allowed to penetrate between hyacinth leaves and fall on the bud. When this happens some of the florets may turn brown.

As already stated, a dry plant may often indicate that it needs water by wilting somewhat. But a plant that has consistently been overwatered is not usually able to give early warning of its troubles. By the time it finally collapses, turns yellow, shows signs of rotting at the base, or what-ever other symptoms the overwatering may cause, it is often too late to save it. All one can do is to keep it almost dry and hope that it may recover. Never on any account feed a sickly plant.

Humidity

To help maintain a certain amount of humidity in the atmosphere of centrally heated rooms or those heated by electricity or gas, there are various types of humidifier available. These are electrically operated. Also troughs that may be filled with water can be bought for attaching to radiators. These aids to greater humidity make the atmosphere more acceptable to humans as well as to the plants.

As with plants in living rooms the provision of adequate humidity in a greenhouse or conservatory is important. In many cases it is possible to shut the house down and pour water on the floor and on the staging several times a day, opening it up again after an hour or so.

There are also automatic devices for doing this as often as required, but again, these are sophisticated and expensive pieces of equipment which few gardeners would consider necessary.

Draughts and Fumes

Few plants are happy in a draughty position. Not many will flourish when temperatures fluctuate wildly – up to 75°F. during the night and down almost to 40°F. in the morning.

The space between the curtains and the window can be a very cold spot indeed on a frosty night. So unless it is possible to arrange that the curtains are fitted so that they are between the glass and the plants, it is best to bring the plants off the windowsill and accommodate them on a table or in a jardinière, or some other container in the room.

Many plants do not like and will not tolerate fumes from a coke boiler or from a gas fire. In fairness it must be added that modern gas fires do not give off fumes, but many of the old types are still in use and they do.

Heating a Greenhouse, Conservatory or a Home Extension

A cold greenhouse, conservatory, lean-to, or a home extension is not as useful as one provided with a modicum of heating sufficient to keep out the frost, or preferably, to maintain a minimum night temperature of 45°F.

Obviously, if the home is heated by gas or oil fired boilers, it would be a simple matter to install another radiator or two in a home extension or a lean-to green-house. It would not be so easy to do this in a free standing greenhouse unless it was very near the dwelling house, and hot water pipes would need to be heavily protected.

A small greenhouse may be heated by one or more free-standing paraffin or kerosene heaters. Normal sizes are 1 in. and 2 in. burner models which will keep frost out of a 600 cubic ft and a 1200 cubic ft greenhouse respectively. It is possible to attach heat distributors to these heaters at an extra cost, and these help to spread warmth under benches. There are now control units which, when connected to a 5 gallon drum of fuel, will assure a burning time of 20 days for the 1 in. model and 9 days with the 2 in. model when the burners are set low. This system obviates the chore of filling the tank every day or two. It is claimed that the carbon dioxide given off by burning paraffin or kerosene stimulates plant growth.

There are also systems of heating greenhouses using either town gas, or gas in cylinders. Again, there is the benefit of carbon dioxide to the plants.

Electricity, however, is a very adaptable source of heating, and once installed can be used for such ancillary purposes as heating frames, propagating cases in the greenhouse or conservatory, for ventilation by extractor fan, and for pest and disease control by means of electrically heated vaporizers. It can also supply supplementary lighting which can be very useful with many plants at certain times of the year.

The cheapest type of electric heater is a fan-assisted or 'blower' heater. This consists of a heating element at one end and a fan at the other. The heater is stood on the floor of the greenhouse at the end furthest from the door, and blows warm air which rises eventually to the roof. Installation is cheap as only one 13 amp. socket is required for each heater.

A little more expensive to install are tubular heaters, but they have several advantages over the fan assisted-type. If a fan-assisted heater breaks down you have no heating until it can be repaired, and this can take a few weeks. But if one element in a bank of tubular heaters should fail it is probable that the other tubes will keep the greenhouse warm enough until a new element can be fitted to the faulty tube.

It is important to use the right type of thermostat – a rod type that is accurate to plus or minus $1\frac{1}{2}°$F.

The positioning of a thermostat is important too. It should be placed a third of the way down from the apex of the roof, and about half way along the house. If the greenhouse runs east-west fix the thermostat on the north facing wall. However, if it runs north-south fix it to the east wall.

Now, whether a greenhouse, conservatory or home extension is to be heated by electricity, solid fuel, gas, or by paraffin or kerosene heaters, it is important to study the economics of the heating system.

Most of the plants the amateur wishes to grow, with the exception of some orchids and other tropical plants, will grow happily in a house with a minimum night temperature of 45°F. provided they have a root temperature of about 55°F.

In nature the soil temperature is always warmer at night than the air temperature. We say for plants 'give them cool heads and warm toes'. Of course, many plants would not grow actively in winter in an air temperature of 45°F. at night. They would stay alive; but with a soil temperature of 55°F. they will grow actively in winter.

Providing the desired soil temperature is simple if electrical soil warming cables are used.

If soil warming cables are to be laid in a soil border in a greenhouse or conservatory, it would be advisable to use a transformer and cables carrying a loading of only 12 volts. In a border there is always the chance that somebody is going to be digging about with a fork or a trowel and may damage a cable. If the cable is carrying mains voltage, this could lead to danger.

On benches, however, the danger of cable damage is much less and the heavily insulated mains voltage heating cables may be used.

The bench should be well constructed and capable of carrying the considerable weight of a sand layer and pots or boxes of plants. The base of the bench may be of corrugated asbestos sheeting, and lengths of old water pipe or something similar should be placed under the asbestos sheeting, the whole length of the bench, to take the weight. On a bench, say 3–4 ft wide, it would be wise to lay two or even three lengths of piping under the corrugated asbestos.

Ordinary builders' sand is spread on the asbestos to a depth of about 2 in. The cables are laid on the sand, and another 2 in. layer of sand is spread on top. The sand is, of course, kept moist so that the heat from the cable can rise to heat the plants' roots. Pots or boxes of plants are placed firmly in contact with the moist warm sand, and spaces between them are filled with peat to prevent the warmth from the cables from escaping. Again, the peat should be kept moist.

Then there are various types of electrical propagating case available which can be kept at temperatures up to 70–80°F. Many plants may be raised from seed or propagated by cuttings in these propagators.

Ventilation is easily done by means of an extractor fan controlled by a thermostat. It is wise to set the thermostat so that it activates the fan when the temperature rises to about 60°F. in winter, but to set it down to operate at 50°F. in summer. The reason for this is that if you set the fan thermostat at 50°F. in winter, you may have a warm sunny afternoon, the fan will go on extracting warm air until dusk, and very swiftly the temperature will fall to below 45°F. and the heating will be switched on. If the fan thermostat is set to operate at 60°F. there will be a reserve of heat from the sun, and the heating will not begin to operate for several hours.

But in the summer, when the heating is not in use, it is desirable to have the ventilation working at 50°F. to cause movement of air, to dry condensed moisture from the leaves of plants, and to minimize the risk of disease spores germinating on the foliage.

There are now, of course, electrical devices which will open and close greenhouse ventilators.

In recent years it has been found useful to install a small fan to direct the warm air which rises into the apex of the house down again, and at the same time this dries unwanted moisture on plant foliage in autumn and winter and thus reduces the incidence of mildew and other diseases.

Such a fan is particularly valuable where fan assisted heaters are used, as these tend to blow the warm air to the roof of the house far more quickly than it would rise by convection over tubular heaters. At times there can be as much as 14°F. difference between the temperature on the floor and at the roof ridge. By redirecting the warm air down again this difference can be reduced to as little as 2°F.

Shading

It is necessary to use some form of shading to protect plants from excessive sun in summer. Plastic roller blinds fitted to the inside of the house on the south- or west-facing roof slope are excellent, and there are various types of material that are dissolved in water and either painted or sprayed on the glass. One type is impervious to rain, but is wiped off easily with a dry cloth. Another type is opaque, but becomes translucent when wet.

There are, of course, even more sophisticated but expensive methods of shading, by automatically operated blinds or louvres.

GREENHOUSES AND FRAMES

If there is space available a free standing greenhouse, a lean-to greenhouse against the house wall, or even a home extension which will normally be made with mainly glass walls, is a wonderful investment.

Generally flowering plants, with a few notable exceptions, do not like prolonged existence in the rather arid and overheated atmosphere of a living room. They may be brought indoors for the span of their flowering period, azaleas, cyclamen, primulas, clivias, and many more, but they like to go back to a greenhouse to convalesce, as it

were, to build up their strength to flower again another year.

So we have the problem of choosing a greenhouse, whether it be of metal or wood, whether it be free standing or a lean-to type.

It is important to study the possibilities carefully. Modern metal houses – aluminium framed – are exceedingly popular. They used to be much more expensive than wooden houses, but not now. The cost of timber and the cost of working it are now so high that aluminium houses are very competitive. Also, aluminium needs no maintenance. It will last a lifetime.

It is often objected that metal houses cost much more to heat than wooden ones. This is not so. Then old gardeners say that you get condensed moisture dropping off the metal glazing bars to the detriment of the plants. This was true of the early models of metal houses, but now modern design has taken care of this problem.

Now we have the question of what type of greenhouse to have – glass to the ground, or with brick or wooden sides up to bench level – 3 feet? If only one house is to be erected, whether free standing or as a lean-to, it is always best to have it with glass to the ground. You can grow plants on benches, under the benches, and even on shelves over the benches, and thereby reap a rich dividend from the house.

Many house plants, particularly foliage plants like ivies, cissus, peperomias, begonias, ferns and the like, grow very happily under the bench.

Where to site the house? If it is to be heated with electricity, and this is the most sensible modern way, it should be as near as practicable to the mains electric supply. When we say 'as near as practicable' this means that the house should receive as much sunlight as possible, and it should not be shaded by buildings or trees. Too often greenhouses are built at the far end of the garden, or well out of sight from the house. But this entails a long run of expensive cable, and the nearer the greenhouse is to the back door of your house, the more you will be willing to go and see that all is well on cold, frosty or snowy nights.

Naturally, if a lean-to or a home extension is to be built against a dwelling house, there may not be much choice. But if there is, it is always best to build it against a south or west facing wall. A free standing greenhouse is probably best sited so that it runs east to west with the door at the west end. Thus it will get all the benefit of the low angled winter sunshine which is so valuable.

You can put heat into a greenhouse reasonably economically, but supplementary lighting can be expensive.

Then it is important to compare prices of various makes

of greenhouses. The significant point to look for is the cost per square foot of growing area covered by glass. This can vary enormously with different types and different sizes of greenhouse.

For example, take a greenhouse 10 ft by 6 ft. You need a path 2 ft wide down the middle. This leaves you a bed or bench on each side of the path only 2 ft wide – total growing area only 40 square ft. But if you have a greenhouse 10 ft by 8 ft, and you have your 2 ft path, you have borders or benches on either side 3 ft wide making a total of 60 square ft of growing area. Compare prices on this basis.

Now let us consider frames. If there is no room for a greenhouse, or if this would be too expensive, a frame or two that can be heated with electrical air warming cables can be most useful. They are economic to heat because wood, breeze block or brick walls are good insulators, and you can always lay mats of hessian (burlap) or old sacks over the glass to keep the heat in on cold nights.

Incidentally, if you invest in a greenhouse you will soon find that you need a few frames, either heated or unheated, to take the plants from the greenhouse for hardening off prior to planting out.

PESTS

Many pests can breed happily and almost continuously in the warm conditions of a living room or a greenhouse. Garden shops and the garden departments of ironmongers or stores offer a variety of chemical sprays or dusts to control the pests that normally infest greenhouse plants. In a greenhouse the insecticidal smokes are very effective as they penetrate all through the foliage and all round the house.

Sometimes, if the same chemical control has been used over a long period, a pest can build up resistance to it so it is desirable to ring the changes with the different insecticides on the market. When resistant strains of, say, peach leaf aphids do appear it is usually worth while turning to a nicotine insecticide. Pests also seldom build up resistance to derris, but it has been known to happen.

Aphids
The commonest pests indoors in Britain are the aphids – greenfly mostly, but they come in other colours; for example, the peach leaf aphid which is a tough variety and pinkish-brown. They infest many different kinds of plant, usually clustering on young tender shoots, often on the undersurface of the leaves and down among the young growing shoots in the heart of a plant. Sometimes one can dip the plants in a sink full of tepid water and drown the aphids. But either spraying or applying from an aerosol a suitable insecticide is usually more immediately effective. The aerosol sprays get right down into the heart of a plant if this is where the aphids are congregated. There are also various systemic insecticides which are available to control aphids and other sap sucking insects. These chemicals are absorbed into the plant, and the insects sucking the sap stream are destroyed.

Ants
These insects are not usually unduly troublesome in the home or greenhouse – more so in the garden. But they can transmit diseases from a sick plant to healthy ones, and they do have the odd habit of 'farming' aphids – they collect them and consume the 'honey dew' excreted by the aphis. When they appear in any noticeable numbers a proprietary ant killer should be used. It should be noted that ants have periods when they feed, and periods when they do not. So if they ignore an ant bait, keep renewing it and they will eventually take it. In America, where mealy bugs are the ranking headache, tiny ants place the bugs in favourite spots. These ants must be eliminated or a new infestation will develop.

Capsid bugs
These insects appear usually in the autumn and cause deformed flowers and holes in leaves. When young the insects are green and wingless; in the adult stage the bugs are yellowish-green with reddish-brown markings. Pyrethrum, malathion or nicotine sprays are usually effective, or a BHC smoke may be used under glass. A European pest.

Carnation tortrix moth
This pest attacks carnations and other plants under glass. The caterpillars spin silken webs to draw leaves and flowers together to form a protective covering. Pinch the caterpillar between finger and thumb, or spray with trichlorphon if possible before the caterpillars have woven their protective shelter. They do not occur as pests in America.

Chrysanthemum eelworm (Chrysanthemum foliar nematode)
This is a serious pest of chrysanthemums, but it will also attack other plants such as calceolarias. It is difficult to control and affected plants should be destroyed. Symptoms are brown or black areas between the veins of the leaves, and a severe attack may kill the plant.

Chrysanthemum leaf miner
A disfiguring pest, the maggots of which tunnel into the chrysanthemum leaves. Other plants, such as cinerarias, may be attacked. The pest may be controlled by spraying with BHC or nicotine, or by smokes of BHC or nicotine.

Earwigs

These are not often troublesome but can sometimes damage chrysanthemums and other plants. Spray or dust BHC on and around the plants or use an insecticide containing carbaryl.

Ground mealy bugs see Root aphids

Leaf hoppers

Many plants may be infested with these pests which cause light mottling of the leaves. The physical damage they do is not serious, but they can transmit virus diseases from sick to healthy plants. They congregate on the underside of the leaves and hop about when disturbed. Spray with malathion, derris or BHC.

Mealy bugs

In greenhouses and indoors these can be troublesome pests. They look like white woodlice (sowbugs), and breed all the year round. Spray with malathion or a systemic insecticide. See also under Ants.

Red spider (Spider mites)

There are several kinds of spider mite and nearly all greenhouse plants are subject to infestation. Use malathion or Kelthane.

Root aphids (Root-mealies, Ground mealy bugs)

There are types of aphid that infest the roots of pot plants and cause them to turn yellow or wilt. Soak the soil in the pot with malathion or nicotine at the strength recommended for spraying.

Scale insects

Troublesome both in the greenhouse and in the home, these insects resemble yellow or white scales on the stems and leaves. These are the female insects. Spray with malathion, nicotine or a petroleum emulsion spray.

Slugs

Not a problem in the home, but sometimes troublesome in frames or a greenhouse. Place metaldehyde slug baits on benches and borders, or water borders with liquid metaldehyde.

Sowbugs see Woodlice

Spider mites see Red Spider

Thrips

Not very serious pests, thrips can cause damage and congregate on flowers and leaves. They suck the sap from leaves, and cause a mottled effect on foliage and flowers. Dust or spray with malathion at the first sign of damage.

White flies

These infest the foliage of plants and feed on the sap. Spray with malathion at the first sign of the pest.

Woodlice (Sowbugs)

These pests feed mainly at night on roots, stems and leaves of various plants, and can be troublesome. Spray or dust with BHC around the plants on benches, and anywhere where the woodlice may hide away during the daytime.

DISEASES

Basal rot

Various fungi can cause bulbous plants such as lilies to rot at the base of the bulb. Quintozene (Terrachlor) dusted on diseased bulbs, after the affected parts have been cut away, is often an effective cure. Badly diseased bulbs should be destroyed.

Black leg

This trouble may be caused by various fungi or bacteria and is particularly troublesome with *Pelargonium* cuttings. Use sterile composts, and destroy affected plants.

Chrysanthemum virus diseases

These cause distortion of blooms, stunting, mottling of leaves, and greening of flowers. There is no chemical cure, and affected plants should be destroyed.

Damping off

Seedlings of many plants may suffer from this disease which affects the stem and causes the seedling to wilt and die. As a precaution, if the disease has appeared before, water boxes or pots of seedlings with cheshunt compound, captan or zineb.

Grey mould

This disease can attack many types of plants outdoors, under glass or in a living room. Remove and burn all affected parts. Dust or spray affected plants with tecnazene or captan. Avoid a damp atmosphere in winter.

Mildew

This disease attacks a wide range of plants and is worst in greenhouses or frames in autumn and winter if the air is over humid and stagnant. Adequate ventilation is necessary. A copper fungicide spray is usually an effective control.

Rust

Many greenhouse plants suffer from rust diseases – chrysanthemums, carnations and pelargoniums in particular. Remove infected foliage, ventilate well, and spray with thiram or zineb every 10–14 days.

Cacti and Succulents

Some experts object to the phrase 'cacti and succulents' because cacti *are* succulents, but it is useful to emphasize certain differences between the cactus family, *Cactaceae*, and the other succulents, which belong to many other families. Unfortunately, uninformed people often refer to other succulents as cacti, but this leads to much confusion and bad cultivation. A proper appreciation of what a succulent plant is, and how it functions, is very important for understanding how to grow it, and a short explanation is now given.

A succulent plant is one which is adapted to store water in adverse conditions. These conditions can include those which make uptake of water difficult, such as salt marshes and places where the roots are frozen, but succulents in general cultivation in house and greenhouse are adapted to cope with very dry conditions, at any rate during part of the year. Although orchids and some hardy plants such as sedums are succulent, they are not usually included when speaking of succulents.

Succulents which store water mainly in the roots are not very often grown in house and greenhouse, where the main kinds either store water in the leaves, for example echeverias, or in the stems, for example cacti. The distinction is not absolute, for echeverias have succulent stems, and a few cacti have leaves.

The main storage organs are usually thick and fleshy, that is to say the volume is large in relation to the surface. In the leaf-succulents the thick leaves are often in tight rosettes, thus further protecting each other from dry conditions. In most stem-succulents the stems perform the usual function of leaves, and plants sometimes approach a spherical shape, since a sphere has the greatest possible volume for a given surface. Other adaptations are a great reduction in the number of stomata (breathing pores) which sometimes open only at night, and the presence of chemicals in the sap which check the evaporation of water. Some stem-succulents produce non-succulent leaves in the wet season, and drop them in the dry season.

Many dry places have a sharp fall in temperature at night with considerable dew, and many succulents can absorb dew. Sharp spines are thought to favour the deposition of dew, and this may explain why many succulents are spiny, though the spines also protect the plants from grazing animals. Probably both factors are important, because although some exceedingly poisonous euphorbias have spines, they are not as spiny as some cacti, which generally have edible flesh.

Cacti are distinguished from other plants by the presence of organs called areoles, which bear fur and spines. Usually, but by no means always, the flowers and new growths arise from or close to the areoles, and so do leaves if present. Sometimes spines are absent, but nearly always there are some, even if very small or temporary.

Contrary to popular belief, few cacti or other succulents grow in extreme deserts where there is almost complete drought. Most of them grow in the ground in areas where there is some, but low, rainfall, and there is sparse vegetation, giving at any rate some shade, and it is these plants which form the bulk of the collections in general. Cacti are found in America, and generally are very adaptable, as are many other American succulents. For example, whether they come from north or south of the Equator, they seem to adapt to our seasons well, growing in our summer and resting in our winter. On the other hand, many African succulents retain their original growth rhythm, and this will be mentioned when dealing with the genera concerned.

It is therefore possible to give general cultural directions to suit a large number of cacti and other succulents. However, there is a very important group of cacti grown in rooms and greenhouses which do not grow in low rainfall areas. These are the epiphytic cacti, which grow in pockets of decaying vegetable matter on trees and rocks in rain forests. There are not many species, but large numbers of hybrids with exceptionally beautiful flowers. Although they require somewhat different treatment from other cacti, they fortunately are also very adaptable, and include some of our finest house plants.

To distinguish them from the epiphytes, some people call cacti which grow on the ground 'desert' cacti, but 'terrestrial' is a better word.

CULTIVATION

The key to successful cultivation of cacti and succulents is to give them a fair amount of water in the growing season, and very little or none in the resting season. The great thing to be avoided is continuous wet round the roots, and stagnant moisture is deadly. Therefore potting, soil and watering all tie together to attain this end.

Soil – Terrestrial Cacti and Succulents

Terrestrial cacti and succulents in their native lands are not accustomed to much decaying vegetable matter in the soil, and their roots have little resistance to some of the organisms which flourish in rotting matter. The basis of potting composts is therefore soil, preferably loam, which has not recently been manured or dressed with such substances as leafmould. Drainage is assured by the addition of sharp sand, or preferably crushed brick, since this retains some moisture without remaining too wet.

Soil containing only these ingredients would, however, dry out rather too quickly in a pot, so something must be added to retain moisture. Rather surprisingly, peat is excellent. It may be that, being already half rotted, it does not sustain dangerous organisms, but whatever the reason, it works. A potting compost of equal parts of loam, peat and crushed brick (or sharp sand) suits a wide range of terrestrial cacti and succulents. Good loam is somewhat scarce nowadays, but not a great deal is needed for the average collection. Concentrated fertilisers are not added to the compost, as they can cause unbalanced growth. After about a year, liquid fertilisers of the high-potash type used sparingly will restore the fertility of the soil.

Lime in some form used to be added to every cactus compost, but although terrestrial succulents frequently grow in limy soils, and many are very tolerant of lime, it is unnecessary for most of them. Very acid soils should be avoided, and lime should be added if the acidity reading is below about pH 6 as shown by a simple soil tester.

Soil – Epiphytic Succulents

Epiphytic succulents, mainly cacti, have different soil requirements. Accustomed to growing in pockets of decaying vegetable matter in trees, they revel in leafmould. Since they are grown mainly for their flowers, fertilisers are added to the soil, because this improves flowering and it does not matter if the shape of the plant is not quite typical of the wild plants – most of the epiphytic succulents cultivated today are hybrids in any event.

There are many composts, but a good one is, by volume, 60 per cent leafmould, 30 per cent garden soil, and 10 per cent drainage material, either sharp sand or horticultural perlite, or a mixture of both. If the garden soil is heavy, drainage material can be increased up to 20 per cent, with a corresponding decrease in the soil. To each bushel (8 British gallons, 10 United States gallons or 36 litres) is added a 4-in. (10 cm.) potful of bonemeal and 4 oz. (120 gm.) of sulphate of potash. If good leafmould is not available, a mixture of equal parts of peat and well-rotted sifted garden compost makes a fair substitute.

Epiphyllums are fairly tolerant of lime, but the *Zygocactus-Schlumbergera-Rhipsalidopsis* group, which includes the popular Christmas Cactus, is sensitive to lime. *Zygocactus* has been carefully investigated, and while it grows best in soil at an acidity reading of about pH 6, it is killed when the soil goes further towards the alkaline at a pH of 7·2, which is just above neutral. It also dies at a pH below 4·8. A good tip is to take soil for the compost from a place where rhododendrons flourish, and no trouble is likely with such soil as it should be suitably acid, though a pH test is always a wise precaution.

Pots

Pots for succulents should not be too small. Around $2\frac{1}{2}$ in. diameter is about the minimum in which watering can be controlled properly, and very small plants are best grown in or transplanted into large pans or boxes. Most succulents grow fairly slowly and can remain two or three years without repotting. When the time comes, the soil is completely replaced. The plant should be well watered the day before repotting, and the old soil shaken off the roots, damaging them as little as possible. Very spiny plants can be held with leather gloves or layers of newspaper.

Plastic or other non-porous pots are greatly preferred by most growers nowadays, chiefly because they are much easier to water correctly. Also the tendency of roots to wind round and round the inside of a clay pot makes them particularly susceptible to damage in repotting.

The pot should hold the roots comfortably with a little, but not too much, room for further growth. This may sometimes mean that the new pot is the same size as the old one. Plants from dry places require very good drainage, and a layer of crocks or pebbles at the bottom of the pot is usually desirable.

Potting and Repotting

The soil should be moist enough to take the shape of the hand when squeezed, but should break up readily when prodded. It should be carefully run in round the roots so that there are no empty pockets, and shaking and tapping the pot frequently while adding the soil is helpful.

The soil should then be pressed down, leaving the usual space at the top of the pot for watering. It is very important not to water a newly potted plant too soon, because some roots are always damaged, and it is very easy for rot to set in unless the roots have time to heal before watering. The plant should therefore be put in a shady place for about a week, and then well watered.

The ideal time for repotting is just after the beginning of the growing season, but there is often a margin of up to three months. Plants should not be repotted in the dormant season, but sometimes it does no harm, for example if the plant is knocked out of its pot accidentally.

Watering
During the growing season, succulents (of course including cacti) usually like a good deal of water, but the frequency of watering varies so much with conditions that one cannot give exact directions on timing. A safe general rule with terrestrial succulents is to give a good soaking, and then no more until the soil is quite dry, much drier than with most pot plants. The epiphytic cacti are exceptions, because if the soil gets quite dry in hot weather the roots can be damaged, and rot often sets in when water is eventually given. Thus, when an epiphytic cactus rots at the root, many people think it has been overwatered, whereas in fact it has been allowed to get too dry in hot weather. The rule with these plants is not to let the soil get bone dry, but to water again when it is fairly dry, as is the rule with the great majority of house plants of all kinds.

The pots should not stand in water. In rooms, where saucers have to be put under the plants to prevent surplus water from the pot damaging furniture or windowsills, it is a good idea to put pebbles in the saucer, so that the pot stands on them away from any drainage water.

In the dormant season, usually the winter, the general rule is to give enough water to prevent the plant from shrivelling, but not enough to cause growth, for, if growth takes place in the weak light of winter, the growth is likely to be thin and elongated. It helps greatly if the temperature can be kept low, because this discourages growth. Frost must of course be excluded, but provided this is done, the cooler the temperature the better for most succulents. Although it is not difficult to keep plants cool in a greenhouse, it is not so easy in a dwelling house, especially if it is centrally heated. The rule here is to put the plants in the coolest frost-free room available, and find out the correct watering procedure by experience.

Some succulents, for example conophytums, must remain absolutely dry in the resting period, or they will

rot. Some require higher temperatures in winter than set out above, but these special cases will be noted in the alphabetical descriptions.

Overhead spraying with a fine mist spray is beneficial to many succulents, as it resembles the natural dew to which they are accustomed. Dew, however, occurs at night, and dries off in the morning, and spraying in daytime followed by hot sunshine can be dangerous because sometimes droplets of water act as burning glasses and scorch the skin of the plants.

PROPAGATION

The natural method of propagation of cacti and succulents is by seed, though some of them have very effective ways of propagating themselves vegetatively. For example, some members of the genus *Bryophyllum* produce tiny plantlets, complete with stems, leaves and roots in the notches of the leaves.

Seed
Growing cacti and succulents from seed is much the same as growing other plants from seed. Ordinary seed compost in pots, pans or boxes is used, and the young plants transplanted into a normal compost used for other plants. Care should be taken to see that the seedlings do not dry out, for when very small many of them have not yet developed their resistance to drought. Some of them grow very slowly in their early stages, and may have to remain where sown for a full year. It is best therefore to use a sterile or sterilized sowing compost to avoid weeds as far as possible, but the damping-off fungus (*Pythium debaryanum*) can spread quickly in sterile soil, and watering with a preventive such as cuprammonium solution (cheshunt compound or liquid copper fungicide) is advisable. Extremes of heat should be avoided, and a night temperature of 50–55°F. and a day temperature not exceeding 70°F. suits most of them. The usual rule of covering the larger seeds with twice their depth of compost and sowing the very small seeds on the surface can be followed.

Epiphyllums again are exceptional. They should always be sown on the surface in full light, and kept in a sealed container of glass, or a seed tray enclosed in a polyethylene bag. Temperatures of 120°F. will not harm them, nor will the dripping of condensation at night; they seem to like it and to be immune from damping-off disease.

The great majority of plants in a collection are true species and come true from seed, but there are pitfalls in saving one's own seed. Many succulents, particularly cacti, are self-sterile and will not set seed with pollen from the same plant. It should be noted that this applies to all plants in a clone, that is to say plants which have been propagated vegetatively from a single plant, and in small collections it is often the case that all the plants come from offsets or cuttings from one original plant. Unfortunately, although a plant may not accept its own pollen, it often happens that it will accept pollen from another species, sometimes even if that species is in a different genus. Thus seed set without special precautions stands a good chance of being hybrid, and since the aim of the enthusiast is to grow true species as closely resembling the wild plant as possible, home-saved seed often causes disappointment.

Fortunately, seed of good quality is obtainable from many sources, and a watch should be kept on advertisements in the gardening papers and the bulletins of cactus and succulent societies. One cannot always get seed of everything one wants all the time. This of course applies to plants as well, and it is one of the ways in which collecting cacti and succulents differs from ordinary gardening. If, for example, one wishes to get a collection of roses, it is usually possible to find several firms which will supply at any rate the more popular varieties, but with cacti and succulents even the commoner ones are not always available.

As has been said, some cacti, such as epiphyllums, are grown entirely for their flowers, and they have been extensively hybridized for many years. Such plants do not come true from seed, and seed is used only for the purpose of breeding new varieties, as is the case with many ordinary cultivated plants such as roses, dahlias and the like. To keep such plants true, vegetative propagation is used, such as cuttings in the case of epiphyllums.

Offsets

The easiest kind of vegetative propagation is by offsets. In addition to the bryophyllums previously mentioned, which produce complete plants in the notches of the leaves, there are some which produce almost complete plants as offsets, such as cacti of the genus *Echinopsis*. In this case one need only pull off the offsets and plant them.

Cuttings

If offsets are not produced, the next expedient is to take cuttings, which may be either leaf or stem cuttings. The difference between succulents and ordinary plants is that it is not necessary to root the cuttings in a moist atmosphere – in fact this is usually to be avoided as it may cause rotting.

Leaf Cuttings

Leaf cuttings, though very interesting, are not as common as some people think, because it is necessary that the leaf should break off cleanly, and not tear off leaving a bit attached to the stem. For example, the leaves of some echeverias break off cleanly, but others do not. If they do, all that is needed is to lay the leaf on sandy soil, half burying the end of the leaf which was formerly attached to the stem. After a few weeks a tiny plant develops which roots in the soil, and draws some of its nourishment from the leaf which ultimately withers away.

Stem Cuttings

In addition to those plants whose leaves do not make good cuttings, there are of course many succulents which do not have leaves, such as most cacti. Here the only possible cutting is the stem cutting. In general, plants with long stems or side branches make the best cuttings, such as for example the Rat's-tail Cactus, *Aporocactus flagelliformis*. Incidentally this cactus and quite a number of trailing cacti are tip-rooting like a blackberry, and this can be used to advantage if one only has a small piece which might rot if planted in the ordinary way. The trick is to insert it upside down; it then roots rather slowly but the side stems which spring up are right way up. However, if a long stem is cut up into sections care should be taken to plant them right way up, as they look decidedly odd if rooted upside down.

Assuming the cuttings are to be inserted with the cut end below the soil, it is advisable to dip the cut end in flowers of sulphur, or a fine alkaline powder such as basic slag, to discourage rotting. Usually the cutting should be dried for a few days before insertion so that some healing takes place, and thus the risk of rotting is reduced. Most succulents do not produce calluses in the correct sense of the word, that is to say undifferentiated scar tissue from which roots spring, but send out roots from parts of the original stem, and thus the drying process does not have to be prolonged. In any case, the cutting should not be dried for so long that it begins to shrivel, and if there are signs of this it must be planted even if there is a risk of rotting.

There is one special trick with some euphorbias which is worth mentioning. The cuttings sometimes bleed excessively, exuding a milky sap or latex (which incidentally can sometimes be poisonous). The trick here is to dip the cut surface in water, which surprisingly usually stops the bleeding. The cutting can then be dried in the usual way.

When dried, the cutting is inserted into the rooting medium. If the natural soil of the district is very sandy it can often be used as it is, but heavier soil is best mixed with sharp sand up to half the total bulk. Some people prefer a mixture of equal parts sand and peat, but, whatever it is, it should wet easily with ordinary watering of the pot.

Adding up to an eighth part of horticultural vermiculite can cause a soil to wet readily.

Pots, pans or trays can be used for rooting cuttings, and again those made of plastic are favoured by most growers. When putting in the soil, allowance should of course be made for a space for watering at the top of the pot.

The depth to insert varies with the size of the cutting, and it is a good rule not to plant deeper than one quarter of the length of the cutting, and with a long cutting not more than 1 in. If the cutting is top heavy, securing it to a stick before insertion is a good idea.

Some succulents grow leggy in the course of years, and often the whole top of the plant can be cut off and rooted as a cutting. If the bottom of the plant is kept, it will often throw up fresh stems which when large enough can be taken off and rooted as cuttings.

Some people cut off the tops of those globular cacti which do not produce offsets, root them as cuttings, and keep the stump of the old plant in the hope that it will then produce offsets, but this is very risky. In fact, this is usually unnecessary, because it will often be found that cacti which do not produce offsets are fairly easy to grow from seed.

The correct time to take cuttings is when the plants are growing freely, usually in summer, but it is surprising how often a piece broken off by accident at the wrong time of the year, will root. If it is necessary to root a cutting in winter, it should be dried off four or five times longer than if taken in summer.

Grafting

Grafting has never been used much with succulents other than cacti, but not long ago many large cacti were grown on stocks as a regular method of cultivation. This has now fallen out of favour for various reasons. For example, Christmas Cacti were often cleft-grafted on to *Pereskia*, and in this way larger specimens were obtained. However, these grafts were never truly permanent, and sooner or later the heads fell off. Moreover, once it was realized that Christmas Cacti were very sensitive to excessive alkalinity in the soil, the difficulty of growing large plants on their own roots was overcome. In what follows, as is usual in describing grafting, the cactus on to which the graft is made will be called the 'stock', and the cactus which is grafted on to the stock will be called the 'scion'.

Some cactus species which were slow and difficult on their own roots were grafted on to strong-growing easy cacti, such as for example *Trichocereus spachianus*, but the trouble was that often the strong-growing stock caused the weak-growing scion to develop in a way uncharacteristic of the species. Nowadays permanent grafting is used by enthusiasts only for cacti which are almost impossible on their own roots, or for freak cacti such as cristate forms or those which contain no chlorophyll. It is also used where a rare specimen has rotted from below, and what remains of the top is too small to root as a cutting, so it is grafted and grown on until it is big enough to be severed and used as a cutting. Seedling grafting will be dealt with later.

In grafting all plants, it is necessary that the tissues which carry the sap, namely the vascular tissues, should be able to pass the sap from stock to scion. In most plants, particularly woody ones, it is necessary that these tissues should be in contact when making the graft. It was thought at one time that this was the case in cacti, and that the main sap-carrying tissues, which show as a ring of circular dots when the top of a globular or spherical cactus is cut off, would have to be in contact. Although it is true that when this is so the graft takes much faster, it is often not practical to do this when the diameters of stock and scion differ. Provided that the central woody part of the stems are in contact, grafts usually take well if the ring of circular dots do not make contact.

The way to go about it is to get everything ready beforehand, so that the cut surfaces do not have time to dry out while the operation is performed; usually there is a margin of a quarter of an hour or so between making the two cuts before there is a risk of drying, so there should be ample time.

The top of the stock should be cut off an inch or two from the top with a clean tool, stainless steel knives or razor blades being a great help. Any ribs on the stock should be slanted down for a quarter of an inch or so, so that they will not stick up as the cut surface dries later on.

The top of the scion is then cut off and pressed firmly on to the stock so as to exclude air. If there has been any undue delay after cutting the stock so that it has become dry, a thin slice is cut off. Stock and scion will adhere owing to the stickiness of the sap, but they should be held under pressure for a few days. A good way to do this is to put a rubber band round the graft and the bottom of the pot. If the scion is soft, or the band thought to be rather tight, a pad of cloth or soft paper will prevent the band cutting into it.

Cleft grafts are made by cutting a v-shaped notch in the stock, and shaping the end of the scion into a wedge to fit the notch. The scion is held in place by pinning it into the stock, and the best pins are cactus spines, cleaning them by pushing them through an unwanted piece of cactus.

All grafting must be done in the growing season, when sap is flowing freely. After grafting the plant should stand in a sunny place for a few days, when if the union is going to take the two parts will be stuck together firmly enough for the plant to be moved with care, and the rubber band

Rebutia senilis scion just placed on *Trichocereus schickendantzii* stock. Two rubber bands have been cut and tied together so as not to press too tightly on the scion.

A successful graft. *Frailea cataphracta* flowering after having been grafted onto *Hylocereus undatus* in a previous year. Fraileas are not easy on their own roots and are best grafted. They are plants for specialists and the genus is not described in this book for that reason.

should then be removed. However, the plant should be treated carefully, because it may take several weeks before the union is really strong. The stock should be watered freely, but the union should not get wet.

Seedling Grafting

While permanent grafting of mature cacti is losing favour, temporary grafting of seedlings is beoming more popular. The chief reason is that seedlings of some species grow very slowly in their early stages, and by growing as grafts for a year or two and then severing from the stock and rooting as a cutting, a great deal of time can be saved.

Seedling grafting is easy. The best stock is a fast-growing seedling, because although there are cases where, in mature cacti, stock and scion are incompatible, this is very seldom so if both are seedlings. Seedlings of *Cereus peruvianus* are often used, because seed is readily available, it germinates

easily and the seedlings grow fast. The cereus seedlings are lined out in boxes 2 in. apart, and when they are 2–3 in. tall they are ready.

Seedlings of the scion are cut off just above the cotyledons when large enough to handle, and the tip of the seedling stock is cut off so that the cut surface is large enough to take the scion, which is merely placed on the stock. Usually there is enough sap for the scion to adhere, but if not squeezing the piece of the stock which has been cut off with a pair of pliers will expel a drop of sap.

There is no need to bother about vascular rings, and they are usually not visible in any event in such small plants. Nor should pressure be put on the scion to hold it in place, or it may get bruised. Obviously, vibration should be avoided for a couple of days, but after that the box of grafts can be moved about without harm.

Some cactus seedlings go through a juvenile stage which

A v-shaped notch has been cut in the stock of
Selenicereus grandiflorus and the *Aporocactus flagelliformis*
scion has been pinned into position with a cactus spine.
As a precaution the graft should also be lightly bound
with string. The scion will grow faster when grafted, and
as it has a trailing habit, a 'weeping standard' will be
formed after about twelve months, as can be seen
on the right.

Grafting a seedling *Epiphyllum* (right) onto a mature plant of *E.* 'Cooperi' (left) to promote quicker growth and earlier maturity. About ½ in. is cut horizontally off a young shoot of the stock, and the same amount is cut, at right angles to the stem, off the tip of the seedling scion.

can last for several years. This is particularly so with epiphyllums, which in their early stages look rather like *Aporocactus*, and they will not flower until the typical flattened stems of the mature stage are produced. The production of mature stems is greatly speeded up if the seedlings are grafted on to a mature epiphyllum plant.

A fast-growing epiphyllum which produces plenty of side shoots, such as the old hybrid 'Cooperi', should be chosen. The mature plant can be used, or cuttings can be taken and rooted 3 in. apart in boxes. For a given stock plant, taking cuttings will ultimately produce far more grafting shoots than a mature plant, but it will take a season longer to produce them.

A very young shoot, 2–5 in. long, is ideal for grafting. About ¼–½ in. of the tip is cut off, and a piece of the seedling about the same length is taken from the tip of a shoot – it may be the entire top of a very young seedling. This is merely placed centrally on the cut surface of the

stock, and adheres by its own stickiness. It sticks very firmly after a day or two. All other young shoots should be removed from the same branch of the mature plant, or the rooted cutting if this is used.

An important point to remember is that the cut on the stock should be horizontal, even if not at right angles to the shoot, and the cut on the scion should be at right angles to the stem. This ensures that it will stand upright on the stock.

The graft usually hangs fire for a few weeks, and then grows very vigorously. It usually produces a forest of young shoots from the base of the scion, and it is wise to reduce these to 2 or 3 to promote early maturity in those that remain. If left to flower on the stock, flowering is early but the blooms may not be typical; so it is best to remove scions which have attained the typical flattened stems of mature plants, and root them as cuttings. Such cuttings usually make fine bushy plants.

The piece of the scion has merely been placed on the cut end of the stock, and adheres by the sticky sap.

PESTS

Nowadays pests should not present any great problems, though before the invention of modern chemicals pests could cause much damage, and still can in neglected collections. Most of them are not specific to cacti and succulents, but can attack many greenhouse plants.

Aphids
Aphids do not usually attack stems or leaves, but sometimes build up rapidly on flowers.

Earthworms
Earthworms in the pot can cause serious damage to roots, particularly to those plants which require rather moister treatment, such as the epiphytic cacti.

Mealy bugs
Mealy bug, which looks rather like a miniature woodlouse (sowbug) covers itself and the plant with a white woolly or mealy substance, needs to be checked at once; if there are only a few they can be painted over with dilute alcohol, eau-de-Cologne used neat being about the right strength. A different species attacks the roots, and the mealy appearance is very obvious if a plant is tapped out of the pot.

Red spider (Spider mites)
Red spider is neither red nor a spider, but is a brown mite which spins webs, flourishes in hot, dry conditions, and sucks the sap of many plants.

Scale insects
Scale insects can be troublesome if not checked. The insects move about freely when young, but later the females settle in one place and develop a hard covering. They suck the sap, and then the eggs hatch and the mobile stage begins again.

For cacti and most other succulents malathion spray will deal effectively with all the pests so far mentioned. Although all horticultural chemicals should be used with care and in strict accordance with the maker's instructions, malathion is far less poisonous than most modern insecticides. Moreover, it begins to decompose as soon as diluted (it must be used within two hours of making up), and leaves no harmful residue which could pollute the environment. While active, it has a most unpleasant smell, so accidental drinking is most unlikely, but the smell vanishes when the solution decomposes.

It is sprayed on the plants in the usual way, and soil pests are destroyed by watering the soil with it. It has one serious disadvantage, namely that it is liable to damage members of the family *Crassulaceae* to which many of the most popular succulents belong. For these plants the best thing to do is to try other insecticides until one is found which is effective for the pest concerned.

Caterpillars

Since the restrictions on the supply of DDT for amateur use, it is difficult to recommend a chemical for the control of caterpillars. BHC is often effective, but the best method is probably picking off by hand, remembering that most, if not all the caterpillars which attack cacti and succulents operate by night.

Eelworm (Nematode)

Attack by root and stem eelworm is mainly confined to plants collected from the wild, which are usually rare species not found in ordinary collections. Removing the upper part of the plant and rooting as a cutting eliminates these pests, but remember to bake or boil the old roots, soil and pot before throwing into the garden.

Nematode see Eelworm

Slugs and snails

Slugs and snails are killed by malathion if they are reached by it, but often they hide some distance away from the plant during the day, coming to attack at night. Metaldehyde will deal with them, but the usual prepared bait is attractive to some animals and children. The safest method is to sprinkle the surface of the soil with pure metaldehyde dust, but of course watering washes it away and it has to be renewed.

DISEASES

Few diseases attack cacti and succulents, and well grown plants should be immune. Sudden drops in temperature, particularly if condensation occurs, can cause spots of rot to develop. Scraping away the rotten patches till healthy tissue is reached, and then dusting with flowers of sulphur, will save the plant, but of course it leaves scars. Rotting at soil level or below is almost always due to bad drainage or overwatering. Often the first sign of root rot is shrivelling of the upper part of the plant. Cutting off the top and re-rooting is usually the only remedy.

Acknowledgments

We would like to thank Mr George Kalmbacher, Taxonomist and Curator of the Herbarium at the Brooklyn Botanic Garden, for his useful advice and comments which have added to the value of so many of the descriptions, and Richard Gorer who has kindly read the text on behalf of the Royal Horticultural Society.

PICTURE ACKNOWLEDGMENTS

The colour photographs were taken by the following photographers:

Bernard Alfieri: 207

Ernest Crowson: 2, 8-11, 14, 15, 17, 20-3, 27, 32-3, 37, 44-7, 49, 50, 54, 57-8, 66-7, 69-72, 74-5, 81-3, 90-1, 93, 95, 98, 101-3, 107-10, 112-13, 115-16, 123, 128, 130-1, 134, 139, 149, 151, 153-6, 159-60, 163, 165-6, 169-70, 177-8, 180, 182, 190, 194, 196-8, 202-5, 215, 221, 224, 228-9, 232-6, 240, 242-6, 248-53, 255, 257-61, 263, 268-70, 273-5, 283, 287, 289, 292, 294, 299, 302-3, 306-9, 311-12, 315, 317, 320, 323-5, 327-9, 331-2, 336, 338, 340, 343, 345-9, 351, 353, 355, 363-5, 370-2, 377-85, 387, 390, 392-3, 397, 399, 400, 403, 405-6, 408, 410-11, 416-17, 428, 431-7, 439, 441, 443, 445, 451, 453, 455-6, 458-60, 465, 469-73, 481-2, 485-8, 491, 500, 502

Valerie Finnis: 31, 86, 96, 158, 266, 280-1, 319, 407, 483, 490, 492

John Gapp: 25, 30, 34, 39, 59, 60-5, 80, 84, 105-6, 118-22, 126-7, 138, 140-1, 145, 147, 164, 171, 173-4, 176, 181, 183-7, 200, 206, 239, 264, 293, 295, 297-8, 333, 356, 359-61, 375-6, 396, 398, 429, 438, 454, 479-80, 494, 496, 501

F. R. McQuown: 208-13, 247, 422, 448-9

Harry Smith: 1, 3, 5, 7, 12, 13, 16, 18, 19, 26, 28, 35-6, 38, 40-1, 48, 51-3, 55-6, 68, 73, 76-9, 85, 87-9, 97, 99, 100, 104, 111, 114, 117, 124-5, 133, 136-7, 144, 148, 150, 152, 157, 161-2, 167-8, 172, 175, 179, 188-9, 191-3, 195, 199, 201, 204, 214, 216-20, 222-3, 225-6, 230-1, 238, 241, 254, 256, 262, 265, 267, 271-2, 276-9, 282, 284-6, 290-1, 296, 300-1, 304-5, 310, 313-14, 318, 321, 326, 330, 334-5, 337, 342, 350, 352, 357-8, 362, 367-9, 373-4, 386, 388, 391, 394, 401-2, 404, 409, 412, 414-15, 418-21, 423-7, 430, 440, 442, 444, 446-7, 450, 457, 461-4, 466-8, 474-7, 484, 493, 495, 497-9, 503-6

Tom Wellsted: 227, 478

Dennis Woodland: 4, 92, 94, 288, 316, 339, 344, 413

We would like to thank Ilford Limited for allowing us to reproduce the following transparencies: 6, 24, 29, 42-3, 129, 132, 135, 142-3, 146, 237, 322, 341, 354, 366, 389, 395, 452, 489

The black and white photographs in the Introduction were taken by Ernest Crowson.

The Plates

I
Abutilon mega-
potamicum

2
Abutilon
striatum
'Thomsonii'

3
Acacia armata

4
Acacia
dealbata

5
Acacia
longifolia

6
Acalypha
hispida

7
Achimenes
heterophylla
'Little Beauty'

8
Adiantum
tenerum

9
Adiantum
trapeziforme

10
Adromischus
cristatus

11
Adromischus
rotundifolius

12
Aechmea
chantinii

13
Aechmea
fasciata

14
Aeonium
arboreum

15
Aeonium
tabulaeforme

16
Aeschynanthus
lobbianus

17
Agapanthus
africanus

18
Agapanthus
campanulatus

19
Agave
americana
marginata

20
Agave
americana
'Mediopicta'

21
Agave
angustifolia
'Marginata'

23
Agave
victoriae-
reginae

22
Agave filifera

24
Aglaonema
commutatum

25
Aglaonema
crispum
'Silver Queen'

26
Aglaonema
treubii

27
Allamanda
cathartica
'Grandiflora'

28
Allamanda
neriifolia

29
Aloe variegata

30
Alonsoa
warscewiczii

31
Amaryllis
belladonna

32
Ananas
bracteatus
'Striatus'

33
Anchusa
capensis
'Blue Bird'

34
Anthurium
andreanum

35
Anthurium
scherzerianum

36
Aphelandra
squarrosa

37
Aporocactus
flagelliformis

38
Araucaria
excelsa

39
Arctotis
breviscapa

40
Arctotis ×
hybrida

41
Ardisia crispa

42
Aristolochia
elegans

43
Arum creticum

44
Asclepias
curassavica
'Aurea'

45
Asparagus
densiflorus
'Sprengeri'

46 Aspidistra
elatior

47
Asplenium
bulbiferum

48
Asplenium
nidus

49
Astrophytum
ornatum

50
Asystasia bella

51
Babiana
sambucina

52
Begonia
coccinea

53
Begonia
fuchsioides

54
Begonia
haageana

55
Begonia
manicata

56
Begonia
masoniana

57
Begonia nitida
'Alba'

58
Begonia rex

59
Begonia
semperflorens

60
Begonia
socotrana
'Regent'

61
Begonia ×
tuberhybrida
'Corona'

62
Begonia ×
tuberhybrida
'Elaine
Tartellin'

63
Begonia ×
tuberhybrida
'Guardsman'

64
Begonia ×
tuberhybrida
'Harlequin'

65
Begonia ×
tuberhybrida
'Mary Heatley'

66
Begonia ×
tuberhybrida
Pendula

67
Beloperone
guttata

68
Billbergia
nutans

69
**Billbergia
pyramidalis**

70
**Blechnum
gibbum**

71
**Bougainvillea
× buttiana
'Mrs Butt'/
'Crimson Lake'**

72
**Bougainvillea
glabra
'Double Pink'**

73
**Bougainvillea
spectabilis**

74
**Bouvardia ×
domestica
'Mary'**

75
Bouvardia ×
domestica
'President
Cleveland'

76
Browallia
speciosa

77
Brunfelsia
calycina
'Macrantha'

78
Bryophyllum
uniflorum

79
Caladium
bicolor

80
Calandrinia
umbellata
'Amaranth'

81
Calathea
insignis

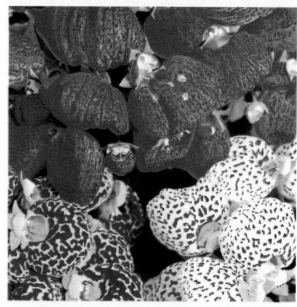

82
Calathea
makoyana

83
Calathea
zebrina

84
Calceolaria ×
herbeohybrida
'Monarch'

85
Calceolaria ×
herbeohybrida
'Multiflora
Nana'

86
Calceolaria
integrifolia

87
Calceolaria
pavonii

88
Callicarpa
rubella

89
Callistemon
citrinus

90
Callistemon
speciosus

91
Camellia
japonica
'Alba Simplex'

92
Camellia
japonica
'Jupiter'

93
Camellia
japonica
'Adolphe
Audusson'

94
Camellia
japonica
'Tricolor'

95
Camellia
reticulata
'Captain
Rawes'

96
Campanula
isophylla

97
Campanula
isophylla
'Alba'

98
Canna ×
hybrida 'J.B.
van der Schoot'

99
Cantua
buxifolia

100
Capsicum
annuum
'Fiesta'

IOI
Capsicum
frutescens
'Chameleon'

IO2
Capsicum
frutescens
'Fips'

103
Caralluma
europaea

IO4
Cassia
corymbosa

105
Cattleya
'Catherine
Subod'

106
Celosia
argentea
Cristata

107
Celosia
argentea
Pyramidalis

108
Celsia
arcturus

109
Cephalocereus
senilis

110
Ceropegia
woodii

111
Cestrum
aurantiacum

112
Chamaecereus
silvestrii

113
Chamaedorea
elegans

114
Chamaerops
humilis

115
Chirita
sinensis

116
Chlorophytum
elatum
'Variegatum'

117
Chorizema
cordatum

118
Chrysanthe-
mum (1) 'John
Rowe'

119
Chrysanthe-
mum (2)
'Parade'

120
Chrysanthe-
mum (3) 'Fred
Shoesmith'

121
Chrysanthe-
mum (4) 'Peggy
Stevens'

122
Chrysanthe-
mum (5)
'Marion Stacey'

123
Chrysanthe-
mum (6)
'Fairie'

124
Chrysanthe-
mum (7)
Cascade/Charm

125
Chrysanthe-
mum (7)
Korean

126
Chrysanthe-
mum (7)
'Portrait'

127
Chrysanthe-
mum (7)
Rayonnante

128
Cineraria
'Berlin Market'

129
Cissus
antarctica

130
Citrus mitis

131
Cleistocactus
strausii

132
Clerodendrum
speciosissimum

133
Clerodendrum
thomsonae

134
Clerodendrum
ugandense

135
Clianthus
formosus

136
Clianthus
puniceus

137
Clivia ×
cyrtanthiflora

138
Clivia miniata

139
Clivia nobilis

140
Cobaea
scandens

141
Coccoloba
uvifera

142
Codiaeum
variegatum
Pictum

143
Codiaeum
variegatum
Pictum
'Volcano'

144
Coelogyne
cristata

145
Coelogyne
ochracea

146
Coleus blumei

147
Coleus
thyrsoideus

148
Coleus blumei

149
Columnea ×
banksii

150
Columnea
gloriosa
'Purpurea'

151
Cordyline
australis

152
Cordyline
terminalis
'Firebrand'

153
Coronilla
glauca
'Compacta'

154
Coryphantha
echinus

155
Crassula
argentea

156
Crassula
falcata

157
Crinum ×
powellii

158
Crocus vernus
'Vanguard'

159
Crossandra
undulifolia
'Mona Walhed'

160
Cryptanthus
bivittatus

161
Cryptanthus
zonatus

162
Ctenanthe
oppenheimiana
'Tricolor'

163
Cunonia
capensis

164
Cuphea miniata
'Firefly'

165
Cuphea
platycentra

166
Cupressus
cashmeriana

167
Cycas revoluta

168
Cyclamen
persicum

169
Cyclamen
persicum

170
Cyclamen
persicum
'Shell Pink'

171
Cymbidium
Rosanna
'Pinkie'

172
Cymbidium
Rosette

173
Cymbidium
Swallow
'Exbury'

174
Cymbidium
Vieux Rose

175
Cymbidium
lowianum

176
Cyperus
papyrus

177
Datura
cornigera
'Grand
Marnier'

178
Datura
sanguinea

179
Datura
suaveolens

180
Dendrobium
aureum

181
Dendrobium
nobile
'Virginale'

182
Dianella
tasmanica

183
Dianthus
'Ballerina'

184
Dianthus
'Brocade'

185
Dianthus
'Fragrant Ann'

186
Dianthus
'Heather
Beauty'

187
Dianthus
'Helios'

188
Dicentra
spectabilis

189
Dicksonia
antarctica

190
Dieffenbachia
picta 'Exotica'

191
Dieffenbachia
picta 'Roehrsii'

192
Dionaea
muscipula

193
Dipladenia
splendens

194
Dizygotheca
elegantissima

195
Dracaena
deremensis

196
Dracaena
fragrans

197
Dracaena
godseffiana

198
Dracaena
marginata
'Variegata'

200
Eccremocarpus
scaber

199
Drosera
capensis

201
Echeveria
harmsii

202
Echinocactus
grusonii

203
Echinocereus
rosei

204
Echium
fastuosum

205
Epidendrum
brassavolae

206
Epidendrum
ibaguense

207
Epiphyllum ×
ackermannii

208
Epiphyllum
'Carl von
Nicolai'

209
Epiphyllum
'Cooperi'

210
Epiphyllum
'London'

211
Epiphyllum
'Eastern Gold'

212
Epiphyllum
'London
Gaiety'

213
Epiphyllum
'Thalia'

214
Episcia
cupreata
'Silver Sheen'

215
Episcia
dianthiflora

216
Episcia fulgida

217
Erica
canaliculata

218
Erythrina
crista-galli

219
Eucalyptus
globulus

220
Eucharis
grandiflora

221
Eucomis
comosa

222
Eupatorium
atrorubens

223
Euphorbia
fulgens

224
Euphorbia
horrida

225
Euphorbia
milii splendens

226
Euphorbia
pulcherrima

227
Euphorbia
pulcherrima
'Mikkel-
Rochford Pink'

228
Euphorbia
resinifera

229
Exacum affine
'Midget'

230
Fabiana
imbricata

231
× Fatshedera
lizei 'Variegata'

232
Fatsia japonica

233
Faucaria
tigrina

234
Ferocactus
latispinus

235
Ficus
benjamina

236
Ficus
diversifolia

237
Ficus elastica
'Decora'

238
Ficus elastica
'Doescheri'

239
Ficus pumila

240
Ficus radicans
'Variegata'

241
Fittonia
argyroneura

242
Fittonia
verschaffeltii

243
Freesia ×
hybrida

244
Fuchsia
'Arabella'

245
Fuchsia
'Impudence'

246
Fuchsia
'Leonora'

247
Fuchsia
'Swingtime'

248
Fuchsia
'Violet Gem'

249
Gardenia
jasminoides
'Florida'/
'Plena'

250
Gasteria
brevifolia

251
Geogenanthus
undarus

252
Gerbera
jamesonii

**253
Gerbera
jamesonii
'Farnell's
Strain'**

**254
Gladiolus
'Columbine'**

**255
Gladiolus
'Charm'**

**256
Gladiolus
tristis
'Christabel'**

**257
Globba
atrosanguinea**

**258
Gloriosa
superba**

259
Guzmania
lingulata

260
Gymno-
calycium
baldianum

261
Gynura
aurantiaca

262
Haemanthus
katherinae

263
Haworthia
attenuata

264
Hedera
canariensis
'Variegata'

265
Hedera helix
'Glacier'

266
Hedera helix
'Gold Heart'

267
Hedera helix
'Lutzii'

268
Hedychium
coccineum

269
Hedychium
gardnerianum

270
Heliocereus
speciosus

271
Heliotropium
× hybridum

272
Hibiscus
rosa-sinensis

273
Hibiscus
rosa-sinensis
'Miss Betty'

274
Hibiscus
rosa-sinensis
'The President'

275
Hibiscus
rosa-sinensis
'Veronica'

276
Hibiscus
waimeae

277
Hippeastrum

278
Hippeastrum
'Jenny Lind'

279
Hippeastrum
'Nivalis'

280
Hippeastrum
aulicum

281
Hippeastrum
× johnsonii

282
Hoya bella

283
Hoya carnosa

284
Hyacinthus

285
Hyacinthus
'Eros'

286
Hyacinthus
'Perle
Brillante'

287
Hydrangea
Hortensia

288
Hydrangea
'Hamburg'

289
Hydrangea
'Nieder-
sachsen'

290
Hymenocallis
caribaea

291
Hymenocallis
littoralis

292
Hypoestes
taeniata

293
Impatiens
balsamina

294
Impatiens
wallerana
petersiana

295
Hypocyrta
glabra

296
Impatiens
wallerana
sultanii

297
Ipomoea
purpurea
'Scarlett
O'Hara'

298
Ipomoea
tricolor

299
Ixia

300
Jacobinia
carnea

301
Jacobinia
coccinea

302
Jacobinia
pauciflora

303
Jacobinia
suberecta

304
Jasminum
mesnyi

305
Jovellana
violacea

306
Kalanchoe
blossfeldiana
'Emma Lord'

307
Kalanchoe
blossfeldiana
'Morning Sun'

308
Kalanchoe
blossfeldiana
'Tom Thumb'

309
Kalanchoe
millotii

310
Kalanchoe
pumila

311
Kohleria
eriantha

312
Lachenalia
aloides

313
Lantana
camara

314
Lapageria rosea

315
Lantana
selloviana

316
Leptospermum
cunninghamii

317
Leptospermum
scoparium
'Nanum'

318
Leucadendron
argenteum

319
Lilium auratum

320
Limonium
suworowii

321
Lippia
citriodora

322
Lithops
salicola

323
Lycaste
Auburn

324
Lycaste
Auburn

325
Malvaviscus
arboreus

326
Mammillaria
bocasana

327
Mammillaria
elongata

328
Mammilaria
hahniana

329
Mammillaria
zeilmanniana
'Alba'

330
Mandevilla
suaveolens

331
Maranta
leuconeura
'Erythrophylla'

332
Maranta
leuconeura
'Kerchoveana'

333
**Martynia
louisiana**

334
Maurandia
erubescens

335
Maurandia
scandens

336
Maxillaria
sanderiana

337
Medinilla
magnifica

338
Miltonia
Everest

339
Mitraria
coccinea

340
Momordica
charantia

341
Monstera
pertusa

342
Moraea
iridioides

343
Musa
cavendishii

344
Mutisia
oligodon

345
Narcissus
'Double Event'

346
Narcissus
'Paperwhite
Grandiflora'

347
Neoregelia
carolinae
'Tricolor'

348
Nepenthes ×
'F. W. Moore'

349
Nephrolepis
exaltata
'Elegantissima'

350
Nerine
bowdenii

351
Nerine
sarniensis
'Miss E. Cator'

35²
**Neriwm
oleander**

353
**Nerium
oleander
'Variegata'**

354
**Nidularium
innocentii**

355
**Nopalxochia
phyllanthoides**

356
**Nymphaea
capensis
'Zanzibariensis
Rosea'**

357
**Odontoglossum
crispum**

358
Nymphaea
stellata
'Dir. G. T.
Moore'

359
Odontoglossum
Kopan
'Lyoth Aurea'

360
Odontonia
Atheror
'Lyoth Majesty'

361
Odontonia
Olga 'Icefall'

362
Ophiopogon
jaburan
'Variegatus/
'Vittatus'

363
Oplismenus
hirtellus
'Variegatus'

364
Opuntia
decumbens

365
Opuntia
microdasys
'Albispina'

366
Ornithogalum
thyrsoides

367
Pachystachys
lutea

368
Pamianthe
peruviana

369
Paphiopedilum
insigne

370
Paphiopedilum
× maudiae

371
Parodia
chrysacanthion

372
Passiflora ×
allardii

373
Passiflora
edulis

374
Passiflora
quadrangularis

375
Pelargonium
crispum
'Variegatum'

376
Pelargonium ×
domesticum
'Doris Frith'

377
Pelargonium ×
domesticum
'Grand Slam'

378
Pelargonium ×
domesticum
'Kingston
Beauty'

379
Pelargonium ×
hortorum
'Distinction'

380
Pelargonium ×
hortorum
'Fiat'

381
Pelargonium ×
hortorum
'Gazelle'

382
Pelargonium ×
hortorum
'Mr Henry Cox'

383
Pelargonium ×
hortorum
'Spitfire'

384
Pelargonium ×
hortorum
'Pink Harry
Hieover'

385
Pelargonium
peltatum
'Sussex Lace'

386
Pellaea
rotundifolia

387
Pellionia
pulchra

388
Pentas
lanceolata

389
Peperomia
argyreia

390
Peperomia
caperata

391
Peperomia
hederifolia

392
Peperomia
magnoliifolia
'Variegata'

393
Peristrophe
angustifolia
'Aurea-
variegata'

394
Philesia
buxifolia

395
Philodendron
andreanum

396
Philodendron
hastatum

397
Philodendron
scandens

398
Phoenix
roebelinii

399
Pilea cadierei

400
Pilea muscosa

401
Platycerium
bifurcatum

402
Pittosporum
tobira

403
Plectranthus
coleoides
'Marginatus'

404
Plectranthus
oertendahlii

405
Pleione
forrestii

406
Plumbago
capensis

407
Polianthes
tuberosa

408
Polypodium
aureum

409
Primula
kewensis

410
Primula
malacoides

411
Primula
obconica

412
Primula
sinensis
'Dazzler'

413
Prostanthera
ovalifolia

414
Protea
cynaroides

415
Punica
granatum
'Flore Pleno'

416
Punica
granatum
'Nana'

417
Rebutia

418
Rebutia
minuscula

419
Rechsteineria
cardinalis

420
Reinwardtia
trigyna

421
**Rechsteineria
leucotricha**

422
Rhipsalidopsis
gaertneri

423
Rhipsalidopsis
rosea

424
Rhododendron
bullatum

425
Rhododendron
simsii
'Perle de Noisy'

426
Rhododendron
simsii
'Vervaeneana'

427
Rhododendron
taggianum

428
Rhoicissus
rhomboidea

429
Ricinus
communis
'Gibsonii'

430
Rochea
coccinea

431
Rondeletia
roezlii

432
Ruellia
macrantha

433
Saintpaulia
ionantha
'Diana Blue'

434
Saintpaulia
ionantha
'Rhapsodie'

435
Santpaulia
ionantha
'Rhapsodie'

436
Saintpaulia
ionantha
'Rhapsodie'

437
Saintpaulia
ionanthe
'Rhapsodie'

438
Salpiglossis
sinuata
'Superbissima'

439
Salvinia
auriculata

441
Sansevieria
trifasciata

442
Sansevieria
trifasciata
'Laurentii'

443
Sarracenia
purpurea

444
Sarracenia
purpurea

445
Saxifraga
stolonifera

446
Schizanthus
pinnatus

447
Schlumbergera
× buckleyi

44⁸
Schlumbergera
'Königers
Weihnachts-
freude'/
'Christmas
Joy'

449
Schlumbergera
'Winter-
märchen'/
'Winter Tales'

45⁰
Scindapsus
aureus
'Marble
Queen'

45¹
Sedum
rubrotinctum
'Aurora'

45²
Sedum sieboldii
'Medio-
variegatum'

453
Sedum
treleasei

454
Selaginella
involvens
argentea

455
Selaginella
vogelii

456
Senecio
citriformis

457
Senecio
grandifolius

458
Senecio
serpens

459
Sinningia
regina

460
Sinningia
speciosa
Fyfiana

461
Smithiantha
'Elke'

462
Smithiantha
'Pink Domino'

463
Solanum
capsicastrum

464
Solanum
wendlandii

465
Sollya
fusiformis

466
Sonerila
margaritacea

467
Sparmannia
africana

468
Spathiophyllum
wallisii

469
Sphaeralcea
umbellata

470
Stapelia
variegata

471
Stephanotis
floribunda

472
Strelitzia
reginae

473
Streptocarpus
× hybridus
'Constant
Nymph'

474
Streptosolen
jamesonii

475
Strobilanthes
dyerianus

476
Tecomaria
capensis

477
Telopea
speciosissima

478
Tetrastigma
voinieriana

479
Thunbergia
alata

480
Thunbergia
gregorii

481
Thunbergia
natalensis

482
Tibouchina
semidecandra

483
Tigridia
pavonia

484
Tigridia
pavonia
'Lutea'

485
Tillandsia
lindeniana

486
Tillandsia
usneoides

487
Torenia
fournieri

488
Tradescantia
fluminensis
'Quicksilver'

489
Trichocereus
candicans

490
Tropaeolum
tricolorum

491
Tulipa
'Brilliant Star'

492
Vallota speciosa

493
Veltheimia
viridifolia

494
× Venidio-
arctotis

495
Venidium
decurrens

496
Venidium
fastuosum

497
Vinca rosea

498
Vriesea
fenestralis

499
Vriesea
splendens

500
× Vuylstekeara

The Dictionary

Symbols used in the text

✽   attractive flowers

🐌   interesting general appearance or foliage

●   interesting fruit

Temperature guide

Cold – unheated, preferably not below freezing

Cool – not below 45°F.

Warm – not below 60°F.

Metric conversion guide

1 in. = 2·54 cm.

1 ft = 0·31 m.

Degrees Fahrenheit to degrees Celsius (Centigrade)
conversion factor $(°F. - 32) \times \frac{5}{9} = °C.$

A

ABUTILON (MALVACEAE) Flowering Maple
A genus of herbs and shrubs mainly from warm temperate climates, which needs greenhouse protection at least in winter. All have simple, undivided leaves and 5-petalled, bell or lantern-shaped flowers. Grow in the cool greenhouse or conservatory border or in pots or tubs of a loam-based compost. In the border they will grow to 6–8 ft tall but in pots they will reach 3–4 ft. Shade from hottest sun and ventilate freely. Propagate by stem cuttings in summer.

darwinii
A large evergreen or semi-evergreen shrub especially suitable for training up pillars. It has large leaves reaching 6 in. in length, the lower being up to 7-lobed, the upper only 3. In spring the velvety calyx opens out to produce striking orange-red flowers, 2 in. across and veined in a full deep red. Brazil.

× hybridum
This is a hybrid between *A. darwinii* and *A. striatum* and forms a neater, branched shrub with large lobed leaves similar to those of the previous species. The flowers, which are pendent, are about 1½ in. across and coloured variously in shades of yellow, orange, red and white. Many named cultivars are grown of which 'Ashford Red' and 'Golden Fleece' are most striking. Garden origin.

insigne
A slender shrub, particularly valuable for its winter flowering habit. The 2-in. flowers are carried on pendulous stalks, each bloom with carmine veins laced across white petals, while the stalks and the calyx are covered with a reddish down in the young stage. Colombia.

megapotamicum
A graceful evergreen shrub reaching 6 ft on a wall but 3–4 ft in pots, with bright green, ovate, pointed leaves. The lantern-like, pendent flowers have a large carmine inflated calyx from which emerge the yellow petals and a cluster of red stamens which protrude beyond them. The total effect is most attractive, the flowers appearing from late spring to October. Brazil. **1.**

× milleri
A hybrid of *A. megapotamicum* and *A. pictum* which is suitable for a greenhouse border. The ovate, toothed leaves are large, reaching 6 in. in length, and have a conspicuous yellow mottling. The flowers, which are orange-yellow with red veins, appear throughout the summer. Garden origin.

striatum 'Thomsonii' Spotted Flowering Maple
A shrubby plant with deeply lobed, maple-like leaves which are dark green and mottled with creamy-yellow. The solitary flowers are bell shaped and a dark orange with rich red veining. It makes a good, undemanding house plant. Brazil, Uruguay, Argentina. **2.**

ACACIA (LEGUMINOSAE) Mimosa
A genus of chiefly Australian evergreen shrubs or trees. A feature of most species is that the leaves are reduced or absent, their place being taken by modified leaf stalks known as phyllodes. Although when fully grown, many are large trees, they are easily grown in the cool greenhouse or conservatory border or pots or tubs and must be grown under cover except in very mild areas. Use a loam-based compost and ventilate freely in warm weather. Propagate by seeds in spring or heeled stem cuttings in summer.

armata Kangaroo Thorn
This is a good indoor shrub reaching 10 ft. The phyllodes are dark green, narrowly oblong and spine-tipped. They contrast well with the rich yellow heads of fluffy flowers borne in April. Australia. **3.**

baileyana Cootamunda Wattle
A beautiful shrub or small tree, with bi-pinnate, grey-green pendent leaves, each composed of numerous tiny leaflets. The rich yellow flowers are carried in hanging clusters up to 4 in. long and open in April. Australia.

cultriformis Knife Acacia
A shrub growing to 6 ft with slender branches and grey-green pointed phyllodes. The flowers, in small yellow pompon heads, are carried in upright clusters and appear in spring. Australia.

dealbata syn. **A. decurrens dealbata** Silver Wattle
A superb tree for the large greenhouse or conservatory, it can attain 25 ft. The silver in its name refers to the fern-like leaves which are covered with silvery down when young. The yellow flowers are borne on long pendent shoots and are fragrant. The value of this plant is increased by the fact that given warm conditions it will come into flower in December. Australia. **4.**

decurrens dealbata see **A. dealbata**

drummondii
A shrub to 10 ft with long dissected leaves and lemon yellow flowers in cylindrical spikes, carried in the axils of the leaves. It makes a good pot plant and flowers in spring. W. Australia.

farnesiana Popinac, Opopanax, Huisache
This is a small tree reaching 20 ft. It has hairless, bi-pinnate leaves and fragrant, yellow pompon flower heads. It flowers in February and March and is a source of perfume. Australia.

longifolia Sydney Golden Wattle
A tree or large shrub attaining 20 ft with distinctive long, leaf-like phyllodes which are somewhat hoary green and give the plant a willow-like appearance. Its bright yellow, globular flower heads are carried in erect, axillary clusters. A good indoor plant where space permits. Australia. **5.**

podalyriifolia Pearl Acacia
A 10 ft shrub with white downy twigs when young. The leaf-like phyllodes are also silvery and set off the axillary clusters of up to 20 globose yellow heads of flowers. These appear in winter, making it a valuable plant. Australia.

riceana
A distinctive small tree of weeping habit attaining 15 ft or more. The phyllodes are spine-tipped and the spikes of globose flower heads a clear yellow. It is particularly attractive treated as a climber and trained up supports. Australia, Tasmania.

verticillata Star Acacia
A compact shrub reaching 10 ft or more. The spine-tipped phyllodes grow in whorls of about 6 and the compact, cylindrical spikes of flowers are bright yellow. The latter appear in spring, often in abundance. This species is suitable for the larger, cool greenhouse or conservatory and responds to pot culture for more restricted areas. Australia, Tasmania.

ACALYPHA (EUPHORBIACEAE)
A genus from warm regions of the world which is grown chiefly for its large, brightly coloured leaves. With the exception of *A. hispida* the flowers are small and inconspicuous. They thrive best in a warm, humid atmosphere, shaded from direct sunlight in summer. Use a loam-based compost or a proprietary peat mix. Propagate by stem cuttings in spring or summer.

hispida Chenille Plant, Red-hot Catstail
A shrub attaining 10–15 ft. It has ovate, slender-pointed evergreen leaves and red flowers in long, pendent, tassel-like spikes up to 20 in. long. It needs a minimum temperature of 60°F. to thrive properly. New Guinea. **6.**

wilkesiana
A shrub of 6 ft or more which is grown for its coppery foliage which is mottled and blotched with crimson. Several varieties with varying leaf markings have been named. New Hebrides.

× Achimenantha see **× Eucodonopsis**

ACHIMENES (GESNERIACEAE)
A genus of tufted herbaceous perennials with curious scaly, tuber-like rootstocks. The flowers which are profusely borne, range from pink and red to purple, yellow and white and somewhat resemble small foxgloves. All species and cultivars are excellent pot plants. Use a peat mix or a loam-based compost, potting the tubers in spring. Water sparingly at first, then more freely. Dry off in autumn. Keep shaded in summer and provide a humid atmosphere. Propagate by separating the tubers at potting time each year.

coccinea
A neat plant about 1½ ft in height. It has whorls of 3 small, ovate,

bright green leaves and small intense crimson scarlet blooms which appear from August onwards. Jamaica, Mexico to Panama, Peru.
   'Pulchella' has blooms yellow-flecked at the centre;
   'Rosea' has a dark eye.

grandiflora
This species grows to about 1½ ft. The leaves are green and rusty beneath, and the flowers rose-purple with a white eye. Mexico.

heterophylla
A slender plant reaching 1 ft or more with rich emerald green leaves. The flowers, which appear in July, are scarlet outside and orange-yellow within. Mexico, Guatemala.
   'Little Beauty', the bright and deep pink flowers are borne on a more bushy plant. **7.**

longiflora
A distinctive perennial with slender trailing stems and ovate, sharply pointed hairy leaves, green above and often reddish below. The flowers, which can reach 3 in. in length, are very variable in colour, usually violet but also occurring in shades of pink and blue. Most have a white eye. Mexico to Panama.
   'Alba' is the most striking cultivar, being almost pure white with a slight purple flush at the centre.

mexicana syn. **A. scheeri**
A bushy perennial with stout, hairy stems and ovate, velvety leaves up to 5 in. long. The flowers reach 1½–2 in. in length and are blue-purple outside, white inside and hairy. Mexico.

scheeri see **A. mexicana**

ACOKANTHERA (APOCYNACEAE)
spectabilis Winter-sweet
A very attractive tall evergreen shrub or tree for the warm conservatory or greenhouse, reaching 15 ft. The leaves are broad and ovate, up to 5 in. long, leathery and shining. The glossy white flowers are very fragrant and form a dense globose head in spring. Grow in the border or in tubs or large pots of a loam-based compost. Maintain a humid atmosphere and shade from the hottest sunshine. Propagate by stem cuttings, preferably with a heel in summer. S. Africa.

ACORUS (ARACEAE)
gramineus 'Variegatus'
A densely tufted, moisture loving grass-like plant. The leaves grow to 8–10 in. in length and are green with a white stripe. The small club-shaped flower spikes are insignificant. This is a good pot plant for an unheated room or a cool or cold greenhouse. Grow in a loam-based compost and keep continually moist. Propagate by division in spring. Japan.

ADIANTUM (POLYPODIACEAE) Maidenhair Fern
A genus of dainty, shade loving ferns with finely cut fronds and wiry black stalks. They need a moist atmosphere and are excellent subjects for the shaded greenhouse and conservatory. Grow in pots of a proprietary peat compost or plant out in a border. Propagate by division or spores in spring.

capillus-veneris Common Maidenhair Fern
An evergreen species with pale green triangular fronds, dissected into deeply lobed segments. Each frond grows upright to about 6–10 in. then arches over and becomes pendent. It grows wild in many parts of the world including western Britain and southern U.S.A. As a pot plant it grows best under cover and will often 'seed' itself on damp shady walls.

cuneatum see **A. raddianum**

hispidulum
A handsome, distinct species with the leaf fronds forked at the base, giving the appearance of branching. The hairy, rounded leaflets are leathery in texture and bronze-red when young. Grow in warmth. Tropics.

raddianum syn. **A. cuneatum** Delta Maidenhair
A fern of similar habit to *A. capillus-veneris* with very finely dissected fronds which arch outwards gracefully. Grow in a warm greenhouse. Brazil. Many forms have received names:

'Fritz-luthii', which has long narrow fronds is frequently grown for its striking appearance;
'Fragrantissimum', which is possibly of hybrid origin, has somewhat fragrant fronds up to 1 ft in length.

tenerum
A species with fronds growing up to 3 ft in length. The leaflets are stalked and often have a rosy flush when young. Grow in warmth. West Indies. **8.**
   'Farleyense' is considered the best form and is possibly the finest *Adiantum* for pot culture. It has strikingly delicate lacy fronds with leaflets which are crisped at the base.

trapeziforme Giant Maidenhair Fern
This species has bold fronds with large bright green leaflets up to 2 in. long, each being undivided and trapezoid in shape. It needs warm, moist conditions to thrive well. Tropical America. **9.**

venustum
An attractive species which grows well in the cool or cold conservatory or greenhouse. It has narrowly triangular fronds and convex leaflets which are bronze-pink when young, becoming green later. Himalayas.

ADROMISCHUS (CRASSULACEAE)
Small perennial plants from S. and S.W. Africa, up to 6 in. across, with tough woody stems often covered with long curly brown hairs (the remains of aerial roots). The thick, fleshy leaves are often marbled or otherwise marked and are the chief attraction, the flowers being less important. Cultivation as for terrestrial succulents, see Introduction. The resting period is in summer but the plants should have a little water. Full light and moderate watering at other times of the year are needed. Sideshoots are seldom produced and propagation is by leaf cuttings or seed. Winter temperatures 50–55°F. for growth, but lower temperatures above freezing will not kill the plants. Formerly included in the genus *Cotyledon*.

cooperi syn. **A. festivus**
The pinkish flowers are ½ in. long and appear in spring. The leaves are cylindrical to pillow-shaped, narrowing below and with the tip narrowing into a wedge-shaped, more or less wavy edge, grey-green with dark markings. Reddish hairs on stem. S. Africa.

cristatus
Very similar to *A. cooperi*, but the leaves are greener and the markings less pronounced. Flowers in spring. S. Africa. **10.**

festivus see **A. cooperi**

maculatus
The flowers, which appear in spring, are ½ in. long and green with pinkish to purplish tips. The leaves are kidney-shaped, flat above, strongly convex beneath, with a horny edge. They are greyish-green, heavily marked with reddish- or purplish-brown. The stems are short and stout. S. Africa.

rotundifolius
The flowers are ½ in. long, pinkish, and appear in spring. The leaves are roundish, green with a waxy covering, concave above, convex below, with a horny edge. The stem is stout, up to 8 in. long, becoming prostrate with age. S. Africa. **11.**

AECHMEA (BROMELIACEAE)
All those commonly grown are epiphytes, having spreading or tubular rosettes of leaves which form a cup or vase at the centre which holds water. The flowers emerge from coloured bracts which last for many weeks. They dislike lime, but any open soil suits, a good one being equal parts of loam, leafmould, peat and sand. Watering should be with rain water, and the cup at the centre should be kept filled. Overhead spraying is beneficial, and plenty of water in summer is needed; they should not get quite dry in winter. Winter temperatures 50–55°F. but lower temperatures are tolerated. Propagation is by severing sideshoots which are produced after the flower fades, when the original rosette dies off. The sideshoots shoots should be cut off with a sharp knife, dried for a day or two and rooted in the growing compost.

barleei see **A. bracteata**

bracteata syn. **A. barleei**
The flowers are pale yellow, with lower bracts red and upper ones green, growing in panicles on a stem up to 12 in. long. The flowers open in September, to be followed by the shiny green and red berries. The leaves are strap-shaped, with stout spines on the margins and up to 3 ft in length. Mexico to Colombia.

chantinii syn. **Billbergia chantinii**
The flowers are yellow to red in a 4–6 in. panicle of salmon to orange bracts. They occur in summer. The leaves are 12 in. long, 2 in. broad and variable in colour, but usually banded with white. The plant spreads by stolons which can be cut off and rooted. Brazil, Peru. **12.**

fasciata syn. **Billbergia rhodocyanea** Urn Plant
The flowers are pale blue, turning pink, surrounded by pink bracts in a compact head about 6 in. long and appear in summer. The leaves are strap-shaped, up to 1½ ft long and 4 in. across, grey green with cross bands of silvery scales. Very popular and easy to grow, the flower heads retaining their colour for several months. The sideshoots grow after flowering, and may be left to form a large plant or detached and rooted. Sometimes incorrectly known as *A. rhodocyanea*. Brazil. **13.**

fulgens
Flowers purple, sepals and flower stem scarlet, up to 50 flowers in a branching panicle up to 6 in. long. The leaves are sword-shaped, up to 1 ft long and 2 in. wide, dusty green in an open rosette up to 10 in. tall. Brazil.
  discolor, has purple undersides to the leaves and is more commonly grown than the type.

rhodocyanea see under **A. fasciata**

AEONIUM (CRASSULACEAE)
A genus very close to *Sempervivum*, which it closely resembles. The fleshy leaves grow in compact rosettes and may be smooth or hairy. Starry flowers are borne in branched clusters. Some species can be grown outside in warm parts of the temperate zone. Grow in a light airy cold greenhouse in a loam-based compost. Keep just moist during the summer and almost dry during the winter. Propagate by offsets in spring.

arboreum
The rosettes of 2–3 in. shining, hairless leaves are borne at the end of the stout light brown branches. Flowers appearing from January to March are bright yellow, carried on slender stalks and forming a rather dense ovoid head about 4 in. long. Total height can reach 3 ft. Portugal, Morocco and eastward to Crete. **14.**
  'Atropurpureum' or 'Foliis-purpureis' has dark purple-flushed leaves.

haworthii
A bushy plant to 2 ft with woody branches carrying the rosettes of leaves. These are grey-green and fleshy with red marginal teeth. The flowers are pale yellow, tinged with pink and open in April and May. Canary Isles.

simsii
A tufted perennial producing frequent offsets. The strap-shaped leaves grow in flattened rosettes and are glandular beneath. The golden flowers are borne in clusters on 4 in. stems. They appear in April and May. Canary Isles.

tabulaeforme
The dense rosette of 100–200 closely packed waxy green leaves makes a flat, saucer-like plant often over 12 in. across. The flowering stem reaches 1–2 ft and carries a much branched cluster of yellow flowers about 12 in. long in July and August. Grow rosette at an angle to permit water to run off. Canary Isles. **15.**

undulatum
An erect unbranched or few-branched plant, 3-4 ft high. The ovate, spathulate leaves grow in a rosette at the top of the woody stems. The numerous bright yellow flowers form a cluster 1–2 ft long and 1–1½ ft across. Canary Isles.

AERANGIS (ORCHIDACEAE)
A remarkable genus of evergreen orchids, the flowers of which bear long tail-like spurs. In the wild they grow on the branches of trees. They are all of tropical origin and should be grown in perforated pans or baskets in a warm greenhouse. Use a compost of equal parts osmunda fibre and sphagnum moss. Shade during the summer and maintain a humid atmosphere. Propagate by division or basal stem cuttings in spring. The genus is sometimes included in *Angraecum*.

biloba
This species has pendulous stems, 6–12 in. long upon which are carried up to 12 white or pink tinged flowers, about 1½ in. across with 2 in. orange spurs. These bloom from October to December and are very fragrant, especially at night. The narrow leaves are thick and blue-green with a notched tip. Tropical Africa.

kotschyana
A distinctive plant with arching, pendulous shoots and white flowers 1–1½ in. across. The most striking feature is the spur which is salmon pink and from 6–9 in. long with 2 spiral twists. The flowers appear from July to September. Tropical Africa.

rhodosticta
An early summer flowering species with white flowers, the lip being twice as wide as the other petals. The spur is green tipped, while each flower has a bright orange-red column. Up to 12 blooms grow on each of the 9 in. pendulous stems. Kenya to Cameroun.

thomsonii
An attractive species with a stout stem 1½–2½ ft high with strap shaped leaves and arching, pendent spikes of flowers, each glistening white, 1½–2½ in. across with 6 in. pale bronze spurs. The flowers are delicately fragrant, especially at night. Central Africa.

AERIDES (ORCHIDACEAE) Fox-tail Orchid
A genus of epiphytic orchids which respond best to basket culture in the warm greenhouse. The somewhat succulent leaves are strap shaped and mid-green with a lobed tip. The waxy flowers, which are fragrant in all species, are borne in cylindrical clusters and have an upturned spur. Grow in perforated pans or baskets of equal parts osmunda fibre and sphagnum moss. Shade during the summer and maintain a humid atmosphere. Propagate by division or basal cuttings in spring.

crispa
The flowers are 2 in. across, white with a purple-rose flush and a 3-lobed lip, the centre lobe having a fringed margin. They are borne on curving pendent stems up to 18 in. long, from June to August. W. India.

falcata
A dwarf species with a short stem and blue-green, leathery cylindrical leaves. The flowers are white, flushed and spotted with rose-purple, each 1½ in. across with a short spur. They are carried on 20 in. pendulous stems from April to July. India, Cambodia.

japonica
The white flowers, which are 1 in. across, are barred with brownish-purple and have a violet line and spots on the lip. They appear from May to July. This species, coming from a more temperate area, needs cooler conditions in the winter. Japan.

odorata
The 1 in. white flowers are red tinged at the tips of the sepals and 2 petals, while the lip has purple spots. They are carried on pendulous stalks up to 18 in. in length which arch from the upright stems. The leaves are dark green and strap shaped. Flowering is from June to August. S.E. Asia.

AESCHYNANTHUS syn. TRICHOSPORUM (GESNERIACEAE)
A genus of perennial, evergreen epiphytes with opposite pairs of fleshy or leathery leaves. The showy flowers are tubular and long lasting. To grow well they need warmth and humidity especially during the flowering season. Grow in pots or baskets of a proprietary peat compost and shade during the summer. Propagate by cuttings of stem tips or sections, in spring or after flowering.

boschianus
A good plant for hanging baskets, about 1 ft in height. The leaves are ovate and entire and the flowers scarlet, the corolla twice the length of the purple-brown bell-shaped calyx. Flowering in July. Java.

lobbianus Lipstick Vine

A generally prostrate or trailing shrub with small glossy, grey-green leaves and terminal clusters of flowers, bright crimson outside and creamy yellow inside the mouth. They have long tubular calyces. The flowers appear from May to July. Java. **16.**

marmoratus Zebra Basket Vine

A trailing plant with beautiful waxy leaves to $3\frac{1}{2}$ in. long, dark green above with a lacy network of yellow-green veins, and purple beneath. The flowers are green with chocolate-brown markings and appear from June to September, but the plant is grown chiefly for its foliage. S.E. Asia.

pulcher Royal Red Bugler

A trailing plant with pendent branches, small waxy light green leaves and bright $1\frac{1}{2}$–$2\frac{1}{2}$ in. tubular flowers which are vermilion red with a yellow throat. The flowers appear chiefly in June and it makes an excellent house plant. Java.

speciosus

A vigorous plant with large pale green leaves and flexible stems to 2 ft long, carrying clusters of showy tubular flowers 4 in. long. These are bright orange to scarlet, shading to yellow at the base and appear from July to September. Java.

African Boxwood see **Myrsine africana**
African Daisy see **Arctotis**
African Evergreen see **Syngonium podophyllum**
African Fern Pine see **Podocarpus gracilior**
African Hemp see **Sparmannia africana**
African Iris see **Moraea iridioides**
African Lily see **Agapanthus**
African Red Alder see **Cunonia capensis**
African Violet see **Saintpaulia ionantha**
African Violet, False see **Streptocarpus saxorum**

AGAPANTHUS (LILIACEAE) African Lily

A genus of perennial plants originating from S. Africa. Many species are hardy in mild areas or when given protection, but they benefit from cool greenhouse treatment in the winter. All have long strap-shaped green leaves and many-flowered rounded heads of funnel shaped blooms on long stems. Grow in tubs, large pots or borders, preferably using a loam based compost. Ventilate freely in summer. Propagate by seeds or division in spring.

africanus Blue African Lily, Lily-of-the-Nile

A very beautiful plant growing to $2\frac{1}{2}$ ft in height, with rich green, evergreen leaves and great showy heads of blue or violet-blue flowers. each 2 in. long and appearing from June to September. It is particularly useful for growing in tubs on the sunny side of the house but is only half hardy and needs protection in the winter. S. Africa. **17.**

campanulatus

A deciduous species growing to $1\frac{1}{2}$ ft, its flowers are sky blue, bell-shaped and opening at the mouth to $1\frac{1}{4}$ in. across. They form dense heads in the late summer. S. Africa. **18.**

inapertus

A tall species growing to 4 ft in height, with deciduous, strap shaped leaves. The drooping flowers are bell shaped, deep to violet-blue, and are borne in many-flowered but loose heads in August. S. Africa.

praecox

Also known as *A. umbellatus*, this species is the most commonly grown in Britain of this genus. It grows to 2–$2\frac{1}{2}$ ft and has evergreen leaves. The flowers are pale to bright blue or white and are borne in dense heads containing as many as 100 blooms from July onwards. It is only half hardy and therefore needs protection from autumn to spring. S. Africa.

umbellatus see **A. praecox**

AGAPETES (ERICACEAE)

A genus of evergreen shrubs grown for their exquisite waxy urn-shaped flowers intricately marked with a dark veining. Some species are epiphytic and all need warmth and humidity to grow well. The narrowly ovate, pointed leaves have a leathery texture. Grow in large pots, or tubs, of a proprietary peat compost. Shade from the summer sun. Propagate by cuttings of lateral shoots, preferably with a heel, in late summer or after flowering.

macrantha

The leaves are short stalked, tapering at both ends, and the flowers which grow to $1\frac{1}{4}$ in. long and $\frac{3}{4}$ in. wide are white, yellow and red and appear in December. N. India.

serpens

This species is considered by some to belong to the genus *Pentapterygium* and will be found under that name in some reference books. It has slender drooping stems and small rich green leaves. The $\frac{3}{4}$ in. long flowers hang from the leaf axils and are bright red with darker markings. S.W. China.

AGAVE (AGAVACEAE)

Grown for their foliage, which consists of a rosette of thick pointed leaves, usually toothed and often variegated, agaves are mostly somewhat big for the living room or small conservatory when fully mature, but growth is not very fast and small plants are as ornamental as large ones. Most species produce sideshoots which can be taken off and rooted, and thus there are usually plenty of small plants to replace those that get too large. Except for *A. americana*, agaves seldom flower in Britain, but they do in the warmer parts of the United States, where they can be grown outdoors. A large flower stem bearing tubular or bell-shaped flowers arises after 7 to 40 years from the centre of the rosette, which then dies. Often the whole plant dies, but sideshoots rooted in previous seasons usually survive. If sideshoots are not produced, propagation is by seed. Soil is that for terrestrial cacti and succulents, see Introduction, and winter temperatures should be above freezing point; full light is advisable. Flowering occurs at almost any time. Various fibres, including sisal, are prepared from the leaves of some species.

americana Century Plant

The flowers are greenish on a branching stem up to 25 ft tall in a large plant. The leaves are grey-green, leathery, spine-tipped with brownish short teeth, up to 3 ft long on mature rosettes. Will grow outdoors in exceptionally mild areas. The name 'Century Plant' arises from the mistaken belief that it takes 100 years to flower; in favourable conditions it can flower in 7 years. Mexico.

marginata, syn. *variegata*, has yellow or white margins to the leaves, **19**;
'Mediopicta', green leaves with a broad yellow central stripe, **20.**

angustifolia

The large rosette comprises long, sword-shaped, spine tipped leaves which are grey-green in colour. It is a very decorative plant reaching 2 ft in height and spread. W. Indies.

'Marginata', the blue-grey leaves have broad white marginal bands, **21.**

filifera Thread Agave

Flowers in 5 ft long spike on an 8 ft stem. The leaves are bright green, leathery, not toothed, 10 in. long by 1 in. wide. They have white lines of horny tissue on the edge which breaks up into loose threads. Many sideshoots are produced. Mexico. **22.**

parviflora

The flowers are in a spike up to 5 ft tall. The erect leaves, 3–4 in. long and $\frac{1}{2}$ in. wide, are in rosettes which often produce offsets. Except in size, the leaves resemble those of *A. filifera*. Mexico, S. Arizona.

striata stricta see **A. stricta**

stricta syn. **A. striata stricta**

The flowers are in a dense spike $2\frac{1}{2}$ ft long, carried on a stem to 7 ft tall. The leaves are green with grey lines, 14 in. long and $\frac{1}{2}$ in. wide, ending in a sharp spine 1 in. long. They are finely toothed and in time form many rosettes. Mexico.

victoriae-reginae

The flowers are in a close spike up to 12 ft long. The leaves are dark green with white markings, 4–12 in. long, broad at the base, narrowing rapidly and ending a black spine. Rosettes are closely packed and solitary, so the whole plant dies after flowering and must be propagated by seed. Needs a winter temperature of 50°F. Mexico. **23.**

AGLAONEMA (ARACEAE) Chinese Evergreens
A genus of small herbaceous perennials with very durable, somewhat leathery, evergreen leaves, usually silver or white variegated. They are of slow growth and will thrive under poor light conditions. The insignificant flowers are surrounded by leaf-like spathes like those of *Arum*. A warm greenhouse provides the ideal conditions, but cooler conditions are tolerated. Grow in pots of a loam-based compost or a peat mix. Maintain a humid atmosphere and shade from direct sunlight. Propagate by division of mature plants or by stem tip cuttings. Stem sections may also be used.

commutatum
A species with dark green, oblong lance shaped leaves with silvery markings. The waxy white spathes appear in July followed by spikes of yellow to red berries. Philippines, Ceylon. **24.**

costatum Painted Drop Tongue
A very decorative evergreen with stiff, ovate dark green leaves marked with white. It has short white spathes up to 1 in. long which are borne in July. Malaya, Borneo.

crispum syn. **A. roebelinii** Painted Drop Tongue
A handsome plant with large ovate leathery green leaves with abundant silver variegation. It is a very good plant for shaded positions in the house and is often sold under the cultivar name 'Silver Queen'. Malaya. **25.**

nitidum see **A. oblongifolium**

oblongifolium syn. **A. nitidum**
A slow growing plant with glossy dark green, un-marked leaves from 8–24 in. long and 4 in. wide. The spathe is green with white margins and appears in July. Malaya.
'Curtisii', has silvery marked leaves.

pictum
A dainty plant with dark green velvety leaves mottled with irregular patches of blue-green and silvery-grey. The 2 in. spathes are creamy-yellow and appear in July and August. Sumatra.

roebelinii see **A. crispum**

treubii Ribbon Aglaonema
A slender plant with narrow bluish-green leaves marked with silver. It has 2 in. white spathes in July and red berries in autumn. As one of the most compact members of the genus it makes a very good house plant. Celebes. **26.**

Air Plant see **Bryophyllum pinnatum**
Albany Bottlebrush see **Callistemon speciosus**

ALBIZIA (LEGUMINOSAE)
julibrissin Pink Mimosa, Silk Tree
A deciduous tree to 20 ft or more in height with large fern-like leaves. Its flowers occur in terminal clusters, the bright pink coloration coming from the long conspicuous stamens which fluff out like a mop. It is suitable for a large cool greenhouse or can be grown outside on warm sheltered walls. Plant in a border or tub, using preferably a loam-based compost. Shade only from the hottest sunshine. Propagate by seeds in spring. Asia.

Alder, African Red see **Cunonia capensis**

ALLAMANDA (APOCYNACEAE)
A genus of evergreen shrubs or climbers of tropical origin which need warm greenhouse conditions to thrive. They have whorled leaves and terminal clusters of showy trumpet shaped flowers, followed by large spiny, globular fruits. Preferably they should be grown in the border, but can be flowered in tubs or large pots of a loam-based compost. A support of canes or wires is needed. Shade from hottest sunshine and maintain a humid atmosphere. Propagate by stem cuttings in spring or summer.

cathartica Golden Trumpet, Common Allamanda
A robust climber reaching 15 ft with strap-shaped green leaves. Two cultivars are commonly grown, both flowering from July to September. Brazil.
'Grandiflora' has 3 in. pale yellow blooms, **27;**

'Hendersonii' has golden-yellow flowers 4 in. across.

neriifolia Golden Trumpet Bush, Oleander Allamanda
An erect or half climbing shrub to 3 ft or more with short-stalked, oblong dark green leaves 3–5 in. long, and smallish, golden-yellow trumpet-shaped flowers 1½ in. across. It grows well as a small bush in pots and flowers in June. S. America. **28.**

Allophyton mexicanum see **Tetranema mexicanum**

ALLOPLECTUS (GESNERIACEAE)
capitatus Velvet Alloplectus
A handsome and erect plant growing to 2–3 ft, the succulent stems are downy red and the 6–8 in. velvety olive green leaves are reddish beneath. The terminal clusters of flowers are bright yellow with a dark red calyx and appear in autumn. It requires shade and moist conditions to thrive, being suitable for a warm greenhouse. Grow in pots of a proprietary peat compost or a loam-based compost. Propagate by cuttings of basal shoots in spring or summer. Venezuela, Colombia.

ALOCASIA (ARACEAE)
A genus of beautiful foliage plants with large, showy long-stalked leaves. The small arum-like flowers are not decorative. All the species are of tropical origin and require warm greenhouse conditions, though they can be used as short term house plants. Pot the tubers in spring using a loam-based compost or a proprietary peat mix. Shade from direct sunlight and maintain a humid atmosphere. Dry off in the autumn and store in the pots until spring. Propagate by offset tubers when repotting each year.

cuprea Giant Caladium
A plant with large, 10–14 in. ovate leaves, dark metallic bronze-green above, violet beneath with deeply depressed veins and which grow on a 12 in. stalk. The spathe has a purple tube and a green blade. Borneo.

indica
A robust plant with waxy, triangular to arrow-shaped leaves, 12–14 in. long and 6–7 in. wide. They are dark green and carried on 16–24 in. stalks. The yellowish-green spathe is 6–7 in. long with reddish spots. Tropical Asia.
'Metallica' has the leaves overlaid with a metallic sheen.

lindenii
A species with heart-shaped leaves reaching 16 in. in length and 6 in. in width. They are green and hairless with yellowish-white veins and grow on 10–12 in. white stalks. When bruised the leaves emit a strong pungent smell. New Guinea.

macrorrhiza Giant Elephant's Ear
A bold showy plant eventually reaching 8 ft or more in height and becoming tree like. Its broadly arrow shaped leathery leaves grow to 2 ft and are carried on 3 ft stalks, their size giving the plant its popular name. The spathe is 5–6 in. long, bluish-green to yellowish. E. Indies, Malaya, Ceylon.

micholitziana
An erect plant to 20 in. high with arrow shaped, wavy-edged leaves which are dark green above with a white mid-rib and lateral veins, and paler beneath. The spathe is green outside and yellowish or whitish-green within. Philippines.

sanderiana Kris Plant
A graceful plant bearing glossy, metallic green leaves with silver-white veins and rather deeply lobed, white-edged margins. The under sides of the leaves are purple and the leaf stalks 10–12 in. long and brownish-green. It is considered by many to be the finest *Alocasia* for pot culture. Philippines.

ALOE (LILIACEAE)
Grown for their foliage, aloes superficially resemble agaves, but the flowers are produced from the leaf axils, the rosettes do not die after flowering, and they are mainly from Africa. They are leaf succulents, the leaves often being variously marked and packed in close rosettes. The flowers are sometimes showy, usually tubular on a slender stem and variable in colour. Growth is often in winter. Autumn is the best time to repot. Soil as for terrestrial cacti and succulents, see Introduction, and

the soil should not be kept too dry even in the resting period. Offsets suitable for propagation are usually freely produced, but if not propagation is by seed. Seed produced in cultivation is often hybridized unless great care is taken to isolate the parent plant. In winter frost must be excluded, but if the plant grows in winter a temperature of 50–55°F. is advisable.

aristata

The orange-red flowers appear in summer on a loose stem 1 ft tall. The leaves are dark green with white tubercles, about 4 in. long and ½ in. wide at the base, tapering to a point. They form a dense, stemless rosette about 6 in. across, which freely produces offsets. The plant somewhat resembles a *Haworthia*. S. Africa.

ciliaris

The red flowers are loosely produced on short stems in winter. The leaves are dark green, not as fleshy as most aloes, having white teeth, on long, slender branching stems. Grows and flowers mostly in winter. S. Africa.

ferox

The flowers are scarlet, in loose branched spikes up to 3 ft tall. They appear in March. The leaves are dull green with a reddish tinge and fleshy. Their margins and other surfaces are covered with reddish-brown spines. The stem can reach 10 ft, but the plant is slow growing. S. Africa.

saponaria

The flowers are red, orange or yellow, in dense clusters on a branched stem. The leaves are green, sometimes reddish, with paler blotches in bands across, 7–8 in. long with horny margins and coarse brown teeth. Rosettes are closely packed, making offsets freely. S. Africa.

striata

Flowers are coral-red on hanging, much-branched stems. The leaves are grey with pink edges, toothless, 15–20 in. long and 4–6 in. broad. The rosettes are usually stemless. S. Africa.

variegata Partridge-breasted Aloe

The flowers are pale red on unbranched stems about 12 in. tall. The leaves are green with cross bands of white spots; they are triangular in section, fleshy with white edges and keel, 6–8 in. long and up to 1½ in. thick. The rosettes of upright leaves are stemless at first, but as the lower leaves die off, a short stem is formed. Many well-rooted offsets are produced. Probably the most popular aloe. S. Africa. **29.**

ALONSOA (SCROPHULARIACEAE) Mask Flower

A genus of S. American perennial plants which make showy pot plants for the conservatory or greenhouse. Although perennials, they will flower in their first year and can therefore be grown as annuals. Grow in cool conditions in pots of a loam-based compost. They may also be planted in the border. Ventilate freely in summer. Propagate by seeds sown in early spring.

acutifolia

A bushy sub-shrub growing to 2 ft. The stalked leaves are broad and ovate with toothed margins. The deep red flowers are saucer shaped and grow in loose spikes; they normally appear from June to October, but will bloom in winter under glass. Peru.

warscewiczii

A compact bushy species reaching 12–24 in. It has heart-shaped, toothed leaves and brilliant scarlet flowers borne on red stems. They open from July to October. A white variety also is grown. Peru. **30.**

Aloysia triphyllia see **Lippia citriodora**

ALTERNANTHERA (AMARANTHACEAE)

This group of plants is grown mainly for the attractive, variously coloured foliage. They are mostly evergreen perennials but need to be propagated annually to maintain strong growth and good leafage. Grow in pots or pans of a loam-based or proprietary peat compost, and shade lightly from the hottest sunshine. Maintain a humid atmosphere in summer. Propagate by stem cuttings in spring or late summer. The following species are suitable for a cold greenhouse.

amoena Parrot Leaf

A dwarf tufted, much branched species having 1–3 in. long broadly oval to elliptic leaves with a sharp slender point. Each leaf is veined and blotched orange and red on a bright green background. Brazil.

bettzickiana Calico Plant

This variable species is represented by dwarf tufted plants only 2 in. tall and larger forms 6 in. or more high. The narrow, often twisted leaves can be blotched or suffused in shades of red and yellow. Brazil.

'Aurea Nana', the Yellow Calico Plant, has spoon-shaped bright green leaves variegated pale yellow.

dentata False Globe Amaranth

A bushy plant up to 1 ft tall having elliptic, pointed-tipped leaves and tiny rounded heads of green-white flowers. It is represented in cultivation by the metallic, ruby-red leaved form known as 'Ruby'. Brazil.

versicolor Copper Leaf, Joseph's Coat

This much branched species has spoon-shaped leaves up to 1½ in. long on stems 1 ft or so tall. Each leaf is wrinkled along the margin, bronze or copper-green veined or suffused pink and crimson. Brazil.

Aluminium Plant see **Pilea cadierei**
Amaranth, False Globe see **Alternanthera dentata**
Amaranth, Globe see **Gomphrena globosa**

AMARYLLIS (AMARYLLIDACEAE)

belladonna Cape Belladonna, Belladonna Lily

A bulbous plant with large trumpet-shaped flowers 4–5 in. across, variable in colour, but usually a shade of rose pink; they grow on solid 2 ft long reddish stalks. The flowers appear from August to October before the green, strap-shaped leaves. It needs large pots to grow well and is best planted out in the conservatory or cool greenhouse border. Pot the bulbs in late summer, preferably using a loam-based compost. Ventilate freely and water regularly when the foliage is well developed. Dry off when the leaves turn yellow. Propagate by removing offsets when repotting every other year. In sheltered spots it can be grown outside. **31.**

'Hathor' with pure white flowers is a most attractive form.

Amaryllis see also under **Hippeastrum**
Amazon Lily see **Eucharis grandiflora**
Amblyopetalum caeruleum see **Tweedia caerulea**

AMICIA (LEGUMINOSAE)

zygomeris

A woody perennial reaching 8 ft with hairy branches and handsome leaves made up of several pairs of leaflets. The somewhat pea-like yellow flowers have a purple keel. They are borne in pendent clusters of from 4 to 5 in autumn. It is just hardy in extremely mild areas but otherwise should be grown under glass in tubs or large pots. Use a loam-based compost and ventilate freely in summer. Propagate by cuttings of young shoots in spring. Mexico.

AMORPHOPHALLUS (ARACEAE)

A genus of plants similar in form to *Arum* with large, fleshy spathes. They make striking and unusual warm greenhouse plants. Grow in large pots or tubs of a loam-based compost and shade from direct sunlight. Maintain a humid atmosphere in summer. Dry off when foliage turns yellow. Repot in spring every other year. Propagate by removing offset tubers at repotting time.

bulbifer

A tall plant with 3 ft leaf stalks carrying leaves divided into 3 main segments, each about 12 in. long and again subdivided. The 6 in. spathes, carried on long stalks are dull green, pink spotted outside, merging to red at the base and yellowish-green inside, they enfold the green and pink club-like spadix. India, Afghanistan.

rivieri syn. **Hydrosme rivieri** Devil's Tongue, Voodoo Plant

A large and curious plant with umbrella-like leaves up to 4 ft wide which have 3 large segments, each further divided and carried on a marbled pink stalk. The lead-blue spadix grows within an impressive purple and green spathe, carried on a 2 ft stalk and smelling of carrion. It makes a most distinctive house plant and is equally effective in a warm greenhouse. E. Indies.

ANANAS (BROMELIACEAE)

A genus of evergreen perennials for a warm, humid greenhouse with spiny, strap-shaped leaves growing in a basal rosette. The flowers are small and form a dense spike and the fleshy fruits include the familiar pineapple. Grow in pots of a loam-based compost or a peat mix and shade in summer. Propagate from suckers or the leafy shoot from the top of the fruit.

bracteatus

'Striatus', variegated Wild Pineapple, is the form which is usually grown; it has coppery green leaves with yellow variegated margins and widely spaced teeth. The flowers are lavender and form a cone, 4–6 in. high which is made conspicuous by its brilliant red bracts, and is followed by a red-brown edible fruit. Brazil. **32.**

comosus syn. **A. sativus** Pineapple

The cultivated pineapple can be grown both for its fruit and its decorative qualities. The grey-green pointed leaves can reach 5 ft in length. The spike of pink purple flowers is small and is followed by the familiar succulent fruits. Continuous warmth is needed to produce edible fruits, but it will grow well in a warm room as long as it is free of draughts. Brazil.

'Variegatus', with variegated leaves makes a most attractive foliage plant.

sativus see **A. comosus**

ANCHUSA (BORAGINACEAE)

capensis

An 18 in. species, usually grown as an annual which makes a pretty house plant. It has narrow, pointed leaves and long clusters of $\frac{1}{4}$ in. flat, bright blue flowers which are at their best in July and August. Grow in pots in a proprietary peat mix, sowing in January. Africa.

'Blue Bird', a more floriferous cultivar with sprays of forget-me-not like flowers. **33.**

ANGELONIA (SCROPHULARIACEAE)

gardneri

A perennial, upright sub-shrubby plant growing to about 3 ft. Its leaves are simple, lance-shaped and grow in opposite pairs up the stem, while the white-centred purple flowers are red spotted and borne on terminal spikes in May. They need a warm airy greenhouse, but will tolerate cooler conditions. Grow in pots of a loam-based compost and shade from hottest sunshine. Propagate from basal stem cuttings from old cut back plants in summer. Pinch the young plants several times to promote bushy growths. Brazil.

Angel's Tears see **Billbergia nutans**
Angel's Trumpet see **Datura arborea**
Angelwing Begonia see **Begonia coccinea**

ANGRAECUM (ORCHIDACEAE)

A genus of beautiful, epiphytic orchids of tropical origin, with fragrant, star-shaped waxy flowers which are very long lasting. They need warm greenhouse conditions and humidity during the growing and flowering season to thrive. Cultivate in perforated pots or baskets of equal parts osmunda fibre and sphagnum moss, shading from the hottest sunshine. Propagate by taking stem-tip cuttings and basal shoots that arise on the old plant after beheading. The genus *Aerangis* is sometimes included under *Angraecum*.

distichum syn. **Mystacidium distichum**

A neat plant with 8 in. pendent stems which carry 2 ranks of light green, fleshy leaves. The slightly fragrant flowers are small and white with $\frac{1}{2}$ in. spurs and appear from July to October. It is best grown in a basket. Of easy culture it is a good orchid for the house. Sierra Leone.

eburneum

An upright species with stiff, strap-shaped leaves to 20 in. long and 2 in. wide. The flowers are borne on a stout stalk which can attain 3–4 ft from the base. The waxy sepals and petals are greenish-white with a broad white lip. It flowers throughout the winter. Madagascar.

sesquipedale Star of Bethlehem Orchid

A superb plant, considered by many to be the best of the genus. It has a single stem which can reach 3 ft and the leaves are 10–15 in. long, dark glossy green, growing in 2 overlapping rows. The flowers, fleshy and fragrant, are 5–8 in. across, ivory-white and have a pale green sinuous spur up to 12 in. long. It flowers from November to March. A plant for the warm greenhouse only. Madagascar.

ANIGOZANTHOS (AMARYLLIDACEAE)
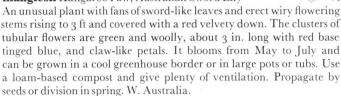

manglesii Kangaroo Paw, Australian Sword Lily

An unusual plant with fans of sword-like leaves and erect wiry flowering stems rising to 3 ft and covered with a red velvety down. The clusters of tubular flowers are green and woolly, about 3 in. long with red base tinged blue, and claw-like petals. It blooms from May to July and can be grown in a cool greenhouse border or in large pots or tubs. Use a loam-based compost and give plenty of ventilation. Propagate by seeds or division in spring. W. Australia.

Anise, Star see **Illicium anisatum**
Anise Tree see **Illicium**

ANTHURIUM (ARACEAE)

A genus of exotic *Arum*-like plants with leathery, evergreen leaves grown for their foliage and colourful leaf-like spathes. They require warm greenhouse conditions with shading from direct sunshine and a humid atmosphere. Grow in baskets or pans of a proprietary peat compost, preferably mixed with a $\frac{1}{2}$ part sphagnum moss. Propagate by division where possible or by seeds in spring.

andreanum Oil Cloth Flower, Tail Flower, Painter's Palette

An erect plant with oblong heart-shaped leaves 6–8 in. long and 3–5 in. wide. The spathe is heart shaped, lacquered reddish-orange or scarlet, 4–5 in. long with a yellow and white pendent spadix. Suitable for the greenhouse but not a very successful house plant. Colombia. **34.**

scherzerianum Flamingo Flower, Flame Plant

A short plant with narrow leaves 6–8 in. long and 1–2 in. wide. The ovate spathe is brilliant scarlet, while the spirally twisted spadix is golden-yellow. It flowers chiefly from February to July and needs keeping moist. The best house plant of the genus. Costa Rica. **35.**

ANTHYLLIS (LEGUMINOSAE)

barba-jovis Jupiter's Beard

An evergreen shrub which, when mature, can reach 8 ft or more. The whole plant is silvery-hairy. The rounded heads of pea-like flowers are pale yellow and borne at the ends of the twigs. Suitable for borders or tubs in the cool greenhouse. Grow in a loam-based compost and support with canes or wires if it is to be trained flat. Ventilate freely in summer. Propagate by stem cuttings with heel in late summer or by seeds in spring. Spain.

ANTIGONON (POLYGONACEAE)

leptopus Coral Vine

A showy perennial climber with slender, smooth stems and arrow-shaped leaves. The clusters of 6 to 15 small flowers are each rose pink with a darker centre. The plant climbs by means of small, branched tendrils, but needs training on supports of wires or strings. Grow in a warm greenhouse, preferably in the border or large tubs. If the latter, use a loam-based compost. Maintain humidity during the summer. Good light is needed for prolific flowering. Propagate by seeds in spring or by stem cuttings in summer. Mexico.

APHELANDRA (ACANTHACEAE)

squarrosa Saffron Spike, Zebra Plant

An evergreen plant: the broad, glossy dark green leaves, 6–10 in. long, are banded with white. The golden-yellow pyramids of flowers make a striking contrast with the leaves. A most attractive plant for the warm greenhouse or house. Grow in a loam-based compost or a proprietary peat mix and shade from the hottest sun. Maintain a humid atmosphere in summer. Propagate by basal stem cuttings, preferably from cut back plants in spring or summer. Brazil. **36.**

'Louisae' is a compact low growing cultivar with shiny elliptic leaves to 5 in. long with white striping. The bright yellow flowers are carried on red stems. One of the best pot plants;

'Brockfeld' has stiffly held oval leaves and more attractive leaf markings, the veins being picked out in cream.

APOROCACTUS (CACTACEAE)
flagelliformis Rat's-tail Cactus
The bright rose pink flowers, 1½–2 in. long and about 1 in. across, appear in April and May. They are funnel-shaped, and are freely produced along trailing green stems, up to 15 in. long; which bear short brownish spines. Culture as for epiphytic cacti, see Introduction. The plant grows well on its own roots, being very suitable for hanging baskets, but owing to its pendulous habit, it is often grafted on a tall cactus to make a standard, a *Selenicereus* species being very suitable. It is not known in the wild state; probably from Mexico originally. **37.**

mallisonii see × **Heliaporus smithii**

Apple, Balsam see **Momordica balsamina**
Apple, Geranium see **Pelargonium odoratissimum**
Apple, May see **Passiflora incarnata**
Arabian Coffee see **Coffea arabica**
Aralia, False see **Dizygotheca elegantissima**
Aralia japonica see **Fatsia japonica**
Aralia sieboldii see **Fatsia japonica**

ARAUCARIA (PINACEAE)
excelsa Norfolk Island Pine
An evergreen, coniferous tree which can, in its native South Pacific region, reach heights of over 200 ft, but which grows happily in its juvenile state from 1–3 ft high for many years, making an easy cool greenhouse or house plant. It has small awl-like soft leaves which lie overlapping close to the branches. Grow in pots or tubs of a loam-based compost or a proprietary peat mix. Ventilate the house freely from spring to autumn and shade lightly during the hottest months. Propagate by seeds sown in autumn or spring. Norfolk Island. **38.**

ARAUJIA (ASCLEPIADACEAE)
sericofera Bladder Flower, Cruel Plant
A vigorous, woody climber with leaves green above and white felted beneath. The salver-shaped flowers are fragrant and white, 1–1¼ in. across and grow in clusters. Moths are often caught at night by the sticky pollen, but are usually able to free themselves when sunshine has dried it out. Grow in large pots or tubs of a loam-based compost, or in a conservatory or cool greenhouse border. Ventilate freely in summer and shade lightly from the hottest summer sun. Propagate by seeds in spring. S. America.

ARCTOTIS (COMPOSITAE) African Daisy
A genus of perennial and annual plants with silvery, densely hairy stems and leaves. The flowers are daisy like. Most of the species in cultivation are grown as annuals and are suitable for borders in a conservatory or cool greenhouse and pots. Use a loam-based compost and ventilate freely from spring to autumn. Propagate by seeds in spring and by basal non-flowering shoots inserted as cuttings in late spring or early autumn.

acaulis
A dwarf plant, almost stemless. Its lobed leaves are densely woolly beneath. The flowers are combined shades of pink and orange, darker in the centre, 3½ in. across and borne on 6 in. stalks. They are produced in July and August. It is a good plant for window boxes. S. Africa.

breviscapa
An annual with deeply cut leaves, green above and white woolly beneath. The flowers, which are carried on short stalks are yellow and orange with a black centre, and are in bloom from July to the frosts. A useful pot plant for the greenhouse where it will often flower earlier in the summer. S. Africa. **39.**

× hybrida
Several hybrids are included under this name, all of which are attractive annual plants with flower colours ranging from white and yellow to orange and brilliant red. Many have centres of contrasting colours. The long stemmed flowers are produced from July onwards. **40.**

stoechadifolia syn. **A. venusta**
A larger plant than the above species, growing to 2½–3 ft. It has narrow, toothed grey-green leaves and the flowers are white with a blue centre

which is encircled with gold. It flowers from July to the first frosts. S. Africa.
'Grandis' has larger flowers reaching 4 in. across and ranging in colour from white to pale yellow.

venusta see **A. stoechadifolia**

ARDISIA (MYRSINACEAE)
crispa Coral Berry
A graceful, slow growing shrub eventually reaching 4 ft with long narrow glossy green leaves to 4 in. and fragrant red or reddish-violet flowers. These are followed in winter by clusters of bright scarlet, waxy berries which can persist until the next flowering season. A most handsome pot plant for the warm or cool greenhouse or the home. Grow in a loam-based compost or a proprietary peat mix and shade from hottest sunshine. Propagate by lateral shoots taken as cuttings from spring to autumn, or by seeds in spring. The latter method provides the best plants. E. Indies. **41.**

ARECA (PALMAE)
catechu Betel Nut
Young plants of this species make excellent pot plants, especially for table use. The arching, slender leaves are composed of numerous, narrow pointed leaflets. When fully adult it can make a tree from 30–100 ft high, but should remain of manageable size in the house for five or six years. Grow in a warm, humid greenhouse shaded from the hottest sunshine. Use a peat mix or a loam-based compost and propagate by seeds in spring. S.E. Asia.

Areca Palm see **Chrysalidocarpus lutescens**

ARISTOLOCHIA (ARISTOLOCHIACEAE) Birthwort, Dutchman's Pipe
A genus of flowering climbers suitable for the greenhouse and conservatory, especially in the border trained up a pillar or trellis. The curious flowers are pendulous with a curved lip and hood. Grow in a loam-based compost or a peat mix. Propagate by seeds in spring, or stem cuttings in summer.

altissima syn. **sempervirens**
An evergreen climber reaching 8–10 ft. Its shiny leaves are heart shaped and bright green. The flowers are yellow with reddish-brown stripes, they reach 1½ in. in length and appear from June to August. Best for the cool greenhouse border. Italy to Israel, N. Africa.

elegans Calico Flower
A graceful climber with broadly kidney-shaped leaves and 5 in. flowers with a pale, yellowish-green tube and rich chocolate-purple lip with white markings. A free flowering species which can be grown in pots in the warm greenhouse. Brazil. **42.**

sempervirens see **A. altissima**

ARTHROPODIUM (LILIACEAE)
cirrhatum Rock Lily
An attractive plant for a cool room or greenhouse, with spreading, narrow light green leaves with translucent margins. The white flowers are carried in loose clusters and have a conspicuous cone-shaped mass of stamens. Grow in pots of a loam-based compost or in a peat mix. Keep the greenhouse well aerated in summer and shade from direct sunlight. Propagate by division or seeds in spring. New Zealand.

Artillery Plant see **Pilea muscosa**

ARUM (ARACEAE)
A genus of distinctive perennials with the small flowers clustered on a pencil-shaped spadix within a large, glossy spathe. Grow in pots of a loam-based compost or in a conservatory or cool greenhouse border. Keep moist when in full leaf, barely so at other times. Those grown in pots may be dried off when the leaves turn yellow. Begin watering again in autumn. Propagate by seed when ripe or offset tubers at potting time or while dormant.

creticum

A plant with 5–7 in. arrow-shaped leaves and a 5 in. long, slender pointed spathe, pale green within and whitish outside, carried on a 10–15 in. stalk and flowering in May. A plant for the cool greenhouse. Crete. **43.**

orientale

An attractive species usually with a deep black-purple spathe on a short stalk appearing in June. The leaves are broadly arrow shaped with a long central lobe and a long stalk. Suitable for the cool greenhouse. Greece to U.S.S.R.

Arum Lily see **Zantedeschia**
Asarina see **Maurandia**

ASCLEPIAS (ASCLEPIADACEAE)

curassavica

A sub-shrub for the cool greenhouse border or pots, having pairs of entire glossy green leaves. From June to October it bears dense clusters of orange-red flowers. If in pots, plant in a proprietary peat-based compost and keep moist at all times. It can be cut back and re-potted in spring, or grown afresh from seeds sown at the same time. Tropical America.
'Aurea', the flowers are yellow with a hint of orange. **44.**

ASPARAGUS (LILIACEAE)

With their graceful, feathery foliage these species make excellent house and cool greenhouse plants. Inconspicuous, greenish to pinkish flowers are followed by red berries. The apparent leaflets are small needle-like branches known as phylloclades. Grow in pots of loam-based compost and lightly shade in summer. Propagate by seeds or division in spring.

asparagoides see **A. medeoloides**

densiflorus

The type species is rarely seen in cultivation.
'Sprengeri', syn. *A. sprengeri*, the cultivar which is commonly grown as a potted plant. It is much branched and has arching, wiry stalks, and soft pale green, glossy phylloclades. The small, pinkish flowers are fragrant and are followed by bright red berries. Natal. **45.**

medeoloides syn. **A. asparagoides, Smilax asparagoides**

This species is the 'Smilax' of florists, the lateral sprays of glossy oval leaf-like phylloclades being used in bouquets and other floral arrangements. The plant is a tall climber with zig-zag stems up to 10 ft or so.
'Aureus', a very pale green form;
'Myrtifolius', Baby Smilax, is smaller than the type in all its parts.

plumosus see **A. setaceus**

scandens

A climbing perennial with much branched stems and the phylloclades lying all in one plane, making a fern-like frond. The flowers are small and whitish and the berries red and globular. S. Africa.
'Deflexus', a similar plant, but with reflexed branches.

setaceus syn. **A. plumosus** Asparagus Fern

An ornamental species much used as a house plant and in flower decoration in its young stages. It has bright green, bristle like phylloclades and when mature becomes a climber. It has red, globular berries. S. Africa.
'Nanus' is the most commonly grown form being smaller and with denser, horizontal fronds.

sprengeri see **A. densiflorus** 'Sprengeri'

ASPIDISTRA (LILIACEAE)

A remarkably tolerant genus which will thrive in almost all living room conditions and can withstand considerable extremes of light and heat. All the species are evergreen and are grown exclusively for their foliage. Grow in a humid, shady, cool or warm greenhouse using a loam-based compost or a proprietary peat mix. Propagate by division in spring or summer.

elatior Aspidistra

The 20 in. dark green, shining leathery ovate leaves narrow into

strong stalks. The flowers are small and dull purple and are produced at soil level. China. **46.**
'Variegata' is an attractive form with variegated leaves striped in cream to white.

ASPLENIUM (ASPLENIACEAE) Spleenwort

A genus of ferns, many of which make attractive house or greenhouse plants. Their fronds are usually glossy and rather tough. Grow in a proprietary peat mix or a loam-based compost. Shade from direct sunlight and keep humid. Propagate by spores or division in spring.

bulbiferum Hen and Chicken Fern, Mother Spleenwort

This species is most remarkable for the bulbils which appear on the fronds, eventually weighing them down, and from which new plants will grow. It has long narrow fronds which are finely dissected and can reach 2 ft. A good house plant and cool greenhouse subject. New Zealand, Australia and India. **47.**

flabelliforme Necklace Fern

An ideal plant for a hanging basket, it has trailing fronds 6–12 in. long, divided into 20–30 small, pale green fan shaped segments alternately on the stalk. Good for the cool greenhouse. New Zealand, Australia.

nidus Bird's Nest Fern

A species with glossy, bright green fronds which are completely undivided and form a shuttle-cock shaped rosette. They are between 2–4 ft long. A warm greenhouse species and a very good house plant. Tropics. **48.**

ASTROPHYTUM (CACTACEAE)

ornatum

The round 8-ribbed plant body, which elongates with age, is grey-green and covered with bands of small white scales. The 2 in. stout spines are borne in clusters of 5–11. The yellow flowers, $2\frac{1}{2}$–$3\frac{1}{2}$ in. across, are daisy like and are produced from June to August. For cultivation see under terrestrial cacti in the Introduction. Enjoys full sunshine. Propagate by seeds sown in Spring. Mexico. **49.**

ASYSTASIA (ACANTHACEAE)

bella syn. **Mackaya bella**

An upright shrub with oval to oblong, wavy edged leaves with slender points. The lilac flowers are somewhat foxglove-like with purple veining. They appear in lax clusters from 5–8 in. long from May to July. Suitable for a conservatory or cool greenhouse. Grow in the border, or in large pots or tubs of a loam-based compost. Shade from hottest sunshine and maintain humidity in summer. Propagate from lateral, non-flowering stem cuttings in summer. S. Africa. **50.**

ATHYRIUM (ATHYRIACEAE)

A genus of ferns with elegant, deeply divided leaves, of which the two following species are most suitable for cool greenhouse and conservatory cultivation. Grow in pots of a proprietary peat compost and shade from direct sunlight. Maintain a humid atmosphere in summer. Propagate by division or spores in spring.

angustifolium syn. **A. pycnocarpon**

A tufted fern with 18–24 in. fronds which are divided into 20–30 oblong segments, each with a wavy margin. Canada.

goeringianum Japanese Painted Fern

'Pictum', the form in cultivation is a small, tufted species with spear-shaped, divided fronds which are sage green with a silvery-grey band. Japan.

pycnocarpon see **A. angustifolium**

Aubergine see **Solanum melongena**
Australian Bluebell Creeper see **Sollya fusiformis**
Australian Fountain Palm see **Livistona australis**
Australian Fuchsia see **Correa × harrisii**
Australian Mint see **Prostanthera**
Australian Sword Lily see **Anigozanthos manglesii**
Australian Tea Tree see **Leptospermum laevigatum**

Autumn Cattleya see **Cattleya labiata**
Autumn Sage see **Salvia greggii**
Aylostera see under **Rebutia**
Azalea, Indian see **Rhododendron simsii**
Aztec Lily see **Sprekelia formosissima**

B

BABIANA (IRIDACEAE)
A genus of attractive bulbous plants with 3–12 in. stems rising from small corms, and tapering, pleated leaves. The flowers are brightly coloured, often with several different colours on the same blossom. They are best grown in pots of loam-based compost and placed in the cool greenhouse. Pot the corms in October and keep just moist. Increase watering when in full leaf and flower. When the leaves turn yellow dry off and store in the pots. Repot annually and propagate by removing cormlets then.

plicata
A fragrant species with a clove-carnation scent. The flowers are a light violet-blue and grow to a height of about 6 in. They open in May and June. S. Africa.

sambucina
The fragrance of this species is akin to that of European elder (*Sambucus nigra*) flowers. The blossoms are blue-purple and appear in April and May. S. Africa. **51.**

stricta Baboon Flower
The most colourful species with multi-coloured, fragrant 2 in. flowers, winter to May; the 3 outer petals being white, the 3 inner, blue with a dark blotch at the base. They are borne on stems about 12 in. high. S. Africa.
'Rubro-cyanea' has petals which are rich crimson towards the base and a brilliant blue at the tips. It is somewhat smaller than the type and most decorative.

Baboon Flower see **Babiana stricta**
Baby Pepper see **Rivina humilis**
Baby Primrose see **Primula malacoides**
Baby Rubber Plant see **Peperomia obtusifolia**
Baby Smilax see **Asparagus medeoloides** 'Myrtifolius'
Baby's Tears see **Soleirolia soleirolii**
Bahaman Globe Mallow see **Sphaeralcea abutiloides**
Ball Fern see **Davallia mariesii**
Balsam see **Impatiens balsamina**
Balsam Apple see **Momordica balsamina**
Balsam Pear see **Momordica charantia**
Bamboo, Heavenly see **Nandina domestica**
Banana see **Musa** and **Chirita**
Barbados Gooseberry see **Pereskia aculeata**
Barbados Pride see **Caesalpinia pulcherrima**
Barberton Daisy see **Gerbera jamesonii**

BARLERIA (ACANTHACEAE)
lupulina
A 2 ft evergreen shrub having long narrowly lance-shaped, leathery green leaves and downward pointing spines borne in the leaf axils. The pinky-yellow flowers are tubular and 1 in. in length and are borne in an overlapping cluster forming a hop-like spike at the ends of the branches. They are produced in August. Grow in pots in a warm greenhouse, planting preferably in a loam based compost, or a proprietary peat mix. Keep well ventilated and water freely in summer. Shade lightly during the hottest months. Propagate by lateral stem cuttings with heel in summer or basal shoots from cut back plants in spring. Mauritius.

BAROSMA (RUTACEAE)
A genus of small evergreen shrubs with strongly fragrant leaves when crushed. The small flowers are borne in clusters in the axils of the leaves. Grow in the cool greenhouse in pots or tubs in a proprietary peat compost, keep moist but do not allow to become waterlogged. Ventilate freely on warm days. Propagate by lateral stem cuttings, preferably with a heel, in late summer.

betulina
A small, densely branched shrub with slender, hairless twigs which bear the ½–¾ in. oval, toothed leaves which taper at both ends. The pink, starry flowers are carried in clusters of 1–3 and are produced in summer. S. Africa.

pulchella
A 3 ft shrub with slender twigs bearing small, crowded leaves, less than ½ in. long and thickened at the edges. The flowers are borne in leafy clusters at the ends of the branches, 1 or 2 growing from each leaf axil. They are small, reddish to purple, and open in June. S. Africa.

serratifolia
The largest species, eventually making a 7–8 ft shrub. The long, narrow leaves reach 1½ in. in length and are finely toothed, blunt at the apex and tapering to the slender stalk. The pure white flowers have purple anthers and are borne in clusters of 1–3 in May. S. Africa.

Basket Grass see **Oplismenus hirtellus**
Basket Vine, Zebra see **Aeschynanthus marmoratus**

BAUERA (SAXIFRAGACEAE)
rubioides River Rose
A small evergreen shrub, growing to 2 ft or more, easily grown in the cool greenhouse. It has opposite pairs of stalkless leaves, each divided into 3 segments, and nodding, solitary, pale red, pink or white flowers which open in succession almost all the year round. Grow in pots or tubs of a proprietary peat compost or in the border. Ventilate on all sunny days. Propagate by cuttings of side shoots with a heel in summer. Avoid lime. New South Wales.

BAUHINIA (LEGUMINOSAE)
A genus of showy, evergreen shrubs and tropical climbers. Many of the climbers have oddly twisted and flattened stems, while the leaves have 2 leaflets which are joined for much of their length. The following two shrubs may be grown in large pots or tubs of a loam-based compost in the cool greenhouse or conservatory. Aerate freely on sunny days. Propagate by seeds or cuttings of young shoots in spring or summer.

acuminata Orchid Bush
A shrub reaching 5–6 ft, with smooth, heart shaped leaves. The stalkless, white, 5-petalled flowers are 2–3 in. across and appear in June. Burma, Malaya, China.

purpurea see **B. variegata**

variegata syn. **B. purpurea** Purple Orchid Tree
A small deciduous tree or bushy shrub with thin, leathery leaves 3–4 in. long. Its 3½ in. flowers which appear in June, are deep pink with dark purple and crimson markings. In shape they resemble a *Cattleya* orchid, hence their popular name. This plant may also be grown in the warmth, with plenty of sun to flower. Tropical Asia.

Bean see **Phaseolus**

BEAUMONTIA (APOCYNACEAE)
grandiflora Herald's Trumpet
A small straggling tree or tall climber with robust rusty-haired young twigs. The broad, oblong-ovate leaves are shiny above and downy beneath. The large fragrant white flowers appear at intervals throughout the year with a main display in winter. They are trumpet-shaped and grow in clusters on the tips of mature stems. It grows best in borders in the warm greenhouse but may also be accommodated in tubs of a loam-based compost if possible. Support with canes or wires. Maintain a humid atmosphere in summer. Propagate by lateral stem cuttings with a heel in summer. India.

Beauty Berry see **Callicarpa**
Beefsteak Begonia see **Begonia** × **feastii**
Beefsteak Plant see **Iresine herbstii**

BEGONIA (BEGONIACEAE)
A large genus of ornamental plants grown both for their foliage and

often profusely borne, richly coloured flowers. In a good collection of begonias it is possible to have some plants in bloom throughout the year. All are suitable for growing in the greenhouse while many make excellent house plants. Begonias have 3 root forms, some growing from tubers, some from rhizomes, while the rest have fibrous roots. The tuberous species are mostly deciduous while the rest are evergreen or partially so. Grow in the greenhouse border, or in pots of a proprietary peat mix or a loam-based compost. Shade from hottest sun and maintain a humid atmosphere in summer. Support the tall-growing kinds with canes. All species and some cultivars may be propagated by seeds, and all by leaf, and stem cuttings in spring or summer. Some tufted and rhizomatous sorts may also be divided. Tubers may be cut into sections after they have been started into growth, each piece with at least one shoot. *B. semperflorens* cultivars are usually raised annually from seeds sown in early spring.

boliviensis
A tuberous begonia which is one parent of many of the more popular hybrid forms. The erect stems carry large, long toothed leaves and drooping succulent stalks bearing scarlet, fuchsia-like flowers which appear in the summer. It is a good greenhouse plant. Bolivia.

boweri Miniature Eyelash Begonia
A 6–9 in. bushy plant with small, waxy leaves, emerald-green with chocolate-brown markings on the margins which are hairy. The $\frac{1}{2}$ in. wide flowers are white or shell-pink and appear from February to May. Suitable for the greenhouse. Mexico.

× carrieri (*B. semperflorens* × *B. schmidtiana*)
A compact plant about 1 ft high, and somewhat similar in growth to *B. semperflorens*. The large white flowers are produced freely throughout the winter. Suitable both for the greenhouse and as a house plant.

coccinea Angelwing Begonia
A shrubby species with a bamboo-like stem. It can exceed 6 ft in height and has glossy-green leaves, finely edged with red. The bright coral-red flowers are 1 in. across and grow in drooping clusters from May to October and occasionally through the rest of the year. Suitable for large pots. Brazil. **52.**
   'President Carnot' is a vigorous hybrid with larger pink flowers and
      silver-spotted leaves.

corallina
A branching, shrubby plant to 7 ft with large olive-green leaves, white spotted above and wine-red beneath. The coral flowers, which appear in spring are borne in drooping clusters. It makes a good house or greenhouse plant. Brazil.

daedalea
Grown for its striking foliage, this is a compact plant reaching 12 in. in height. The large green leaves have a scarlet network when young which later turns mahogany-brown. The flowers are white, tinged with rose-pink and are carried in loose clusters in the summer. Mexico.

diadema
A 2 ft plant with fleshy stems, grown for its deeply cut, glossy leaves which are pale green, irregularly blotched with white and having a red centre. The flowers are pink and very small and appear in spring. A plant for the warm greenhouse. Borneo.

dregei Miniature Maple-leaf Begonia
A small plant good for both house and greenhouse, with fleshy, red stems and thin, bronze-green, deeply toothed leaves which are reddish beneath. The flowers are white and open in summer. S. Africa.

× feastii (*B. hydrocotylifolia* × *B. manicata*) Beefsteak Begonia
A good foliage plant with leathery, mid-green leaves, dark red beneath with white hairs on the margins. The stalks have shaggy red hairs up to 3 in. in length. The pale pink flowers appear from January to May and are carried in clusters on long stalks. Good for house or greenhouse. Garden origin.
   'Bunchii' is the form most frequently grown and is a very decorative
      plant with ruffled and crested leaf margins.

fuchsioides Fuchsia Begonia
A compact shrub to 4 ft with slender arching stems and glossy, ovate, toothed leaves. The fuchsia-like flowers range from deep scarlet to pink and are freely borne in drooping clusters from October to March. Chiefly for the greenhouse, though it can be grown as a house plant. Mexico. **53.**

haageana syn. B. scharfii Elephant Ear Begonia
A large handsome, hairy plant with 8–10 in. leaves, shaped like elephants' ears, which are deep glossy green above with red veins and purplish-red beneath. The rose-pink flowers grow in clusters and appear from June to September. Brazil. **54.**

luxurians Palm-leaf Begonia
A plant for the greenhouse with a fleshy, softly hairy stem growing to 6 ft in height, with decorative leaves cut into 5–17 narrow leaflets, red and hairy above, green below. The small, cream flowers grow on long reddish stalks and open in spring. Brazil.

manicata
A small, winter flowering species with pointed, fleshy mid-green leaves with shining green veins beneath and narrow, red, hairy margins. Most conspicuous is the curious collar of red, scaly bristles at the top of the red spotted leaf stalks. The pink flowers are small, but borne in large airy clusters. A plant suitable for pot growth in either house or greenhouse. Mexico. **55.**

masoniana Iron Cross
One of the most striking begonias in cultivation, it seldom flowers, but is grown for its handsome foliage. It has mid-green, hairy, puckered leaves marked with a contrasting pattern in brownish-red, forming a cross, hence its popular name. Older leaves become silvery, and all have bristly red hairs on their surfaces. The leaves are carried on reddish, white-haired stems. An outstanding pot plant for house and greenhouse. S.E. Asia. **56.**

metallica
A bushy, silvery haired plant with branched stems and shining, metallic-green leaves and depressed purple veins above and crimson veins below. The pink flowers appear in September. A good plant for house or greenhouse. Bahia, Brazil.

nitida
The first species of *Begonia* to be grown in England, it is a shrubby plant 4–6 ft high with glossy dark green, wavy leaves and pale pink to carmine flowers which are most profuse in winter, but can appear throughout the year. Central America, Jamaica.
   'Alba', a white flowered form, **57.**

rex
The true species is seldom grown, but many hybrids and cultivars derive from it. They have very varied leaf shape and markings with patterning in silver, pink, red, copper and bronze on a background of all shades of green. All make good house and greenhouse plants. The small, pale pink flowers appear from June to September on mature plants but are not particularly noteworthy. Assam. **58.**

× richmondensis
A bushy, somewhat spreading plant with lustrous, wavy margined leaves on red stalks, and a year round succession of pink flowers. Good as a plant for the greenhouse or the home.

scharfii see B. haageana

semperflorens
An unusually dwarf, bushy species with rounded, shining green leaves. Flowering time is May to October. Many strains and cultivars are on the market from 6 in. dwarfs to 18 in. bushy plants, some with purple tinted leaves and flowers ranging through white to deep crimson. All are good plants. Brazil. **59.**
   'Coffee and Cream' is pure white with purple-brown foliage;
   'Pandy' has blood-red flowers.

serratipetala
An ornamental species with glossy, pleated, deep green leaves carried on arching stems, and rich pink flowers with distinctively notched petals. It flowers from spring to autumn and is a most attractive pot plant for house or greenhouse. New Guinea.

socotrana
The type is now rarely grown, having been largely superseded by cultivars derived from it by hybridization. It has round leaves and deep pink flowers in the winter. The hybrids fall into 2 main groups, the pink Lorraine begonias and the larger flowering Hiemalis group which has a wider colour range, from white through orange to pink. All are excellent pot plants for house and greenhouse. Socotra.
Lorraine group
   'Ege's Favourite', rich pink;

'Red Marina', deep reddish-pink;
'Regent', carmine-pink, **60**;
'White Snow', glistening white.
Hiemalis group
'Eveleen's Orange', deep orange flowers;
'Thought of Christmas', a white, double-flowered cultivar;
'Van de Meer's Glory', with salmon-orange flowers.

× tuberhybrida ❀

A series of hybrids to which many cultivar names have been given. They fall into 2 groups, the Double or Rose-flowered sorts which have mid-green leaves and 3–6 in. flowers opening from June to September, and the Pendula group which are smaller with slender, pendent stems and single or semi-double flowers 2–3 in. across. The following cultivars are particularly attractive.
Rose-flowered
'Corona', yellow with fine rose edge, **61**;
'Diana Wynyard', with large white flowers;
'Elaine Tartellin', overall rich rose pink, **62**;
'Guardsman', clear and bright orange scarlet, **63**;
'Harlequin', white with a rose-pink edge, **64**;
'Mary Heatley', bright orange, **65**;
'Olympia', bright crimson;
'Rhapsody', rose-pink;
'Seville', yellow with pink margins.
Pendula, **66**
'Red Cascade', scarlet;
'Golden Shower', golden-yellow;
'Lou-Anne', rose-pink.

Belladonna Lily see **Amaryllis belladonna**
Bell Flower, Chilean see **Lapageria rosea**
Bellflower, Chimney see **Campanula pyramidalis**
Bell-Vine, Purple see **Rhodochiton volubile**

BELOPERONE syn. DREJERELLA (ACANTHACEAE)
guttata Shrimp Plant ❀

A popular plant for the house or greenhouse with soft, somewhat shining green leaves and spikes of white, tongue-shaped flowers which protrude from overlapping, pinky-brown bracts, fancifully appearing like the body of a shrimp. Flowers appear almost throughout the year. Grow in the cool greenhouse in pots of a loam-based compost or a proprietary peat mix. Shade from hottest sunshine. Propagate by stem cuttings, preferably from cut back plants in spring or summer. Mexico. **67**.

Bermuda Buttercup see **Oxalis cernua**

BERTOLONIA (MELASTOMATACEAE) Jewel Plant
A genus of dwarf evergreen plants grown primarily for their beautifully marked foliage. The small, rosy-purple flowers are not a noteworthy feature. They are excellent plants for small pot culture and both for the house and warm greenhouse. Grow in a proprietary peat mix and shade from direct sunlight. Maintain a humid atmosphere. Propagate by basal stem cuttings in summer or seeds sown in spring.

maculata ✿

A creeping plant with bristly stems and oval to heart-shaped, hairy leaves, patterned with silvery white spots. Brazil.

marmorata syn. **Eriocnema marmorata** ✿

A beautiful, delicate plant with vivid, bright green leaves streaked above with silvery-white, and purple beneath. Brazil.

BESSERA (LILIACEAE)
elegans Coral Drops ❀

A lily-like plant with 1–2 ft prostrate narrow leaves growing in a basal tuft. The long, stalked flowers are scarlet or scarlet and white, bell-shaped with purple stamens. Grows best in an airy cool greenhouse, and flowers from July to September. Pot the bulbs in pans of a loam-based compost in spring and keep just moist until the leaves are well developed, then water more freely. When the leaves yellow after flowering, dry off and store in a frost free place. Propagate by offsets at potting time or seeds when ripe. Mexico.

Betel Nut see **Areca catechu**

BIGNONIA (BIGNONIACEAE)
unguis-cati syn. **Doxantha unguis-cati** Cat's Claws ❀ ✿

A climber with leaves composed of a pair of narrow, opposite leaflets and claw-like tendrils by which it holds on to supports. It has solitary, bell-shaped, 5-lobed flowers which are yellow and open in the summer. It is seen to best advantage grown in a cool well ventilated greenhouse or conservatory border, trained up pillars or trellis work. It can also be grown in tubs of a loam-based compost. Propagate by stem cuttings in spring. Argentina.

BILLBERGIA (BROMELIACEAE) Queen's Tears
A genus of easy, attractive house and greenhouse plants with rosettes of graceful, strap-shaped leaves. The flowers, or bracts that enfold them, are showy, mostly in shades of pink, red, purple and green. In most species they are carried on long, arching stems. They appear throughout the summer. Grow in a proprietary peat mix or equal parts of a loam-based compost and sphagnum moss. Shade from direct sunlight and maintain a humid atmosphere. Propagate by division or removing offsets in summer. Seeds may also be sown in spring but the plants take several years to reach maturity.

chantinii see **Aechmea chantinii**

nutans Angel's Tears ❀ ✿

The erect, dark green leaves with a silvery sheen, grow to 18 in. in height. The tubular green, purple-blue edged flowers appear between rosy-pink bracts and are carried in 3 in. drooping clusters in long, arching stems. A species very tolerant of temporary cold spells. Brazil. **68**.

pyramidalis Summer Torch ❀ ✿

The broad, bright green leaves grow in a vase shaped rosette, from the centre of which rises an erect, 4–6 in. spike of crimson, purple tipped flowers with scarlet bracts, borne on a woolly stem. A very showy plant. Brazil. **69**.

rhodocyanea see **Aechmea fasciata**

× windii (*B. decora* × *B. nutans*) ❀ ✿

A hybrid with firm, somewhat grey-green leaves and small, greenish-blue flowers almost hidden within the large, bright pink bracts. They are borne in pendent clusters on arching, 18 in. stems. Garden origin, Belgium.

Bird of Paradise Flower see **Strelitzia reginae**
Bird's Nest Fern see **Asplenium nidus**
Birthwort see **Aristolochia**
Black-eyed Susan see **Thunbergia alata**
Black Leaf Panamiga see **Pilea repens**
Black-throated Calla see **Zantedeschia melanoleuca**
Black Tree Fern see **Cyathea medullaris**
Bladder Flower see **Araujia sericofera**

BLECHNUM (POLYPODIACEAE)
A genus of handsome, decorative ferns of which the following species respond best to pot culture in a greenhouse or house. Grow in a proprietary peat compost and shade from direct sunlight. Maintain a humid atmosphere from spring to autumn. Propagate by division or spores in spring.

brasiliense Rib Fern

A large fern which, with age, develops a small scaly 'trunk' and has upright fronds from 2–4 ft in length and 6–16 in. broad. They are deeply cut, with each segment finely toothed and wavy edged. It needs warmth and humidity and is best grown in a warm greenhouse. Brazil, Peru.

capense ✿

An erect fern with 1–3 ft fronds having long, narrow segments 3–12 in. in length and ½–1 in. broad, rounded or heart-shaped at the base. The spores are borne on separate fronds which are narrow and only 6 in. long. It is suitable for both house and greenhouse. South Africa, Polynesia.

gibbum

A large fern with 2–3 ft densely scaly stalk, and 2–3 ft fronds divided into narrow, 4–6 in. segments which are held stiffly. A good greenhouse plant which can be grown indoors. New Caledonia, **70.**

moorei syn. **Lomaria ciliata**

A smaller species with a rosette of stiff, divided fronds 8–12 in. long having uncut, wavy edged segments. These are broad on the sterile fronds and narrower on those bearing spores. If kept moist, it can make a good house plant and also grows well in the greenhouse. New Caledonia.

Bleeding Heart see **Dicentra spectabilis**
Bleeding Heart Vine see **Clerodendrum speciosissimum**
Blood Flower see **Haemanthus katherinae**
Bloodleaf see **Iresine lindenii**
Blood Lily see **Haemanthus**
Blue African Lily see **Agapanthus africanus**
Blue-flowered Torch see **Tillandsia lindeniana**
Blue Cape Plumbago see **Plumbago capensis**
Blue Glory Bower see **Clerodendrum ugandense**
Blue Gum see **Eucalyptus globulus**
Blue Lotus of Egypt see **Nymphaea caerulea**
Blue Passion Flower see **Passiflora caerulea**
Blue Sage see **Eranthemum pulchellum**
Blue Water-lily, Cape see **Nymphaea capensis**

BLUMENBACHIA (LOASACEAE)

A genus of attractive plants, but with stinging hairs which makes them unpleasant to handle. They have deeply lobed leaves and unusual, showy flowers usually in shades of red or orange. Grow in a conservatory or cool greenhouse border or in pots of a loam-based compost. Ventilate freely on sunny days. Propagate by seeds sown in spring. Wear gloves to handle the young plants.

grandiflora

A climbing plant suitable for climbing up a wall. It has deeply cut, rather triangular leaves and orange-red flowers 1½–2 in. across in late summer. Peru, Ecuador.

laterita syn. **Caiophora laterita**

A useful creeping plant with dissected leaves, the segments being rather saw-toothed. The large bell-like flowers are a bright, brick-red and are borne on long stalks. Chile.

Blushing Philodendron see **Philodendron erubescens**
Boat Lily see **Rhoeo spathacea**

BOMAREA (AMARYLLIDACEAE)

A genus of twining plants which can be grown in large pots of a loam-based compost, but are at their best in a cool greenhouse border. The flowers appear to have 6 petals, but in fact the outer 3 are coloured sepals, only the inner 3 being true petals. Plant in spring and provide cane or wire supports. Shade from hottest sunshine and ventilate freely. Propagate by seeds or division in spring.

caldasii

An attractive species with broad-lanceolate leaves and golden-yellow lily-like flowers, 1½ in. long in 6–20-flowered clusters. The 3 outer sepals are golden-yellow, tipped with green and the 3 inner ones bear red spots. Summer is the main flowering season. Ecuador.

kalbreyeri

rather saw-toothes. The large bell-like flowers are a bright, brick-red leaves hairy beneath, and terminal clusters of flowers, the outer sepals a vivid orange-red, the inner rather longer and deep yellow, spotted with red. Colombia.

BORONIA (RUTACEAE)

A genus of graceful, evergreen shrubs, most of which have fragrant blooms and light, dissected foliage. They grow well in pots of a proprietary peat compost in the cool greenhouse, and may be placed outside from July to September. Under glass, ventilate freely whenever

possible and water sparingly. Propagate by seeds in spring or cuttings of lateral shoots with a heel in summer.

alata

A 4–6 ft shrub with hairless, pinnate leaves, the leaflets small and finely toothed. The flowers which grow in clusters in May, are a rich pink, each narrow, slender pointed petal having a red line running along its length. W. Australia.

megastigma

A smaller shrub than the preceding species, attaining only 2 ft with the leaves divided into 3 narrow, linear leaflets. The solitary flowers which open in spring, are maroon-purple outside and yellow inside and are borne on long spikes. Intense perfume. W. Australia.

Botany Bay Tea Tree see **Correa alba**
Bo-tree, Sacred see **Ficus religiosa**
Bottlebrush see **Callistemon**
Boucerosia mammillaris see **Caralluma mammillaris**

BOUGAINVILLEA (NYCTAGINACEAE)

A genus grown for its showy blooms which are made up of large, brightly coloured, papery bracts surrounding the small, insignificant tubular flowers. They are all climbers and make good cool or warm greenhouse and conservatory plants, either in pots or borders. In pots, use a loam-based compost and provide cane or wire supports. Ventilate freely on warm days. Propagate by stem cuttings in summer.

× **buttiana** (*B. glabra* × *B. peruviana*)

A vigorous woody climber with large spines and thick, oval leaves. The large clusters of flowers are surrounded by brilliant, crimson bracts that fade to magenta, making cascades of colour in summer.
  'Kiltie Campbell' has deep orange bracts;
  'Mrs Butt' or 'Crimson Lake' has rose-crimson bracts, **71.**

glabra Paper Flower

A similar plant with smaller, bright green leaves and brightly coloured bracts. When young it makes an excellent pot plant, but can reach 10 ft when fully grown. Brazil.
  'Double Pink', an unusual semi-double form, **72;**
  'Variegata', with showy creamy-bordered leaves.

spectabilis

The most colourful and also the strongest growing species which can reach 30 ft in the greenhouse border. When young it makes a good pot plant with large clusters of brilliant bracts varying in colour from pink to scarlet, appearing from July to September. Brazil. **73.**

BOUVARDIA (RUBIACEAE)

A group of pretty evergreen shrubs with showy clusters of fragrant tubular flowers produced at the ends of the branches. They make good plants for the cool greenhouse and are suitable for the home when in full bloom. Grow in a loam-based compost and shade from the hottest sun. Pinch the young plants several times when young to promote bushy growth. Propagate by stem cuttings with a heel, preferably from cut back plants, in spring.

× **domestica**

A 2 ft shrub of hybrid origin with clusters of white, pink or red, 4-petalled flowers appearing from June to November.
  'Mary' has pure pink flowers, **74;**
  'President Cleveland', with scarlet flowers, **75.**

humboldtii see **B. longiflora**

longiflora syn. **B. humboldtii** Sweet Bouvardia

A beautiful, but somewhat straggling, autumn flowering shrub reaching 3 ft in height. It has glossy leaves and loose clusters of snowy white, waxy flowers which are fragrant. Mexico.

ternifolia see **B. triphylla**

triphylla syn. **B. ternifolia** Scarlet Trompetilla

A 2–3 ft shrub with 3-angled branches and leaves in three's. It has clusters of fiery red blooms, appearing spasmodically throughout the year with the main season from June to February. Mexico.
  'Alba', a neat, white flowering cultivar with hairy foliage.

Bower Plant see **Pandorea jasminoides**
Bow Lily see **Cyrtanthus mackenii**
Bowstring Hemp see **Sansevieria**
Boxwood, African see **Myrsine africana**
Bracken, Trembling see **Pteris tremula**
Brake see **Pteris**
Brake, Cliff see **Pellaea**
Brake, Sword see **Pteris ensiformis**
Brassaia actinophylla see **Schefflera actinophylla**

BRASSOLAELIOCATTLEYA (ORCHIDACEAE)

This comprises a number of hybrids between the 3 genera, *Brassavola*, *Laelia* and *Cattleya*. They have flowers up to 6 in. across which are produced between October and March. Grow in perforated pots or baskets, using a compost of 3 parts osmunda fibre and one part sphagnum moss. Shade from direct sunlight and maintain a humid atmosphere. Propagate by division in spring. Many named forms are grown. The following can be recommended.
    'Nugget', with yellow flowers;
    'Norman's Bay', magenta-pink flowers with a deeper red lip and gold veining in the throat.

Brazilian Edelweiss see **Rechsteineria leucotricha**
Brazilian Nightshade see **Solanum seaforthianum**
Bread Fruit, Mexican see **Monstera deliciosa**

BREYNIA (EUPHORBIACEAE)

nivosa Snow Bush
An unusual species for the warm greenhouse, or when small as a house plant. It is a densely branched but slender shrub bearing green ovate leaves about 1 in. in length and marbled with white. It grows best in the greenhouse border and also makes a good tub or pot plant. Use a proprietary peat compost, shade from direct sunlight and maintain a humid atmosphere. Propagate by lateral stem cuttings, preferably with a heel, in summer. Pacific Islands.
    'Roseopicta', Leaf Flower, is the form most frequently grown, the mottling on the leaves including pink and red markings as well as the green and white of the species.

Bridal Wreath see **Francoa sonchifolia**
Brier, Cat or **Horse** see **Smilax rotundifolia**

BRODIAEA (ALLIACEAE)

A genus of attractive bulbous plants with long, tubular leaves and umbrella-like heads of blue-purple, tubular flowers which are borne on leafless stems. They can be grown either in pots or in a border in the greenhouse. Pot the bulbs in a loam-based compost in autumn. Water sparingly at first, more freely when the leaves are growing vigorously. When the foliage fades, dry off and store in a warm place. Propagate by offset bulbs at potting time or seeds in early spring or when ripe.

coronaria syn. **B. grandiflora** Triplet Lily
A showy species with loose clusters of violet-blue flowers, 1½ in. across, which open during June and July. Pacific N. America.

grandiflora see **B. coronaria**

laxa syn. **Triteleia laxa** Grass Nut
A charming plant with many flowered clusters of blue-purple, funnel shaped flowers, reaching 2 ft in height. They open in July. California.

BROWALLIA (SOLANACEAE)

A genus of profusely flowering, bushy annuals which make beautiful plants for pots in the cool or warm greenhouse. They have blue-purple, tubular flowers which appear from spring to autumn if sown in succession. Grow in a loam-based compost, for preference, and shade from hottest sunshine. Pinch young plants to promote bushy growth. Propagate by seeds sown in spring or summer.

speciosa
A compact plant growing to about 2 ft, it has oval, slender pointed leaves and violet-blue flowers, 2 in. across. Many cultivars are grown, some of hybrid origin. These make excellent pot plants. Colombia. **76.**
    'Major', deep blue flowers with a white edge;
    'Silver Bells', with white flowers.

viscosa
A plant growing to 12 in. or more with ovate clammy leaves. The 1 in. bright blue-violet flowers have white centres. Peru.
    'Sapphire' has blue flowers and a more neat form of growth, attaining only 6–9 in.

Brugmansia see **Datura**

BRUNFELSIA (SOLANACEAE)

Handsome evergreen shrubs with abundant, attractive flowers at their best from June to October, though blooming almost throughout the year. They grow best in pots in the warm or cool greenhouse and need plenty of ventilation in the summer. Use a proprietary peat compost and shade from the hottest sunshine. Propagate by stem cuttings in summer.

calycina syn. **C. floribunda** Yesterday, To-day and To-morrow
A floriferous shrub with shining green, leathery leaves, 2–4 in. in length and 2 in. flowers, rich purple with a white eye, the deep colour fading with age. Brazil.
    'Macrantha' has larger flowers to 3 in. across, **77.**

floribunda see **B. calycina**

undulata White Raintree
A strong growing evergreen shrub reaching 4 ft. It has long mid-green, elliptic leaves and very fragrant white flowers turn to cream, with 3 in. tubes opening to 1½ in. across at the mouth. W. Indies.

BRYOPHYLLUM (CRASSULACEAE) Life Plant

There is some dispute as to whether these plants should now be included in the genus *Kalanchoe*. They are leaf-succulents and should be treated as terrestrial cacti and succulents, see Introduction. Many of them produce minute complete plants in the notches in the margins of the leaves, and these can be taken off and rooted. Sideshoots can also be rooted as cuttings. They flower in late spring and summer, not freely in cultivation indoors. Minimum winter temperature 40°F., but 45–50°F. is better.

crenatum
The flowers are yellowish to red, some with reddish calyces and pedicels. Grown for the leaves which are about 3 in. long and 1 in. wide, grey-green, margined red, rounded and with plantlets in the crenations, on stems up to 15 in. tall. Tropical Africa, Brazil.

daigremontianum
The flowers are grey-violet to yellowish-pink, not freely produced. The leaves are sea-green, paler beneath and patterned with red-purple narrow markings on both surfaces, 3–6 in. long on stems up to 2½ ft. Plantlets are freely produced in the teeth at the edge of the leaves. Madagascar.

pinnatum Air Plant
The flowers are green and pink, 1½ in. long and 1 in. across. The leaves are about 3 in. long, green, tinged with red, the lower ones simple, notched, the upper ones pinnate; they are borne on stems up to 3 ft tall. Tropics of Old and New Worlds.

tubiflorum syn. **Kalanchoe verticillata**
Flowers reddish. Grown for the leaves which are dull green with deep purple markings, 3 in. long and ¼ in. thick, cylindrical in shape with pointed teeth at the end, in whorls of 3. Plantlets develop in the teeth at the end of the leaves. Stem to 3 ft tall. Madagascar.

uniflorum
Flowers pinkish, 1–3 on a stem. The leaves are green, rounded, ½ in. across with up to 5 crenations. They are borne on prostrate stems which root at the nodes. Madagascar. **78.**

Buchu see **Diosma ericoides**

BULBOPHYLLUM (ORCHIDACEAE)

A very large genus of tree-dwelling (epiphytic) orchids many of which have curiously formed flowers. Grow in hanging pots or baskets of 3 parts osmunda fibre to 1 part sphagnum moss in the warm greenhouse. Keep humid and shaded from direct sunlight. Propagate by division of plants in spring when it is necessary to repot.

barbigerum ✳
A dwarf plant with 3 in., dark green leaves. The flowers, which are borne on long spikes, at first horizontal then upward curving, have greenish-brown petals and sepals and a strange, long lip, very slender with the end covered with brown hair like a small powder puff. It is hinged so loosely that it moves with the slightest movement of the air. The flowers are produced in spring. Sierra Leone, West Africa.

careyanum ✳
A summer flowering species having small reddish or greenish-brown flowers borne in a dense spike at the end of the slender stems. India.

dayanum ✳
An attractively coloured species having rich, deep red petals with yellow margins and a green lip marked with red ridges. The blooms are 1 in. across and borne in clusters at the ends of the short stalks. The 3 in. elliptic leaves are suffused with red on the reverse side. The flowers are produced in spring. India.

umbellatum ✳
A pretty species, the long, slender yellow flowers marked with dark purple spotting, the lip being entirely purple. They are borne in stalked clusters of 4–5 blooms, all radiating out from the top of the stem like the spokes of a wheel and are produced in spring. The bulbs bear a single long oval leaf. India.

Bunny Ears see **Ochna atropurpurea**
Burro's Tail see **Sedum morganianum**
Bush Coleus see **Coleus thyrsoideus**
Busy Lizzie see **Impatiens wallerana holstii**

BUTIA (PALMAE) Yatay Palm
yatay syn. **Cocos yatay** 🐚
A palm tree growing to 15 ft when mature, with 9 ft arching frond-like leaves, with 50–60 slender, pointed leaflets on either side of the midrib. When young, it makes a particularly decorative pot plant for the house, keeping its elegant form, but in small proportions. Grow in the warm greenhouse, using a loam-based compost or a proprietary peat mix. Shade from hottest sunshine and maintain a humid atmosphere in summer. Propagate by seeds in spring. Brazil, Argentine.

Buttercup, Bermuda see **Oxalis cernua**
Buttercup Tree see **Cassia**
Butterfly Flower see **Schizanthus pinnatus**
Butterfly Lily see **Hedychium coronarium**
Butterfly Orchid see **Oncidium papilio**
Butterfly Pea see **Clitoria ternatea**
Butterwort see **Pinguicula**
Button Fern see **Pellaea rotundifolia**

C

Cabbage Palm see **Cordyline**
Cabbage Tree, New Zealand see **Cordyline australis**
Cabbage Tree, Spiked see **Cussonia spicata**
Cactus, Christmas see **Schlumbergera × buckleyi**
Cactus, Crab see **Schlumbergera truncata**
Cactus, Desert Pincushion see **Coryphantha deserti**
Cactus, Devil's Tongue see **Ferocactus latispinus**
Cactus, Feather see **Mammillaria plumosa**
Cactus, Mistletoe see **Rhipsalis cassutha**
Cactus, Old Man see **Cephalocereus senilis**
Cactus, Peanut see **Chamaecereus silvestrii**
Cactus, Rat's-tail see **Aporocactus flagelliformis**
Cactus, Redbird see **Pedilanthus tithymaloides**
Cactus, Ribbon see **Pedilanthus tithymaloides**
Cactus, Sea Urchin see **Echinopsis**
Cactus, Sun see **Heliocereus speciosus**

CAESALPINIA syn. **POINCIANA** (LEGUMINOSAE)
A genus of sun-loving shrubs with divided leaves made up of a number of small leaflets and with striking flat to cup-shaped flowers. They are excellent plants for the large cool or warm greenhouse. Grow in the border or tubs of a loam-based compost, and ventilate freely in summer. Propagate by seeds in spring. Cuttings of young shoots may be tried, but are difficult to root.

gilliesii syn. **Poinciana gilliesii** ✳ 🐚
A shrub or small tree with fine, doubly divided leaves and hairy stems terminating in clusters of 30–40 flowers produced in July and August. Each bloom is carried on a downy stalk, and has 1½ in. golden-yellow petals and a tassel of long, scarlet stamens which make a striking combination of colour. Argentina.

japonica ✳ 🐚
An extremely thorny shrub with stout, down-curved spines. It has bi-pinnate leaves and erect clusters of flowers, each comprising 20–30 bright yellow blooms which open in June and July. The plant needs support to reach its full height. Japan.

pulcherrima syn. **Poinciana pulcherrima** Barbados Pride ✳ 🐚
A handsome, prickly shrub with feathery, divided leaves and showy flowers with red to golden-yellow, wavy-edged petals and a pendent mass of scarlet stamens, 2½ in. long, appearing in July. Tropics.

Caiophora laterita see **Blumenbachia laterita**

CALADIUM (ARACEAE) 🐚
bicolor
A superb foliage plant for the warm humid greenhouse, with arrow-shaped leaves on long stalks and tuber-like rootstocks. Pot the tubers in spring, using a proprietary peat compost. Water sparingly at first, then freely as the leaves expand. Shade from direct sunshine. Dry off in autumn and store in a warm place. Propagate by offset tubers at planting time. Many cultivars are grown, all with different leaf patterning, **79.** The following are particularly striking, growing to about 15 in. tall.
  'Candidum', glistening white leaves with a lacy network of green veins;
  'Exposition', dark glossy green with carmine veins;
  'Pink Cloud', dark green, mottled with pink, and fine white veining;
  'Seagull', dark green with broad white veins;
  'Stoplight', carmine-red leaves with a narrow green edging;
  'Texas Wonder', green and white mottled leaves with carmine veins.

Caladium, Giant see **Alocasia cuprea**
Calamondin Orange see **Citrus mitis**

CALANDRINIA (PORTULACACEAE)
The two attractive species described are low-growing plants suitable for pots in a conservatory or greenhouse. They flower from July to September. Grow in a loam-based compost and ventilate freely in summer. Water sparingly in winter. Propagate by division or seeds sown in spring.

discolor ✳ 🐚
A perennial species, but often grown as an annual. It has fleshy, spoon-shaped leaves, light green above and purple beneath, and long clusters of bright purple, saucer-shaped flowers with yellow stamens. Chile.

umbellata Rock Purslane ✳ 🐚
A compact plant with narrow, hairy leaves. In July and August it is densely covered with clusters of bright crimson-magenta, cup-shaped flowers. Peru.
  'Amaranth', a very compact form only 4 in. in height with vivid crimson-purple flowers, **80.**

CALANTHE (ORCHIDACEAE)
A genus of handsome deciduous and evergreen orchids of which the following two species are best grown in a greenhouse. Pot in spring as growth starts, using a loam-based compost, setting the bulbs with the bases just under the soil. Water sparingly at first, then more freely as the leaves expand. When the mature foliage yellows dry off. Usually, no water is needed at flowering time. The evergreen species are kept moist all the year. Propagate by division or offsets at potting time. Burma.

masuca ✳

An evergreen species with 2 ft spikes, carrying from June to August, dense heads of violet-purple flowers. India.

vestita ✳

This species is deciduous and has spikes of up to 25 blooms borne on a 3 ft nodding stem. White flowers with a white or variously red lip appear in winter. Many variously coloured cultivars are known. Malaysia.

CALATHEA (MARANTACEAE)

A genus of handsome foliage plants which make most decorative pot plants for both house and warm greenhouse. They have simple, oval, leathery leaves which are variously marked in a wide range of colours. They need a high humidity to thrive well. Use a proprietary peat mix or a loam-based compost. Shade from direct sunlight, particularly in summer. Propagate by division in early summer.

insignis syn. **C. lancifolia** Rattlesnake Plant 🐦

The long parallel-sided leaves are wavy edged and a rich, velvety green, marked with dark olive-green blotches above and purple beneath. The plant is bushy and slow growing, usually to 1 ft in height, though it can reach 2 ft under favourable conditions. Brazil. **81.**

lancifolia see **C. insignis**

lindeniana 🐦

A tufted species with 6 in. oval leaves, dark green on top, with paler, feathery markings on either side of the midrib and near the edges. The underside is purple, except for a central green stripe. Brazil.

louisae 🐦

The 5 in. ovate leaves are dark green with olive or grey-green feathering outwards from the central vein, and green-purple on the underside with green margins. Brazil.

makoyana Peacock Plant 🐦

Often considered the finest of the genus, this species has silvery-green leaves above, with a fine, lacy design of darker green lines and alternate large and small ovals on either side of the mid vein. The pattern is also on the underside of the leaves, but the lines and ovals are purplish-red. An excellent house plant. Brazil. **82.**

ornata 🐦

This species has long, narrowly oval, green leaves with various striped markings above and is purplish beneath. It is grown as a pot plant in its younger stages when it is about 18 in. high, but when mature it can reach 8 ft. It is suitable for the warm greenhouse. Colombia.

'Roseo-lineata', dark, olive-green leaves with closely set pairs of pink stripes becoming ivory white in older plants.

zebrina Zebra Plant 🐦

A vigorous plant for the warm greenhouse. It has large, oblong leaves to 18 in. in length on 12 in. stalks. They are a soft, velvety green with yellow-green bands that are purple beneath. Brazil. **83.**

CALCEOLARIA (SCROPHULARIACEAE) Slipperwort

A genus including many annual and shrubby plants cultivated in pots both in the cool greenhouse and indoors. They are grown for their curious pouch-shaped flowers with the inflated lip coloured in yellows and reds. Propagate the annual *C. × herbeohybrida* by seeds sown in June. If possible grow the seedlings in an open cold frame until September then bring into the cool greenhouse. Place in final pots of a loam-based compost if available the following February. The shrubby species are propagated by cuttings of lateral non-flowering shoots in late summer. All species require good ventilation and a light shading from the hottest summer sun.

bicolor ✳

A weak-stemmed plant with thin, heart-shaped, toothed green leaves, and loose clusters of ¾ in. flowers, clear yellow with white at the base. It flowers from July to November. Peru.

× herbeohybrida ✳

This name covers a number of hybrids with large, rounded flowers, to 2½ in. in length, coloured variously yellow, orange or red, and spotted or blotched with darker red. They are best grown in the greenhouse where they flower from May to July.

'Grandiflora', flowers yellow, marked in orange-red to maroon, 3 in. across;

'Monarch', 15–18 in. high in a wide range of colours, **84**;

'Multiflora Nana', a dwarf plant, ideal for pot culture. It has clusters of similar shaped yellow or orange flowers flushed and spotted with crimson, **85**.

integrifolia syn. **C. rugosa** ✳

A shrubby perennial with narrow, wrinkled leaves hairy beneath and smooth above. The flowers are small, but open in dense masses making a blaze of colour from yellow to red-brown, throughout the summer. Chile. **86.**

'Angustifolia' has long, narrow leaves and longer stalks to the flower clusters.

pavonii ✳ 🐦

A large square-stemmed species reaching 6 ft; its large, densely hairy, toothed leaves are oval and winged at the base. The clusters of 1 in. flowers are deep yellow to brown and open in summer. Peru. **87.**

rugosa see **C. integrifolia**

Calico Flower see **Aristolochia elegans**
Calico Plant see **Alternanthera bettzickiana**
California Geranium see **Senecio petasites**
Californian Pitcher Plant see **Darlingtonia californica**
Calla see **Zantedeschia**

CALLICARPA (VERBENACEAE) Beauty Berry

A genus of evergreen shrubs grown chiefly for their large clusters of lilac or violet berries, and the autumn coloration of their leaves. The species described require cool greenhouse treatment in all but the mildest parts of Britain. Plant in the border, in large pots or tubs of a loam-based compost. Ventilate freely on warm days. Propagate by lateral stem cuttings with a heel in late summer.

americana French Mulberry 🐦 ●

A 6 ft shrub with oval, downy leaves, blunt toothed and tapered at both ends. The flowers are blue, pink or white and insignificant, but followed by clusters of globular, violet berries which persist through the autumn. S.E. U.S.A., W. Indies.

rubella 🐦 ●

A taller shrub reaching 10 ft with long, slender-pointed leaves and small, pinkish flowers which open in July. The fruits are brilliant red-purple, and often remain on the bush throughout the winter. S.E. Asia. **88.**

Callisia elegans see **Setcreasea striata**

CALLISTEMON (MYRTACEAE) Bottlebrush

A genus of evergreen trees and shrubs which make attractive plants for the cool greenhouse. Their chief feature is the cylindrical, brush-like flower spikes, usually scarlet, and at their best during the summer. Grow in the border or in tubs of a loam-based compost. Ventilate freely whenever possible. Propagate by stem cuttings, preferably with a heel in summer.

citrinus syn. **C. lanceolatus** ✳ 🐦

A graceful shrub or small tree growing to 6 ft or more, with silky twigs and long narrow leaves, coppery when young and bright green when fully grown. The flower spikes have a mass of thread-like, brilliant red stamens and can grow to 6 in. in length. Australia. **89.**

lanceolatus see **C. citrinus**

salignus Pink Tips ✳ 🐦

A bushy shrub, 5–8 ft high, or tree to 30 ft, with narrow tapered leaves 2–4½ in. long emerging coppery pink. The 3 in. spikes of flowers are pale yellow. Suitable for a cold greenhouse. Australia.

speciosus Albany Bottlebrush ✳ 🐦

A very showy species, to 6 ft or more, with long narrow leaves and a broad, dense, rich scarlet flower spike, 5 in. long and carried on a downy stalk, May to August. The best species for greenhouse culture or for tubs. Thrives in wet conditions. W. Australia. **90.**

CALOCEPHALUS syn. **LEUCOPHYTA** (COMPOSITAE)

brownii Cushion Bush 🐦

A small wiry, woolly shrub growing 1–3 ft in height. It has insignificant heads of yellow flowers and is grown for the dense covering of white hairs on all parts of the plant, especially the stems and the narrow leaves. A good foliage plant for pots in the cool greenhouse. Grow in a loam-based compost and ventilate freely wherever possible. Water sparingly. Propagate by lateral stem cuttings, preferably with a heel in late summer. Australia.

Camelia see **Camellia**

CAMELLIA (THEACEAE) Camelia
A genus of ornamental, evergreen shrubs with glossy, leathery, deep green leaves and handsome single, semi-double or double, rose-like flowers which make a superb show from late winter to late spring. They are excellent conservatory subjects and also for the cool or cold greenhouse. Grow in large pots or tubs of a loam-based compost without lime, or in a proprietary peat mix. Shade from hottest sun and ventilate freely. Ideally, stand the plants outside in a shady place from April or May to October. Propagate by stem or leaf-bud cuttings in late summer or early autumn.

japonica
A large, woody evergreen to 15 ft or more with glossy, ovate leaves. The flowers, which are carried on the ends of the branches, are 3–5 in. across, single or double and white, pink, red or variegated. Many cultivars are grown and some hybrids. It flowers from February to May. Japan.
 'Adolphe Audusson', large semi-double blood-red flower and compact growth form, **93;**
 'Alba Simplex', the best single white with conspicuous stamens, **91;**
 'Anemoniflora', vigorous and erect with dark crimson blooms;
 'Chandleri', large, semi-double flowers which are bright red and sometimes white marked;
 'Drama Girl', very attractive, large semi-double form with deep salmon-pink blooms and somewhat pendent growth;
 'Jupiter', the flowers are deep pink with darker veins with a prominent boss of yellow stamens, single to semi-double, **92;**
 'Lady Vansittart', semi-double, wavy-edged petals which are white and striped with pink;
 'Magnoliiflora', semi-double with flower form rather like that of *Magnolia stellata*. Pale rose pink;
 'Mathotiana Rosea', large fully double of almost perfect classical form, medium pink;
 'Nagasaki', large semi-double, rose pink flower with white marbling. Leaves often with yellow mottling;
 'Tomorrow', a very large double to semi-double form with rose pink blooms;
 'Tricolor', blush pink, streaked red, semi-double, **94.**

reticulata
A usually thinner, more erect shrub or small tree reaching only 10 ft or more. It has duller green, leathery, elliptic leaves which are net-veined, and single or double blooms 6 in. across which range from a soft rose to deep red. Flowering season is from February to April. China.
 'Buddha', very large, semi-double, rose-pink flowers with wavy petals;
 'Captain Rawes', a magnificent shrub with large, bright rose-pink, semi-double flower, **95;**
 'Noble Pearl', large semi-double, deep red flowers;
 'Shot Silk', large semi-double with vivid pink, wavy-petalled flowers.

CAMPANULA (CAMPANULACEAE)
A genus of chiefly hardy plants, but the two species below do best with protection. The flowers are bell or star-shaped, in shades of white, blue and violet. Grow in a loam-based compost and ventilate whenever possible. Propagate *C. isophylla* by division or cuttings of basal shoots in spring. Sow seeds of *C. pyramidalis* in spring.

isophylla
A dwarf perennial trailing plant which makes an excellent house or cold greenhouse plant, and is especially decorative when grown in hanging baskets. The blue, starry flowers are 1 in. across and cover the plant in August and September. N. Italy. **96.**
 'Alba', a white form, **97.**

pyramidalis Chimney Bellflower
A large species reaching 5 ft, which makes a very good May flowering plant for large pots or tubs. It has bright green, heart-shaped leaves and long pyramidal spikes of blue or white, open bell-shaped flowers with darker centres. Biennial. S. Europe.

CAMPELIA (COMMELINACEAE)
zanonia 'Mexican Flag' syn. Dichorisandra albo-lineata
A striking foliage plant, the 8–12 in. fleshy, lance-shaped leaves striped longitudinally with creamy-white, red and green, the colours of the Mexican flag, hence its cultivar name. They are borne on a 3 ft, thick fleshy stalk. The purple and white flowers are borne on short stalks in the axils of the leaves. Grow in pots in the warm greenhouse or home, in a proprietary peat compost. Shade from the hottest sunlight and maintain a humid atmosphere in summer. Propagate by division or basal stem cuttings in early summer. Mexico.

Canary Island Banana, Musa cavendishii see under **M. acuminata**
Canary Island Ivy see **Hedera canariensis**
Canary Island Palm see **Phoenix canariensis**
Candle Plant see **Plectranthus coleoides** and **Senecio articulatus**

CANNA (CANNACEAE)
Striking tropical plants, 3–6 ft high with erect stalks, broad leaves, often red or bronze tinted and brilliant coloured, orchid-like flowers. They make very good cool or warm greenhouse plants for pots or borders. Plant the tuberous rootstocks in spring, using a loam-based compost or a proprietary peat mix. Water sparingly at first, then freely while in full growth. Dry off in autumn and store in a warm place. Propagate by dividing the rootstock at potting time or by seeds in spring. Tropical Asia and America.

× hybrida
A group of cultivars, derived by hybridization. The broadly ovate leaves reach up to 2 ft in length and the scarlet, orange or yellow, orchid-like flowers open from June to September. They do not come true from seed.
 'Di Bartolo', deep pink;
 'J. B. van der Schoot', yellow with red speckling, **98;**
 'Lucifer', dwarf growing with bright red flowers edged yellow;
 'Orange Perfection', free flowering; salmon-orange.

CANTUA (POLEMONIACEAE)
buxifolia
A slender shrub grown as a climber and suitable for the cool greenhouse. It has narrow, often hoary leaves and terminal clusters of short stalked, long-tubed flowers, purplish-red with yellow striping on the tube. The bud tips spiral and the blossoms, at first erect, later become drooping. The blooms appear in April. Ideally grow in the border, or in tubs of a loam-based compost. Provide canes or wires for support. Ventilate freely on warm days. Propagate by lateral stem cuttings, preferably with a heel, in summer. Peru, Bolivia, Chile. **99.**

Cape Belladonna see **Amaryllis belladonna**
Cape Blue Water-lily see **Nymphaea capensis**
Cape Cowslip see **Lachenalia**
Cape Grape see **Rhoicissus capensis**
Cape Honeysuckle see **Tecomaria capensis**
Cape Jasmine see **Gardenia jasminoides**
Cape Plumbago, Blue see **Plumbago capensis**
Cape Primrose see **Streptocarpus**

CAPSICUM (SOLANACEAE) Red Pepper
A genus chiefly grown for the shiny, brightly coloured fruits which ripen from late summer to winter. They make most attractive pot plants for a winter display. The fruits of allied cultivars are used for culinary purposes, giving cayenne and paprika as well as the green and red peppers. Grow in a cool greenhouse or frame, ventilating freely during the summer. Alternatively, stand outside in a sheltered, but sunny spot, from May to September. Propagate by seeds sown in spring.

annuum ●
Ornamental and green and red Chilli peppers. The forms grown as pot plants are mostly hybrids, often between *C. annuum* and *C. frutescens* and vary chiefly in the shape and colour of the fruits. They have whitish, starry, pendent flowers from June to September, from which the variable fruits develop.

'Christmas Greeting', 18 in. plant with 1–1½ in. fruits in a medley of colours including shades of green, violet, yellow and red;
'Fiesta', about 9 in. tall with 2 in. long, slender, pointed fruit changing from green to pale yellow, orange then red, **100**;
'Rising Sun', also 18 in. high, this has bright red, tomato-like fruits.

frutescens ●
A larger plant from 1½–6 ft, of which the smaller forms make good pot plants. They have slender, ovate to oblong leaves and erect, ornamental fruits, in colours from white, yellow and green to red and purple. Tropical America.

'Chameleon', a 12 in. plant bearing fruit which change colour as they ripen from green through yellow to purple and red, **101**;
'Fips', a more compact plant, only 7 in. high, with fruit changing from green through yellow to red, **102**.

CARALLUMA (ASCLEPIADACEAE)
Stem succulents closely resembling *Stapelia*; see under the latter for general description and cultivation.

europaea ✳ 🐦
The flowers are pale yellow, banded with dull purple. They are small and grow in clusters near the top of the stem in summer. The leaves are rudimentary. The green, 4-angled stem is channelled between the angles and has small teeth. Mediterranean Islands. **103**.

mammillaris syn. **Boucerosia mammillaris, Piaranthus pullus** ✳ 🐦

The black purple flowers occur in clusters in the grooves of the stem in summer. The 5–6 angled stem is green and has stout, sharp conical spines on the ridges. As with the previous species, the leaves are rudimentary. S. Africa.

Cardinal Flower see Rechsteineria cardinalis

CAREX (CYPERACEAE) Sedge
A large group of mainly tufted grassy plants grown for their attractive tufts of often glossy, slender, tough, leaves. They make durable pot plants for the home or greenhouse. Grow in greenhouse borders or pots of loam-based compost and shade from hottest sunshine. Ventilate on all warm days. Propagate by division or seeds sown in spring.

japonica see **C. morrowii**

morrowii syn. **C. japonica** 🐦
This sedge is represented in gardens by the variegated form, *C.m.* 'Variegata'. It is a tufted species having narrow, stiff, arching, long pointed leaves margined with white lines. The tiny flowers are borne in catkin like spikes in spring, but they are not a noteworthy feature. *C. morrowii* can be grown in a cold greenhouse or unheated room and makes a long-lived plant. Japan.

scaposa 🐦
A very broad-leaved, 1–2 in. wide, species forming a bold, spreading tuft 1 ft tall. Catkin-like spikes of flowers appear in winter. A cool greenhouse plant. S. China.

CARICA (CARICACEAE)
papaya Pawpaw, Melon Tree 🐦 ●
An evergreen tropical tree with male and female flowers on separate trees. It makes an interesting plant for the border or large tub in a large warm greenhouse where it will grow to 8 ft or more and the female plants will produce the 6–12 in. delicious melon-like fruit. This species can be grown in pots as a foliage plant but is not likely to bear fruit. The leaves are cut into 7 lobes which are again cut, making an intricate shape. They grow on long stalks from the top of the palm-like trunk. Grow in a proprietary peat compost and maintain a humid atmosphere from spring to autumn. Shade from the hottest sunshine. Water freely in summer, less in winter. Propagate by seeds sown in spring.

Caricature Plant see Graptophyllum pictum
Carnival Bush see Ochna atropurpurea
Carrion Flower see Stapelia

CARISSA (APOCYNACEAE)
grandiflora Natal Plum ✳ 🐦 ●
A spiny, evergreen shrub 5–7 ft high. It has deep, glossy green leathery leaves, which are oval and 2–3 in. in length and borne on hairless branches which also carry forked spines. The white fragrant flowers have a short tube, opening out to 1⅓–3 in. across the lobes. They grow in small clusters and open in May. In July they bear scarlet, ovoid berries up to 2 in. in length. An attractive shrub for the cool greenhouse border or for large pots and tubs. Use a proprietary peat compost and water freely during the summer, less at other times. Ventilate on warm days and provide light shade during the hottest months. Propagate by seeds sown when ripe or in the spring, or by lateral stem cuttings, preferably with a heel in summer. S. Africa.

Carnation see Dianthus

CASSIA (LEGUMINOSAE) Senna, Buttercup Tree
A large genus of mainly woody plants with elegant foliage and showy clusters of flowers. They are best grown in the greenhouse border where they can grow to a mature size, but can be flowered in large pots or tubs of a loam-based compost or a proprietary peat mix. Ventilate freely on warm days and shade lightly during hot spells. Propagate by seeds sown in spring or by lateral stem cuttings with a heel in summer.

australis ✳ 🐦
A 6 ft erect shrub with mid-green leaves of 9–12 pairs of leaflets. The cup-shaped, 1 in. golden-yellow flowers are in clusters of 3–6 in the axils of the upper leaves, and open in May and June. Australia.

corymbosa Golden Senna ✳ 🐦
A 5–6 ft shrub with only 2–3 pairs of leaflets, and large rich yellow, cup-shaped, 1 in. golden-yellow flowers are in clusters of 3–6 in September. Tropical America. **104**.

fistula Golden Shower, Pudding Pipe Tree ✳ 🐦
A small tree of 10 ft or more, with 4–8 pairs of leaflets to each 12 in. leaf, and drooping clusters of 5 in. golden-yellow flowers, opening in summer. A very beautiful plant, but needs a large greenhouse. India, Ceylon.

Castor Oil Plant see Ricinus communis
Cat Brier see Smilax rotundifolia
Catharanthus roseus see Vinca rosea
Cathedral Bells see Cobaea scandens
Cat's Claws see Bignonia unguis-cati
Cat's Jaws see Faucaria
Cat's Whiskers see Tacca chantrieri

CATTLEYA (ORCHIDACEAE)
A genus of superb, tropical orchids which, in cultivation, needs the humid atmosphere of the warm greenhouse. Each bulb bears from 1–3 fleshy leaves and magnificent flowers which in some species can measure 8–10 in. across the flower. In the wild they grow on tree branches and need special orchid pots or baskets to thrive in the greenhouse. Use a compost of two parts osmunda fibre and one part sphagnum moss. Maintain a humid atmosphere and shade from spring to early autumn. Keep cooler and expose to full light in autumn to aid flower bud initiation. Propagate by division in spring or summer. Many hybrids are grown, 'Catherine Subod' being one with fine white flowers, **105**.

aurantiaca ✳
An early flowering species with 3–20 flowers on a short, erect stem. The petals are orange, about 1 in. long with a crimson-spotted lip and wavy margins; they rarely open fully. Mexico, Guatemala.

bowringiana Cluster Cattleya ✳
A beautiful, autumn flowering species with 5–20 flowers, each up to 4 in. across and a rich rosy-purple with a darker, maroon-shaded lip and a yellow white throat. The 2 stiff leaves are 4–6 in. long. Central America.

citrina Tulip Cattleya ✻
A delightfully fragrant species with somewhat bell-shaped, solitary, lemon-yellow, waxy flowers which open from May to August. The 2–3 narrow leaves are pale grey-green, 6–10 in. long. Suitable for a cool greenhouse. Mexico.

dowiana Queen Cattleya ✻
A one-leafed species about 12 in. high with superb, large, fragrant flowers composed of crisp, golden-yellow petals and a frilled, golden veined, rich purple, rose-shaded lip. 3–6 blooms are carried on each 5 in. stalk, opening in autumn. It has been widely used as a parent for hybridisation and needs more warmth than most species of this genus. Colombia, Costa Rica.

intermedia Cocktail Orchid ✻
An 18 in. species with soft, rose coloured petals, and a rich violet-purple lip. The blooms are 5 in. across and open in spring and early summer. They are long lasting and remain fresh on the plant for 5–6 weeks. Brazil.
'Alba' is pure white with a crisped lip.

labiata Autumn Cattleya ✻
The 5–7 in. blooms of this species are pale rose with beautifully waxy petals and a rich, velvety crimson lip having a frilled edge and yellow throat. It flowers from August to November with 3–7 blooms on each spike. Brazil, Trinidad.

mossiae Easter Orchid, Spring Cattleya ✻
One of the easiest species to grow. It has dark green, shining leaves and fragrant flowers which are a pale lavender-pink with a frilled, crimson, mottled rose lip and a yellow throat. The 4–7 in. blooms are produced from March to June. Venezuela.

skinneri ✻
A 12–18 in. spring flowering species with spikes of 5–12 blooms which are rose-purple and about 3 in. across. The lip is darker purple with a wavy margin and pales to a yellowish-white throat. Guatemala.

trianaei Christmas Orchid, Winter Cattleya ✻
A beautiful winter flowering species with spikes of 2–3 flowers. Each bloom is up to 7 in. across with rose-pink or white petals and a deep purple lip, having a yellow throat. The colouring is very variable and many cultivars are grown. Colombia.

CELOSIA (AMARANTHACEAE)
argentea syn. **C. plumosa** ✻
A compact plant growing to 2 ft with light green, narrow leaves and dense, feathery plumes of tiny, silky flowers which are produced from July to September. Grow in a cool greenhouse, using pots of a loam-based compost or a proprietary peat mix. Ventilate freely on warm days and shade from hottest sunshine. Propagate by seeds sown in spring. Tropical Asia. Many cultivars are grown of which the following are the most noteworthy.
  Cristata: Cockscomb. Shorter plant to 12 in. with small, oval leaves and thick, fan-shaped heads 6–10 in. wide, usually bright red, but also in orange and yellow, **106;**
  Pyramidalis: Spectacular plumes of flowers in brilliant colours and mid-green, oval leaves. Make good indoor plants, **107.**
  'Golden Feather' is a yellow flowered cultivar;
  'Fiery Feather', a good scarlet cultivar.

CELSIA (SCROPHULARIACEAE)
arcturus Cretan Bear's Tail ✻ 🐾
A 2 ft or more, shrubby perennial plant with upper leaves ovate and basal leaves lobed. The flower spikes are rather similar to the mulleins (*Verbascum* sp.) with flat yellow blooms and purple, bearded stamens which are produced from July to September. When young it makes a good pot plant for the cool greenhouse. Grow in a loam-based compost and ventilate freely whenever possible. Propagate by seeds sown in spring. Crete. **108.**

Century Plant see **Agave americana**

CEPHALOCEREUS (CACTACEAE)
These columnar cacti are grown chiefly for the long white hairs which occur mainly at the top of the plant. Although in the wild they are large plants, small specimens are very suitable in the house and greenhouse, and they grow slowly. If it gets dirty, the plant may be shampooed with a shaving-brush and soap, syringing off the soap with clean water. Cultivation as for terrestrial cacti, see Introduction. Propagation by cuttings or seed. Winter temperature 40°F.

chrysacanthus ✻ 🐾
In summer, the nocturnal whitish to rose-red flowers grow on a side of the plant where there is a lot of hair. There are no leaves but the columnar stem is glaucous-green with about 12 ribs, golden spines and white hairs. Up to 15 ft high it branches from the base and above. Mexico.

senilis Old Man Cactus ✻ 🐾
The nocturnal pale yellowish white or pink flowers grow from the thick tawny wool at the top of the plant during the summer. The glaucous-green columnar stem, up to 40 ft long, branches from the base and is covered with long white hairs and weak, greyish bristle-like spines. There are no leaves. Mexico. **109.**

CEREUS (CACTACEAE) Torch Thistle
Columnar cacti with marked ribs, areoles bearing spines but no long hairs. In the wild they grow up to 30 ft and branch at the top. They do not flower until they are large, and the flowers are nocturnal. They grow very quickly and soon give height to a collection. If they grow too tall, the top foot or so of the stem can be cut off and rooted as a cutting; the lower part will then produce branches which can also be used as cuttings. Propagation is, however, mainly by seed, which germinates readily and the seedlings grow quickly. Culture as for terrestrial cacti, see Introduction. Winter temperature 40°F.

jamacaru 🐾
Although rarely produced in cultivation, the flowers are white, 12 in. long and occur in summer. There are no leaves. The stem is green, almost blue when young, and has 5 ribs and variable, often yellow, spines. The young plants are very popular. Brazil.

peruvianus 🐾
The white, 8 in. long, thick-tubed flowers appear in summer, but not often in cultivation. The leafless stems are tall, green or grey-green with 6–9 ribs and slender brown-black spines. Seedlings are much used as stock for grafting. Found in many parts of S. America but apparently not in Peru.

repandus 🐾
The greyish-green, stout, branched stem has 9–10 rather low ribs and numerous spines. The 3 in. long flowers, dark green outside and white inside open in summer but, as with the previous species, they are rare in cultivation. This plant is also without leaves. Curaçoa.

triangularis see **Hylocereus undatus**

CEROPEGIA (ASCLEPIADACEAE)
Usually twining, these succulents mostly bear leaves. The flowers resemble stapelias, but the tips of the corolla lobes often remain united, forming a canopy over the tubular lower part of the flower. Culture as for stapelias. Flowering times vary in cultivation, usually in summer.

haygarthii ✻
The flowers are pale mauve with darker spots, funnel-shaped, the corolla lobes forming partitions in the centre of the flower, where a thin stem produces a hairy knob. The oval leaves are barely succulent and are borne on twining blue-green stems. S. Africa.

sandersonii ✻
The pale green flowers have dark markings and narrow corolla lobes which expand to form a canopy, edged with white hairs, over a funnel-shaped tube. The leaves occur mostly at the tips of the purplish, succulent stems. S. Africa.

stapeliiformis ✻
The white flowers are marked with purple on the outside and expand to form a wide funnel, 2 in. long. The corolla lobes are not united, being erect or recurved. The leaves are rudimentary. The short-jointed grey-green stems are also marked with purple and the whole plant resembles a *Stapelia*. S. Africa.

woodii String of Hearts 🐾
The small flowers of this species are purple with the dark corolla lobes

united at the tips. The succulent, oval leaves are dark green, variegated with silvery-grey and are purple beneath. The slender, purplish, trailing stems grow from a large tuber. Tubers are also produced on the stems. S. Africa. **110.**

CESTRUM (SOLANACEAE)
A genus of very ornamental shrubs grown for the profusely borne clusters of tubular flowers. The following four species make excellent cool greenhouse plants where they are at their best in borders, growing as climbers. They will also grow in tubs or large pots of a loam-based compost. Canes or wires will be needed for support. Ventilate freely on warm days and lightly shade from the hottest sunshine. Propagate by stem cuttings from lateral non-flowering shoots in spring or summer.

aurantiacum
An 8 ft semi-evergreen shrub with 2–4 in. shining ovate leaves and 6–8 in. pendent clusters of bright orange-yellow flowers which open from June to September. Guatemala. **111.**

elegans see **C. purpureum**

fasciculatum
A 5–8 ft evergreen shrub with long, oval leaves 3–5 in. in length, and compact clusters of deep rose, pitcher-shaped flowers at the ends of the slender, somewhat arching stems. Flowering season is from April to early June. Mexico.

× newellii
An evergreen shrub of hybrid origin, probably *C. fasciculatum × C. purpureum*, with larger, narrow pitcher-shaped, brilliant orange-crimson flowers which appear from May into summer.

purpureum syn. **C. elegans**
A 10 ft graceful, evergreen shrub with pendent shoot tips and narrow, dark green leaves. The dense clusters of bright, reddish-purple, tubular flowers are borne from May to September and are succeeded by small round to ovoid purplish berries. Mexico.

CHAMAECEREUS (CACTACEAE)
silvestrii Peanut Cactus
The orange-scarlet, 2 in. long flowers are funnel-shaped, expanding at the top. They are freely produced. The stems are 1–3 in. long, $\frac{1}{4}$–$\frac{1}{2}$ in. thick. They are prostrate and have low ribs and soft whitish spines. There are no leaves. Culture as for terrestrial cacti. Care must be taken not to handle the plants roughly as the stems break off very readily. However, the broken-off stems root easily and propagation is usually by this means, though seed germinates readily. Argentina. **112.**

CHAMAEDOREA (PALMAE)
elegans syn. **Collinia elegans, Neanthe elegans** Dwarf Mountain or Parlor Palm
A small, graceful palm growing to about 4 ft. It has pendent, cut leaves 2–4 ft long with thin, leathery leaflets tapering at both ends. It is an excellent foliage plant for the home or warm greenhouse, perhaps the best of all palms for this purpose. Grow in pots of a loam-based compost or a proprietary peat mix. Maintain a humid atmosphere and shade from hottest sunshine. Propagate by seeds sown in spring. Mexico. **113.**

CHAMAERANTHEMUM (ACANTHACEAE)
A genus of small, herbaceous plants making good ground cover in the warm greenhouse. They also provide plants for small pots or pans. The white or yellowish flowers have a long, slender tube opening to 5 flat, spreading petals. Grow in a peat-based compost and shade from direct sunlight. Maintain a humid atmosphere. Propagate by division in spring.

beyrichii
A small slender plant with ovate leaves, variegated with white. The white flowers, which open during spring and summer, have a slender tube and are 1$\frac{1}{2}$ in. long; they are borne in dense terminal clusters. Brazil.

pictum
A low growing plant, grown for its large leaves, 9 in. long and 4 in.

wide, covered with orange hairs in the juvenile stage and becoming hairless when mature. They are attractively marked, having an orange margin and a silvery blotch at the centre, contrasting with a dark green background. Brazil.

CHAMAEROPS (PALMAE)
humilis European Fan Palm
An evergreen shrub or small tree with 18 in. fan-shaped leaves, divided almost to the base into long narrow segments and borne on 3–4 ft spiny stalks. This palm can reach 20 ft but is usually smaller. When young it makes an excellent palm for pots and tubs in unheated rooms. Use a loam-based compost or a proprietary peat mix. Ventilate freely on warm days. Propagate by seeds in spring, or by suckers detached close to the base in summer. Mediterranean. **114.**
'Elegans', an elegant, smaller form which is the best for indoor cultivation.

Chenille Plant see **Acalypha hispida**
Cherry Pie see **Heliotropium × hybridum**
Chilean Bell Flower see **Lapageria rosea**
Chilean Glory Bean see **Eccremocarpus scaber**
Chilean Guava see **Myrtus ugni**
Chilean Jasmine see **Mandevilla suaveolens**
Chilli Pepper see **Capsicum annuum**
Chimney Bellflower see **Campanula pyramidalis**
Chincherinchee see **Ornithogalum thrysoides**
Chinese Evergreens see **Aglaonema**
Chinese Fan Palm see **Livistona chinensis**
Chinese Hat Plant see **Holmskioldia sanguinea**
Chinese Lanterns see **Sandersonia aurantiaca**
Chinese Primrose see **Primula sinensis**

CHIRITA (GESNERIACEAE)
A useful genus of decorative foliage plants with attractive flowers. They are somewhat succulent, their small, tubular flowers being produced throughout spring and summer. They make good house and greenhouse plants. Grow in a loamy or a proprietary peat compost and keep in a warm and humid atmosphere, *C. sinensis* requiring warm greenhouse treatment while *C. lavandulacea* and *C. micromusa* will grow in the cool greenhouse. Shade from direct sunlight. Propagate by leaf cuttings in summer or by seeds in spring or summer.

lavandulacea Hindustan Gentian
An erect, 1–2 ft plant with light green, oval, downy leaves up to 8 in. in length. The flowers have a white tube, 1–1$\frac{1}{4}$ in. long opening to 5 rounded, spreading petals, the lower 3 larger than the upper 2 and a pale lavender-blue with a yellow marking in the throat. They may be flowered from early spring to late autumn if sown in succession. Malaya.

micromusa Little Banana
The stout 1 ft stems carry very large, shiny green leaves which are oval with a heart-shaped base and taper to a rounded apex. The flowers are a brilliant yellow and have a slightly curved, 1 in. tube opening to small rounded lobes. Thailand.

sinensis Silver Chirita
A beautiful stemless plant, 6 in. high. It has large fleshy, oval leaves 3–4 in. long, dark green, one form with silver variegation, and a fine covering of white hairs. The tubular lavender-coloured flowers are 1$\frac{1}{2}$ in. long, opening to wide, rounded lobes and are borne on red stalks in summer. China. **115.**

CHIRONIA (GENTIANACEAE)
A genus of small evergreen perennials and shrubs with opposite, stemless leaves and reddish-pink flowers opening wide from a narrow tube. Grow in pots using a proprietary peat compost and water sparingly especially in winter. Keep in the cool greenhouse except when flowering when it can be brought into the house. Propagate by cuttings of lateral stems taken with a heel in summer, or by seeds sown in spring.

baccifera
A small 1–2 ft shrub having very slender leaves and reddish-pink flowers which open in June. S. Africa.

floribunda

A 2 ft shrub with a profusion of wide open, pink flowers which are borne in June. The small narrow leaves are pointed and carried in opposite pairs on the soft stems. S. Africa.

CHLOROPHYTUM (LILIACEAE)

elatum syn. **C. capense, C. comosum** Spider Plant

A rosetted or tufted evergreen perennial with broad, grassy foliage. In the true species, the 6–18 in. arching leaves are mid-green. The small, starry-white flowers appear in loose clusters on stems up to 6 ft long throughout the year. Mixed with the flowers are small plantlets, which, if pegged down, or detached and potted will root and produce new plants. S. Africa.

'Variegatum' is the form commonly grown, with leaves longitudinally striped in creamy-white. It makes a very good foliage pot plant for cool and warm greenhouses and homes. Use a loam-based compost or a proprietary peat mix. Shade from hottest sunshine. Propagate by division or plantlets any time from spring to autumn. **116.**

CHORIZEMA (LEGUMINOSAE) Flame Pea

Evergreen shrubs with leathery and shiny leaves and clusters of showy, pea-like flowers. They can be pruned to keep to a small size, and make good pot plants for the greenhouse. If allowed to grow to their full size, they are best in an indoor border, trained up a wall or trellis. If grown in pots, use a loam-based compost or a proprietary peat mix. Ventilate freely on warm days and shade lightly in summer. Propagate by seeds in spring or cuttings of lateral shoots with a heel.

cordatum

A 2–4 ft shrub with slender shoots and spine-toothed, ovate leaves. The 6 in. clusters of 5–10 flowers, with orange or red, yellow-marked standards and purplish wings, appear in April. Australia. **117.**

ilicifolium Holly-leaved Glory Pea

An almost prostrate shrub with glossy green, spine-toothed, holly-like leaves on wiry branches. The small flowers are a bright orange streaked red with a yellow basal spot and purple to crimson wings. This species makes a good house plant when regularly pruned. W. Australia.

Christmas Cactus see **Schlumbergera × buckleyi**
Christmas Cheer see **Sedum rubrotinctum**
Christmas Cherry see **Solanum pseudocapsicum**
Christmas Heather see **Erica canaliculata**
Christmas Orchid see **Cattleya trianaei**
Christmas Pride see **Ruellia macrantha**

CHRYSALIDOCARPUS (PALMAE)

lutescens Areca Palm

The graceful, yellowish stems grow in dense clusters forming a bushy plant to 10–20 ft tall. The rich green leaves are deeply divided into long, narrow segments. In its juvenile stage it makes a decorative indoor or warm greenhouse plant, needing humidity and light shade during the summer. Grow in large pots or tubs of a loam-based compost or a proprietary peat mix. Propagate by seeds in spring or when ripe. Mauritius.

CHRYSANTHEMUM (COMPOSITAE)

Although 200 species of chrysanthemum are known – several are suitable for the rock garden or herbaceous border – it is the many hybrids and cultivars derived from the Asiatic *C. morifolium* and *C. indicum* that most people know. These are the familiar florists' chrysanths which now rank as the most popular of all flowering plants. Grow in pots of loam-based compost. Preferably stand outside in a sunny sheltered spot from May to September or October. Bring into a cool greenhouse and ventilate freely whenever possible. Make sure the plants never lack water or flower buds may suffer. Propagate by cuttings of leafy shoots that grow from the base of the previous year's plants in spring. Pinch the young plants when 6 in. tall and support with a cane. Depending on the cultivar, the shoots may need pinching again or the flower buds thinned to one per stem. The cultivars differ so widely in the form of the flowers and in leaf outline and stature that specialists have classified them into 7 major groups, mainly based upon flower shape.

1. **Incurved:** globose blooms with firm, incurving florets (petals).
   'John Rowe', the large yellow flower head is solid and formed of cupped petals, **118.**
2. **Reflexed:** wig or mop-like flowers with long florets, often waved or crisped, curving outwards and downwards.
   'Parade', spiky petals of an intense crimson with a full centre, **119.**
3. **Intermediate:** loose and somewhat irregularly globular blooms halfway between groups 1 and 2.
   'Escort' 5–6 in., red flowers, the petals yellow backed.
   'Fred Shoesmith', a fine white flower shading to cream in the centre and opening in December, **120;**
4. **Single:** open centred, daisy-like flowers.
   'Peggy Stevens', large, golden-yellow flowers borne in November and December, **121.**
5. **Anemone centred:** single flowers with a cushion-like centre of short, quilled florets.
   'Marion Stacey', purple-red flowers, 5–6 in. across, **122.**
6. **Pompon:** clusters of small button-shaped or globular flowers, having short, tightly packed florets.
   'Fairie', a true pompon with one inch, pink flowers borne in August, **123.**
7. **Miscellaneous:** this covers a number of less common flower forms such as the spider and thread-petalled cultivars with long, slender florets, and the Cascade and Charm plate **124**, and Korean groups, plate **125** bearing sprays of small single or semi-double blooms.
   'Portrait', magenta flowers, 2½ in. across with short, narrow petals, at their best in November, **126;**
   Rayonnante type, spidery blooms with slender petals, **127.**

CHRYSOTHEMIS (GESNERIACEAE)

pulchella

A 2 ft erect plant with ovate, shining, roughly bristly 6 in. leaves and small tubular flowers, bright yellow with red markings inside. These grow within a brilliant red calyx which colours before the flowers appear, and remains after the petals have fallen. A colourful pot plant at its best in April. Grow in a proprietary peat mix or a loam-based compost. Shade from direct sunlight and maintain a humid atmosphere in summer. Propagate by division or basal stem cuttings in summer. Trinidad.

Chufa see **Cyperus esculentus**

CIBOTIUM (CYATHACEAE) Treefern

A genus of large ferns, the fronds growing on long stalks which rise from a central tuft. They grow best in pots or tubs. Use a peat-based compost and shade from direct sunlight. Maintain a humid atmosphere from spring to autumn. Propagate by offsets when possible or by spores in spring.

schiedei Mexican Treefern

A graceful plant with 2–5 ft deeply dissected, pale green, thin fronds. While young it makes a very decorative tub or pot plant with arching fronds. If grown in the cool greenhouse border the trunk can eventually reach 10 ft or more. Mexico.

wendlandii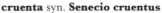

A smaller but similar plant with fronds divided into narrow segments 1 ft or more long which are again cut. It needs more humidity and warmth than the preceding species. Guatemala, Mexico.

Cigar Flower see **Cuphea platycentra**

CINERARIA (COMPOSITAE)

cruenta syn. **Senecio cruentus**

An 18 in. perennial, usually grown as a biennial with ovate, dark green leaves and variously coloured, daisy-like flowers.

The name *C. hybrida* is often given to the large range of hybrids and cultivars which make very good pot plants, flowering from December to June providing valuable winter colour. They vary in colour from white through pinks, reds, mauves and purples to blue, and there are also many bi-coloured forms. Grow in pots of a loam-based compost when available. Ventilate freely at all times and, if possible, stand the young plants outside from May to September in an open cold frame. If under glass, lightly shade from direct sunshine in summer. Sow seeds in spring for winter flowering plants and in summer for the following spring. Cuttings from the base of cut-back plants may also be rooted easily but give inferior plants to those raised from seed. There are three main groups based upon flower size and stature.

1. Hybrida Grandiflora: from 18–24 in. high, large flowered with broad petals.

   'Exhibition Mixed', large flowers, 3 in. across in a wide variety of colours, often with a white centre. The plants to 16 in., in height.

2. Multiflora Nana: a more dwarf selection, not exceeding 15 in. with broad petals.

   'Berlin Market', mixed colours, with large heads made up of many flowers, a compact habit, growing to 15 in., **128.**

3. Stellata: a narrow-petalled group with star-shaped flowers. They are more open plants and grow from 18–30 in.

   'Mixed Star', syn. Stellata mixed, clusters of starry flowers in a wide variety of colours.

CISSUS (VITIDACEAE)

A large genus of foliage plants, the following species making good subjects for cultivation as house plants, or in the greenhouse. The genus divides into two groups, the succulent species which are cultivated for their curious growth form, and the climbing species which have conspicuously marked foliage. Grow the succulent species in pots or tubs of a loam-based compost mixed with $\frac{1}{3}$ part of coarse sand. Grow in a cool greenhouse, freely ventilated in summer. Propagate by seeds or cuttings from the tips of branches in summer. The climbers may be grown in a peat mix or a loam-based compost. Provide canes or wires for support. *C. discolor* requires humidity and shade from hottest sunshine.

antarctica Kangaroo Vine

An attractive, tall, shrubby climber, suitable for house or cool greenhouse culture. It has leathery, shining, 3–6 in. leaves with wavy edges and a somewhat metallic sheen. It is grown for its foliage. Australia. **129.**

bainesii

A shrubby species with a single, succulent, somewhat irregular turnip-like trunk, usually 2 ft high, but which in the wild can reach 6 ft, and from which grow the large, 3-lobed leaves which are wavy edged and thick textured. The plant loses its leaves in autumn, being dormant throughout the winter. The terminal clusters of small, yellow, starry flowers grow on long, stiff stalks and are produced in July, followed by coral-red berries. It needs a warm greenhouse. Tropical Africa.

cactiformis

A thick, succulent climber with tendrils at the joints in the stalks. It can reach 10 ft and looks somewhat like a smooth cactus. It has a few broad leaves and small, green flowers produced in summer and followed by pea-sized, red berries. Warm greenhouse cultivation is necessary. S. Africa.

capensis see **Rhoicissus capensis**

discolor Rex Begonia Vine

A beautiful shrubby climber with thin, dark red stems and superbly marked, long, ovate leaves which are heart-shaped at the base. The leaf colour is a deep coppery-bronze with sunken deep green veins and the ridges between a shining, silvery-white. The undersides are maroon. Perhaps the most gorgeous of vines, it does need warmth and humidity and is best grown as a pot plant in the warm greenhouse. Java, Cambodia.

juttae

A curious, succulent shrub with a thick, 6 ft branched stem at the top of which grows a tuft of large, toothed leaves, shining green above and with red markings beneath. The small flowers grow in flat heads on long branched stems, and are followed in autumn by yellow or red berries. S.W. Africa.

striata Miniature Grape Ivy

A dainty shrubby climber with delicate red stems and tendrils. The 1–2 in. leaves have 5 leaflets radiating from the stalk, and are bronze-

green on the upper surface and reddish-purple beneath. It will grow in a cool or warm greenhouse. Chile.

CITRUS (RUTACEAE)

A genus of evergreen shrubs and small trees including the commercial citrus fruits, orange, lemon and grapefruit. Young plants of most species make excellent foliage pot plants for indoor growing, but when more mature need a greenhouse to flower and fruit. Grow in large pots or tubs of a loam-based compost. Ventilate freely whenever possible and ideally stand outside in a sheltered sunny place from May to September. Propagate by seeds in spring or by grafting named cultivars on to seedling rootstocks.

aurantium Seville Orange

Cultivated as an ornamental, it is a small, 3–4 ft tree with spiny branches bearing slender, glossy, oval leaves. The 1 in. white, fragrant flowers are produced from April to June. In a large tub or greenhouse border the tree will bear fruit. Tropical Asia.

limon Lemon

A small tree with spiny branches and oval, toothed, dark green leaves. The white flowers are tinged with red and appear from April to June, they are followed by the familiar lemon fruits. It makes a good ornamental species for the warm greenhouse. Asia.

mitis Calamondin Orange

A small, spineless bush, growing to a tree when mature. In its young state it makes an ideal pot plant for the house, with its oval, leathery leaves setting off the white, fragrant flowers and 1–1$\frac{1}{2}$ in. globular, orange fruits. It flowers and fruits when very small, bearing almost all the year round. A most rewarding plant. Phillipines. **130.**

paradisi Grapefruit

An attractive species, making a bushy shrub with large, dark green leaves and 1 in. white, solitary flowers. It is sensitive to cold draughts and does not always make a satisfactory house plant; it can however be grown in the warm greenhouse where it will flower from April to June and bear its large, globular, yellow fruits. E. Asia.

reticulata Mandarin, Tangerine

The hardiest of the fruit-bearing citrus, it makes an attractive shrub with narrow, dark green leaves and clusters of white flowers from April to June followed by the small, wrinkled, orange fruits. A useful ornamental species. China.

sinensis Sweet Orange

When young it makes a good house plant up to 3–4 ft in height with spiny stems. The leaves are broadly to narrowly ovate and dark green. The fragrant white flowers appear from April to June. Fruiting trees are much larger, reaching 10 ft or more in a greenhouse border. China.

CLEISTOCACTUS (CACTACEAE)

Slow-growing columnar cacti, grown mainly for the large numbers of fine spines which give the plants a striking appearance. The flowers are not freely produced in cultivation until the plants are well established; they are tubular and do not open fully. Culture as for terrestrial cacti, see Introduction. Propagation by seeds or stem cuttings.

baumannii

A summer-flowering species with 1–3 in. long, orange-scarlet flowers bending down at the tip with the stamens protruding. The columnar stems are stout and erect, later bending, up to 6 ft long, with shallow ribs. The areoles bear yellowish-brown wool and up to 20 whitish spines, about 1 in. long. There are no leaves. Argentina, Paraguay, Uruguay.

strausii

The carmine to dark red tubular flowers are up to 3$\frac{1}{2}$ in. long with the stamens protruding at the end. They occur during the summer. The green, erect stem branches at the base only and grows up to 3 ft tall; it has many shallow ribs. The closely packed areoles produce white wool and numerous spines which obscure the body of the stem. There are no leaves. Argentina, Bolivia. **131.**

CLERODENDRUM (VERBENACEAE)

A genus of tropical shrubs and climbers with brightly coloured clusters of bell-shaped flowers borne at the ends of the branches. The following species are most attractive plants for the warm greenhouse. Grow in the border, or in pots or tubs of a loam-based compost or a proprietary peat mix. Shade from hottest sunshine and maintain a humid atmosphere. Propagate by seeds in spring or by stem cuttings in summer. An alternative spelling is *Clerodendron*.

fallax see **C. speciosissimum**

paniculatum ✽ 🦢
A 2–4 ft shrub with ovate leaves 3–6 in. wide, lobed and heart shaped at the base. The vivid, scarlet flowers have long, protruding stamens and are borne in compact clusters, 9–12 in. across, from July to October. A warm greenhouse plant. S.E. Asia.

speciosissimum syn. **C. fallax** Java Glorybean ✽ 🦢
A very showy, summer flowering, evergreen species with large heart-shaped leaves on white, hairy stems and loose, erect clusters of fiery, scarlet flowers up to 10 in. across, each separate bloom measuring 1½–2 in. long with long stamens. This species also needs warmth to thrive. Java, Ceylon. **132.**

splendens ✽ 🦢
A striking climbing shrub, up to 12 ft or more which needs light and warmth to thrive. It has 3–5 in. long, oval, heart-shaped leaves and in June and July, drooping clusters of scarlet flowers with a narrow tube and flat lobes, 1 in. across with long pendent stamens. W. Africa.

thomsonae Bleeding Heart Vine ✽ 🦢
A twining, evergreen climber reaching 10 ft or more. It has glossy, oval, deep green leaves and very showy, loose clusters of flowers with the starry, scarlet blooms carried within white, inflated calyces which open from June to September. W. Africa. **133.**

ugandense Blue Glory Bower ✽ 🦢
A climbing shrub reaching 10 ft, bearing ovate, bright green toothed leaves and clusters of bright blue flowers with the front lobe violet, and long blue, protruding stamens which arch outwards. It is at its best in spring, but will produce some flowers throughout the year. Uganda to Rhodesia. **134.**

CLIANTHUS (LEGUMINOSAE)
A genus of evergreen shrubs with large showy flowers somewhat resembling a parrot's bill, and feathery leaves, each divided into 12–24 small leaflets. Use a loam-based compost if possible and ventilate freely whenever possible. Propagate by seeds in spring. *C. puniceus* can also be raised from stem cuttings with a heel in summer.

dampieri see **C. formosus**

formosus syn. **C. dampieri** Glory Pea ✽ 🦢
A semi-erect or prostrate sub-shrub up to 2–3 ft high, covered with silvery-grey hairs. The 2 in. scarlet, black-centred, beaked flowers grow in clusters of up to 6, and open in May and June. It is best grown in pots or hanging baskets in a dry atmosphere, but is not easy to keep long in cultivation. Never water from above. Australia. **135.**

puniceus Parrot's Bill, Lobster Claw ✽
An evergreen, spreading shrub which is best grown in a greenhouse border where it can be given support and can attain 12 ft. The clusters of 6–15 brilliant red, claw-shaped flowers grow on pendulous stalks and open in May and June. New Zealand. **136.**
'Alba', creamy white flowered.

Cliff Brake see **Pellaea**
Climbing Fig see **Ficus pumila**
Climbing Gazania see **Mutisia**

CLITORIA (LEGUMINOSAE)
ternatea Butterfly Pea ✽
A short lived tropical perennial, often treated as an annual. Its leaves are divided into 5 oval leaflets. The solitary, showy 2 in. flowers are bright blue and beautifully marked with yellow or white in the throat. Best for a warm greenhouse. Grow in pots of a loam-based compost and shade from the hottest summers' sunshine. Propagate by seeds in spring or take cuttings of side shoots with a heel in summer. India.

CLIVIA syn. **IMANTOPHYLLUM** (AMARYLLIDACEAE) Kaffir Lily
Popular house and greenhouse plants, which flower freely, but tend to become rather large in course of time, because they are not easy to split up, since the fleshy roots get very matted. The flowers are trumpet-shaped and 2–3 in. long, in clusters on stems 8–15 in. long. The leaves are strap-shaped, up to 24 in. long. As the new leaves appear in the centre, an approximately equal number die off at the base of the plant. Any good potting soil suits, and the plants should have plenty of water in the summer, and only enough in winter to avoid the soil becoming dust dry. Put into 5 in. pots in spring and when the roots fill the pot, pot on to the next size. When plants fill a 12 in. pot, split up carefully to avoid breaking the roots, potting the pieces into 5 in. pots. Propagation is by detaching offsets and by division as described above. Seed germinates at 60°F., but the plants produced are variable, and bearing seed tends to stop the plants flowering. Winter temperature 40°F.

× **cyrtanthiflora** ✽
The flowers are light flame-coloured, but can vary between yellow and red. They are 2–3 in. long, pendent, and borne from March to May. The glossy, dark green leaves are strap-shaped and up to 24 in. long. This is a cultivated hybrid between *C. miniata* and *C. nobilis*. **137.**

miniata ✽
This species is valuable for its long flowering period, from March to August. The 2–3 in., orange to red flowers are held erect in clusters of 10–20. The leaves are similar to the preceding species. Propagation by seed produces very variable plants, some very good, others poor. Natal. **138.**

nobilis ✽
The narrow pendent orange-red flowers are tipped with green, 2–3 in. long and are borne in clusters of up to 60 in May. The blunt, dark green glossy leaves are strap-shaped with rough margins. **139.**

Clock Vine see **Thunbergia**
Club Moss see **Selaginella lepidophylla**
Cluster Cattleya see **Cattleya bowringiana**

CLYTOSTOMA (BIGNONIACEAE)
callistegioides ✽ 🦢
An evergreen climber for the warm greenhouse border or a tub, with 2 oblong wavy-edged leaflets per leaf. The pale purple and yellow trumpet-shaped flowers, borne in pairs at the ends of the small branches, are at their best in spring and early summer. If grown in tubs, use a loam-based compost. Maintain a humid atmosphere in summer and shade from the hottest sunshine. Propagate by stem cuttings of 2 or 3 joints in spring. Brazil, Argentine.

COBAEA (POLEMONIACEAE)
scandens Cathedral Bells, Cup-and-saucer Plant ✽ 🦢
This climbing plant is usually grown as a half-hardy annual outside, where it dies in winter; but under glass it flowers continuously from mid-summer. The flowers open cream with a flat calyx and a bell-shaped tube 2½–3 in. long, which turns purple after a day or so. The green, pinnate leaves have 3 pairs of leaflets and end in branched tendrils which support the plant, which can grow to 20 ft but may be cut back in autumn or spring. Grow in an 8–10 in. pot in the greenhouse, in soil which is not too rich and provide some support, such as a trellis. Propagation is by seed sown in an upright position in March or April and germinated at 65°F. For winter flowering maintain a temperature of 45°F.; for survival without flowering keep above freezing point. Central, S. America. **140.**
'Alba' is a form with flowers which do not turn purple.

COCCOLOBA syn. **COCCOLOBIS** (POLYGONACEAE) 🦢
uvifera Seaside Grape
The only member of this large group of tropical trees likely to be found in cultivation. It needs warm greenhouse or conservatory conditions and can reach 20 ft in a border. It is best grown in large pots or tubs where it can display its bold, broadly heart-shaped leaves to advantage. These are leathery in texture, rich glossy green above, paler beneath. Mature specimens can produce terminal clusters of fragrant white

flowers followed by grape-like clusters of red-purple berries. They are not produced on pot specimens. Use a proprietary peat or loam-based compost. Shade from hottest sunshine and maintain a humid atmosphere in summer. Propagate by lateral stem tip cuttings in summer. Tropical America. **141.**

Coccolobis see **Coccoloba**
Coccothrinax argentea see **Thrinax argentea**
Cockle-shell Orchid see **Epidendrum cochleatum**
Cockscomb see **Celosia argentea** Cristata
Cockspur Coral Tree see **Erythrina crista-galli**
Cocktail Orchid see **Cattleya intermedia**
Cocos yatay see **Butia yatay**

CODIAEUM (EUPHORBIACEAE) Croton
variegatum Pictum
A very decorative foliage pot plant which makes an excellent subject for the warm greenhouse. It has entire, leathery, glossy leaves variously shaped and coloured. Use a loam-based compost or a proprietary peat mix. Shade from direct sunshine and maintain a humid atmosphere. Propagate by stem tip or basal cuttings in summer. **142.**
Many cultivars are grown:
'Aucubaefolium', bushy with small, bright glossy-green 3–4 in. elliptic leaves which are spotted and marked with yellow;
'Carrierei', oblong, blunt leaves starting yellow-green and later becoming darker with a red centre. The contrast between the two leaf colourings is very striking;
'Disraeli', yellow blotched leaves with a dark green background, the whole leaf red beneath;
'Norwood Beauty', lobed leaves somewhat reminiscent of an oak leaf, dark bronze-green with yellow veining and red margins;
'Punctatum Aureum', a dwarf form with yellow blotchings on a narrow, dark green glossy leaf;
'Reidii', dark green ovate leaves, slightly wavy with yellow veins and an overall pink flush as the leaves age;
'Volcano', large oval pointed leaves, strongly flushed yellow when young, ageing to pink. **143.**

COELOGYNE (ORCHIDACEAE)
A genus of attractive, evergreen orchids with fragrant flowers which range from white and yellow to beige-pink and tan. Most species will thrive in cool greenhouse conditions and a few are suitable as house plants. Grow in pans or baskets of equal parts osmunda fibre and sphagnum moss. Shade from direct sunshine and maintain a humid atmosphere in summer. Propagate by division in spring, or when the young growths are visible.

asperata
The pale green leaves are borne on the 6 in. bulbs which carry 8–12 in. pendulous flower spikes, each bearing up to 15 flowers from April to June. These are about 3 in. across with pale cream petals and the lip striped and veined in yellow and chocolate brown with an orange-red centred ridge and some red spotting. Borneo.

cristata
A very good orchid for indoor culture, thriving on a cool window sill. The bulbs carry thin, narrow leaves to 12 in. long, and pendulous clusters of sweetly fragrant 3–5 in. flowers which are pure white with orange markings on the lip. They open from December to March. Nepal. **144.**

massangeana
A vigorous species with dark green, strongly veined leaves and magnificent, pendulous flower heads 1½–2 ft long with up to 25 well spaced blooms appearing from January to April. Each is about 3 in. across, pale ochre and having a chocolate-brown lip, marked with yellow and white. Assam.

mooreana
A species having 12–16 in. narrow, somewhat fleshy leaves and 4–12 white flowers with golden markings and hairs on the lip. India.

ochracea
A beautifully fragrant species bearing 7–9 flowers on each erect spike. Each bloom is 1½ in. across, white, with the lip blotched and marked with bright ochre. A spring flowering plant. India. **145.**

speciosa
A beautiful species with 3 in. olive-green flowers having a yellowish fringed lip decoratively marked with dark red, chocolate and coffee brown and bearing a pure white apex. The 9 in. dark green leaves are borne singly on the small bulbs. The flowers appear singly at intervals throughout the year. Java.

COFFEA (RUBIACEAE) Coffee
Evergreen shrubs with fragrant, white flowers and red berries that yield the coffee 'beans' of commerce. An attractive tub or large pot plant for the warm greenhouse. Use a proprietary peat or a loam-based compost. Shade from hottest sunshine and provide humidity in summer. Propagate by seeds in spring or by lateral stem cuttings with a heel in late summer.

arabica Arabian Coffee
A 5–15 ft shrub with willowy branches bearing 3–6 in. dark glossy green oblong, slender pointed leaves. The white flowers grow in compact clusters in the leaf axils and appear in September. Ethiopia.

liberica Liberian Coffee
A more robust species than the above plant with longer, wider leaves. The white flowers are borne in dense clusters. This plant is the source of most domestic coffee. Liberia.

Coffee see **Coffea**

COLEUS (LABIATAE)
This genus provides some of the foremost colourful foliage plants grown today. There are also several species with showy flowers in attractive shades of blue. Both kinds are good pot plants for the cool greenhouse or the home. Grow in a loam-based compost for preference. Shade lightly from direct sunshine in summer. Propagate by seeds in spring or by stem tip cuttings in spring or late summer. Remove flower spikes when small of *C. blumei* to maintain bushy leafy specimens.

blumei
A sub-shrubby plant, grown for the brightly coloured, ornamental foliage. It is correctly a perennial, but is grown as an annual or a biennial and kept to about 18 in. by pinching out flower buds and leading shoots. Many cultivars are known, representing plants with red, yellow, green and multi-coloured foliage. **146, 148.**

fredericii
A relatively new species in cultivation grown for its flowers. It is a 4 ft annual or biennial with ovate, bristly, hairy leaves and showy 4–5 in. clusters of intense blue flowers which appear in December. Angola.

thyrsoideus Bush Coleus
A most attractive winter flowering shrub, 2–3 ft in height, producing its 9 in. spikes of bright blue tubular flowers from November to March. The ovate, heart-shaped, mid-green leaves are 7 in. long. It makes a good house plant. Central Africa. **147.**

Coleus, Prostrate see **Plectranthus oertendahlii**
Collinia elegans see **Chamaedorea elegans**

COLUMNEA (GESNERIACEAE)
Mainly pendulous plants with neat foliage and large, showy, red or yellow flowers. The species mentioned here are excellent for hanging baskets in the warm greenhouse or home. Use a soil comprising equal parts of a loam-based compost and sphagnum moss or a peat-based mix. Shade from direct sunshine in summer and provide humidity. Propagate by stem cuttings in summer.

× **banksii** (*C. oerstediana* × *C. schiediana*)
A rambling, sub-shrubby plant with somewhat box-like, waxy, dark green leaves, red beneath. The hooded, vermilion flowers are 2½–3 in. long and appear from November to April. Garden origin. **149.**

gloriosa
A trailing or pendent species with pale green, hairy leaves. The 1½–3 in. long solitary, bright scarlet blooms with a yellow throat and underside of tube, open throughout the year but are at their best between October and April. Costa Rica.
'Purpurea' has young leaves purple, becoming bronze at maturity, **150.**

microphylla Goldfish Vine
A slender trailing or pendent species with stems 3 ft or more long, covered in small coppery leaves with purple hairs. The glorious 2-lipped flowers, borne between November and April, are 1½–3 in. long and a vivid scarlet with yellow markings. It makes an excellent plant for a hanging basket. Costa Rica.

schiediana
A semi-climbing or trailing plant with 3–4 ft purple-hairy stems. The 5 in. pale green leaves are also silky-hairy, as are the 2 in. flowers with large red or yellow calyces and corolla which appear from May to July. Mexico.

teuscheri see **Trichantha minor**

COMMELINA (COMMELINIACEAE) Day Flower
A group of plants renowned for their sky-blue flowers which emerge from curious, boat-shaped, leaf-like bracts. Grow in pots of a loam-based compost and shade from hottest sunshine. Propagate *C. benghalensis* by stem cuttings in summer and *C. coelestis* by seeds or division in spring.

benghalensis Indian Day Flower
A delicate evergreen trailer with green, ovate, wavy-edged leaves, 2–3 in. long. The small blue flowers appear from late spring to autumn. For house or a warm greenhouse. Tropical Africa and Asia.
  'Variegata' has the leaves striped and edged white.

coelestis
An upright plant reaching 18 in. with long, wavy-edged leaves and bright blue flowers growing from an ovate pointed sheath. Suitable for the cool greenhouse. Mexico.

Common Calla see **Zantedeschia aethiopica**
Common Geranium see **Pelargonium × hortorum**
Common Ivy see **Hedera helix**
Common Maidenhair Fern see **Adiantum capillus-veneris**
Common Passion Flower see **Passiflora caerulea**
Common Stag's-horn Fern see **Platycerium bifurcatum**
Cone Plant see **Conophytum**

CONOPHYTUM (AIZOACEAE) Cone Plant
Small plants from the southern parts of Africa, which resemble the stones among which they grow. Each plant consists of a pair of leaves fused together except for a slit at the top through which the flowers appear. In some species the top of the pair of leaves is rounded, and in others each leaf is lobed, giving a notched appearance. The plants rest from December until July. They should have very little water from December until March, and none at all during May and June, when the leaves shrivel and dry up, and new leaves form inside the old ones. Sometimes two pairs form inside the former single pair, and in this way the plant increases. In July the new leaves burst through the old ones, which can be carefully removed, and the plants begin to flower, going on until the resting period begins. The soil should be as for terrestrial succulents, see the Introduction; good drainage is very important, but the plants like plenty of water while flowering. Propagation is by seed sown in May, the seed being very fine and sown on the surface of the compost, a temperature of 70°F. being needed. Minimum winter temperature 40°F.

bilobum
The yellow flowers are 1 in. across and appear in September and October. The leaves are grey-green, sometimes becoming red, and have 2 lobes with blunt tips. S. Africa.

calculus
The small yellow flowers are ½ in. across and appear in October. The body of the plant is rounded above with a short slit across the top. The leaves are grey-green. S. Africa.

ernianum
An August flowering species with small mauve flowers, ½ in. across. The grey-green leaves have 2 lobes. S. Africa.

scitulum
The flowers are white, ½–1 in. across and occur in October. The leaves

are grey-green netted red-brown, and the plant body top-shaped with narrow slit. S. Africa.

truncatum
A spherical, clump-forming plant with pale greyish-green leaves, spotted with many dots. The flowers, which are produced in October, are straw coloured to white and ¾ in. across. S. Africa.

CONVALLARIA (LILIACEAE)
majalis Lily-of-the-valley
The familiar hardy lily-of-the-valley can be used as a short term pot plant if a temperature of 65–70°F. can be maintained during the forcing period. Plant a dozen plump single crowns in a 5 or 6 in. pot of a proprietary peat compost in October or November and place in a cold greenhouse or frame. In January bring into a warm greenhouse or room which can be maintained at about 70°F. Water freely and keep dark until the leaves are well developed. Once the flower spikes are visible bring into a light position. The large-flowered cultivar 'Fortin's Giant' is a good one to use for this practice.

Cootamunda Wattle see **Acacia baileyana**
Copper Leaf see **Alternanthera versicolor**
Coral Berry see **Ardisia crispa**
Coral Blow see **Russelia**
Coral Drops see **Bessera elegans**
Coral Gem see **Lotus bertholetii**
Coral Plant see **Russelia juncea**
Coral Tree see **Erythrina**
Coral Vine see **Antigonon leptopus**

CORDYLINE (LILIACEAE) Cabbage Palm
Shrubs or small trees in the wild, but making good, handsome foliage pot plants when young. Some species are suitable for cool greenhouses, others for warmer conditions, either in pots or borders. Pot or tub specimens should be grown in a loam-based compost or a peat mix. Ventilate freely for *C. australis* and *C. indivisa* but maintain a humid atmosphere for *C. terminalis*. Shade the latter from the hottest sunshine. Propagate by suckers or stem sections in summer.

australis New Zealand Cabbage Tree, Grass Palm
A 2–3 ft pot plant, but reaching 25 ft when mature. It has narrow, strap-shaped, leathery, arching leaves which grow from the top of a single stem which branches after the plant has reached flowering size. The small, cream, fragrant flowers are borne in large plume-like clusters in June and July. New Zealand. **151.**

indivisa
This is also a tree-sized plant which can be grown as a pot plant in its juvenile stage. It has a single stem throughout and tough, sword-shaped, mid-green leaves with orange midribs. Mature specimens produce pendent clusters of white flowers in June and July, followed by globular, purple berries. New Zealand.

marginata see **Dracaena marginata**

terminalis syn. **Dracaena terminalis**
An excellent foliage plant with rosettes of deep green, sword-shaped leaves flushed with bronzy-red, purple or cream. They make most decorative pot plants when young. The mature tree bears its leaves on a 10 ft palm-like trunk. Many cultivars are grown. Tropical Asia.
  'Firebrand', stiff, slender, bright red glossy foliage, **152;**
  'Tricolor', variegated red and cream on green.

Corn Lily see **Ixia**

CORONILLA (LEGUMINOSAE)
The two species mentioned here are small shrubs with neat, attractive foliage and showy, yellow pea-like flowers. They are suitable for large pots or cold greenhouse borders. Pot specimens do well in a loam-based compost. Ventilate freely whenever possible. Propagate by seeds in spring or use lateral stem cuttings with a heel in summer.

glauca
A 5–9 ft evergreen bush with blue-grey divided leaves, each carrying

5–7 leaflets. The deep yellow, fragrant flowers are borne in clusters of up to 10 blooms from April to June. S. Europe.

'Compacta', syn. *C.g. pygmaea*, a dwarf, compact rounded form, 1½–2 ft high, **153.**

valentina

An attractive, 4 ft evergreen bush, with 7–11 grey-green leaflets, making up each of the leaves. The rich yellow flowers grow in clusters of 10–14; they are fragrant and open from May to July. S. Europe.

CORREA (RUTACEAE)

A genus of evergreen shrubs with pendent, tubular, somewhat fuchsia-like flowers. Although best grown in the cool greenhouse border, they will make satisfactory plants for pots and large tubs. If grown in the latter, use a peat-based mix or a loam-based compost. Ventilate freely whenever possible. Propagate by lateral shoots with a heel in late summer.

alba Botany Bay Tea Tree

A 2–4 ft stiff shrub, covered with dense, short hairs on the stems and the undersides of the ovate to roundish leaves. The white or pale pink, bell-shaped flowers are carried in groups of 1–3 at the ends of the stems and open from April to June. Australia.

× harrisii Australian Fuchsia

A shapely, hybrid shrub with rusty, hairy twigs and entire, softly downy leaves. The brilliant scarlet flowers are 1 in. long and have protruding, yellow-tipped stamens; they open in April and May.

reflexa see **C. speciosa**

speciosa syn. **C. reflexa**

A small shrub, rarely up to 4 ft but sometimes more, with densely hairy shoots and undersides of the leaves. The bright red blooms are similar to *C. × harrisii* and also open in April and May. Australia.

CORYPHANTHA (CACTACEAE)

At one time these cacti were included in the genus *Mammillaria*. They are round or cylindrical plants with marked tubercles, which are grooved on top for their full length. The flowers develop near the growing point of the plant, and are often large and showy. All the species described below are summer-flowering; none of them has leaves. Cultivation as for terrestrial cacti. Minimum winter temperature 40°F.

clava

The green club-shaped stem has a red gland at the base of the groove and about 8 spines, the central one being stouter and longer than the rest. The large flowers are pale yellow. Mexico.

deserti Desert Pincushion Cactus

The large cylindrical stem is densely covered with whitish spines, the central ones red or blackish at the tip. The flowers are pale pink or yellowish. California, Nevada.

echinus

The flowers are yellow. The whitish spines are pressed against the green, spherical to almost conical stem, virtually obscuring it. Texas. **154.**

elephantidens

This species has large pink flowers and a hemispherical green stem with large woolly-based tubercles. There are 8 short spines; no central one. Mexico.

erecta

The green, cylindrical stems grow in clusters and are prostrate at the base, erect at the end. The young part of the plant is very woolly. There are 8–14 radial spines and 2 central ones. The flowers are yellow and large. Mexico.

ottonis

This species has a round or cylindrical blue-green stem, with up to 16 spines, 4 of them central. It has white flowers. Mexico.

salm-dyckiana

A yellow-flowered species with a green spherical stem, sometimes growing in clusters. It has short tubercles and up to 15 whitish radial spines. There are up to 4 reddish-black central spines which grow to 1 in. in length. Mexico.

Costa Rican Nightshade see **Solanum wendlandii**

COSTUS (ZINGIBERACEAE)

A genus of perennial plants with attractive foliage and showy cone-like spikes of flowers borne at the ends of the branches. They make decorative pot plants for the warm greenhouse. Grow in a loam-based compost or proprietary peat mix and maintain warmth and humidity, watering freely. Shade from direct sunshine in summer. Propagate by division in spring.

igneus Fiery Costus

A beautiful tropical plant reaching only 15 in. in height. The 3–6 in. leaves are long oval, tapering to a narrow point, shiny green above and a reddish-purple beneath. The large flowers have a deep orange-yellow tube, 2 in. long and open to orange scarlet lobes, the lip exceeding 2 in. across. A most striking species. Brazil.

sanguineus Spiral Flag

An attractive small plant, the long narrow fleshy leaves tapering at the apex to a slender point, and at the base into a deep red stalk. The velvety surface is a bluish green with a silvery central vein, the whole having a glossy patina. C. America.

speciosus Spiral Ginger

A large and rather variable species, exceeding 6 ft in height. It has somewhat woody stems which bear slender pointed, narrowly-oval leaves, 6–8 in. long arranged in spirals and 5 in. spikes of flowers. These have a short tube opening to 2 in. lobes and are red or white. The 4 in. lip is always white and has an orange central marking. India.

Cotton see **Gossypium**
Cotton Rose see **Hibiscus mutabilis**

COTYLEDON (CRASSULACEAE)

Mostly stem and leaf succulents, but some are deciduous, being almost or entirely leafless during the summer. The deciduous ones must be rested in summer when the flowers appear, the leaves appearing again at the growing tip from autumn through the winter. The evergreen ones also flower in summer, but they need not be kept dry during this period, though too much water spoils the appearance of the leaves, which may become green and bloated. Culture as for terrestrial succulents, see Introduction, full sunshine being desirable. Propagation is by stem cuttings. If the plants become leggy, the tops of the evergreen kinds may be cut off and rooted as cuttings. The best time for taking cuttings is late summer. Winter temperature 40°F.

agavoides see **Echeveria agavoides**
californica see **Echeveria cotyledon**
elegans see **Echeveria harmsii**

orbiculata

The ½–1 in. long, tubular flowers are yellowish-red in colour. The leaves are whitish-grey with a red edge, rounded but narrowing towards the base, evergreen, and are borne on a branching stem. S. Africa.

'Oophylla', with small egg-shaped leaves.

paniculata

The flowers, which are produced during the resting period, are red with a green border, tubular and 1 in. in length. The grey-green deciduous leaves are 2–4 in. long, 1–2 in. wide, forming a crowded rosette at the top of the stout, fleshy stem which grows up to 6 ft tall. Complete rest in summer. S. Africa.

reticulata

This species is also deciduous, requiring complete rest during summer when it produces its flowers. These are greenish-yellow, striped red, ½ in. long and tubular. 4–6 grey-green, almost cylindrical leaves grow at the top of the broad stems which branch from the base and are about 9 in. tall. S. Africa.

teretifolia

The yellow, tubular flowers are ½ in. long. The pale green, almost cylindrical but pointed evergreen leaves are 4 in. long and are covered with soft hairs. The branching stem reaches a height of 4–8 in. S. Africa.

undulata

The tubular, orange-yellow to red flowers are ¾ in. long. The leaves are grey-green under a thick covering of white meal, narrow at the base but wide at the top with a wavy edge. The stems grow to 2 ft. A very popular plant for its beautiful evergreen leaves; these must not be wet or touched as this will spoil their appearance. S. Africa.

Cowslip, Cape see **Lachenalia**
Crab Cactus see **Schlumbergera truncata**
Crape Jasmine see **Ervatamia coronaria**
Crape Myrtle see **Lagerstroemia indica**

CRASSULA (CRASSULACEAE)

Grown for their succulent leaves, these plants are fairly easy provided that they are not given too much water, which causes the leaves to lose colour and become bloated. Culture as for terrestrial succulents, see Introduction, full sun being desirable. Mostly they are propagated by stem cuttings, but seeds and leaf cuttings are also used. Most of them are found in S. Africa, but some occur in other parts of the Old World. Minimum winter temperatures 40°F.

arborescens

The flowers are white, becoming pink, and are borne in terminal panicles, 2–4 in. across, in summer, although they are rarely produced in cultivation. The leaves are rounded, narrow at the base, and are a light grey-green colour with a red margin. It is a shrubby plant with branching stems, up to 3 ft tall. S. Africa.

argentea syn. C. portulacea

The pink flowers are produced in terminal panicles in summer. The oval leaves are bright green and shiny. The stems branch, forming a shrubby plant which, after many years, will reach a height of 10 ft. S. Africa. **155.**

cooperi

The few-flowered panicles of pink flowers are produced in summer. The ½ in. long leaves are pale green with sunken red dots above, red beneath, and are borne on long, thin, branching stems which form mats. S. Africa.

deceptor see C. deceptrix

deceptrix syn. C. deceptor

A late autumn flowering species, bearing its very small, white or pale pink flowers in sparse clusters. The ¾ in. long, whitish-grey leaves are very thick and closely packed on the short branched stems, forming clumps. This species grows in winter, when temperatures should be 45°F. or above. S.W. Africa.

falcata syn. Rochea falcata

The scarlet flowers are borne in closely packed, flat heads, 3–4 in. across, in summer. The grey, sickle-shaped leaves are 3–4 in. long and fold into each other on the stem which is fleshy and up to 2 ft tall. S. Africa. **156.**

portulacea see C. argentea

Cretan Bear's Tail see **Celsia arcturus**

CRINUM (LILIACEAE)

A genus of showy, bulbous plants with long, tapering, strap-shaped leaves and clusters of lily-like flowers. Among the many species, some are suitable for cool, others for a cold greenhouse, either in pots or in the border. Use a loam-based compost if available, and pot in spring. Water freely when in full leaf, sparingly at other times. Shade from hottest sunshine. Repot every 2–3 years. Propagate by offsets removed at potting time or by seeds when ripe.

giganteum (of gardens) Giant Spider Lily

A beautifully scented species with 2–3 ft leaves and clusters of 5–6, showy, white, bell-shaped flowers, with 6 large segments, the tube 4–6 in. long, in summer. Best in a cool or warm greenhouse. The true species is not in cultivation. W. Africa.

× powellii (C. bulbispermum × C. moorei) Swamp Lily

A spectacular plant with 3–4 ft leaves and a stiff, 3–4 ft stem upon which are borne about 8, rose red, trumpet-shaped flowers, the overall petal length often up to 7 in. It thrives well in a cold greenhouse. Garden origin. **157.**

CROCUS (IRIDACEAE)

All members of the genus *Crocus* are hardy and thrive best in the open garden. However, several species and cultivars respond well to container culture, providing a welcome splash of colour early in the new year. A cold or only slightly heated greenhouse or room are essential for success. If conditions are too hot, the flower buds will fail to develop properly. Plant the corms in pans or bowls of a loam or peat-based compost in October and plunge in a bed of ashes, sand or peat outside. Alternatively place in a cool room or cellar and keep dark. When the shoots are 1–1½ in. tall bring into the light but keep as cool as possible. Among suitable cultivars to try are:

chrysanthus (flowering from January to February)

'Blue Pearl', soft blue with bronzy base;
'Cream Beauty', soft creamy-yellow, rounded shape;
'E. A. Bowles', butter yellow.

vernus (flowering from February to March)

'Jean d'Arc', pure white;
'Purpureus Grandiflorus', deep rich purple;
'Vanguard', pale blue, shaded silvery-grey **158.**

CROSSANDRA (ACANTHACEAE)

The two species described here are somewhat shrubby plants with pleasing foliage and terminal heads of showy yellow or orange flowers. They are good pot plants for the warm greenhouse and the home. Use a proprietary peat mix or a loam-based compost. Shade from direct sunshine in summer and provide humidity. Propagate by basal stem cuttings from cut back plants in summer or by seeds in spring.

infundibuliformis see C. undulifolia

nilotica

A 1–2 ft plant with long, narrowly oval leaves. The brick-red flowers are borne in dense spikes at the ends of the erect stems, and appear in summer. E. Africa.

undulifolia syn. C. infundibuliformis

An erect plant, 1–3 ft high, with pointed, oval, wavy-margined leaves and large, orange-yellow to salmon-pink flowers carried on 4 in. spikes. E. Indies.

'Mona Walhed', a hybrid form with broad oval leaves and larger flowers of bright orange-yellow, **159.**

CROTALARIA (LEGUMINOSAE) Rattle-box

juncea Sunn Hemp

A downy annual plant, suitable for greenhouse culture. It has long oval to oblong leaves and deep yellow, broom-like blossoms, 1½ in. long, carried in a terminal spike up to 1 ft long. The flowering period is July to September. Grow in pots of a loam-based compost and place in a cool greenhouse. Ventilate freely on warm days. Propagate by seeds sown in spring. Tropical Asia, Australasia.

Croton see **Codiaeum**
Crown of Thorns see **Euphorbia milii splendens**
Cruel Flower see **Araujia sericofera**

CRYPTANTHUS (BROMELIACEAE)

A genus of evergreen bromeliads grown for their attractive coloured and patterned leaves borne in neat, often flattened or starfish-like rosettes. They are excellent pot or pan plants for the shadier parts of warm greenhouses or homes, thriving in any of the proprietary peat composts.

acaulis Green Earth Star

A small flattened rosette, 3–6 in. across, with leaves mid-green above and scaly-white beneath with prickly margins. The small, white, 3-petalled flowers appear spasmodically throughout the year. The plant produces small offsets from the base which can easily be rooted in peat. Brazil.

'Rubra', the leaves have a purple-bronze flush particularly along the margins.

bivittatus

The leaves of this species are up to 9 in. long and have a dark green central stripe on a background of olive-green, tinged with rose. Like

C. acaulis, it can be increased by offsets. Brazil. **160.**

'Atropurpureus', a smaller plant with dark, red leaves.

bromelioides Rainbow Star

A striking, upright plant reaching 12 in. with fresh-green, wavy-edged, slightly spiny leaves. Brazil.

'Tricolor', a variegated cultivar having leaves striped bronze-green and ivory-white with rose margins.

fosterianus Pheasant Leaf

A large plant with long, thick, fleshy leaves making a rosette up to 30 in. across. They are copper to purple-brown, cross banded with light grey scales. Brazil.

undulatus

A very small species, similar in growth and colour to *C. acaulis* but with leaves reaching only 2 in. in length. Mainly represented in cultivation by *C.u.* 'Ruber' which has dark green leaves. Brazil.

zonatus Zebra Plant

A spectacular plant with 6–9 in. waxy, scaly, leathery leaves having alternate coppery-green and dove-grey horizontal banding above, and silvery scales beneath. Brazil. **161.**

CTENANTHE (MARANTACEAE)

A group of handsome foliage plants closely allied to *Calathea*. They are tufted evergreen perennials, the leaves of which are shaded, patterned or splashed with shades of cream, pink, silver or grey. Grow in pots or pans of a proprietary peat compost in a warm greenhouse. Shade from direct sunshine and maintain a humid atmosphere in summer. Propagate by division or cuttings of basal shoots in early summer.

lubbersiana

This 1–1½ ft tall species has slender, forking stems set with narrowly oblong, long-stalked leaves. These are deep green above, lined and mottled with yellow, paler beneath. Brazil.

oppenheimiana Never-never Plant

A strong-growing clump forming species producing lance-shaped dark green leaves bearing bands of silver grey on the upper surface. The lower surface is wine-purple. Brazil.

'Tricolor', has the leaves splashed cream and pink, **162.**

CUNONIA (CUNONIACEAE)

capensis African Red Alder

A small, evergreen tree which can attain 40 ft, but which makes a good tub or house plant when young. It has reddish twigs and shiny-green, glossy leaves divided into 5–7 leaflets which are reddish-brown when young. The spikes of small, white flowers appear in August. Also very suitable for the cool greenhouse. S. Africa. **163.**

Cup-and-saucer Plant see **Cobaea scandens**

CUPHEA (LYTHRACEAE)

Bushy perennial or shrubby plants grown for their curious and often showy, tubular flowers. The species described are suitable for a window or cool greenhouse, in pots or the border. Propagate by stem cuttings in spring and pinch the young plants to promote a bushy habit.

cyanea

An 18 in. sub-shrub, having a curiously clammy feeling. It has small, oval, hairy leaves and 1 in. tubular flowers enclosed in a calyx which is orange at the base and yellow above, the blue-purple petals only just protruding from it. Mexico.

ignea see **C. platycentra**

miniata

A 2 ft evergreen sub-shrub having oval, slender pointed leaves which are green and have a sparse covering of white bristles. The 1½ in. pale vermilion, tubular flowers are produced from June to September. Mexico.

'Firefly', a smaller, more bushy cultivar growing to 12–15 in. in height, with bright cerise flowers, **164.**

platycentra syn. **C. ignea** Cigar Flower

A bushy, 12 in. plant having smooth, narrow leaves and 1 in. tubular,

scarlet flowers with the petal tips reflexed to show dark purple and white markings, like the ash on a cigar. They are at their best from April to November but often produce a few blooms throughout the year. Mexico. **165.**

CUPRESSUS (CUPRESSACEAE) Cypress

cashmeriana Kashmir Cypress

Considered one of the most beautiful cypresses, it is a graceful, pyramidal tree with blue-green, scale-like leaves borne on pendulous branches. An excellent species for cultivation as a pot plant or in tubs of all sizes, but not suitable for the greenhouse border as it can reach 60 ft. Tibet. The green form of this species is not impressive. **166.**

CURCUMA (ZINGIBERACEAE)

roscoeana Hidden Lily

A robust plant with an 18 in. stalk and 6–8, handsome, evergreen, glossy, sword-shaped leaves. In August it produces showy, 8 in. spikes of yellow flowers with conspicuous, at first green then vivid orange-scarlet bracts below each bloom. A plant for pots in the warm greenhouse needing a humid atmosphere and shade from the summer sun. Propagate by division in spring. Malaya.

Curly Sentry Palm see **Howea belmoreana**
Cushion Bush see **Calocephalus brownii**

CYANOTIS (COMMELINACEAE)

A genus of semi-succulent creeping plants somewhat similar to *Tradescantia*, of which the following species are most suitable as greenhouse or house plants. Plant in pots or hanging baskets, in which they look particularly attractive, in a loam-based or proprietary peat compost. Keep well watered in summer, sparingly at other times, and do not allow to become cold. Propagate by cuttings of young stems in summer.

kewensis Teddy-bear Vine

The whole plant is covered with a rusty-brown, densely woolly hair; the deep green, triangular, fleshy leaves are borne on trailing, succulent stems, and are purple beneath. The small, 3-petalled flowers are a reddish-violet and are produced during winter and spring. India.

somaliensis Pussy-ears

A creeping plant having long ovate, glossy green leaves 1½ in. in length, white hairy on both surfaces with particularly long hairs along the margins. The 3-petalled blue-purple flowers open in spring. Somaliland.

CYATHEA (CYATHEACEAE) Treefern

A genus of majestic treeferns, the full beauty of which can only be appreciated when planted out in a large, high greenhouse or conservatory. While small, they are suitable for culture in tubs or large pots. Ideally a humid atmosphere should be maintained by regular damping down. Propagate by spores or suckers in spring.

dealbata Ponga or Silver King Fern

One of the most handsome of treeferns for a cool greenhouse. It has a slender trunk up to 10 ft or more, and a palm-like head of leaves 6–12 ft long, each frond deeply dissected into a lacy pattern, pale green above and intense blue-white beneath. It requires plenty of headroom if planted out in a greenhouse border or can be accommodated in a large tub. New Zealand.

medullaris Sago or Black Tree Fern

Similar in size and appearance to *C. dealbata* with a slender blackish trunk and spreading, leathery, dark green fronds, paler beneath 6–15 ft long. It is best in a warm greenhouse but will grow satisfactorily under cooler conditions. New Zealand, Australia.

mexicana Monkey-tail Fern

A rather more robust treefern than the above species, rarely exceeding 6 ft in cultivation, but with a shorter, thicker trunk and spreading, 6–9 ft long mid-green fronds. It needs a tub or greenhouse border to produce fine specimen plants. Mexico.

CYCAS (CYCADACEAE)

Palm-like plants with a woody trunk and head of stiff, arching fronds.

While young, the species described make handsome tub or pot plants for the cool or warm greenhouse. Propagate by seeds in the spring.

circinalis Fern Palm 🦢
A palm-like plant with a heavy trunk from which grows an elegant rosette of stiff, shining fronds divided to the mid-rib into 80–100 long, narrow segments. In the wild it can reach 40 ft but responds well to tub culture. Madagascar, E. Indies, Ceylon to Guam.

revoluta Sago Palm 🦢
The stout, bulky trunk which grows to 7 ft or more carries 2–7 ft stiff, leathery fronds divided into about 120 narrow, spine-tipped segments. Like a small palm in appearance. China, Japan. **167.**

CYCLAMEN (PRIMULACEAE)
These are herbaceous, perennial plants grown for their attractively silver patterned foliage and uniquely lovely, shuttlecock-shaped flowers. They are excellent pot plants for the home or cool greenhouse. Propagate by seeds sown in autumn or spring and when potting keep the top of the corm above ground level.

indicum see **C. persicum**

persicum syn. **C. indicum** ✳ 🦢
A fine plant with round- to heart-shaped, evergreen leaves with silver marbling on the upper surface. The 1–1½ in. flowers are pink in the wild species with narrow petals, but cultivars, often listed as *C.p. giganteum*, range from white to deep carmine, often with larger petalled blooms. It flowers from autumn to spring. E. Mediterranean. **168.**
A group of some of the very fine modern silver marked leaf varieties is shown in plate **169;** other recommended cultivars are listed below.
  'Butterfly', frilled, salmon to rose-pink petals;
  'Cattleya', orchid-mauve flowers;
  'Rex', silver marbled leaves;
  'Rosalie', very fragrant, pale salmon to rose;
  'Shell Pink', with prettily marbled leaves, **170;**
  'Silberstrahl', red flowers with a delicate silver margin;
  'White Swan', superb white flowers.

rohlfsianum ✳ 🦢
A delightful, autumn flowering species with round, faintly lobed leaves and fragrant flowers, with pink, red based overlapping petals. When the petals drop, the flower stalk spirals downwards, carrying the seed pod to ground level. N. Africa.

CYMBIDIUM (ORCHIDACEAE)
A popular genus of orchids for cool greenhouse conditions, the beautifully shaped and subtly coloured flowers of which are much in demand by florists. The tougher species and cultivars may also be grown in the home. Shade from hot sun in summer but expose to autumn sunshine to promote flowering. Propagate by division at re-potting time after flowering. A suitable compost comprises equal parts loam, fibre or shredded bark, osmunda fibre, and sphagnum moss. A large number of cultivars have been named, almost all of which have derived from hybridization between species.
  Babylon 'Castle Hill' has deep pink flowers;
  Rosanna 'Pinkie', delicate blush pink with a deeper lip, **171;**
  Rosette, greenish-yellow with dark red marking on the lip, **172;**
  Swallow 'Exbury', yellow, slightly tinged with light green with
    reddish spotting on the lip, **173;**
  Vieux Rose has rose-pink flowers, **174.**

aloifolium syn. **C. simulans** ✳
From the 3 in. bulbs grow stiff, very narrow leaves which are held erect, and 18 in. pendulous stems bearing in July and August numerous, 1½ in. fleshy flowers with purple-marked, pale yellow petals and a yellow-brown lip. It grows best in a hanging basket in a warm greenhouse or room and needs some shade. S.E. Asia.

dayanum ✳
A good species for the cool greenhouse with long, narrow leaves and 3 in. pale yellow to white flowers, with a wine-coloured central streak and a purple and yellow lip bearing white markings. They are carried on long, pendent stalks about 12 in. in length and open in autumn. Assam.

devonianum ✳
A spring flowering species having light brown, fleshy, 1–1½ in. flowers,

marked with dull purple, as is the white lip. They grow in many flowered, drooping spikes. India.

eburneum ✳
A delightfully fragrant species flowering in March to June. It has 2–3 creamy-white flowers with a yellow-marked lip on each 8–12 in. stem, and long, narrow, bright green leaves. Can be grown in the home. India.

elegans ✳
The arching stems carry up to 40 bell-like blooms, 1½ in. long with straw-yellow sepals, petals and lip, the lip marked with 2 bright orange lines, opening in October and November. The narrow, curving leaves can reach 2 ft in length. A plant for the warm greenhouse. Nepal.

giganteum ✳
A large flowered, fragrant species, the 2–3 ft arching stem bearing in autumn, 7–15 blooms, each 4–5 in. across, light yellow-green with purple markings, and having a yellow lip blotched with a bright reddish-brown. The stems and long, sword-like leaves grow from a 6 in. bulb. A plant for cool greenhouse or room cultivation. N. India.

lowianum ✳
The 4–5 in. yellow-green flowers have a whitish-yellow lip with crimson, central markings. They appear from March to May and are borne in spikes of 15–40 blooms on an 18 in. pendulous stalk. A good species for the cool greenhouse or home. Burma. **175.**

simulans see **C. aloifolium**

tigrinum ✳
The smallest of the species described here, it has 2–5 flowers, about 2 in. across which open in May and June. Each bloom has greenish-yellow, red spotted and striped sepals and petals, with a large white lip bearing very distinct red-purple markings. It is best in the warm greenhouse. S.E. Asia.

tracyanum ✳
A very distinctively marked species the 4–5 in. fragrant flowers are brown and red striped on a yellow background. The hairy lobed lip has similar coloration with a white fringed margin. The blooms are borne on 2 ft stems between November and January. It thrives in the house or cool greenhouse. Burma.

CYPELLA (IRIDACEAE)
Bulbous plants for the cool greenhouse having slender grassy leaves and elegant iris-like flowers in contrasting colours. Each blossom lasts a few hours only, but is followed by a daily succession over a long period. Repot annually during the dormant season using a loam-based compost. Propagate by offsets at potting time or by seed in spring.

coelestis see **C. plumbea**

herbertii ✳
A variable flowered species having petals spotted or lined; centre yellow and dull purple with red spots. The overall height of the plant is about 1 ft and the flowers appear in July. Argentina, Uruguay, Brazil.

plumbea syn. **C. coelestis** ✳
A taller plant than the preceding species with well-spaced, sword-shaped leaves and 3 or 4 dull lead flowers, yellow at the base, appearing in autumn. Brazil, Argentine.

CYPERUS (CYPERACEAE) Galingale
A group of handsome grass-like plants for the cool and warm greenhouse and frames. Some species make excellent pot plants. The genus is also the source of Egyptian papyrus and the tiger-nuts of commerce. Propagate by division in spring. Grow in a loam-based compost and keep *C. papyrus* and *C. alternifolius* constantly moist by standing the pot in a saucer of water. *C. esculentus* needs better drained soil and should be kept just moist. Pot the nut-like tubers of the latter in spring.

alternifolius Umbrella Grass 🦢
A good plant for room decoration with many, dark green stems, growing from 1–1½ ft in height and crowned with a rosette of long, arching, leaf-life bracts growing from the end of the stem like the ribs of an umbrella. Madagascar.
  'Variegatus', stems and leaves are white or white-striped.

esculentus Tiger-nut, Chufa
A dark green, grassy plant with slender, pointed, arching leaves. It may be grown in cool or warm greenhouse or house, but dies down in autumn. The small, nut-like root tubers are edible, having a sweet nutty flavour and crisp texture.

papyrus Egyptian Paper Rush, Papyrus
A tall, evergreen, aquatic species for a large, warm greenhouse. The dark green stems grow from 4–10 ft and carry a mop-like cluster of fluffy, yellow-green flower heads, each growing on a 6–18 in. drooping or spreading, thread-like stalk. It is a most striking plant for an indoor pool or in a tub stood in a tray of water. W. Mediterranean. **176.**

Cypress see **Cupressus**
Cypress, Summer see **Kochia scoparia trichophylla**
Cypress Vine see **Quamoclit pennata**
Cypripedium see **Paphiopedilum**

CYRTANTHUS (AMARYLLIDACEAE)
Attractive bulbous plants with narrow strap-shaped leaves and heads of curved, tubular flowers in shades of red, yellow and white. Those mentioned here are suitable for a cool greenhouse or home. Pot the bulbs in spring and repot at least every other year after flowering. *C. sanguineus* should be dried off after flowering until repotting. Use a loam based compost. Propagate by offsets when repotting or by seeds in spring.

mackenii Bow or Ifafa Lily
A delightful plant with 15 in. narrow leaves and 12 in. stalks bearing a cluster of 4–10, almost erect ivory-white or pink, fragrant flowers which open in the spring. Natal.

macowanii
A striking species with 6–8 bright scarlet, nodding flowers with a 1½ in. tube and opening to a bell shape at the mouth. They are carried on a 12 in. purplish stem and open in spring. The leaves are from 6–12 in. long and dark green. Cape Province.

o'brienii Red Ifafa Lily
A very similar plant to *C. macowanii* but carries lighter coloured scarlet flowers. S. Africa.

sanguineus Fire or Inanda Lily
A large flowered species with bright red trumpet-shaped flowers having a 3 in. tube and opening to 1 in. across at the mouth with 1½ in. lobes. 1 to 3 are carried on a 12 in. stem in August. The leaves grow to 16 in. and green and glaucous forms occur. S. Africa.

CYRTOMIUM (POLYPODIACEAE)
falcatum Fish-tail Fern
A handsome fern with the divided leaves of shining, dark green, oval leaflets, pointed at the tips and arranged alternately on the 1–2 ft dark, wiry stalk. It is an extremely tolerant plant and grows well as an indoor pot plant thriving in ordinary garden soil with extra humus. It prefers cool conditions and is best propagated by division. S.E. Asia.

'Rochfordianum', Holly Fern, has larger leaflets with wavy, spiny margins very reminiscent of holly. More compact than the species, rarely exceeding 12 in.

D

Daffodil, Peruvian see **Pamianthe peruviana**
Daffodil, Sea see **Panacratium maritimum**

DAIS (THYMELAEACEAE)
bholua
A small evergreen shrub with long, ovate leaves having slightly waxy incurved margins, The small, fragrant flowers are white with a faint pinkish tinge and grow from a purplish-pink, silky calyx. They are carried in clusters of 3 or more and open from January to March. A good plant for the cool greenhouse which can be propagated by layers or cuttings. India.

Daisy, African see **Arctotis**
Daisy, Barberton see **Gerbera jamesonii**

Daisy, Namaqualand see **Venidium fastuosum**
Daisy, Transvaal see **Gerbera jamesonii**
Dancing Doll Orchid see **Oncidium flexuosum**

DARLINGTONIA (SARRACENIACEAE)
californica California Pitcher Plant
A remarkable insectivorous plant with curious, upright, tubular leaves 3–30 in. long and ½–3 in. wide, bright yellow-green, swelling towards the top into an arched hood marked with a network of red veins. From the tip hangs a two-lobed, purple spotted 'tongue', very smooth inside and with down-pointed hairs which prevent any insect which is attracted in, from escaping. The pendent globe-shaped flowers have red petals and greenish sepals appearing during April and May. It makes a fascinating plant for the cool greenhouse growing best in a compost of peat and sphagnum moss which must be continuously moist and needs a humid atmosphere. Propagate by seed or division in spring. California.

Date Palm see **Phoenix**

DATURA syn. **BRUGMANSIA** (SOLANACEAE)
A genus of mainly shrubby plants with bold foliage and striking trumpet-shaped flowers in shades of cream, white and red. All the species described here may be grown in tubs or large pots in a cool greenhouse, but are best grown in the border. Prune back the flowering shoots to a short stub in late winter. Propagate by cuttings in spring.

arborea syn. **Brugmansia arborea** Angel's Trumpet
A shrub or small tree reaching 10 ft, softly hairy all over with ovate, nearly entire, leathery leaves and white, pendent trumpets 6–8 in. long, beautifully fragrant, especially in the late evening, and produced in August. Peru, Chile.

cornigera syn. **Brugmansia knightii**
A downy shrub, reaching 10 ft. having large ovate leaves and 6 in. ivory flowers from June to August. They are strongly fragrant. Mexico.
'Grand Marnier', a robust, vigorous plant with larger cream flowers, **177;**
'Knightii', the semi-double form, is most usually seen in cultivation.
'Nairobi Yellow', creamy-yellow flowers.

fastuosa syn. **D. metel**
A 2–3 ft annual, with 7–8 in. narrowly ovate leaves and erect 6–7 in. flowers, produced in July. They are violet-purple on the outside and show the contrasting white inside at the mouth of the trumpet-shaped blooms. India.

metel see **D. fastuosa**

meteloides
A bushy, shrubby perennial, short lived so often replaced annually. The leaves are unequally ovate and have a strong, pungent smell when bruised. The flowers are fragrant, white or bluish-lilac and 4–8 in. long. S.W. U.S.A.

rosei see **D. sanguinea**

sanguinea syn. **Brugmansia sanguinea**
An evergreen, shrubby species reaching 6 ft. It has 7 in. ovate, wavy-edged, mid-green leaves which are softly hairy. The 8 in. flowers are orange-scarlet and open in July and August. Peru. The correct name for this plant is probably *D. rosei*. **178.**

suaveolens
A large, 6–15 ft tree-like shrub. It has 12 in. entire, smooth leaves, sometimes downy beneath. The pendent, showy, white flowers can reach 12 in. in length and are very fragrant. They open in August. Mexico. **179.**

Daubentonia punicea see **Sesbania punicea**

DAVALLIA (POLYPODIACEAE)
Elegant ferns having finely dissected fronds which are borne on distinctive, furry stems (rhizomes). The species described here are suitable for a cool greenhouse or home. Use a peat-based compost and repot every second or third year. Propagate by division or cuttings of the rhizomes in early spring.

canariensis Hare's-foot Fern

A good species for house or greenhouse, it gets its popular name from the brown, hairy-rootstock which hangs over the edge of the pot, resembling a hare's foot. The fronds are leathery, deeply dissected and somewhat reminiscent of a carrot leaf. It reaches 12–18 in. W. Mediterranean.

mariesii Ball Fern

A cool greenhouse species with fibrous rhizomes which are sometimes trained to grow into curious ball shapes. The light green fronds are 8–12 in. long and deeply dissected· giving it a feathery appearance. Japan.

Day Flower see **Commelina**
Delta Maidenhair see **Adiantum raddianum**

DENDROBIUM (ORCHIDACEAE)

Superbly showy orchids bearing elegant blooms in contrasting colours. Among the species described here are those suitable for cool and warm greenhouses and for the home. Propagate by division just as the young shoots appear, using a compost of 3 parts osmunda fibre to one part sphagnum moss. Keep shaded and humid during the summer, allowing more light in autumn.

aureum syn. **D. heterocarpum**

A warm greenhouse species having clusters of 4–6, creamy-yellow flowers rising from slender 12–18 in. leafy bulbs. Each bloom has a velvety-golden lip marked with brown and purple and is delightfully fragrant. India. **180.**

bigibbum

A species needing humidity and a temperature above 81°F. to thrive. It has graceful, arching spikes of 6–12 rich, rose-purple flowers with a white-crested lip which open in September and October. The overall height is 12–18 in. Australia, New Guinea.

brymerianum

An attractive evergreen with golden-yellow sepals and petals and a whiskery, fringed margin to the lip, which has a deeper orange throat. It flowers from February to April, the 3 in. blooms being carried with the 5 in. sword-shaped, light green leaves at the top of the 12–24 in. bulbs. It needs a warm greenhouse. Burma.

densiflorum

A most handsome, sturdy species needing warmth in the growing season. The 1–1½ ft bulbs, each bear about 5 dark green, leathery leaves and dense, drooping trusses of 50–100 blooms which open from March to May. The flowers are a shining, golden-yellow, 1½ in. across with a deeper golden lip. India, Burma.

fimbriatum

A beautiful species with 2 in. light orange blooms and an almost circular lip with a golden fringe. The flowers are borne on pendulous stalks in loose clusters of 12–20 blooms. The mid-green leaves grow along the length of the 2–4 ft high bulbs. Flowers March–April. India, Burma.

'Oculatum', a free flowering cultivar with a maroon throat.

heterocarpum see **D. aureum**

kingianum

A charming small plant for the cool greenhouse with 2–12 in. bulbs bearing dark green leaves and in April and May, 6 in. spikes of 2–6, white marked and white lipped, violet-purple blooms, 1 in. across. Australia.

loddigesii sym. **D. pulchellum**

The fragrant solitary blooms are 1½ in. across with elliptic, rose-lilac petals and an almost circular orange-yellow lip with a broad, white, shortly fringed margin. They are borne along the 3–6 in. stem from February to April, and contrast with the narrow, dark green leaves. China.

moschatum

A large, light-demanding species for the warm greenhouse with 5 ft cane-like bulbs and 20–30, large, leathery leaves. The drooping spikes of 7–15 flowers are fragrant and produced from May to July; each bloom has palest yellow, rose-tinged petals and a slipper-shaped, downy, yellow lip with a deep purple patch at each side of the fringed lines at the centre. India, Burma.

nobile

One of the easiest and most variable members of this genus, bearing an abundance of 2–3 in. fragrant flowers. Each blossom has white petals suffused pink or lilac, and a yellow lip bearing a deep velvety-maroon blotch at the throat and a pink to purple margin. They are borne from January to March on 18 in. bulbs, together with the bright green leaves. N. India, Assam, China.

'Album', pure white flowers;
'Virginale', white with a pale primrose-yellow blotch on the lip, **181.**

pulchellum see **D. loddigesii**

speciosum

A cool greenhouse species with stout, 6–15 in. bulbs bearing dense spikes of fragrant, creamy-white, waxy flowers having a purple speckled, white lip. They open from February to April. Australia.

thyrsiflorum

A fine, showy species in habit rather like *D. densiflorum*. It has 18 in. slender bulbs, many dark green leaves and massive pendulous clusters of 80–100 flowers opening from March to May. Each bloom is 1½–2 in. across with white rose-flushed petals and a hairy, golden-range lip. Burma.

victoriae-reginae

A pretty, deciduous species for the cool greenhouse with 6–12 in. pendulous bulbs bearing dark green leaves, and from April to October, clusters of 3–7 purple-blue streaked petals fading to white at the centre. Philippines.

Montrose 'Lyoth Gold', a hybrid with large yellow petals and a brown throat.

Denmoza rhodacantha see **Echinopsis rhodacantha**
Desert Pincushion Cactus see **Coryphantha deserti**
Desert Privet see **Peperomia magnoliifolia**

DESMODIUM (LEGUMINOSAE) Tick Trefoil
gyrans syn. **D. motorium** Telegraph Plant

A fascinating annual plant. Each leaf is composed of a large elliptic, central leaflet and two very small, lateral leaflets. These small leaflets are mobile, and during warm days move quite rapidly with a circular motion. Small, violet flowers are borne in dense, branched spikes, opening in late summer. A really warm, humid greenhouse is needed for the best results, using a loam or peat-based compost. India.

Devil Flower see **Tacca chantrieri**
Devil's Ivy see **Scindapsus aureus**
Devil's Tongue see **Amorphophallus rivieri**
Devil's Tongue Cactus see **Ferocactus latispinus**

DIANELLA (LILIACEAE)

A genus of sub-shrubs having fans of dark green, strap-like leaves and unique purple-blue berries. They are best grown in cool greenhouse borders but can be accommodated in pots, using a loam-based compost. Propagate by division or seeds, in spring.

caerulea

The dark green, rough leaves grow along the 2 ft stem which bears a terminal cluster of blue flowers in May, followed by purple-blue berries. Australia.

intermedia

A white flowered species with 10–18 in. panicles of blooms, opening in spring. The purple-blue berries are freely produced in autumn. New Zealand.

tasmanica

A much larger plant than the other two species described, reaching 5 ft, with narrow, stiff, 3–4 ft spine-toothed leaves. The loose clusters of pale blue flowers appear in spring and are followed by ½–¾ in. persistent, blue-purple berries. Tasmania, Australia. **182.**

DIANTHUS (CARYOPHYLLACEAE) Pink, Carnation

This genus of 300 or so species contains many beautiful cultivated plants, but for greenhouse use the perpetual-flowering carnation is really the only one which needs to be considered. It is grown commercially on a large scale in Britain and the United States and in many other countries. The origin of this plant is not quite clear, but it is probably a hybrid between *D. caryophyllus*, the wild carnation of S. Europe, and *D. chinensis* (incorrectly *D. sinensis*), the Chinese or Indian Pink from E. Asia. It tends to flower in bursts at any time of the year, but the period can be controlled by stopping (removing the tips of the branches) and by the temperature of the greenhouse. For good winter flowering a temperature of 50°F. is needed for full production of blooms, though a fair number of flowers will be produced at 45°F. Below these temperatures flowering is very erratic, and will take place in the following spring or summer. The plants will not die provided frost is excluded.

A greenhouse with full light and full ventilation is needed, and since some ventilation is required even in winter, heating must be adequate. Perpetual-flowering carnations need a drier atmosphere than many plants, and condensation of moisture must at all times be avoided. In their first year they grow 3–4 ft tall, and in their second year up to 6–7 ft, so a fairly tall greenhouse is necessary; second-year plants may be on staging close to the ground. The 'Sim' varieties, highly popular with commercial growers, tend to be taller than this, and most of them should be avoided by amateurs having low greenhouses.

Young rooted plants are potted into 2½ in. pots in late February or March, and when the roots reach the side of the pots they are potted on to 4 in. and then 6 in. pots. An ordinary loam-based compost is suitable for the young plants, but a richer one should be used for the 6 in. pots, in which the first season's flowers will be produced. When the plants have made 10 or so pairs of leaves, break out or cut out the top at the 7th to 9th joint. When the side shoots grow, break them out to leave 5 to 7 joints on each – do not do them all at once but over a period of 10–14 days as they become ready. The next stopping controls the time of flowering. Up to the middle of June autumn flowering will result. Mid-June to mid-July produces winter flowers. Stopping from mid-July to mid-August early, spring flowers, but if these plants are not given the third stopping they will flower in autumn. After this, cutting the blooms will act as stopping.

When the flower stems develop, remove all pea-sized buds except the one at the top of the stem, called the crown bud. At this stage proprietary carnation manure should be given, once each two weeks in autumn and spring, and once a month in winter.

In hot weather overhead spraying, and damping down the house helps the plants, but it should be done early so no moisture remains on the plants at night. Open or opening blooms must not be wetted. Support is needed as the plants grow, wire rings which clip on to a bamboo cane being very suitable.

For the second year, pot on into 8 in. pots of a medium rich, loam-based compost. After two seasons, the plants may be planted outdoors in spring to produce blooms until they are killed by frost. Propagation is by cuttings taken in February. Side shoots about 6 in. long are cut off cleanly just below a joint and the bottom pair of leaves is removed; they are then inserted 1 in. apart in pans of very sharp sand, and put in a propagating case in the greenhouse, with enough bottom heat to ensure a temperature of 60–65°F. The atmosphere is kept close until the tops of the cuttings begin to grow, when air is gradually increased and the temperature allowed to fall over a period of 7–10 days to that of the greenhouse. The rooted cuttings are then potted singly into 2½ in. pots and grown on as described above.

New varieties are grown from seed sown in January or February in a temperature of 60°F., the seedlings afterwards being potted on as with cuttings, but only one stopping is given so that early blooms are produced; the inferior plants can then be thrown away before the winter.

Various pests can attack carnations. Aphids can spread virus diseases as well as causing direct damage. Thrips can mark flowers. Caterpillars are rare under glass. Red spider mites can be troublesome if the house gets too dry. It is good practice to alternate various insecticides, such as malathion. BHC or kelthane wettable powder and pyrethrum.

Various fungi can attack the plants, and for those which cause spots or mould on the leaves, alternation of captan, thiram, zineb and liquid copper fungicides will usually provide a cure. Virus and wilt diseases are usually considered incurable, and the plants should be destroyed to protect the healthy ones. Since these incurable diseases can be carried by apparently healthy cuttings, many growers do not propagate but get stock from a certified source each year.

There are many good varieties, and new varieties are continually being introduced. It is generally true that varieties which are listed by the specialist growers are good, particularly those which have been in the catalogues for several years, since competition is keen and it costs no more to propagate a good variety than a poor one. Some good ones are:

'Alec Sparkes', crimson;
'Bailey's Splendour', pink;
'Ballerina', rich cerise, **183;**
'Bonny Charlie', orange;
'Brigadoon', yellow;
'Brocade', white with dark red stripes, **184;**
'Deep Purple', purple;
'Fragrant Ann', white. **185;**
'Heather Beauty', pinky-mauve, scented, **186;**
'Helios', pale yellow, **187;**
'Joker', crimson;
'Paris', pink;
'Tetra', salmon;
'Viking', cerise;
'Zuni', dark cerise, marked crimson.

DICENTRA (FUMARIACEAE)

spectabilis Bleeding Heart, Dutchman's Breeches
A hardy plant, delightful also for the cool or cold greenhouse border or in pots, with grey-green, feathery leaves and arching spikes of dainty rose-red, heart-shaped flowers having white inner petals. They are produced from April to June. Propagate by division in winter, or by seeds. E. Asia. **188.**

Dichorisandra albo-lineata see **Campelia zanonia** 'Mexican Flag'

DICKSONIA (CYATHEACEAE)

Majestic treeferns for the cool greenhouse with fibrous palm-like trunks and umbrella-like heads of large, dissected fronds. They are best grown in borders or large tubs for maximum ornamental effect, but make attractive pot plants while young. Use a proprietary peat compost, shade from direct sunshine during the late spring to early autumn period and maintain a humid atmosphere. Propagate by suckers or spores in spring.

antarctica Woolly Treefern
The most useful of these species for tubs and pots as it is very slow growing and almost hardy. The deeply dissected, leathery fronds have yellowish veins and are carried in a close, palm-like cluster which crowns the fibrous trunk. At maturity this treefern can reach 25 ft or more, but it takes many years to do so planted out in a border. Tasmania, Australia. **189.**

fibrosa Golden Treefern
A medium sized treefern eventually reaching 15 ft or more. Its stout trunk is covered with golden brown, fibrous rootlets and carries a mass of bright green 3–6 ft dissected fronds. New Zealand.

squarrosa
The slender, dark trunk is crowned with somewhat rough, deep green, dissected fronds which are carried almost at right angles to the trunk, giving a flat top to the head. Each plant may have several stems in a cluster. A useful pot plant when small, with fronds to 18 in. long, it can reach 20 ft with 8 ft fronds at maturity. New Zealand.

DIEFFENBACHIA (ARACEAE) Dumb Cane

Handsome foliage plants having robust, somewhat fleshy stems and clusters of large leaves spotted or suffused with yellow or white. All the species and cultivars grown make fine pot plants when young, or may be grown as large specimens in the greenhouse border. Good results can be obtained with either a loam-based or an equivalent peat compost. Shade from direct sunshine in summer and maintain a humid atmosphere. Propagate by 3 in. long stem sections just buried in peat in a warm frame.

amoena
The oval, dark green, glossy leaves are feathered with white and pale yellow markings. They are borne on a central stem which thickens and becomes trunk-like with age. It makes a good house plant which tolerates poor light. Tropical America.

picta

A handsome, robust plant bearing 10 in. oval, blunt leaves which have ivory-white markings, leaving only the veins and margins green. Many cultivars are grown. Brazil.

'Exotica', pale yellow markings on a dark green leaf, possibly a hybrid. **190;**

'Roehrsii' or 'Rudolf Roehrs', chartreuse yellow leaves with white markings leaving only the midrib and marginal areas green, **191;**

'Superba', thick, glossy leaves, heavily flecked with ivory white.

seguina

A robust species having long, fleshy, dark green leaves and irregular white spots in cultivation. An interesting pot plant but perhaps not as striking as the two species mentioned above. W. Indies, N.S. America.

Dietes bicolor see **Moraea bicolor**
Dietes grandiflora see **Moraea iridioides**

DIONAEA (DROSERACEAE)
muscipula Venus's Fly Trap

A remarkable insectivorous plant with a flat rosette of 1–5 in. leaves, the lower half flattened and light green, the upper half oblong, jointed at the centre making two upward folding halves. The margins have long teeth which enmesh when the two halves come together. The mechanism is triggered off by 3 sensitive hairs on the upper surface of each part, and the trap can close in a fraction of a second when a small insect touches them. The plant has attractive clusters of white flowers in July and August and can be grown in a pot with a mixture of peat and sphagnum moss placed in a dish of water to maintain constant moisture. Propagate by division, bulblets or seed. N. and S. Carolina. **192.**

DIOSCOREA (DIOSCOREACEAE) Yam

A genus of climbing plants, some species of which have beautifully coloured, heart-shaped leaves. The species mentioned make attractive plants for the warm greenhouse or home. Several other species yield the tropical root vegetables known as yams. Use a loam-based compost and make sure the plants never dry out during the growing season. Shade from direct sunshine during the summer. Propagate by division of the tuber or cutting of young shoots in the late spring.

discolor Ornamental Yam

A handsome twining plant with large, 5–6 in. leaves, a rich dark green with paler yellow marbling overlaid with a silvery-white band along the midrib. The underside of the leaf is red-purple. It needs supports to climb, and is best in a warm greenhouse. N.S. America.

elephantipes syn. **Testudinaria elephantipes** Elephant's Foot, Tortoise Plant

An extraordinary plant with a huge, roundish or pyramidal tuber growing above ground, eventually reaching 3 ft in height. From it, annual, climbing stems, 6 ft or more in length arise, carrying oval to kidney shaped leaves and small clusters of greenish-yellow flowers in the autumn. S. Africa.

multicolor

Rather similar to *D. discolor*, with 3–5 in. leaves mottled in shades of green, pale purple beneath. Many cultivars are known. Brazil, Colombia.

'Argyraea', with silvery-grey markings on the leaf;
'Metallica', bronze-green with copper markings.

DIOSMA (RUTACEAE)
ericoides Buchu

A twiggy, 1–2 ft heather-like shrub with very small, entire, needle-like leaves and terminal clusters of 2–3 small, pinkish flowers. It makes a good pot plant for the cool greenhouse, thriving in a proprietary peat compost. Grow under well-ventilated conditions and in full light. Propagate by cuttings of small, lateral shoots in summer. S. Africa.

DIPLADENIA (ASCLEPIADACEAE)

Showy, evergreen woody climbers with twining stems and trumpet-shaped flowers during the summer. They may be grown in the warm greenhouse border or in pots trained to a structure of wires or sticks. Use a loam-based or an equivalent peat compost. Propagate by cuttings of 3 in. long stem sections comprising one pair of leaves, and insert in a case with bottom heat during spring.

boliviensis

A small, slender climbing plant with clusters of 3–4 beautiful, 2 in. white flowers with yellow. They are set off by the shining green, oval, slender pointed 2–3 in. leaves. Bolivia.

splendens syn. **Mandevilla splendens**

A striking plant with shining, broad leaves which is covered in summer by 6–8 in. clusters of rose-pink flowers, which open singly in succession. It grows well when twined around wire or twiggy supports, eventually reaching 15 ft if allowed. It will however flower when only 9 in. high, making a good pot plant. Brazil. **193.**

DISSOTIS (MELASTOMATACEAE)
plumosa syn. **D. rotundifolia**

A small, shrubby, prostrate plant rooting from its stems as it spreads. The broad oval leaves are up to 1½ in. long, and the 5-petalled, purple-pink flowers are solitary, with petals slightly reflexed. They appear in summer. Suitable for a warm greenhouse where it grows best in a peat or loam-based compost. It needs some shading from the sun in summer and the atmosphere should be kept moist. Propagate by cuttings in spring. Sierra Leone.

DIZYGOTHECA (ARALIACEAE)
elegantissima False Aralia

As an excellent ornamental foliage plant to 4 ft or more high, ideal for the house and warm greenhouse when young. In its juvenile state it has graceful leaves, divided from the centre into 7–10 leaflets each of which is cut into lobed segments, and which is a metallic, coppery colour. As the plant matures the leaves become dark green and its height increases, eventually becoming a small tree. Some shade from direct sun is needed during the summer, and the plants should be repotted at least every second year. Propagate by seeds sown in early spring. New Hebrides. **194.**

DOMBEYA (STERCULIACEAE)

A genus of evergreen shrubs resembling *Abutilon*, with heart-shaped or maple-like leaves and flowers borne in dense spherical heads. They require cool greenhouse conditions and large pots of a loam-based compost to thrive well. Ideally, they should be planted out in a border and trained out on a wall or pillar. Propagate by cuttings of young shoots in spring.

× **cayeuxii** (*D. mastersii* × *D. wallichii*)

An attractive shrub with dark green heart-shaped leaves, distinctly net-veined, and dense, 3–4 in. pendent clusters of rose-pink blooms which are richly fragrant and open in winter. Garden origin.

mastersii

A similar plant to the species described above having softer, more velvety leaves and fragrant white flowers with a faint rose-pink flush. Tropical Africa.

Doxantha unguis-cati see **Bignonia unguis-cati**

DRACAENA (LILIACEAE)

Evergreen foliage shrubs or trees with a somewhat palm-like appearance. They make fine pot plants, being grown for their colourfully variegated leaves. Some kinds are suitable for the cool greenhouse or home, others for warmer situations. Grow in a loam-based compost and shade from direct sun in summer. Propagate by suckers or 3 in. stem sections in a warm case in spring or summer.

deremensis

A handsome plant with striking leaves, 18 in. long and sword-shaped, with 2 silvery-white bands running the length of the dark-green, glossy leaves. It is a good house or warm greenhouse plant. Africa. **195.**

'Bausei' has one central white stripe on the dark green leaf.

draco Dragon Tree

A curious tree which makes a very decorative plant in its juvenile stages, up to about 3 ft high. It has thick, smooth, fleshy leaves with a translucent margin. A fully grown specimen can reach 60 ft. It tolerates cool conditions. Unlike the other species mentioned here it needs full light. Canary Isles.

fragrans

A warmth loving species with arching leaves having green and gold

stripings, arranged variously in a number of cultivars. Guinea. **196.**
   'Massangeana', has a central golden-yellow stripe with mid-green
   margins.

godseffiana Gold-dust Dracaena
A charming, small-leaved species suitable for the home. It has branching, wiry stems carrying 3 in. oval, laurel-like leaves in twos or threes.
Each leaf is a deep, glossy green, spotted with yellow. Small, yellow-
green flowers are occasionally produced, and are followed by red
berries. Congo. **197.**

marginata syn. **Cordyline marginata** Madagascar Dragon Tree
A tree-like species which makes a durable house plant while young. The
long, narrow rigid leaves can reach 18 in. and are dark green, edged
with red; they are carried on a slender stem forming a dense, terminal
rosette. At maturity the plant can reach 4–5 ft in height and develops a
thick trunk. Madagascar.
   'Variegata', an attractive cultivar with dark green cream-striped
   leaves, **198.**

sanderiana Ribbon Plant
A good pot plant for the home with 7–10 in. narrow, arching leaves
growing from the 18 in. stem. Leaf markings are somewhat variable,
but the coloration is usually a grey-green with broad, white margins.
At maturity the plant can reach 7–10 ft and if kept in large pots makes
a very striking plant for the warm or cool greenhouse.

terminalis see **Cordyline terminalis**

Dragon Tree see **Dracaena draco**
Dragon Tree, Madagascar see **Dracaena marginata**
Drejerella see **Beloperone**

DROSERA (DROSERACEAE) Sundew
Intriguing carnivorous plants, the leaves of which bear prominent red-
tipped sticky glands which trap small insects. Once a capture is made,
the leaf folds over the victim and enzymes break down the body tissues.
Nitrogen and other compounds are released and then absorbed by the
leaf tissue. Droseras grow in heathy or boggy areas where nitrogen is
almost lacking. Grow in a mixture of equal parts peat and chopped
sphagnum moss in pans placed in a cool greenhouse or room. Water
regularly from spring to autumn, sparingly in winter. Propagate by
division or seeds in spring.

binata
A slender plant, 6–18 in. in height with long-stalked, reddish, narrow
leaves deeply cut into two lobes and covered with sticky, glandular
hairs to which small insects are attracted. It has large, white flowers
in a long-stalked spike, opening from June to September. Australia.

capensis
A more squat plant than the preceding species attaining only 6 in. in
height. The leaves are linear-oblong, uncut and borne on a long stalk
and equipped with hairs similar to those described above. The flowers,
which open in June and July are purple. S. Africa. **199.**

Dudleya cotyledon see **Echeveria cotyledon**
Dumb Cane see **Dieffenbachia**
Dutchman's Breeches see **Dicentra spectabilis**
Dutchman's Pipe see **Aristolochia**
Dwarf Lily Turf see **Ophiopogon japonicus**
Dwarf Mountain Palm see **Chamaedorea elegans**
Dwarf Painted Feather see **Vriesea psittacina**

E

Easter Lily see **Lilium longiflorum**
Easter Orchid see **Cattleya mossiae**

ECCREMOCARPUS (BIGNONIACEAE)
scaber Chilean Glory Flower
A colourful, fast growing climber with ribbed stems which can reach
10–15 ft. It has fast growing dark green compound leaves, the central
stalk of which ends in a tendril. From June to October the whole plant

is covered with spikes of vivid orange, 1 in. tubular flowers. Chile. **200.**

ECHEVERIA (CRASSULACEAE)
Attractive house and greenhouse plants grown mainly for their rosettes
of fleshy leaves. Some species are used for summer bedding. The bell-
shaped flowers, usually about 1 in. long, are borne on branching stems
arising from among the leaves in the rosette. The leaves have a waxy
bloom, which is easily dislodged by handling, and many are brightly
toned in dry conditions. Water freely in summer but keep moisture
away from the leafy rosettes; feed occasionally with liquid manure of
a high potash type. Root offsets in March under glass protection; take
leaf cuttings in July, or propagate from new shoots which form after the
old plants are cut back after flowering. Winter in a cold frame in a
minimum temperature of 41–45°F.

agavoides syn. **Cotyledon agavoides**
The rosettes are composed of 3 in. long, brown-tipped, pointed leaves
which turn outwards like those of an agave. In full sun the whole leaf
turns brownish-red. The flower stem is 18 in. long and topped with
red and yellow blooms in July. Mexico.

cotyledon syn. **Cotyledon californica, Dudleya cotyledon**
In summer the whitish-yellow flower sprays arise from a rosette of
3–4 in. long, strap-shaped leaves which are powdery white and of great
interest. California.

derenbergii
The rosettes are 2–3 in. across, with leaves rounded underneath but
flat on the upper surface. They are spoon-shaped, pale green with a
greyish tinge and tipped with red. The reddish-yellow flowers grow on
3–5 in. stems in June. Mexico.

elegans see **E. harmsii**
fulgens see **E. retusa**

gibbiflora
The blue-mauve leaves are 5–10 in. in length, spoon-shaped and keeled
at the base. They form a rosette at the top of the stem, which can reach
a height of 18 in. The reddish-yellow flowers grow on a 20 in. long stem
arising from the leaf rosette during the autumn and winter, but they
are infrequent in cultivation. Mexico.
   metallica, has redder-toned leaves with a metallic sheen. More
   popular than the type.

glauca syn. **E. secunda glauca**
A good house plant, also very attractive in summer bedding schemes.
The tight leafy rosettes are 4 in. in diameter, the leaves themselves
being ¾ in. across with a heavy waxy coating, giving them a grey
appearance. The yellow, red-tipped flowers are freely produced in
summer on a stalk 6–8 in. long. Mexico.

harmsii syn. **E. elegans, Cotyledon elegans, Oliveranthus
elegans**
The 12–18 in. long flower stems are topped with red, yellow-tipped
blooms in summer. The leaf rosettes, 2–3 in. across, are composed of
strap-shaped leaves with pointed ends and covered with fine soft hairs.
Mexico. **201.**

retusa syn. **E. fulgens**
An attractive summer flowering plant with bright scarlet flowers on
stems 18 in. long arising from the loosely set rosettes of bluish-green,
wavy-edged leaves. These are about 2 in. long and ¾ in. wide. Mexico.

runyonii
The small rosettes of 3 in. spoon-shaped, bluish-green leaves form
offsets freely. The pink flowers appear in September. Water sparingly,
otherwise the foliage tends to lose its blue tints and become soft and
green. Mexico.

shaviana
A very beautiful species with a tightly packed rosette of incurved
leaves having pinkish, transparent margins. The rosettes reach about
4 in. across. Mexico.

secunda glauca see **E. glauca**

setosa
Attractive white hairs cover the leaves which form 3 in. high, stemless
rosettes. The red, yellow-tipped flowers are borne on 3–4 in. long stems
at any time during the summer, though not freely in cultivation.
Mexico.

ECHINOCACTUS (CACTACEAE)

Grown for their attractive spines, these round to cylindrical cacti need a position in full light to flourish. Set the plants in small pots initially, but as they grow, pot them on until they are finally in 6–12 in. containers, according to species. For culture see under terrestrial cacti in the Introduction. Use a compost that drains freely, such as 1 part sharp sand to 2 parts loam-based compost. Give plenty of air in summer and water freely throughout the growing season. Keep fairly dry from October to March. Minimum winter temperature 45°F. Propagate by seeds sown in spring in gentle heat in a propagating frame.

grusonii Golden Barrel
Probably the most handsome species, forming a 3 ft ball of whitish-yellow spines, up to 2 in. long when mature. It has about 30 ribs. Growing slowly, the plants seldom produce their 2 in. diameter yellow flowers in cultivation. These form in the white woolly crown at the top and open in May. Mexico. **202.**

horizonthalonius
The pink, 2 in. wide funnel-shaped flowers form freely in April and May, even on young plants. This species grows to about 10 in. tall, is globe-shaped and blue-grey in colour, with 7–13 pronounced ribs set with golden-yellow spines. Water carefully and never when the soil is wet as soggy compost can rot the roots. Texas, Arizona, Mexico.

minuscula see **Rebutia minuscula**

ECHINOCEREUS (CACTACEAE)

This genus is unusual among cacti in that the branches begin to form deeply within the main stem and break out through the outer skin. The flowers develop on the areoles as usual, but only on the sides of stems, never on top. They are often large, usually scarlet, crimson or purple in colour and appear in summer. The spiny fruits are edible. The stems are round or cylindrical, ribbed, with spiny areoles. For culture see terrestrial cacti in the Introduction. Plants do best in wide shallow pans, 6–8 in. across, in well-drained soil. Water freely in summer but keep completely dry from October to March. Minimum winter temperature 38–40°F. Propagate by seed sown shallowly in pots of gritty compost in early spring and germinate in a temperature of 70°F. Alternatively, take stem cuttings of branching species from April to August.

engelmannii
Forms a large clump of erect cylindrical stems, 4–10 in. high, with 11–14 ribs. All spines are yellowish-brown or white, the 10–12 radials spreading, the 5–6 centrals curved and very stout. The flowers are red-purple and up to 3 in. across. S.W. United States.

knippelianus
The dark green, globular to oval stems are about 2 in. across and slow growing. The woolly areoles develop 1–3 small white bristle-like spines. The funnel-shaped flowers, about 1½ in. long, are brown outside and carmine-violet inside. Mexico.

pectinatus
The rounded to columnar stems branch from the base and grow to 9 in. high, 2–2½ in. wide. They are greenish in colour and covered with short white spines, about 25–30 to each areole. Cerise pink flowers are 2½–3½ in. long and develop into wide bells in June. C. Mexico.

pentalophus
About 5 in. high and 1 in. wide, the green sprawling stems have 5 ribs, ridged along the crest; sometimes spiral. The woolly areoles bear 3–5 whitish radial spines, about 1 in. long, but no centrals. Rosy-pink, bell-shaped blooms, about 4 in. long, appear in mid-summer. Mexico.

pentalophus procumbens see **E. procumbens**

procumbens syn. **E. pentalophus procumbens**
Easily grown and forming a low, spreading plant with prostrate stems, 6 in. long and ¾ in. wide. The 4–5 ribs are usually spirally arranged. Up to 8 short spines are borne on each of the closely set areoles. The funnel-shaped flowers are freely produced, about 3 in. across and 4 in. long, violet-red in colour but whitish at the base. Mexico.

rosei
The large clumps are 4–8 in. high and have 8–11 ribs. The whole stem is covered with areoles each bearing reddish spines and becoming grey with age. The flowers are 1½–2½ in. long and a bright scarlet. Mexico. **203.**

scheeri
The dark green, glossy stems, erect or sprawling, are 4–9 in. long and 1 in. thick. There are 7–9 short, yellowish radial spines to each areole, and 3 longer centrals, brown, tipped with red. The pink, funnel-shaped flowers are 4–5 in. long. Mexico.

ECHINOPSIS (CACTACEAE) Sea Urchin Cactus

A delightful range of ball-shaped cacti, becoming cylindrical with age, with flowers that open at evening and last for about 2–3 days. They are tubular, 4–8 in. long, pinkish or white in colour and sometimes richly scented. For culture see under terrestrial cacti in the Introduction. Grow in full light but shade from hottest sun. Fairly hardy if kept dry in winter, and to promote better flowers, at a minimum temperature of 36–40°F. Propagate by offsets, or by seed.

eyriesii
Most species grown under this name are hybrids, the true species being rarely found. The globe-shaped stems, producing numerous offsets, have about 12 sharp ribs and grow to 6 in. across. The areoles are covered with greyish wool and bear reddish-brown spines which darken with age. The flowers are 9 in. long, 2–3 in. across and white in colour, though the hybrids often have a tinge of pink or mauve. S. Brazil.

multiplex
The rounded stems grow to 6 in. high and have 12 sharp ribs bearing the robust brownish spines. The large pinkish flowers are richly scented, 5 in. across and 8 in. long. The stems branch freely and form many offsets at the base. S. Brazil.

rhodacantha now called **Denmoza rhodacantha**
The dark green, 6 in. high spherical stems elongate with age. An attractive species with 12–15 pronounced ribs set with scarlet spines which gradually turn brownish-red, then grey. Stamens, style and stigma protrude brush-like from the 3 in. long scarlet flowers. Argentina.

rhodotricha
Growing to 2½ ft or so, this is one of the larger species. The matt green, oval or cylindrical stems are woolly on top and have 8–12 ribs. Up to 8 brownish-yellow spines arise from each areole, 4–7 radials ¾ in. long, and a single central which can reach 1½ in. in length. The white, unscented flowers, about 6 in. long and 3 in. across, are borne on the side of the stems in early summer. Argentina, Paraguay.

ECHIUM (BORAGINACEAE) Viper's Bugloss

Evergreen plants with bold spikes of flowers, and suitable for a sunny, airy, cool greenhouse. Use a loam-based compost and large pots or tubs, or plant out in the border. Propagate by seeds or cuttings of short, non-flowering lateral shoots in summer.

bourgeauanum syn. **E. wildpretii**
An attractive biennial with long silvery hairy, mid-green, narrow leaves from which rises a flowering stem sometimes exceeding 6 ft in height. This takes the form of a pyramidal spire made up of short branches of rose-pink, tubular flowers, often blue-tinted, which open from May to July. Canary Isles.

callithyrsum
A bristly, very robust species having a woody stem and lance-shaped, mid-green leaves with prominent veins. The flowers which appear in May and June are from pink through all shades to violet, and are borne in large, branching spikes. Canary Isles.

fastuosum
A 2–4 ft well-branched shrub having the stem clothed with ranks of down-pointing, long narrow evergreen leaves which are white downy. The deep blue flowers are carried in dense broad spires on leafy stems and appear from April to August. Canary Isles. **204.**

wildpretti see **E. bourgeauanum**

Edelweiss, Brazilian see **Rechsteineria leucotricha**
Egg Plant see **Solanum melongena**
Egyptian Paper Rush see **Cyperus papyrus**
Egyptian Star Cluster see **Pentas lanceolata**

EICHHORNEA (PONTEDERIACEAE)
speciosa syn. **E. crassipes** Floating Water Hyacinth
A beautiful evergreen floating plant which can be put in outdoor pools

during the summer, but needs greenhouse protection in winter. The plant floats by means of the inflated and spongy bases to the rosettes of roundish glossy green leaves. The lavender-blue flowers have a golden eye and are carried in long spikes, which are held stiffly above the water in summer. Increase by removing the new plants which grow on the stolons produced during the summer. Tropical America.

Elder, Yellow see **Tecoma stans**
Elephant Ear Begonia see **Begonia haageana**
Elephant's Ear see **Philodendron hastatum**
Elephant's Foot see **Dioscorea elephantipes**
Elk-horn Fern, Regal see **Platycerium grande**
Emerald Ripple see **Peperomia caperata**
English Ivy see **Hedera helix**

EPIDENDRUM (ORCHIDACEAE)

A genus of orchids of diverse habit, some with short plump bulbs, others with long cane-like ones. The mainly small flowers are borne in dense terminal spikes and can be brightly coloured. Grow in a compost of equal parts osmunda fibre and sphagnum moss. Propagate by division, or cuttings of the cane-stemmed kinds after flowering.

brassavolae ✳
A graceful orchid with small, pear-shaped bulbs from which rise erect, 18 in. stalks bearing in July and August, clusters of very fragrant, somewhat spidery, flowers with long, narrow straw-yellow petals and a white or pale yellow lip, purplish towards the point. It needs a cool greenhouse to thrive. Guatemala, Costa Rica. **205.**

ciliare ✳
A delicately flowered species with short bulbs and 10 in. stems carrying up to 8 flowers. The petals are pale green, long, narrow and somewhat reflexed. The pale blue or white lip has a long slender central and deeply fringed outer lobes. For the cool greenhouse. Tropical America.

cochleatum Cockle-shell Orchid ✳
A cool greenhouse plant often also grown as a house plant where the temperature remains above 55°F. It has pear-shaped bulbs and erect flower spikes bearing curious blooms which have narrow greenish-white petals and a deep purple black-violet veined lip. The latter is shaped like a cockle-shell, and owing to the fact that the flower stalks are twisted, is at the top of the bloom. Flowers are produced spasmodically throughout the year, but are at their best from January to July. W. Indies, Central America.

crassilabium see **E. variegatum**

endresii ✳
This species has slender bulbs up to 12 in. high and an erect spike with up to 15 flowers, the petals white with violet or green tips and the 4-lobed lip blotched and spotted purple and orange. The blooms appear from January to May and the plant needs cool greenhouse conditions. Costa Rica.

falcatum see **E. parkinsonianum**

fragrans ✳
A spicily fragrant species with 2–4 in. bulbs each bearing only 1 leaf. The individual flower stalks are twisted, making the 2 in. waxy-white blooms appear upside down. The lip is heart-shaped and striped with red-purple lines. A plant for the cool greenhouse. Tropical America.

ibaguense syn. **E. radicans** ✳
A distinctive plant with a cane-like, leafy stem reaching 3 ft or more. The leaves are pale green and fleshy, and the long stems terminate in a brilliant globular or ovoid cluster of 1 in. flowers, ranging in colour from orange to red, and sometimes pink or lilac. Many hybrids have been raised, in varying combinations of colours. Grows well in the cool or warm greenhouse. Colombia, Peru, Guatemala, Mexico. **206.**

nocturnum ✳
A species with a strong fragrance at night, it has usually solitary, pale yellow or greenish-white blooms, 5 in. across with narrow, shapely petals and a white 3-lobed lip, the central lobe slender and pointed, the lateral lobes shorter, triangular. The flowers appear over the year, though are most frequent from March to May, and are borne on 1½–2 ft stout stems. A warm greenhouse plant. Tropical America.

parkinsonianum syn. **E. falcatum** ✳
A plant with pendulous stems which must be grown in a hanging basket or raft. It has narrow, fleshy, tapering leaves and 2–5 flowers, up to 4 in. across, at the end of the 12 in. stems. The blooms have narrow, creamy-white petals and a white or cream, 3-lobed lip with a narrowly triangular, pointed central lobe. Good for a cool greenhouse. Mexico.

prismatocarpum Rainbow Orchid ✳
A striking fragrant species for the cool greenhouse with narrowed bulbs bearing 2, 1 ft, mid-green leaves and 15 in. spikes of 10–20 very decorative, long lasting, waxy flowers. These are 2 in. across, the petals a yellowish-green with deep maroon blotches and a narrow, pointed rose to purple lip having a white margin and a yellow tip. The flowers are produced from May to August. Central America.

radicans see **E. ibaguense**

variegatum syn. **E. crassilabium, E. vespa** ✳
A species with 6–9 in. bulbs having long, narrow, thin-textured leaves. The 12 in. stems carry numerous, fragrant blooms which have pale yellow-green petals marked with brownish rose, and a small white or pale rose lip. It flowers during the winter and does best in the cool greenhouse. S. America.

vespa see **E. variegatum**

EPIPHYLLUM (CACTACEAE)

This genus of epiphytic cacti is not a large one, and was formerly known as *Phyllocactus*, an invalid name. Unfortunately there is some confusion, because the plants formerly known as *Epiphyllum* (and still so labelled from some German nurseries) are now included in *Schlumbergera*. Although few of the species are suitable for the amateur's greenhouse, the hybrids, which include hybrids with other genera such as *Heliocereus*, *Selenicereus*, and *Nopalxochia*, are among the most beautiful and easy greenhouse and room plants, having gorgeous flowers, in some cases 6–7 in. across, in a wide range of colours, and many are deliciously scented. Unless otherwise stated, the main flowering period is May and June, but sometimes there is a second flowering period in autumn, when the colours are sometimes different. The usual height is 1–2 ft, and the plants are normally staked. There are no true leaves, but the stems are usually flattened so that they have the appearance of thick leaves of a mid-green colour. The habit of growth is to replace the old stems with fresh growth from the base, unusual in cacti. Culture as for epiphytic cacti, see Introduction, and fierce sunshine should be avoided. Minimum winter temperature 35°F. unless otherwise stated.

ackermannii syn. **Nopalxochia ackermannii** ✳
This species has weak, flat stems, and large crimson flowers, about 4 in. across, in summer. It is rare and not recommended for amateurs, but mentioned here as the parent of many beautiful hybrids. The plant widely grown under this name is a hybrid, see below. Probably Mexico.

anguliger ✳ ☙
Grown mainly for the stems, which are flattened with deeply serrated margins, and for the scent of the small papery-white flowers, 4 in. long and 1½–2 in. across, produced in autumn. The scent is rich, and unlike that of the hybrids mentioned below, persists for several days. Mexico.

oxypetalum ✳
This plant grows 3–4 ft tall and has flattened, very leaf-like stems. The large white flowers, 3–4 in. across, open at dusk, so rapidly that the movement is often seen. It is popular in the southern United States as a room plant; also in Malaya where much folk lore has grown up around it. Mexico, Guatemala, Venezuela, Brazil.

strictum ✳
The flattened stems bear the extremely elegant large white flowers in early summer. These are 3–4 in. across with narrow petals, pale yellow anthers, carmine style and deep yellow stigma. They last but a single night, and a winter temperature of 50°F. is needed. Mexico, Guatemala to Panama.

truncatum see **Schlumbergera truncata**

Hybrids ✳
There are probably thousands of hybrids, mostly of British, United States or German origin. Unrooted cuttings are a convenient way of buying, since they root easily (see propagation of epiphytic cacti in the Introduction) and travel well. A brief selection of varieties follows:
× *ackermannii*, very floriferous and popular, probably a hybrid

between *Heliocereus speciosus* and *E. ackermannii*, with which it is often confused. Stems triangular, moderately spiny, 18 in. long; flowers flame-red, of medium size. **207.**

'London Beauty' is a clone of this hybrid, with flame-red flowers in May, and azalea-pink flowers in autumn.

'Carl von Nicolai', pink. **208;**

'Cooperi', with large white, strongly scented flowers. Very popular. **209;**

'Doctor Werdermann', vermilion with blue sheen;

'Eastern Gold', yellow, waved petals, **211;**

'Little Sister', white;

'London', mixed varieties, **210;**

'London Delight', salmon flushed rose in summer, orange-red with blue sheen in autumn;

'London Gaiety', salmon-pink outer petals, shading to rose-pink in centre. Very floriferous, **212;**

'London Glory', flame-red with magenta overlay. Very easy and reliable;

'London Magic', pale rose-pink;

'London Majestic', outer petals purple, shading to pink in centre. Strongly scented;

'London Sunshine', yellow, scented;

'Midnight', deep purple;

'Padre', large pink flowers, often at odd times;

'Professor Ebert', large, mauve;

'Reward', large, deep yellow;

'Sunburst', large, orange;

'Thalia', orange-red, overlaid magenta, **213.**

EPISCIA (GESNERIACEAE)

Trailing evergreen plants for the warm greenhouse or home, grown for their ornamental foliage and small colourful flowers. They are suitable for hanging baskets or pans and grows well in the proprietary peat composts. Shade from direct sunshine during the spring to autumn period and maintain a humid atmosphere. Propagate by division or cuttings in spring or summer.

chontalensis syn. **E. lilacina**

A 6 in. plant with oval leaves, pale green above and a dull purple beneath. The attractive flowers are tubular with 5 broad, spreading lobes about 2 in. across, white or lilac tinged, with a yellow eye, and are produced in November and December. Nicaragua.

cupreata

A distinctive creeping plant grown chiefly for its multicoloured foliage. The downy, wrinkled, ovate leaves are mid-green with a red and silver band down the centre. There are many named cultivars with different patterning. The flowers are scarlet and carried singly or in small clusters. Colombia, Venezuela.

'Metallica', coppery leaves with silvery markings, and orange-scarlet flowers;

'Silver Sheen', bright, silvery leaves with coppery margins and orange-red flowers. **214.**

dianthiflora

A charming small plant with small, 1–1½ in. dark green, softly hairy leaves and delicate white, shining flowers, the margins of which are deeply fringed. Summer flowering. Mexico. **215.**

fulgida syn. **E. reptans**

A small plant bearing 3–5 in. ovate, wrinkled, dark green, almost copper-coloured leaves, having paler contrasting mid-rib and lateral veins. The flowers, which appear in July, are flame-coloured with narrowly fringed petals. N.S. America, Brazil. **216.**

lilacina see **E. chontalensis**
reptans see **E. fulgida**

ERANTHEMUM (ACANTHACEAE)

atropurpureum see **Pseuderanthemum atropurpureum**

pulchellum syn. **E. nervosum** Blue Sage

A small 2–4 ft shrub with 4–8 in. rough, oval leaves having prominently marked veins. The dark blue flowers have a purple eye. Valuable for its winter flowering habit. It needs warm greenhouse culture, and as the foliage is best in young plants, is often raised annually from cuttings taken in spring. India.

ERICA (ERICACEAE) Heath

Evergreen shrubs grown for their freely produced bell-shaped flowers in a wide variety of colours. A well ventilated, sunny, cool greenhouse is needed and a lime-free peat compost. Propagate by cuttings of young lateral stems in late summer. Species are often given the incorrect common name of Heather (*Calluna*).

canaliculata syn. **E. melanthera** Christmas Heather

A 2 ft winter flowering shrub with tiny needle-like, hairless leaves and abundantly produced clusters of white or pinkish, open bell-shaped flowers showing conspicuous black anthers. S. Africa. **217.**

cerinthoides Red Hairy Heath

A rich crimson-flowered species with 2–2½ in. dense clusters of blooms borne on the downy shoots from May to October. The typical, heather-like leaves grow in whorls of 4–6 on the twiggy branches. Grown in a large pot or tub this shrub reaches 2–3 ft in height. S. Africa.

coccinea

An erect shrub to 2 ft or more, bearing clusters of pendulous, long tubular bells which, though usually red, can be orange, yellow or green. They appear from August to October, sometimes earlier and later. S. Africa.

gracilis syn. **E. nivalis** Rose Heath

A dainty, bushy shrub rarely exceeding 18 in. with pale green leaves and from October to January an abundance of clusters of tiny rose bells which are very long lasting. S. Africa.

'Alba', a white form sometimes called *E. nivalis*.

× **hyemalis**

An erect species growing to 2 ft with needle-like mid-green leaves and terminal racemes of ¾ in. tubular white flowers having a rose-pink flush; they open from November to January. Unknown garden origin.

mammosa Red Signal Heath

A 4 ft shrub with leaves in fours and tubular flowers which are reddish-purple, bright red or white and grow in pendulous, dense clusters. They are produced from July to October. S. Africa.

massonii

A 1–3 ft shrub having densely packed thread-like leaves which end in a hair point. The clusters of 10 or 12 flowers are somewhat sticky, reddish-orange, darker at the base of the petals and becoming paler towards the tips; they are produced in summer. S. Africa.

melanthera see **E. canaliculata**
nivalis see **E. gracilis**

tumida

A stocky, glandular shrub bearing a profusion of large tubular orange flowers from June to October. S. Africa.

Eriocnema marmorata see **Bertolonia marmorata**

ERVATAMIA (APOCYNACEAE)
coronaria Crape Jasmine

A handsome 5–8 ft shrub, reminiscent of a gardenia, having glossy green, elliptic leaves 3–5 in. long. The 1½–2 in. waxy white flowers have wavy-edged petals and are borne in small clusters. It is a very fragrant species, especially at night. Grow in pots or tubs of a loam-based or proprietary peat compost and shade from direct sunlight in summer. Maintain humidity and ventilate on warm days. Propagate by lateral stem cuttings, preferably with a heel, in summer. India.

ERYTHRINA (LEGUMINOSAE) Coral Tree

Trees or shrubs, often prickly, bearing large spikes of showy red pea-shaped flowers. They make good plants for the cool greenhouse, preferably in large pots or tubs. Planted in the border they will get too large for the smaller greenhouse. Use a loam-based compost, keep moist during the growing period and almost dry in winter. Propagate by seeds or cuttings of young shoots in spring.

corallodendron

A prickly, woody plant which will reach 6–12 ft, with leaves of 3 broad, pointed leaflets on short, thornless stalks and superb, long, pendent clusters of scarlet flowers which are produced in May and June after the leaves have fallen. W. Indies.

crista-galli Cockspur Coral Tree ✳
A most spectacular small tree for the cool greenhouse, eventually reaching 10 ft. The leathery, grey-green leaves have 3 leaflets, borne on spiny stalks, while the dense spikes of waxy, 2 in. flowers are a vivid scarlet, and are produced in June and July. Brazil. **217.**

'Compacta', a dwarf form.

EUCALYPTUS (MYRTACEAE) Gum Tree, Iron-bark Tree
Handsome trees grown mainly for their decorative and aromatic foliage. Some species are also very showy when in flower. They are too big for all but the largest greenhouse but make attractive pot or tub plants when young. Grow in a loam-based compost and keep in a well ventilated greenhouse in full light. Propagate by seeds sown in spring and make sure the young plants never become dry or rootbound.

citriodora Lemon-scented Gum 🐌
A shrub or small silver-barked tree noted for its delightful lemon scented leaves. Grow in pots in a large greenhouse where it will fill the air with its fragrance. In the young stage its leaves are ovate, 3–6 in. long, at maturity becoming spear-shaped. It has small terminal clusters of 3–5 petalless flowers. Queensland.

ficifolia Red Gum, Scarlet Flowering Gum ✳ 🐌
A richly coloured tree becoming 20 ft or more in height at maturity. The juvenile leaves are long ovate, the adult are up to 6 in. in length, long and narrow with slender points. The flowers are borne in clusters 6–7 in. across, each having no petals, but comprising a mass of scarlet stamens carrying deep red anthers. They are produced in August. S.W. Australia.

globulus Blue Gum ✳ 🐌
A species with attractive foliage which is grown in its young state for the blue-grey, oval leaves which are heart-shaped at the base and clasp the stem. After the third year, long, narrow, deep green leaves grow, making a good foil for the globular heads of creamy-white flowers which are borne in winter and spring. It can eventually reach 50 ft or more. Victoria, Australia; Tasmania. **219.**

EUCHARIS (AMARYLLIDACEAE)
grandiflora syn. **E. amazonica** Amazon Lily ✳
A superb bulbous plant, bearing 8 in. broadly ovate, glossy green leaves and shining, white star-like fragrant flowers with a short tube and 6, wide-spreading lobes, up to 5 in. across. They are carried on 2 ft stems in clusters of 3–6 blooms which open in summer or irregularly at other times. It needs a warm, humid atmosphere and is best grown in large pots. Propagate by removing offsets from the bulbs in spring. Colombia. **220.**

× **EUCODONOPSIS** syn. × **ACHIMENANTHA** (GESNERIACEAE) ✳
A charming group of plants derived from crossing *Smithiantha* and *Achimenes*. Branched stems and bell-like to tubular flowers resemble a blend of the parent plants. They are suitable as pot plants for the home or cool greenhouse and need the same treatment as *Smithiantha*.

EUCOMIS (LILIACEAE) Pineapple Flower
Striking bulbous members of the lily family having rosettes of strap-shaped leaves and dense columnar spikes of starry flowers. Grow in cool greenhouse borders or in pots. A loam-based compost gives good results. Plant the bulbs 3 in. deep in spring, watering sparingly until growth appears. Keep almost dry when the plants die down in autumn and repot each spring. The leafy bracts above the flowers give the genus its English name.

bicolor ✳
A robust species with oblong, upright leaves with a closely-waved margin. The dense oblong clusters of pale green flowers are 3–4 in. long and the petals have a narrow, purple edge. Natal.

comosa syn. **E. punctata**
The long narrow leaves of this species are up to 2 ft long and spotted with purple beneath. The small green flowers are borne in a cylindrical spike up to 12 in. long in July or later. Excellent as a cut flower lasting for weeks in water. S. Africa. **221.**

pole-evansii Giant Pineapple Flower ✳
A tall species which can reach 6 ft but is usually nearer 3 ft in height.

The leaves have wavy margins and the 12 in. dense, flowering spike carries greenish-white blooms. Berries following the flowers remain ornamental for months. Swaziland.

punctata see **E. comosa**

zambesiaca Pineapple Lily ✳
The bright green leaves of this species are purple spotted beneath, and the greenish, waxy flowers are borne in late summer in a dense cylindrical spike, topped by a rosette of green bracts with red margins. E. Africa.

EUGENIA (MYRTACEAE)
A genus of evergreen shrubs and trees, some species being suitable as pot or tub plants for cool and warm greenhouses. The flowers have a large central boss composed of numerous coloured stamens which in some species are followed by edible fruits. Grow in a loam-based compost or an equivalent peat mixture and shade from the hottest summer sunshine. Propagate by cuttings of lateral shoots in summer or seeds in spring.

brasiliensis syn. **E. dombeyi** ✳ ●
A small tree with dark green, oblong leaves 3–5 in. long and 1–2 in. wide. The clear white flowers are carried in leafy, terminal clusters each comprising 2–6 blooms, and are produced in April, followed by small, round berries which can be red, white or deep purple. Brazil.

dombeyi see **E. brasiliensis**

jambolana syn. **Syzygium cuminii** ✳ ●
A tall shrub with 6 in. oval leaves and large pyramidal spikes of fragrant flowers, composed of smaller round heads each bearing a number of small, red flowers. They are produced in August, while in autumn the plant bears roundish 1½ in. deep purple edible fruits of pleasant flavour. Tropical Asia.

EUPATORIUM (COMPOSITAE) Mist Flowers
Shrubby or herbaceous plants with handsome foliage and pretty clusters of small flower heads. The shrubby species described here are suitable for the cool greenhouse border and make good pot plants for the home while in bloom. Grow in a loam-based compost and shade from the hottest summer sun. Propagate by cuttings of lateral shoots taken in spring.

atrorubens ✳ 🐌
An autumn and winter flowering species bearing abundant, reddish, lilac-tinged flowers in loose clusters and large, toothed, oval leaves with a covering of reddish hairs. Mexico. **222.**

ianthinum syn. **E. sordidum** Violet Mist Flower ✳ 🐌
A 3 ft winter flowering species having purple flowers growing in large terminal clusters and with large, softly hairy leaves which are coarsely toothed. Mexico.

ligustrinum see **E. micranthum**

micranthum syn. **E. ligustrinum** ✳ 🐌
A large, bushy shrub which normally reaches 5 ft or more in height. It has 2–4 in. narrowly elliptical leaves and 8 in. flattish clusters of fragrant, white or rose-tinged flowers on hairy stalks. These are produced from September to November. Mexico.

sordidum see **E. ianthinum**

EUPHORBIA (EUPHORBIACEAE) Spurge
A fascinatingly varied group of plants including succulent, herbaceous, and shrubby species, which are suitable for cool and warm greenhouses. The species mentioned here are either shrubs or succulents. The latter group need a cool airy greenhouse with good light and a compost of equal parts of a loam-based compost and grit or coarse sand. Propagate by seeds in spring. The shrubby species can be grown in a loam-based compost or a proprietary peat mix. Propagate by cuttings from cut back plants in spring and grow on in good light with a humid atmosphere. Keep on the dry side in winter and cut back *E. pulcherrima* and *E. fulgens* hard in early spring.

fulgens Scarlet Plume ✳
A beautiful shrub growing to 6 ft or more, but most attractive as a house plant when young. It has long, slender leaves and orange-scarlet

blooms borne along the slender, arching stems, which often also terminate in a cluster of flowers. It can be brought into flower at almost any time of the year. Mexico. **223.**

horrida
A cactus-like plant with angled, fleshy stems bearing spines along the rib-like ridges. The surfaces between are deeply concave. Fully grown it can reach 3 ft in height, but in cultivation is usually much smaller. S. Africa. **224.**

milii splendens Crown of Thorns
A very spiny 3 ft fleshy shrub with sparse, thin, bright green leaves and flat clusters of salmon-red flowers, borne on slightly sticky, red stems, which open in spring. Madagascar. **225.**
   'Bojeri', syn. *E. bojeri*, a dwarf cultivar with grey branches and grey-green leaves. Flowers deep red.

pulcherrima Poinsettia
A showy species very popular for house decoration, especially at Christmas when it is usually at its best. The true leaves are oval to elliptical, or bold, mid-green. The spectacular coloration is found in the scarlet leaf-like bracts which grow like a thick ruff beneath the small, yellow cluster of flowers. To produce really good colour they need both warmth and light. Cultivars with white, pink or crimson bracts are also popular. Mexico. **226.**
   'Mikkel-Rochford Pink', a good form with pink bracts. **227.**

resinifera
A hummock forming shrub, 16 in. high, branched from the base, each branch erect, 4-angled and bearing pairs of spines. The surfaces between the angles are concave at first, becoming smoother later, and grey-green. Morocco. **228.**

European Fan Palm see **Chamaerops humilis**

EXACUM (GENTIANACEAE)
Bushy, leafy, annual or short lived perennial plants grown for their freely borne, small rounded blooms and lustrous foliage. They make good pot plants for the house or cool greenhouse. Grow in a proprietary peat or loam-based compost. Propagate by seeds sown in spring or summer.

affine Persian Violet
A charming, compact, bushy plant about 6 in. high with shining, ovate, deep green leaves and abundantly covered from June to November with 1 in. saucer-shaped, fragrant flowers, which are lavender-blue with deep yellow stamens. Socotra.
   'Midget', a delightful form, smaller in all parts, **229.**

macranthum
A larger plant than *E. affine* reaching 18 in. It has 2 in., deep blue-purple blooms with similar conspicuous bright yellow stamens. These are borne in flat-topped clusters on square stems, and the leaves are narrowly ovate and pointed. Ceylon.

Eyelash Begonia, Miniature see **Begonia boweri**

F

FABIANA (SOLANACEAE)
imbricata
A 3-6 ft heather-like, evergreen shrub with minute, overlapping, triangular leaves on softly hairy shoots. The slender, tubular white or violet flowers are carried in abundance at the ends of the twigs and are produced from June to August. A useful plant for the conservatory, cold or cool greenhouse in a sunny site. Propagate by cuttings taken in late summer. Chile. **230.**

Fairy Lachenalia see **Lachenalia glaucina**
Fairy Primrose see **Primula malacoides**
False African Violet see **Streptocarpus saxorum**
False Aralia see **Dizygotheca elegantissima**
False Globe Amaranth see **Alternanthera dentata**
False Jerusalem Cherry see **Solanum capsicastrum**
False Mallow see **Malvastrum**

Fame Flower see **Talinum**
Fan Palm, European see **Chamaerops humilis**
Fan Palm, Chinese see **Livistona chinensis**

× **FATSHEDERA** (*FATSIA* × *HEDERA*) (ARALIACEAE)
lizei (*Fatsia japonica* 'Moseri' × *Hedera helix* 'Hibernica') Ivy Tree
An evergreen shrub which, if given some support, can reach 6 ft or more. The 5-10 in. leaves are leathery, 3-5 lobed and similar in shape to common ivy. The pale green flowers grow in terminal clusters and open in October and November. A hardy plant in England, it also makes an attractive specimen grown either in a conservatory border, or indoors in pots or tubs of loam-based compost. Pot annually in spring and propagate by stem cuttings in July and August.
   'Variegata', has creamy-white margins to the glossy leaves, **231.**

FATSIA (ARALIACEAE)
japonica syn. **Aralia japonica, A. sieboldii**
A handsome, erect shrub often exceeding 10 ft in height it will survive outdoors in mild localities and sheltered places. It has bright green, glossy 5-9-lobed leaves when mature. Small, round heads of white flowers are arranged in large, loose clusters and appear in late autumn. For pot growth use a loam-based or proprietary peat compost. Propagate by removing suckers in spring for cuttings, or by seed. Japan, Formosa. **232.**

FAUCARIA (AIZOACEAE) Tiger's or Cat's Jaws
Almost stemless greenhouse or conservatory perennials, formerly included in *Mesembryanthemum*, typified by the criss-cross arrangement of thick fleshy leaves. These are edged with jagged teeth, interlocking in young plants, separating later to give the appearance of gaping jaws. Large yellow flowers open in the afternoon. The main growth is in autumn when the plants need plenty of water, but they may be watered freely from May onwards. Keep fairly dry throughout winter at a minimum temperature of 40°F. They enjoy full sun. For further culture see under terrestrial succulents in the Introduction. Divide and repot when clumps become crowded; raise new plants from cuttings or seed. Sow seed in spring in gentle heat, keeping seedlings moist through first winter. Cuttings are quicker and should be taken from June to August. Dry off their stem bases and insert them in a mixture of equal parts sharp sand and moist peat.

felina
Similar to *F. tigrina* but the narrower leaves have fewer white dots and teeth. S. Africa.

tigrina
4-5 pairs of leaves form a cluster 2 in. high and covered with white dots which screen their greyish-green appearance; they have 9-10 hooked teeth terminating in bristles. The bright yellow flowers are 2 in. across and appear in autumn. S. Africa. **233.**

tuberculosa
A fairly large plant, to 6 in. across and about 3 in. high, with 3-4 pairs of dark green leaves. These are covered with white tubercles above and edged with 3-5 stout teeth. The yellow flowers, 1½ in. across, are borne in autumn. S. Africa.

Feather Cactus see **Mammillaria plumosa**
Feather Duster Palm see **Rhopalostylis sapida**
Fern, Asparagus see **Asparagus setaceus**
Fern, Ball see **Davallia mariesii**
Fern, Bird's Nest see **Asplenium nidus**
Fern, Button see **Pellaea rotundifolia**
Fern, Common Maidenhair see **Adiantum capillus-veneris**
Fern, Fishtail see **Cyrtomium falcatum**
Fern, Floating see **Salvinia auriculata**
Fern, Giant Maidenhair see **Adiantum trapeziforme**
Fern, Grotto Lace see **Microlepia speluncae**
Fern, Hare's-foot see **Davallia canariensis** and **Polypodium aureum**
Fern, Hen and Chicken see **Asplenium bulbiferum**
Fern, Holly see **Cyrtomium falcatum** 'Rochfordianum'
Fern, Japanese Painted see **Athyrium goeringianum**

Fern, Maidenhair see **Adiantum**
Fern, Monkey-tail see **Cyathea mexicana**
Fern, Mule's see **Phyllitis hermionitis**
Fern, Necklace see **Asplenium flabelliforme**
Fern Palm see **Cycas circinalis**
Fern Pine, African see **Podocarpus gracilior**
Fern, Ponga see **Cyathea dealbata**
Fern, Regal Elk-horn see **Platycerium grande**
Fern, Rib see **Blechnum brasiliense**
Fern, Sago see **Cyathea medullaris**
Fern, Silver King see **Cyathea dealbata**
Fern, Silver Table see **Pteris ensiformis** 'Victoriae'
Fern, Stag's-horn see **Platycerium**
Fern, Sword see **Nephrolepis**

FEROCACTUS (CACTACEAE)

Round or cylindrical cacti with strikingly coloured prominent spines, often hooked. The stems are sharply ribbed, and the funnel-shaped flowers arise from the top of the plants, but seldom in cultivation. For culture see under terrestrial cacti in the Introduction. They thrive better in the conservatory than the house, as they need full sunlight. Stand plants outside in summer sun to intensify the spine colour. Minimum winter temperature 40°F. and keep very dry. Propagate by seed.

acanthodes
The perfectly spherical blue-green stem has 13–27 ribs and grows to 3 ft tall, becoming cylindrical with age. The woolly areoles have about 10 pink or red radial spines and 4 centrals, which can grow 4–5 in. long, flattened and yellow to reddish with a curved tip. The yellow to orange flowers, 2 in. across, are borne in June and July. S. and Lower California, Arizona, Nevada.

histrix see **F. melocactiformis**

latispinus Devil's Tongue Cactus
Large globose plant, to 12 in. high, with 15–23 ribs and pronounced clusters of 4 stout reddish central spines and 6–12 white or red radials. The lowest central, the 'devil's tongue' spine, grows to $1\frac{1}{4}$ in. long and $\frac{1}{4}$ in. thick. It is hooked and has transverse scoring. The whitish, reddish or purple, sweetly scented flowers, enclosed by papery scales, are produced in summer, though rarely in cultivation. Mexico. **234.**

melocactiformis syn. **F. histrix**
A single globe-shaped stem, 1–2 ft high, elongating with age, develops in cultivation but wild plants often produce offsets. The stems are greeny-blue with up to 25 ribs and areoles bearing reddish spines, 9 or so recurved radials and 1–4 centrals up to $2\frac{1}{2}$ in. in length. Pale yellow flowers, about 2 in. across, appear in June and July. Mexico.

wislizenii
Round cactus whose stems lengthen with age up to $6\frac{1}{2}$ ft. Ribs 13–25, 12–20 very slender whitish or yellow 2 in. long radial spines and 4 yellow to reddish-brown centrals which are longer, very thick and flattened, the lower central tipped with a hook. They are borne on large oval areoles. The bell-shaped flowers, about 2 in. long, are yellow to reddish with green outer petals and produced in summer. Texas, Arizona, Mexico.

FICUS (MORACEAE) Fig

A genus of trees and woody climbers with ornamental foliage. The species described here are good pot plants while young, either in the warm greenhouse or home. Use a loam-based compost or an equivalent peat mix and shade from direct sunlight during the summer. Propagate by stem or leaf-bud cuttings in summer.

benjamina Weeping Fig
An attractive pot or tub plant while small, eventually making a 40 ft tree. The long ovate, slender pointed leaves are shining, light at first, becoming darker as the plants age, and borne on pendulous shoots. India. **235.**

deltoidea see **F. diversifolia**

diversifolia syn. **F. deltoidea** Mistletoe Fig
A slow growing bushy plant with 2 in. leathery, rounded to triangular dark green leaves which are brown-spotted above and fawn below. It has abundant small, dull yellow berry-like fruits which it will produce

when very small, adding to its attraction as a house plant. India. **236.**

elastica Rubber Plant
A frequently grown pot plant which is almost entirely represented in cultivation by forms or cultivars. Tropical Asia.
'Decora', a broad leaved plant with elliptical, shiny, dark green leaves 10–12 in. in length, carried at right angles to the trunk and growing to about 10 ft under tub cultivation. In the wild it makes a superb 100 ft tree. **237;**
'Doescheri', a variegated cultivar with young leaves pale green with a pink flush and white margins. **238;**
'Variegata', creamy-yellow and grey striped on a dark green leaf.

lyrata syn. **F. pandurata** Fiddleleaf Fig
The 1–2 ft fiddle-shaped leathery leaves are dark green and glossy with yellow-green veins and a wavy edge. They are borne towards the top of the stem and make a most decorative plant when young. At maturity this species makes a 40 ft tree. W. Tropical Africa.

pandurata see **F. lyrata**

pumila Climbing Fig
A climbing plant which holds on to walls with small ivy-like roots; as a pot plant it needs some form of support or may be grown as a trailer. The young ovate leaves are small, stiff, dark green and remain while the plant is of manageable size. At maturity it has larger, oblong leaves. China. **239.**

radicans Rooting Fig
A good plant for a basket or where a trailing form of growth is required, it spreads by rooting from the stem and has 2 in. narrow, leathery, slender-pointed leaves. In cultivation it is largely replaced by the variegated cultivar. E. Indies.
'Variegata', the long, narrow leaves have cream margins and blotches. **240.**

religiosa Sacred Bo-tree, Peepul
A distinct species with slender, arching branches bearing pendulous, grey-green, heart-shaped leaves with a curiously elongated tip and marked with light-coloured veins. E. Indies.

Fiddle Leaf see **Philodendron panduriforme**
Fiddleleaf Fig see **Ficus lyrata**
Fiddler's Trumpet see **Sarracenia drummondii**
Fiery Costus see **Costus igneus**
Fig see **Ficus**
Fingernail Plant see **Neoregelia spectabilis**
Fire Bush see **Kochia scoparia trichophylla**
Firecracker Plant see **Manettia inflata**
Fire Lily see **Cyrtanthus sanguineus**
Fire-wheel Tree see **Stenocarpus sinuatus**
Fish Geranium see **Pelargonium** × **hortorum**
Fish-tail Fern see **Cyrtomium falcatum**

FITTONIA (ACANTHACEAE)

Highly ornamental foliage plants, suitable for the warm conservatory, greenhouse or home. The broad, paddle-shaped leaves have a fine network of coloured veins. Shade from direct sunlight and grow in pots or pans of a proprietary peat compost. Propagate by division in summer.

argyroneura Silver Net Leaf
A dwarf herb with ovate, 4 in., bright green leaves beautifully netted with white veins giving a quilted appearance. The inconspicuous flowers are best pinched out, and the plant needs a warm greenhouse to thrive. Considered by some a variety of *F. verschaffeltii*. Peru. **241.**

verschaffeltii Painted Net Leaf
A somewhat similar plant to *F. argyroneura* but less exacting, making a good room plant. The network of veins is bright carmine giving a purple sheen to the leaves. Peru. **242.**

Five Fingers see **Syngonium auritum**
Flame of the Woods see **Ixora coccinea**
Flame Pea see **Chorizema**
Flame Plant see **Anthurium scherzerianum**
Flamingo Flower see **Anthurium scherzerianum**
Flaming Sword see **Vriesea splendens**
Flax, Yellow see **Reinwardtia trigyna**

Floating Fern see **Salvinia auriculata**
Floating Water Hyacinth see **Eichhornea speciosa**
Florida Anise Tree see **Illicium floridanum**
Flowering Inch Plant see **Tradescantia blossfeldiana**
Flowering Maple see **Abutilon**
Flower of the Western Wind see **Zephyranthes candida**
Fountain Palm, Australian see **Livistona australis**
Fox-tail Orchid see **Aerides**

FRANCOA (SAXIFRAGACEAE)
sonchifolia Bridal Wreath
A 2 ft perennial, best grown in pots in cool conditions. The mid-green, lyre-shaped leaves are net-veined. Flowering branches have handsome spikes of 4-petalled flowers on long leafless stalks in July. Each petal is white or deep pink with a darker marking near the base. The plants can be divided, but are best propagated by seed in early spring. Chile.

Frangipangi see **Plumeria rubra**
Freckle-face see **Hypoestes sanguinolenta**

FREESIA (IRIDACEAE)
× **hybrida** syn **F.** × **kewensis**
A genus of bulbous plants with beautifully scented flowers much in demand for house decoration. All those in cultivation are hybrids and are usually grouped under the name × *hybrida*. They have long, narrow sword-like leaves and slender, branching stems which carry the 1–2 in. funnel-shaped flowers. They are best suited to cool greenhouse or conservatory culture and the corms should be planted in a loam-based compost. Propagate by seeds in spring, or by separating offsets from the corms in late summer. **243.**

French Mulberry see **Callicarpa americana**
Friendship Plant see **Pilea involucrata**

FUCHSIA (ONAGRACEAE)
A popular group of flowering shrubs renowned for their pendulous bell-like flowers, usually in two contrasting colours. Among the many species there is a great diversity of growth habit, from small trailers to tree-sized giants. Grow in pots or tubs of loam-based compost or a peat mix and shade from the hottest sunshine. They are best in a well aerated cool greenhouse or conservatory, but make good short term pot plants for the home. Propagate by stem cuttings in spring or late summer.

boliviana
A 2–4 ft shrub with abundant, pendent clusters of rich crimson, slender trumpet-shaped flowers, the tube 2–3 in. in length. The leaves are oval, toothed and slightly pointed. Peru to Argentina.

boliviana luxurians syn. **F. corymbiflora**
Somewhat similar to *F. boliviana* with arching stems carrying pendent clusters of long tubular bright crimson flowers from June to September. The leaves are light green and have pink veins. Ecuador to El Salvador.

corymbiflora see **F. boliviana luxurians**

fulgens
A 3–4 ft shrubby species with fleshy, red stems carrying large, oval to heart-shaped leaves and pendulous, leafy clusters of scarlet flowers. The narrow tube is 2–3 in. long and bears green-tipped lobes. Mexico.

magellanica
A deciduous shrub, hardy in mild areas but at its best with some protection. It has long, narrow, mid-green leaves and clusters of pendent, 1½–2 in. flowers with a crimson tube and petal-like sepals and 4 purple petals which form a bell. Many hybrids are grown, most of which have been derived from *F. magellanica* crossed with several other species. They vary chiefly in flower shape and coloration, but also in leaf form and general habit. Peru, Chile.
 'Arabella', white sepals and rosy-red petals. **244;**
 'Cascade', a pendent plant with pink flushed, white sepals and deep crimson petals;
 'Citation', pale rose-pink tube with 4 white petals opening to saucer shape;
 'Impudence', brilliant scarlet sepals form the tube, while the protruding petals are white and almost flat, **245;**

'Jack French', a well branched cultivar with deep red sepals and purple petals;
'Leonora', a single pink with a good rich colour and bell-shaped petals, **246;**
'Swingtime', a most attractive, showy species with shining scarlet sepals and frilly white petals **247;**
'Thalia', the dark pinky-red tubular flowers are slender and borne in dense clusters;
'Traudchen Bonstedt', pale salmon flowers and very light green leaves;
'Violet Gem', a large plant with carmine-red sepals and violet petals, **248;**
'Winston Churchill', a double-flowered cultivar with pink sepals and blue-tinged petals.

serratifolia
A bush to 4 ft or more with reddish branches bearing pendent flowers with pinkish-red sepals and short, scarlet petals, appearing in summer. The leaves which grow in whorls are oblong, narrow and slender pointed. Peru, Chile.

splendens
A densely branched shrub attaining 6 ft or more with light green, pointed heart-shaped leaves and drooping flowers; the petals a vivid scarlet with pale green tips, opening in June. Mexico.

triphylla
A 2 ft, downy shrub with whorls of long, ovate leaves, green above and purplish below. The flowers which are produced from June to October are a brilliant vermilion. W. Indies.

Fuchsia, Australian see **Correa** × **harrisii**
Fuchsia Begonia see **Begonia fuchsioides**

G

Galingale see **Cyperus**

GARDENIA (RUBIACEAE)
jasminoides syn. **G. florida** Cape Jasmine
A beautiful 1–6 ft evergreen shrub for the greenhouse, represented in cultivation by the double flowered cultivar 'Florida' or 'Plena'. It has glossy, dark green, long-oval leaves and 3 in. white, waxy flowers which are superbly perfumed. They are carried singly towards the apex of the branches, from June to September. They grow well in pots in a loam-based compost or a proprietary peat compost and can be propagated by taking stem cuttings early in the year. China, Formosa, Japan. **249.**
 'Fortuniana', 4 in., waxy, double white flowers, yellowing with age.

Garland Flower see **Hedychium coronarium**

GASTERIA (LILIACEAE)
A group of succulents grown for their handsomely marked, greatly thickened leaves which are arranged in 2 ranks, or in a rosette. An easy house plant with reddish tubular flowers, about 1–2 in. long, borne on a 12 in. arching stem throughout the growing season of March to September. For culture see terrestrial cacti in the Introduction. Grow in sun or light shade. Water freely in the growing season, less so in winter. Minimum winter temperature 40°F. Propagate by seed, cuttings, or offsets which form freely.

brevifolia
A stemless plant, the 3½–6 in. leaves erect at first, later spreading. They are broad and thick with a flat upper surface and concave lower, tapering to a rounded apex with a short point. The dark green surface is covered with white spots arranged in bands across the leaves. S. Africa. **250.**

liliputana
Striking keeled dark green leaves, blotched white, are arranged spirally. Growing no more than 2–3 in. high, this is the smallest member of the group. S. Africa.

maculata
The strap-shaped horny-tipped leaves, green blotched white and 6–8 in.

long, are arranged in 2 ranks, forming a plant 6–8 in. high. The flowers are scarlet. S. Africa.

verrucosa

Raised grey spots mask the dark green, 4–6 in. long pointed leaves. They have rounded edges and grooved upper surfaces. Growing in a distinctive manner, in pairs one above the other, they form a plant 6 in. high. The flowers are small and red. S. Africa.

GAZANIA (COMPOSITAE)

Mat-forming plants with pleasing dark green or grey foliage and showy large daisy flowers often contrastingly patterned with another colour. The flowers only open fully in bright sunlight. They make handsome pot or border plants for the well ventilated cool or cold conservatory. Grow in a loam-based compost and propagate by cuttings in late summer or spring.

× hybrida (G. longiscapa × G. nivea)

The dark green foliage is light grey on the underside, and the long, narrow leaves provide a foil for the 2–3 in. flowers which range through shades of yellows, oranges and browns to pinks and reds. Many hybrids have been given cultivar names.

   'Hazel', deep chocolate to red with deep yellow tips;
   'Monarch Mixed', including a complete range of colour forms.

× splendens

The leaves are spoon-shaped, dark green above and white silky beneath. The 3 in. flower heads are bright orange with black and white spotting at the centre. They are produced from July to September.

Gazania, Climbing see **Mutisia**
Gentian, Hindustan see **Chirita lavandulacea**
Gentian Sage see **Salvia patens**

GEOGENANTHUS (COMMELINACEAE) Seersucker Plant
undatus

A low growing plant with dark green, oval leaves having curious wavy lines running longitudinally above, and maroon red beneath. The surface of the leaves is also wavy like quilting. A plant for warm conditions which can be propagated by cuttings or division. Peru. **251.**

Geranium see **Pelargonium**
Geranium, California see **Senecio petasites**
Geranium, Strawberry see **Saxifraga stolonifera**

GERBERA (COMPOSITAE)

Tufted perennials with elegantly showy large daisy flowers in a variety of colours and shades. They are best grown in a cool, well-ventilated conservatory or greenhouse but make good short term pot plants for the home. Grow in a loam-based compost and propagate by seeds or division in spring.

jamesonii Barberton Daisy, Transvaal Daisy

A 12–15 in. perennial with 5–10 in., deeply lobed, woolly hairy leaves and striking, solitary orange-scarlet flowers, 3–5 in. across borne on erect 10–18 in. stalks. **252.** Many hybrids have been raised using this species as a parent, and these can be single or double-flowered and occur in a great range of colours from yellows to pinks. S. Africa.

   'Farnell's Strain' is a double form, **253.**

Giant Caladium see **Alocasia cuprea**
Giant Elephant's Ear see **Alocasia macrorrhiza**
Giant Granadilla see **Passiflora quadrangularis**
Giant Maidenhair Fern see **Adiantum trapeziforme**
Giant Pineapple Flower see **Eucomis pole-evansii**
Giant Potato Vine see **Solanum wendlandii**
Giant Spider Lily see **Crinum giganteum**
Ginger, Kahili see **Hedychium gardnerianum**
Ginger Lily see **Hedychium**
Ginger, Spiral see **Costus speciosus**
Ginger, Yellow see **Hedychium flavum**
Gippsland Waratah see **Telopea oreades**

GLADIOLUS (IRIDACEAE)

A popular genus of bulbous plants, the many hybrid cultivars of which

are mainly grown in the garden. They also make good short-term pot plants for the cool greenhouse and home. There are also several wild species from S. Africa which bloom in early spring and cannot be grown in the open garden. These are particularly suited to pot culture. Set the bulbs (corms) in pots of a loam-based compost and keep well ventilated. Propagate by cormlets or seed sown in spring or summer. Several of the smaller species have been hybridized to produce various groups of elegant plants suitable for pot culture. The main groups are Butterfly, Colvillii, Nanus, and Primulinus, 'Columbine', **254**, belonging to this last group. The more recent cross, Tubergenii, is also used for this purpose 'Charm', **255**, being particularly effective.

blandus

The 12–18 in. stem bears 4 strap-shaped leaves and in June, spikes of 4–8 white, pink-tinged or reddish flowers, the side petals having a pink-flush and the lowest often with a purplish spot in the centre. S. Africa.

× colvillii (G. cardinalis × G. tristis)

A dainty hybrid with a lax, 10 in. spike of bright red flowers, the lower 3 petals having a central, bright yellow spot. The blooms are 3 in. across and open in July. The narrow, pointed leaves have conspicuous nerves and the overall height of the plant is 12–24 in. Garden origin.

papilio

A large, vigorous species with the flowering stems reaching 6 ft, in height. The 2–3 ft leaves are long and narrow, and the yellow bell-shaped blooms, which are violet edged and with two large deep purple blotches, grow in long lax spikes in summer. S. Africa.

primulinus

A distinctive species much used in hybridization, with a spike of 4–5 primrose-yellow blooms having the central upper petal forming a hood and up to 1¼ in. long. The central lower petal is recurved, helping to give a nodding effect. The overall height of the plant is 1½ ft, and the ribbed, narrow, arching leaves are up to 1 ft in length. Tropical E. Africa.

tristis

A fragrant species with 2 in., upturned, yellowish-white flowers, the petals sometimes pink-tinged. They are borne in lax spikes of 3–4 blooms on 18 in. stems, opening in July. The 3 leaves are almost round in section and are up to 1–1½ ft in length. S. Africa.

   'Christabel', with dark veined petals. **256.**

GLOBBA (ZINGIBERACEAE)

Erect tufted perennials with bright green narrow leaves and slender stems bearing curious, orchid-like flowers, often protected by coloured bracts and sometimes mixed with bulbils. They are best grown in warm conditions, but tolerate cooler temperatures. Grow in a loam-based compost and shade from the hottest sunshine. Propagate by division in spring.

atrosanguinea

A 1½–3 ft plant with slender, arching stems having 6–8 in., deep green, yellow margined leaves with a covering of fine hairs beneath. The tubular yellow flowers have red bracts at their bases and occur at intervals throughout the year. Borneo. **257.**

schomburgkii

A smaller plant than G. atrosanguinea with 3 in. clusters of flowers, 4–5 on each branch. The yellow petals are joined below into a tube up to ¾ in. in length, and the divided lip is marked with red spots. The flowers are protected by light green bracts, some of which bear bulbils. They open in August. Siam.

winitii

An erect plant, to 3 ft with large, sword-shaped leaves, the lowest bladeless sheath the stem. The drooping clusters of flowers are 6 in. long and carry small yellow blossoms with a curved tube and large, rose-purple bracts which are at their best in autumn. Siam.

Globe Amaranth see **Gomphrena globosa**
Globe Amaranth, False see **Alternanthera dentata**
Globe Mallow see **Sphaeralcea**

GLORIOSA (LILIACEAE) Glory Lily

A genus of strikingly attractive climbing lilies with tuberous roots.

They can be grown in pots or borders in conservatories. Twiggy sticks, strings or wires are needed for support. Plant or pot the snake-like tubers in spring. Propagate by offset tubers at potting time.

rothschildiana ✽
A showy species producing flowers with 6 brilliant scarlet 4 in. petals, curved backwards to reveal a golden-yellow flash at the base. The glossy, lily-like leaves taper into tendrils which enable them to climb suitable supports reaching up to 6 ft in height. They flower from June to August. Tropical Africa. **258.**

superba ✽
A plant of similar habit and form to *G. rothschildiana*, but with smaller flowers, having narrower 3 in. petals which are curled and crisped along the edges and change colour as they develop, from a yellow-green, through orange to red. Late summer to autumn. Tropical Asia and Africa. **258.**

Glorybean, Java see **Clerodendrum speciosissimum**
Glory Flower, Chilean see **Eccremocarpus scaber**
Glory Lily see **Gloriosa**
Glory Pea see **Clianthus formosus**
Glory Pea, Holly-leaved see **Chorizema ilicifolium**
Gloxinia see **Sinningia**
Gold Dust Dracaena see **Dracaena godseffiana**
Golden Barrel see **Echinocactus grusonii**
Golden Calla see **Zantedeschia elliottiana**
Golden Guinea Flower see **Hibbertia**
Golden Pothos see **Scindapsus aureus**
Golden Senna see **Cassia corymbosa**
Golden Shower see **Cassia fistula**
Golden Spider Lily see **Lycoris aurea**
Golden Treefern see **Dicksonia fibrosa**
Golden Trumpet see **Allamanda cathartica**
Golden Trumpet Bush see **Allamanda neriifolia**
Golden Wattle, Sydney see **Acacia longifolia**
Goldfish Vine see **Columnea microphylla**
Gold-rayed Lily see **Lilium auratum**
Goldvine, Guinea see **Hibbertia volubilis**

GOMPHRENA (AMARANTHACEAE)
globosa Globe Amaranth ✽
An attractive erect, annual pot plant to bring in from the cool greenhouse, reaching to 2 ft in height. It has pale green, oblong, hairy leaves and round to oval, clover-like flower heads at the ends of the branches, which can be white, yellow, orange, red or purple. Propagate by seed. India.
  'Buddy', a 6 in., dwarf form with bright purple, long-lasting flowers; 'Nana compacta', also a dwarf form with fine dark red flowers.

Gooseberry, Barbados see **Pereskia aculeata**

GOSSYPIUM (MALVACEAE) Cotton
Erect annuals or perennial subshrubs with somewhat maple-like leaves and funnel-shaped flowers. The large bulbous seed pods contain the raw cotton of commerce. The species mentioned here are mainly grown for interest, though the short-lived flowers are attractive. Grow in pots of loam-based compost and keep in a humid warm greenhouse or conservatory. Propagate by seeds sown in spring.

arboreum Tree Cotton ●
A shrub or small tree with deeply 5–7-lobed leaves. The showy, 5-petalled purple flowers have spreading petals opening in summer, and followed by a hard almost circular fruit which bursts when ripe, exposing the seeds which are attached to and surrounded by the soft white cotton fibres. India.

herbaceum Levant Cotton ●
A 3–4 ft hairy, shrub rather similar to *G. arboreum* but having leaves shallowly cut into five rounded lobes and purple centred yellow flowers in early summer. The rounded fruits split to reveal the fluffy greyish-white cotton fibres. Asia.

Granadilla see **Passiflora edulis**

Granadilla, Giant see **Passiflora quadrangularis**
Granadilla, Yellow see **Passiflora laurifolia**
Grapefruit see **Citrus paradisi**
Grape Ivy see **Rhoicissus rhomboidea**
Grape Ivy, Miniature see **Cissus striata**
Grape, Rose see **Medinilla magnifica**
Grape, Seaside see **Coccoloba uvifera**

GRAPTOPHYLLUM (ACANTHACEAE)
pictum syn. G. hortense Caricature Plant 🐾
A tropical shrub with oval, leathery leaves curiously blotched with white, the markings often resembling faces, hence its popular name. The crimson flowers grow in small clusters. The plants need warm conservatory or greenhouse treatment and plenty of water and light in summer. They soon become leggy, and are best renewed frequently. Propagate by stem cuttings from March to June. E. Indies.

Grass Nut see **Brodiaea laxa**
Grass Palm see **Cordyline australis**
Greater Butterwort see **Pinguicula grandiflora**
Great White Strelitzia see **Strelitzia augusta**
Greenbrier see **Smilax**
Green Earth Star see **Cryptanthus acaulis**
Green Ixia see **Ixia viridiflora**

GREVILLEA (PROTEACEAE)
Trees and shrubs grown for their attractive flowers and, or, foliage. The species described are all suitable for pot or tub culture in a well ventilated cool conservatory or greenhouse. Use a loam-based compost and propagate by seed (*G. robusta*) or cuttings of lateral shoots in late summer or spring.

banksii ✽ 🐾
A tree or shrub growing to 15 ft or more. It has rich green leaves divided into 5–11 narrow lobes which are silky-white beneath. The bright red flowers grow in 4 in. crowded spikes and are produced in the spring. Queensland.

juniperina see G. sulphurea

robusta Silk Oak 🐾
In cultivation this tall tree species is usually kept as a 3–6 ft non-flowering pot plant, and is grown for its fern-like foliage. The 18 in. finely divided leaves are mid-green at first, darkening as they mature. New South Wales.

rosmarinifolia ✽ 🐾
A 6 ft shrub having dark green, rosemary-like narrow leaves which are paler beneath, and 1 in. rose-red flowers in dense terminal spikes which open from May to September. New South Wales.

sulphurea syn. G. juniperina ✽
A 6 ft shrub with narrow, needle-like light green leaves and clusters of yellow flowers borne at intervals along the upright leafy stems, and opening from May to September. Each bloom is yellow and about ½ in. long with a conspicuous, protruding yellow style giving a feathery look to the flower clusters. New South Wales.

Grotto Lace Fern see **Microlepia speluncae**
Guava, Chilean see **Myrtus ugni**
Guernsey Lily see **Nerine sarniensis**
Guinea Goldvine see **Hibbertia volubilis**
Gum Tree see **Eucalyptus**

GUZMANIA (BROMELIACEAE)
Rosette-forming plant, the leaves of which overlap to form a water-holding vase. The flowers rise from deep in the centre of the rosette and are surrounded by brightly coloured leaf-like bracts. They make good pot plants for the warm greenhouse or home. Grow in a peat-based compost, preferably mixed with equal parts of sphagnum moss. Shade from direct sunlight. During the spring to autumn period, keep the central part of the leaf rosette filled with water. Propagate by offsets in summer.

lingulata ✽ 🐾
A most striking species with 18 in. green, spear-shaped, rigid leaves

and a 12 in. flowering stem bearing a cluster of short-lived, yellow-white flowers enfolded by brilliant crimson bracts, 2½ in. long and holding their colour for many weeks after the petals have dried. W. Indies, Central to S. America. **259.**

monostachya syn. **G. tricolor**
From the large rosette of narrow, light green leaves rises a 15 in. flower spike, the inconspicuous white flowers almost completely covered by the bracts which at the base of the spike are green with narrow, brownish-purple stripes and white tips, becoming flushed with red until at the apex of the spike they are a vivid, shining scarlet. Florida, W. Indies, Central to S. America.

sanguinea
A very decorative species with a flat rosette of long, almost parallel-sided leaves, recurved at the tips and yellow at the centre, shading to scarlet on the upper leaves when in blossom and green on the lower. The small yellow, tubular flowers appear at the centre. The whole plant is about 12 in. high. Costa Rica, Trinidad, Ecuador, Colombia.

tricolor see **G. monostachya**

GYMNOCALYCIUM (CACTACEAE)

Ball-shaped cacti divided into 2 groups: those with appressed spines which tend to lie flat and hug the stems, and those with spines more outward curving although tending to follow the outline of the plant. Stems are heavily ribbed, with a protuberance called the 'chin' projecting below the areole. The variously coloured and fairly large flowers are produced freely in summer. For culture see under terrestrial cacti in the Introduction. Easy to grow and enjoying sun and plenty of water during the spring and summer. Minimum winter temperature 40°F. Propagate from offsets rooted in a mixture of equal parts of sharp sand and moist peat, or from seed.

baldianum
Round bluish-grey plant, 2½ in. high, with 11 flattish ribs with 'chins' beneath the areoles, the latter surrounded by about 7 radiating white spines, brownish at the base. The purple to red flowers, 2 in. long and 1 in. across, appear freely even on young plants. Seeds are regularly produced as this is self-fertile. An extremely handsome species. Argentina. **260.**

gibbosum
A blue-green ball-shaped plant, later becoming column-shaped up to 3½ in. across and 8 in. tall, the straight ribs broken up by chin-like, prominent warts. About 10 pale brownish spines, which eventually turn grey, grow from each areole. The white, often rose-tinted flowers, 2½ in. long, produce a ball of colour on mature plants, making this a very popular species. Argentina, Patagonia.
  nobile, a very fine form with most attractive spines; should not be coddled as it hails from a cool moist climate.

multiflorum
Glaucous bluish-green stems, 3½ in. high and 5 in. in diameter, have 10–15 fleshy ribs with areoles surrounded by 10 awl-shaped 1 in. long yellow spines, red or blackish at the base. The funnel-shaped flowers, almost 2 in. long, have brownish-green outer petals and whitish-rose inners. Argentina.

saglione
Large plants, roughly ball-shaped and up to 12 in. across, with 10–30 ribs. The large woolly areoles bear 7–12 handsomely curved radial spines, 1–1½ in. long, and up to 3 centrals. All the spines are browny-black with a reddish tinge, turning white with age. The flowers are white or pinkish, about 1½ in. long. Argentina, Bolivia.

GYNURA (COMPOSITAE)

Attractive foliage plants of erect or semi-climbing habit for the warm or cool conservatory or greenhouse. Grow in a peat-based mix or a loam-based compost and shade from the hottest summer sunshine. Propagate by stem cuttings in spring or summer. To promote more leafy branches the young flowering stems should be pinched out.

aurantiaca Velvet Plant
A 3 ft shrub with long, ovate dark green leaves covered, as are the stems, with a thick covering of bright purple hairs, giving the plant a velvety appearance. The flowers are small, rather like 1 in. orange petalless daisies, and open in February. Java. **261.**

sarmentosa syn. **G. scandens**
A rather similar species considered by some authorities to be a variety of *G. aurantiaca*. It is, however, a climber and needs support up which it will twine. The leaves have the same purple hair cover, but the flowers are paler and smaller and open in March and April. India.

scandens see **G. sarmentosa**

H

HABRANTHUS (AMARYLLIDACEAE)
robustus
A large, bulbous lily-like plant with 3½ in. long trumpet-shaped blooms, opening a purplish-rose and fading to white, borne on a stout 2 ft stem. The grey-green leaves are very long and narrow with a marked central vein. They grow best in a sunny position in a cool conservatory, or on a suitable window sill in the home. Propagate by offsets from the bulbs, or by seed in spring. Argentina.

HAEMANTHUS (AMARYLLIDACEAE) Blood Lily
Unusual bulbous plants with clusters of tiny flowers grouped into brush-like heads surrounded by petal-like bracts. Some species have larger flowers arranged in spherical heads lacking floral bracts. Apart from one or two evergreen species, they all flower before the new leaves expand. Grow in cool conservatory or greenhouse borders or in pots of loam-based compost, setting the bulbs so that no more than half is buried beneath the compost. When the foliage dies down withhold water until the flower heads show, then start watering gradually as the leaves appear. The evergreen species must be kept just moist at all times.

albiflos White Paint Brush
A low, somewhat succulent evergreen species with thick fleshy, curving leaves and a 2 in. brush-like mass of greenish white flowers with long protruding stamens which open in June. Each flower cluster is surrounded by whitish petal-like bracts. S. Africa.

coccineus Ox-tongue Lily
The 2¼–3¾ in. orbicular heads of bright, salmon-red flowers and bracts open on bare stems in August and September, and only after they have died does the plant produce the long prostrate mid-green leaves. S. Africa.

katherinae Blood Flower
A striking plant with 1–1½ ft soft, fleshy green, wavy-edged leaves and a large head of deep red flowers with protruding crimson stamens carried on a long stout stalk, sometimes borne on the plant at the same time as the leaves or just before. The flowers appear in July. S. Africa. **262.**

multiflorus Salmon Blood Lily
A superb species with 6 in. spherical heads of up to 100 deep coral-pink to red flowers, borne on a 3 ft stalk in April. The deciduous leaves are 1 ft long, broad and mid-green and are joined to the stem at the base. Tropical Africa.

Hairy Heath, Red see **Erica cerinthoides**
Hairy Mallow see **Malvastrum scabrosum**

HAKEA (PROTEACEAE)
Wiry shrubs with needle or dagger-like leaves and usually profusely borne small flowers. The latter are without petals but have narrow fleshy sepals, often brightly coloured, fused to the stamens. They require a cool, well ventilated conservatory or greenhouse with full light to grow and flower well. Large pots or tubs are best, but they can be grown in the borders. A peat-based mix or loam-based compost can be used. Propagate by seeds in spring.

laurina Sea Urchin, Pincushion Flower
A shrub reaching 10 ft or more with 4–6 in., narrowly oblong leaves and globular clusters of red, flowers with long, golden-yellow styles protruding from them like soft spines. They appear in summer and grow directly upon the leafy branches of the plant. W. Australia.

microcarpa
A 6 ft shrub forming a compact bush. The leaves are up to 4 in. long

and very slender while the yellowish-white flowers, which appear in May, form heads up to 1 in. across are fragrant. Tasmania, Australia.

saligna

A very fragrant species with short-stalked clusters of white flowers borne in the axils of the long, tapering leaves from March to July. The plant is almost completely hairless. It can grow to 10 ft or more. Queensland, N. S. Wales.

suaveolens ✳

An 8–15 ft silky hairy shrub with needle-like leaves and small dense clusters of white, fragrant flowers carried in summer near the ends of the shoots. W. Australia.

HAMATOCACTUS (CACTACEAE)

The round or cylindrical stems have a soft texture and often spiralling ribs. The funnel-shaped or tubular flowers are followed by small red fruit. The central spines are long and at least one of them has a pronounced hook. For culture see under terrestrial cacti in the Introduction. They enjoy full sun or light shade. Minimum winter temperature 40°F. Raise new plants from seeds or offsets.

hamatacanthus ✳ 🦋

Ball-shaped stems when young, 4–6 in. across, elongating up to 2 ft with age, dark green and with up to 13 ribs, separated by deep grooves. The yellowish-white areoles have 9–12 radial spines and 1–4 centrals, of which the lowest is up to 4½ in. long and hooked downwards at the tip. The spines are all red, fading to white. The yellow flowers, flushed red in the throat, are brownish-green outside and up to 3 in. wide. They form freely throughout the summer. Texas, New Mexico.

setispinus ✳ 🦋

Attractive spines and freedom of flowering are notable features. The spherical stems, which lengthen with age, have 13–15 wavy ribs. The woolly white areoles bear 12–15 white or brownish radial spines about 1¼ in. long, and up to 3 white centrals, longer and stouter and hooked at the tips. The fragrant flowers are yellow with glowing scarlet throats, about 3 in. long and follow each other in quick succession. Mexico.

HARDENBERGIA (LEGUMINOSAE)

A genus of slender climbers with bi- and tricoloured pea flowers. They may be grown up a structure of twigs or wires in pots or borders. Grow in a cool conservatory, where it is shaded from the hottest sunshine. Propagate by seeds or stem cuttings in summer.

comptoniana ✳

An attractive evergreen twining plant which can reach 7 ft or more. The leaves are divided into 3 or 5 smaller leaflets, and the purplish-blue flowers have a greenish-white mark on the base of the petals. They are borne from January to April in 3–6 in. clusters in the axils of the leaves and at the ends of the shoots. W. Australia.

violacea ✳

A climbing or scrambling evergreen species, having undivided leaves and clusters of violet flowers with yellow markings. They open in March and April. Australia.

Hare's-foot Fern see **Davallia canariensis** and **Polypodium auratum**

HAWORTHIA (LILIACEAE)

Thickened and marked leaves, usually white on green, form attractive rosettes producing racemes of slender branched greenish-white pitcher-shaped flowers in summer. These are very small and of little interest. For culture see terrestrial succulents in the Introduction. Plants thrive in full sun or light shade. Water freely in spring and summer, less in autumn and not at all during the winter. Minimum winter temperature 40°F. Raise new plants from offsets, or seed sown in spring in gentle heat.

attenuata 🦋

Attractive leaves marked with scattered white tubercles on the upper surface, which are in transverse lines on the underside. The leaves, thick at the base and tapering, form rosettes 2–3 in. across. Offsets are freely formed. Insignificant flowers are produced in summer.

Numerous varietal forms occur, some of which have been named. S. Africa. **263.**

margaritifera 🦋

Narrow tapering leaves form broad rosettes, varying in spread but about 3 in. high and attractively marked with white tubercles. Loosely set on slender branches, the greenish-white bell-shaped flowers are borne from early summer to autumn. Forms offsets freely. S. Africa.

truncata 🦋

Dark upright leaves form a stemless rosette, variably sized but 1–2 in. high. The leaves are cylindrical, seemingly cut off sharply at the tip which is transparent forming a 'window' through which the plants get light during the dry season, when, in their native habitat, they are almost buried in sand. Greenish-white flowers are produced in summer. S. Africa.

Heart-leaf Philodendron see **Philodendron scandens**
Heath see **Erica**
Heather, Christmas see **Erica canaliculata**
Heavenly Bamboo see **Nandina domestica**

HEDERA (ARALIACEAE) Ivy

A genus of most valuable evergreen climbers from which many decorative cultivars have arisen. These make excellent pot plants when grown in a loam-based or proprietary peat compost, and either given some form of support to enable them to climb, or grown in a hanging position. They need shading from direct sunlight in summer and can be kept in a cold room in winter.

canariensis Canary Island Ivy 🦋

A handsome species with 5–8 in. leathery leaves which are somewhat more rounded than those of the Common Ivy (H. helix). Canary Isles.
> 'Variegata', syn. 'Gloire de Marengo', is a fine form with dark, glossy green leaves marked and edged with creamy white, **264.**

helix Common Ivy, English Ivy 🦋

A familiar species of which the following are some of a great number of named cultivars. Europe.
> 'Buttercup', syn. 'Golden Cloud' or 'Russell's Gold', a very fine golden variegated cultivar;
> 'Chicago', small, dark green leaves with purple to bronze markings;
> 'Digitata', broad leaves divided into 5 finger-like lobes;
> 'Discolor', a small, neat plant having the dark green leaves marbled with cream, often with a rose flush;
> 'Eva', a dwarf sturdy plant with pointed 3-lobed leaves having a broad white margin;
> 'Glacier', small leaves with a silvery sheen and white margins, **265;**
> 'Gold Heart' syn. 'Jubilee', neat tapering leaves with a gold splash on the dark green background, **266;**
> 'Green Ripple', the lobes are jaggedly cut, the central one tapering to a point;
> 'Lutzii', with marbled leaves, **267;**
> 'Sagittifolia', arrowhead-shaped leaves, the central lobe long and triangular;
> 'Tricolor', small greyish-green leaves with a white margin which turns pink in autumn and winter.

HEDYCHIUM (ZINGIBERACEAE) Ginger Lily

Erect unbranched herbaceous perennials with stems that arise annually from a thick creeping rootstock (rhizome). Each stem has 2 ranks of narrow leaves and terminates in a dense spike of somewhat orchid-like flowers. They are best grown in a cool or warm greenhouse or conservatory border, but can be accommodated in tubs. Use a loam-based compost and shade from the hottest summer sunshine. Water freely in summer, but keep only just moist in winter. Propagate by division of the rhizomes in spring.

coccineum Scarlet Ginger Lily ✳ 🦋

A 4 ft species with narrow leaves, 18 in. long and 1½–2 in. wide which encircle the stem at their base. The stems terminate, from July to September, in spikes of orange-red flowers with long slender stamens which far exceed the 2 in. blooms. India, Burma, Ceylon. **268.**

coronarium Butterfly Lily, Garland Flower ✳ 🦋

A beautifully perfumed species reaching 6 ft, having narrow 2 ft long leaves which are mid-green above and downy beneath. The pure white flowers are carried in 8 in. spikes and the lip is sometimes marked with yellow. India.

flavum Yellow Ginger
A yellow-flowered species with 20 in. long, mid-green leaves arranged along the 5 ft stem, and spikes of 3 in. long fragrant flowers which have orange markings at the centre and open from July to September. N. India.

gardnerianum Kahili Ginger
A particularly beautiful species remarkable for the long bright red stamens which protrude far beyond the yellow petals. The 12 in. spear-shaped leaves are mid-green above and downy white below and are borne on a stiff, 6 ft stem. The flowers are produced from July to September. India. **269.**

Heeria elegans see **Schizocentron elegans**

× **HELIAPORUS** (CACTACEAE)
smithii syn. **Aporocactus mallisonii**
Long thought to be a species of *Aporocactus*, this is now believed almost certainly to be a hybrid between *A. flagelliformis* and either an *Epiphyllum* hybrid or *Heliocereus speciosus*. It is very similar to *A. flagelliformis* though larger, with stems twice as thick and about 22 in. long, The red flowers are also twice the size. Culture as for epiphytic cacti, see Introduction.

HELIOCEREUS (CACTACEAE)
Somewhat resembling spiny epiphyllums with usually 4-angled stems to 3 ft high, and areoles on the crenations of the ribs. Plants may be branched, erect or pendulous. Clusters of 5–8 attractive yellowish-brown spines are borne on the areoles which are about 1 in. apart. Roots very readily at the tips of the branches, like a bramble. Flowers 6–7 in. long, 3–4 in. or more across are borne singly, remaining in blooms for 2–3 days. Very striking. For culture see epiphytic cacti in the Introduction; minimum winter temperature 40°F. Propagate by cuttings or seed. Probably the parents of many hybrid flowering cacti.

amecamensis
Exactly similar to *H. speciosus* but with white flowers. Probably a wild sport of that species.

cinnabarinus
Striking blooms, 2–2½ in. wide and 3½–6 in. long, with green outer petals and vermilion inners, produced in early summer. The deeply ribbed stems, erect or lax and spreading, have up to 10 yellowish spines around the woolly areoles. Guatemala.

speciosus Sun Cactus
The stems, arching or pendent, sometimes prostrate, are usually 1–1½ in. thick, reddish when young, turning dark green and grow to 3 ft and have 3–4 ribs. The striking funnel-shaped scarlet flowers with a bluish sheen appear in late spring and are about 6–8 in. long. A long-lived species often hybridized with epiphyllums in the search for new colour breaks. Mexico, C. America. **270.**

Heliotrope see **Heliotropium**

HELIOTROPIUM (BORAGINACEAE) Heliotrope
× **hybridum** Cherry Pie
A favourite, very fragrant house plant which can also be grown in the cool greenhouse. It has dark to mid-green oval leaves which are closely veined and wrinkled. The dense flat clusters of flowers can measure 6 in. across and range in colour from lavender-pink to violet. White forms are also grown. The main flowering season is summer and early autumn, but they can flower at any time of the year. Grow in a good loam-based or soilless compost in 4–6 in. pots and bring into a warm place to induce flowering. Shade from the strongest summer sun and keep moist. They are best repotted annually in spring. Propagate by stem cuttings in autumn or early spring. **271.**

Helmet Flower, Vermilion see **Rechsteinera macropoda**
Helxine soleirolii see **Soleirolia soleirolii**

Hemp, African see **Sparmannia africana**
Hemp, Bowstring see **Sansevieria**
Hemp, Sunn see **Crotalaria juncea**
Hen and Chicken Fern see **Asplenium bulbiferum**
Herald's Trumpet see **Beaumontia grandiflora**
Herring-bone Plant, Red see **Maranta leuconeura 'Erythrophylla'**

HETEROCENTRON (MELASTOMATACEAE)
roseum
A warm conservatory or greenhouse sub-shrub, 1 ft in height with entire, elliptic leaves, somewhat rough above, bearing in autumn terminal clusters of 1 in. bright purplish pink, 4-petalled flowers. It needs warmth in winter. Grow in a proprietary peat compost and propagate by cuttings taken in February and March. Mexico.

HIBBERTIA (DILLENIACEAE) Golden Guinea Flower
Vigorous evergreen flowering climbers suitable for unheated conservatories. They are best grown in a bed or border and trained up canes or wires, but can be accommodated in tubs or large pots of loam-based compost. Shade from the hottest sunshine. Propagate by stem cuttings of short side shoots in summer.

dentata
A downy species when young, it has oval, slightly-toothed leaves, 1½–3 in. in length and carries handsome 1–1½ in. wide golden-yellow blooms with widely spaced, somewhat folded petals, which are borne singly on short stalks in the axils of the leaves. They flower in spring and summer. Australia.

scandens syn. **H. volubilis** Guinea Goldvine, Snake Vine
This shrub can be allowed to grow to its full height of 30 ft or more, but will grow happily as a 4 ft shrub if kept well pruned. The dark green, oval leaves grow up to 4 in. in length and are shiny above and silky hairy beneath. The showy 2 in. diameter flowers have widely spaced petals with the 1 in. green, pointed sepals visible between them. They are produced in summer. Australia.

volubilis see **H. scandens**

HIBISCUS (MALVACEAE) Rose-mallow
A genus renowned for the colourful flowers of its tropical shrubby members. These are evergreen and bear funnel or trumpet-shaped blossoms in a wide variety of colours and sizes. Although eventually forming large bushes, they can be flowered when small and make good pot or tub plants. Use a loam-based compost and grow in a cool or warm greenhouse or conservatory. Propagate by stem cuttings in summer.

× **archeri** (*H. rosa-sinensis* × *H. schizopetalus*)
A hybrid very similar in appearance to *H. rosa-sinensis*, one of its parents, but with darker red flowers which open in August and September. It makes an erect, bushy shrub up to 6 ft.

mutabilis Cotton Rose
An unusual species, with solitary 4 in. flowers which change colour during the day, opening a very pale pink, almost white, and deepening to a clear red by evening; they are produced almost continually in August and September. It is a shrub to 6 ft or more with heart-shaped, mid-green, slightly hairy leaves, but can be grown to 3 ft as a pot plant. China.

rosa-sinensis Rose of China
A most attractive shrub 6 ft or more tall, with ovate dark green, shining somewhat toothed leaves, making a splendid foil for the profusion of 5 in. deep crimson single flowers each with a central mass of long red stamens and yellow anthers. They are produced from June to September. **272.** Many cultivars of hybrid origin are grown having double or single flowers with yellow, pink or salmon petals. China.
'Apricot', apricot yellow with a large crimson eye;
'Cooperi' has leaves variegated with cream and dark red, and somewhat smaller flowers;
'Hubba', bright, clear pink with recurving, wavy-margined petals;
'Miss Betty', large, single pale yellow flowers, **273**;
'The President', cerise red, deeply waved petals and yellow stamens, **274**;
'Veronica', white-veined, yellow petals, suffused with rosy mauve, with a purple eye, **275.**

schizopetalus Japanese Lantern ✷
A very attractive tall shrub with pendulous branches bearing oval, toothed, glossy green leaves and small clusters of brilliant orange-red flowers hanging on long slender stalks. Each flower is 3 in. across, with deeply cut flared petals and a 2 in. column of fused stamens protruding far beyond them. They open in August and September. Tropical Africa.

waimeae ✷
A tall species with colourful twigs, at first a dull purple, later becoming grey. The wide oval to roundish leaves are up to 8 in. in length, smooth above and softly hairy beneath. The solitary flowers are white with 4½ in. spreading petals and a striking long tube of fused red stamens, over 6 in. long, and are borne in autumn. Hawaiian Islands. **276.**

Hibiscus, Sleeping see **Malvaviscus**
Hidden Lily see **Curcuma roscoana**
Hindustan Gentian see **Chirita lavandulacea**

HIPPEASTRUM (AMARYLLIDACEAE)
Striking bulbous plants with lily-like flowers which make excellent house plants as well as being suitable for a cool greenhouse. They have long, strap-shaped, deep green leaves and stout flowering stems. In many of the species the flowers open after the leaves have died down. Plant the bulbs singly in a loam-based compost, leaving the top half of the bulb exposed. Keep moist until the leaves die down. Propagate by seed in March, or by offsets. Most of the plants obtained in cultivation are of hybrid origin. They bear large trumpet-shaped flowers varying in colour from white, through crimson to deep red, sometimes variously striped with a different shade or colour. **277.** Generally sold as 'Amaryllis', some recommended varieties are:
    'American Express', crimson scarlet with a satin lustre;
    'Bouquet', salmon-pink with a red eye and veining;
    'Candy Cane', white, veined and sometimes flushed with red;
    'Jenny Lind', with large cerise flowers, **278;**
    'Nivalis', pure white with a yellow throat, **279.**

× **ackermannii** ✷
A deep red, trumpet-flowered hybrid with flowers 5–6 in. long, opening in winter and spring, and borne on 18–24 in. stems. Garden origin.

aulicum ✷
The 18 in. stems of this species carry from 2–4 flowers, each 5–6 in. long, a rich red increasingly darker inwards with green at the base of the petals. The blooms are produced in winter. Brazil. **280.**

candidum ✷
A summer flowering species with 2–3 ft stems bearing two or more drooping white blooms, yellow or green-tinged which are very fragrant. The long narrow leaves appear with the flowers. Argentina.

equestre ✷
A 1½–2½ ft plant with long leaves which develop after the flowers have died. The blooms which are carried in groups of 2–4 on the long stem, are 4–5 in. across and somewhat variable in colour, red with a green tinge being the most usual form. They are produced in winter and spring. Many cultivars are known, mostly of hybrid origin. S. America.
    'Fulgidum', bright orange, white edged petals;
    'Splendens', red flowers, much larger than those of the type.

× **johnsonii** (*H. reginae* × *H. vittatum*) ✷
A robust plant producing large, deep red flowers, opening at the mouth into 6 segments, each of which has a central white line. It flowers freely and is a spectacular specimen plant for the conservatory or window. **281.**

reticulatum ✷
The 1 ft leaves have a clear, central white stripe, while the 3 in., soft pink and white flowers are marked with red veins. They are carried on a long stem, 5 or 6 together, opening in autumn. A warmth demanding species. Brazil.

rutilum ✷
The 3–4 in., bright crimson flowers are shaded and streaked with green, and borne in spring in 1 ft scapes of 2–4. Venezuela, Brazil.

vittatum ✷
The 6–8, 2 ft, bright green leaves appear before the flowers which are 4–5 in. across and white with red stripes. They are borne on 3 ft stems in groups of 3–6 blooms. Peru.

Holly Fern see **Cyrtomium falcatum** 'Rochfordianum'
Holly-leaved Glory Pea see **Chorizema ilicifolium**

HOLMSKIOLDIA (VERBENACEAE)
sanguinea Chinese Hat Plant ✷
A straggling shrub which can reach 30 ft but in cultivation is usually kept below 6 ft. It has 4 in., evergreen, ovate, slender-pointed leaves and clusters of scarlet, tubular flowers growing from the centre of the almost circular, flat reddish calyx. It needs a warm greenhouse to thrive, and should be propagated by cuttings. India.

Honey Bush see **Melianthus major**
Honeypot Sugarbush see **Protea cynaroides**
Honeysuckle, Cape see **Tecomaria capensis**
Honeysuckle, Jamaica see **Passiflora laurifolia**
Horse Brier see **Smilax rotundifolia**
Horse's Head see **Philodendron panduriforme**
Horseshoe Geranium see **Pelargonium zonale**

HOWEA syn. **KENTIA** (PALMAE)
A genus of palm trees containing only two species, both of which make very decorative plants for tubs or pots in the home, and are also good greenhouse plants. In the wild they can reach 60 ft or more but are generally kept below 10 ft in cultivation. Grow in loam-based compost keeping in good light, though some shade is advisable in summer and repot every other year. Propagate by seeds in warmth.

belmoreana Curly Sentry Palm ➤
The handsome leaves are deeply divided into many, long, slender-pointed upward arching leaflets giving it a feathery appearance. The stiff, reddish stalks are erect when young, but curve over at maturity, and finally become pendent at the tips. Lord Howe Island.

forsteriana Kentia or Paradise Palm ➤
A plant with many features in common with *H. belmoreana* but carrying its fronds in a more upright position when young, making it a more compact plant. Lord Howe Island.

HOYA (ASCLEPIADACEAE)
Evergreen, climbing or trailing plants with flexible stems and leathery or fleshy shiny leaves and clusters of star-like, waxy flowers. They make good greenhouse and house plants and are best trained up supports. Grow in a loam-based or proprietary peat compost and shade from hottest sunshine. Keep in a humid atmosphere in summer, but allow to be cooler and drier in winter. Propagate by stem cuttings in summer, or by layering.

bella ✷ ➤
A dwarf, spreading, shrub-like species with pendulous branches, which grows well in a hanging basket. The small, dark green leaves are narrowly oval, occasionally with white spotting. The fragrant white flowers have a red-purple centre and are borne in wide clusters in the axils of the leaves May to September. India. **282.**

carnosa Wax Plant ✷ ➤
A good house plant with mid-green fleshy leaves growing on long stems, climbing by means of aerial roots. The flowers are pinkish-white with a red, star-shaped marking in the centre and are fragrant, opening from May to September. Queensland. **283.**
    'Variegata', an attractive form with bluish-green leaves having red shading and creamy-white margins.

imperialis ✷ ➤
A plant for the warm greenhouse, it is a strong climber with 6–9 in. shiny, but slightly downy leaves and clusters of large reddish-brown flowers having white centres. They are borne in pendent clusters in summer. Borneo.

Huisache see **Acacia farnesiana**
Humble Plant see **Mimosa pudica**

HUMEA (COMPOSITAE)
elegans ✷
A fragrant biennial suitable for the cool greenhouse. It grows to 5 or

6 ft in height and has large, oblong to lance shaped sticky leaves and elegant drooping clusters of tiny pink, glossy red or brownish-red flowers which are produced from July to October. The seeds should be sown in July and the seedlings transferred to small pots of loam-based compost as soon as possible. Move on to larger pots regularly to prevent their getting root bound and thus checking growth. Australia.

HYACINTHUS (LILIACEAE)

orientalis Common Hyacinth ✳

A popular hardy bulbous plant that responds well to cool greenhouse or home culture. It has several narrow glossy green leaves and dense oblong spikes of strongly fragrant waxy bell flowers. Double and single bloomed sorts are known in a wide variety of colours. Flower and spike sizes vary, the latter ranging from 4–8 in. or more in length. For indoor culture, plant the bulbs during September in bowls or pots of loam-based compost or a proprietary peat mix. Bulb fibre may also be used, but the bulbs will be exhausted after flowering. Place the bulbs so that the tip just shows above the compost. Keep the newly potted bulbs in a cool cellar or buried under sand, ashes or soil. In December, or when the shoots are 2–3 in. long, remove the pots to a cool room or greenhouse that is well ventilated, and make sure that the compost does not dry out. They will bloom in early spring. For really early flowering in December, specially prepared bulbs must be bought. Eastern Europe. **284.** Among the many cultivars, the following can be recommended:

'Amethyst', violet mauve;
'City of Haarlem', pale yellow, long spike;
'Eros', large full bloom of bright rose, closely set bells, **285;**
'King of the Blues', Oxford blue, large;
'Lady Derby', pale pink, large;
'La Victoire', brilliant red;
'L'Innocence', pure white, large;
'Ostara', bright blue, good for forcing;
'Perle Brillante', blue outside, paler inside; suitable for late forcing, **286;**
'Rosalie', a light pink;
'Victory', double, bright carmine;
'Yellow Hammer', golden-yellow.

HYDRANGEA (HYDRANGEACEAE)

macrophylla ✳

A familiar and popular hardy shrub often grown in pots for the home. It has broadly oval, prominently veined leaves and large, flattened or domed heads of bloom in shades of pink, red, blue, purple and white. The wild species has each flower head composed of many small greenish or bluish starry florets surrounded by much larger, more strongly coloured sterile ones. There are several different cultivars of this type which are called Lacecaps. The 'double' flowered or Hortensia group is the common hydrangea of gardens and indoor culture. Here, the flower heads are domed and almost entirely composed of sterile florets, with just a few fertile ones hidden between. Grow in a cool greenhouse or room and shade from the hottest sun. When the flowers are finished place outside, preferably plunged in soil, and keep moist. Cut back the flowered shoots and repot annually. Propagate by stem cuttings in spring or late summer and pot on as soon as rooted. Use a proprietary peat mix, or loam-based compost without lime, if good blue flowers are required. Limy composts or soils may be treated with aluminium sulphate at $2\frac{1}{2}$ lb to each 1 cwt of soil, or with bluing compounds used to manufacturers instructions. Japan. **287.**

The following cultivars can be recommended:
'Altona', rose pink, large;
'Hamburg', pink, **288;**
'La France', pink or blue;
'Miss Belgium', red; dwarf habit;
'Niedersachsen', pink or purplish blue, **289;**
'Souvenir de Madame E. Chautard', pale pink, mauve or blue compact habit.

HYDROCLEYS (LIMNOCHARITACEAE)

commersonii syn. **H. nymphoides** Water Poppy ✳ ☙

A beautiful tropical, aquatic herb for an aquarium or tub of water. It has 2–3 in. glossy green, roundish, leathery leaves with spongy tissue to allow them to float. The large, solitary, yellow, poppy-like flowers open in succession in May. The stems root as they grow and propagation by division is simple.

Hydrosme rivieri see **Amorphophallus rivieri**

HYLOCEREUS (CACTACEAE)

These climbing plants are mostly epiphytic and cling to trees by means of aerial roots. The stems are usually 3-angled; flowers are nocturnal, large and white, often purplish outside. For culture see epiphytic cacti in the Introduction. They require light shade, and in summer plenty of water and warmth to produce flowers. Minimum winter temperature 45°F. Propagate by cuttings.

undatus miscalled **Cereus triangularis** ✳ ☙

The dark green triangular stems, 2 in. in diameter and $1\frac{1}{2}$ ft or more long, are erect or pendulous with numerous branches. The spines are very short and inconspicuous. The flowers are funnel-shaped, up to 12 in. long and produced in late summer. This species is frequently used as a stock for grafting, when flowers are not encouraged and a minimum winter temperature of 40°F. is sufficient. W. Indies.

HYMENOCALLIS (AMARYLLIDACEAE) Spider Lily

A delightful genus of bulbous plants for the greenhouse, best grown in pots. They have long strap-shaped arching leaves and fragrant flowers with a trumpet shaped centre surrounded by spreading narrow petals, borne on stout stems. Plant in loam-based compost allowing the top of the bulb to show above the surface and keep watered during the growing season. Shade during the summer and repot every second or third year in spring. Propagate by removing bulb offsets when potting.

amancaes ✳

A 2 ft species with net-veined leaves sheathing the lower half of the stem, and $4\frac{1}{2}$–5 in., yellow or yellow-white drooping flowers which are greenish at the base of the tube. They are borne singly and in a warm greenhouse appear in April, but open later in cooler conditions. Chile.

americana see **H. littoralis**

calathina syn. **H. narcissiflora** ✳

A deciduous species often exceeding 2 ft in height. The large flowers are 4–6 in. across, white with a green flushed tube and jagged edges to the crown. They are borne between March and July depending on temperature. Brazil.

caribaea Caribbean Spider Lily

The pure white fragrant flowers are 6 in. long and have long, narrow outer petals and a toothed, central tube. They open in summer. The 2–3 ft leaves are strap-shaped and deep green. W. Indies. **290.**

× **festalis** (*H. calathina* × *Elisena longipetala*) ✳

A strong growing hybrid with 4–5 in. white flowers with a fringed crown and long, recurved, slender petals, borne on an 18 in. stalk, opening between April and August depending upon the warmth of its surroundings. Garden origin.

harrisiana ✳

A small species with arching leaves and a 12 in. stalk bearing very spidery, large, white flowers measuring 6–8 in. across. They open in June and July. Mexico.

littoralis syn. **H. americana** ✳

A magnificent species with leaves 3 ft and over. The flower has a large white funnel shaped crown surrounded by very long, slender, pendent petals. The flowers are produced in May. S. America. **291.**

× **macrostephana** (*H. calathina* × *H. speciosa*) ✳

A semi-evergreen species with 5–7 in., white, fragrant flowers which open between April and August depending upon heat available. The tube is shaded green. Northern S. America, Mexico, Guatemala.

narcissiflora see **H. calathina**

HYPOCYRTA GESNERIACEAE

A small genus of which the following species are low growing and rather shrubby with small entire leaves, pouch-like flowers and a petal-like calyx. They need a warm, humid greenhouse to thrive and should have the old flowering stems removed to keep them small and bushy. Propagate by soft cuttings.

glabra ✳ ☙

An unbranched species with an erect, purplish, fleshy stem and velvety hairy, shining, oval leaves. The small but striking flowers form bright red-orange-yellow pouches, and open in June and July. S. America. **295.**

nummularia
A dainty, prostrate, creeping species with oval, downy leaves carried on red-hairy stems, and curious flowers with a vivid scarlet tube, and the pouch edged with small yellow lobes. It is a good summer flowering plant for hanging baskets. Mexico.

HYPOESTES (ACANTHACEAE)
A genus of evergreen shrubs and perennial herbs, mostly tropical, needing high temperatures. Grow in a loam-based or proprietary peat mixture. Propagate by young cuttings in spring using bottom heat.

sanguinolenta Freckle-face
A small downy-stemmed species 6–12 ins. high. It is a beautiful foliage plant for culture in the warm greenhouse or home, the downy, dark green, roundish leaves having wavy margins and red veins and spotting. The pale lilac and white flowers have dark purple markings, and are borne throughout the summer. Grow in a proprietary peat mixture and water freely in summer, keeping just moist in winter. Propagate by stem cuttings in summer. Madagascar.

taeniata
A bushy perennial species with ovate or oblong leaves and large terminal clusters of flowers borne on long stems and raised well above the level of the foliage. The tubular blooms are dull purple and grow from a ring of pink bracts. The flowering period extends from autumn into early winter. Madagascar. **292.**

I

Iboza riparia see **Moschosma riparia**
Ifafa Lily see **Cyrtanthus mackenii**
Ifafa Lily, Red see **Cyrtanthus o'brienii**

ILLICIUM (MAGNOLIACEAE)
A genus of evergreen shrubs with entire, glossy, leathery leaves and solitary flowers like small magnolias, comprising as many as 30 petals. Nearly completely hardy they may be grown in a cool greenhouse. Best grown in a lime free compost, though a little lime may be tolerated. Propagate by layering or cuttings in spring or late summer.

anisatum Star Anise, Japanese Anise Tree
A shrub or small tree with distinctively fragrant wood and leaves, the latter narrowly oval, up to 4 in. in length. The flowers are borne one or two in the axils of the leaves, each flower 1–1½ in. across with up to 30, narrow, pale greenish-yellow petals; they are produced in May. Japan, Taiwan.

floridanum Florida Anise Tree
A 6–10 ft evergreen with up to 6 in. long, narrow, tapering leaves and solitary flowers which are borne on nodding stalks and are 2 in. across, having 20–30 red-purple, narrow petals. They open in May. S.E. U.S.A.

IMPATIENS (BALSAMINACEAE) Touch-me-not
A genus of somewhat succulent annuals and perennials which make very good house and greenhouse plants. They have simple leaves and clusters of brightly coloured cup-shaped or flat pansy-like flowers with long spurs. These species should be grown in a loam-based or proprietary peat compost and watered well during the growing season. Shade from direct sunlight. Propagate by seed sown in March, or in the case of perennial species by 3–4 in. tip cuttings at any time.

balsamina Balsam
A compact annual which makes a good pot plant. It has long, narrow, light green leaves and 1½ in. red flowers with an incurved spur. Several double-flowered named cultivars have derived from this species. Malaya. **293.**

hawkeri
A 2 ft perennial species with densely branching, red, succulent stems bearing 4½ in. oval leaves and 3–4 in. red-bronze flowers with creamy markings and a deep red spur. S.E. Asia.

holstii see **I. wallerana holstii**

marianae
An annual species grown almost entirely for its very attractive foliage, the deep-green, fleshy leaves having paler, almost silvery markings between the veins. The light-purple flowers grow in small, crowded clusters and have a slender hooked spur; they open in June. Assam.

oliveri
A large, perennial species reaching 4 ft or more, with long, oval dull green, fleshy leaves, 6–8 in. long. The pale lilac flowers reach 2½ in. across and have a long, slender spur. A good species for more shaded positions. E. Africa.

petersiana see **I. wallerana petersiana**
sultanii see **I. wallerana sultanii**

wallerana holstii Busy Lizzie
A sub-shrubby species with red succulent stems and green or brown tinged, ovate leaves. The 1–1½ in., bright scarlet flowers have flat petals and a long, down-turned spur, and are produced from April to October. Tropical Africa.

wallerana petersiana
A densely branched, shrubby species with very distinctively coloured stems and foliage, both being a dark, bronze red. The leaves are long, elliptic and the flowers a bright red, 1–1½ in. across with long slender spurs, opening from April to October. W. Africa. **294.**

wallerana sultanii
A much branched perennial with green, fleshy stems, narrow elliptical leaves narrowing to long points at both ends. The large flat flowers with a long spur are known in shades of orange and red, also white. They are produced from April to October. Zanzibar. **296.**
'Variegata', with white-rimmed leaves.

Inanda Lily see **Cyrtanthus sanguinea**
Inch Plant see **Tradescantia albiflora**
Inch Plant, Flowering see **Tradescantia blossfeldiana**
Inch Plant, Striped see **Setcreasea striata**
Indian Azalea see **Rhododendron simsii**
Indian Day Flower see **Commelina benghalensis**
Indian Lotus, Sacred see **Nelumbo nucifera**
Indian Pink see **Quamoclit pennata**
Indigo see **Indigofera**

INDIGOFERA (LEGUMINOSAE) Indigo
pulchella
A dainty 5 ft shrub with neat small elliptical leaflets. The purple-red and lilac pea-like flowers are borne in erect spikes in the axils of the leaves. Grow in a cold or cool greenhouse and shade from the hottest sunshine. Best results are obtained in a border, but large pots or tubs can be used. Propagate by stem cuttings with a heel in summer or seeds in spring. East Indies.

IOCHROMA (SOLANACEAE)
A genus of attractive shrubs or small trees with clustered, tubular flowers. They make good plants for the cool greenhouse border or for pots. Grow in a proprietary peat compost and keep well ventilated especially in summer. Provide light shade during the summer months. Propagate by lateral stem cuttings in summer.

coccinea
A scarlet-flowered shrub having pendulous clusters of 8 or more small blooms with a 1½–2 in. tube, opening to ¾ in. across, shallowly lobed and creamy-yellow in the throat. They are borne at the end of long, downy twigs with the 3–5 in., oblong to ovate pointed leaves. Easily cultivated reaching 4 ft or more in cultivation. Central America.

grandiflora
A tall, downy shrub having broad ovate leaves up to 5 in. in length, somewhat heart-shaped at the base. The rich purple flowers, which are borne in clusters at the ends of the shoots, have a 1½ in. tube opening to 5 pointed lobes, 1¼ in. across, produced in autumn. Ecuador, Peru.

tubulosa
A 4–6 ft shrub bearing large clusters of up to 20 deep purple blooms.

Each has a cylindrical tube, $1\frac{1}{2}$ in. long, opening to 5 lobes, $\frac{1}{2}$ in. across and a paler purple. The flowers open in August. The leaves are long oval, up to 5 in. in length and greyish-green. Tropical America.

IPOMOEA (CONVOLVULACEAE) Morning Glory
A showy genus of climbing plants with large flowers which open early in the morning and begin to fade soon after mid-day. They need some form of support to make a good display, and are also very good pot plants. Grow in a loam-based compost. Propagate by seed in March or April.

batatas Sweet-potato Vine
A tuberous rooted species which can be grown in a hanging basket. The leaves are broadly triangular and toothed, and the 2 in. funnel-shaped flowers, purple, reddish to white, grow in clusters of 3 or 4 on long stalks. The tuberous roots are edible. E. Indies.

biloba syn. **I. pes-caprae**
A large prostrate or climbing, hairless perennial with broad, 2-lobed, fleshy leaves and 1–2 in., bell-shaped pinkish or purple flowers borne in groups of 1–3 blooms. Tropics.

bonariensis
A purple-stemmed twining species having leaves cordate at base and divided into 3–5 rounded lobes and 3–7 flowered clusters of purplish-pink blooms which open in summer one at a time. A plant for the warm greenhouse. Argentine.

horsfalliae
A handsome, evergreen climber for the warm greenhouse. It has deeply cut glossy leaves with 5 very pointed leaflets and clusters of large, rose pink trumpet-shaped flowers with slightly reflexed petals, opening in winter. W. Indies.

pes-caprae see **I. biloba**

purpurea syn. **Pharbitis purpurea**
An annual climbing species having entire, heart-shaped leaves and beautiful purple blooms 3 in. across. Although these are short lived, the plant bears flowers continuously from July to September. Tropical America.
'Scarlet O'Hara', a good form with deep crimson flowers, **297.**

rubro-caerulea see **I. tricolor**

tricolor syn. **I. rubro-caerulea**
A twining climber with thin stems which can grow to 8 ft or more. Between July and September it bears an abundance of pale blue-purple flowers which open to 5 in. across each morning and die during the afternoon to be replaced by blooms the next day. Mexico. **298.**

Ipomoea, Star see **Quamoclit coccinea**

IRESINE (AMARANTHACEAE)
A genus of ornamental foliage plants which make attractive pot plants for house or greenhouse. They should be grown in a loam-based compost or proprietary peat mix, and must be kept rather dry through the winter. Propagate by stem cuttings in spring or autumn.

herbstii Beefsteak Plant
A 12–18 in. plant with bright red stems and branches and distinctive, round to heart-shaped leaves, notched at the apex and purplish-red above with lighter veins and crimson beneath. Keep in sunshine to bring out the colours at their best. S. America.
'Aureo-reticulata' has bright green leaves with yellow veins, and deep red stems.

lindenii Bloodleaf
A narrower leaved species than *I. herbstii* with spear-shaped, pointed leaves which are a rich, deep red with a lighter central stripe. Ecuador.
'Formosa' has yellow leaves with light green markings, and red stems.

Iris, African see **Moraea iridioides**
Iris, Peacock see **Moraea glaucopsis**

Iron-bark Tree see **Eucalyptus**
Iron Cross see **Begonia masoniana**
Isolepis see **Scirpus**
Isoloma see **Kohleria**
Ivy see **Hedera**
Ivy Arum see **Scindapsus**
Ivy, Devil's see **Scindapsus aureus**
Ivy, Grape see **Rhoicissus rhomboidea**
Ivy-leaved Geranium see **Pelargonium peltatum**
Ivy-leaved Peperomia see **Peperomia hederifolia**
Ivy, Miniature Grape see **Cissus striata**
Ivy, Parlour see **Philodendron scandens**
Ivy, Swedish see **Plectranthus oertendahlii**
Ivy Tree see × **Fatshedera**

IXIA (IRIDACEAE) Corn Lily
viridiflora Green Ixia
A delightful species of bulbous plants having long, stiff, grass-like leaves and tall, wiry stems bearing spikes of starry flowers. It has been much used for hybridization. The true species has up to 18 in. stems of greenish flowers with a darker, bluish centre. The hybrids are generally more robust reaching 18 in. in height and have a wide range of colour forms, **229.** Plant in pots in loam-based compost and only water when the plant is in growth. Propagate by offsets from the corms or by seed sown in March.
'Afterglow', soft pink outside, orange-fawn inside with a dark red centre;
'Artemis', white with black centre with carmine backs to the petals;
'Blue Bird', white with a vivid red eye;
'Conqueror', deep yellow with dark red eye, carmine on the reverse;
'Rose Queen', the whole flower a soft rose-pink;
'Venus', deep carmine-red with a dark eye.

IXORA (RUBIACEAE)
coccinea Flame of the Woods
A 3–4 ft evergreen shrub having oblong, heart-shaped stalkless, leathery leaves and clusters of beautiful, vivid scarlet flowers, the tube almost 2 in. long with 4 spreading pointed lobes. A number of colour variants are known in cultivation. A striking plant for the warm greenhouse, best in pots, in a loam or peat-based compost. It is propagated by cuttings. E. Indies.

J

JACARANDA (BIGNONIACEAE)
mimosifolia syn. **J. acutifolia, J. ovalifolia**
An ornamental semi-evergreen shrub or tree to 10 ft or more high, with 18 in. fern-like leaves, the primary axis with 20–40 branches each with 700–1500 leaflets in fully grown specimens. The showy, blue, drooping flowers are borne in 8–12 in. erect clusters in June but only on large specimens. When small its decorative foliage makes it a good house plant, but it is best grown in the cool or warm greenhouse border. Propagate by cuttings of half-ripe shoots taken in summer. Brazil.

Jacobean Lily see **Sprekelia formosissima**

JACOBINIA (ACANTHACEAE)
A genus of colourful, evergreen sub-shrubs with 2-lipped, tubular flowers and entire leaves. They grow well in the warm greenhouse, most species flowering in winter. Keep moist throughout the year. Propagate by cuttings of young shoots in April.

carnea
A 6 ft shrub with dark green, glossy, slender-pointed leaves, and tight 4–6 in. clusters of pink to carmine flowers borne at the ends of the shoots in August and September. Brazil. **300.**

chrysostephana
A 4 ft shrub with long, mid-green leaves with tapering points, the veins

showing red on the underside. The yellow flowers are carried in dense terminal heads and open from November to February. Mexico.

coccinea syn. **Pachystachys coccinea**　✳
The bright scarlet flowers of this species are borne in February in crowded 2 in. clusters at the ends of the stems. The leaves are elliptic to oval and carried on branches which make a 5 ft shrub. Brazil. **301.**

pauciflora syn. **Libonia floribunda**　✳
A plant having a very different appearance from the other species mentioned here, its long, yellow-tipped scarlet flowers growing singly from the axils of the leaves. They are produced from October to May. The shrub is much branched and grows to 2 ft in height. It makes a very decorative potted plant and can be grown in a cool greenhouse. Brazil. **302.**

pohliana
A strong growing plant reaching over 4 ft with dense, 6 in. oval leaves and clustered terminal ovoid heads of bright crimson flowers. They are borne in August and September. Brazil.
velutina has softlyhairy leaves and 2 in. long, pale pink flowers.

suberecta　✳　🐦
A low, spreading species reaching only 18 in. in height. It has grey velvety hairy twigs and leaves and small terminal clusters of orange-scarlet flowers which are open from July to September. It makes a good basket plant. Uruguay. **303.**

Jamaica Honeysuckle see **Passiflora laurifolia**
Japanese Anise Tree see **Illicium anisatum**
Japanese Lantern see **Hibiscus schizopetalus**
Japanese Painted Fern see **Athyrium goeringianum**
Japanese Pittosporum see **Pittosporum tobira**
Jasmine see **Jasminum**
Jasmine, Cape see **Gardenia jasminoides**
Jasmine, Chilean see **Mandevilla suaveolens**
Jasmine, Crape see **Ervatamia coronaria**
Jasmine, Madagascar see **Stephanotis floribunda**

JASMINUM (OLEACEAE) Jasmine
A popular genus of garden shrubs of which the two species described below need cool greenhouse treatment. The flowers are tubular opening out to become flat and star-like. Although they will grow in large pots, they are best in the greenhouse border and need supports for climbing. Keep the plants moist. Propagate by taking stem cuttings in spring or in August and September.

mesnyi syn. **primulinum** Primrose Jasmine　✳
A somewhat rambling, evergreen shrub which needs training up supports to show its full beauty. The 1–3 in. leaves are divided into 3 oval leaflets, while the semi-double, 2 in., primrose-yellow flowers are borne from March to May in the axils of the leaves. China. **304.**

polyanthum　✳
A semi-evergreen climber which grows up to 10 ft in height, and can reach 20 ft in a greenhouse border. It has dark green divided leaves, 3–5 in. long with 5–7 leaflets and the white and pale pink budded, white flowers are borne in 2–4 in. clusters from November to April. They will flower as young specimens in pots. China.

primulinum see **J. mesnyi**

Java Glorybean see **Clerodendrum speciosissimum**
Jelly Beans see **Sedum rubrotinctum**
Jerusalem Cherry see **Solanum pseudocapsicum**
Jerusalem Cherry, False see **Solanum capsicastrum**
Jerusalem Thorn see **Parkinsonia aculeata**
Jewel Plant see **Bertolonia**
Joseph's Coat see **Alternanthera versicolor**

JOVELLANA (SCROPHULARIACEAE)
A genus of plants grown for their curiously beautiful helmet-shaped flowers which are related to and reminiscent of *Calceolaria*. They are good cool greenhouse plants and make pleasing short term specimens for the home. Use a peat mix or loam-based compost for pot culture. Propagate by seeds in spring or stem cuttings in summer.

sinclairii　✳
An upright, hairy sub-shrub with toothed elliptic leaves downy above and smooth beneath, and loose, branching heads of white to pale lilac flowers, spotted with red and markedly 2-lipped, the upper shorter than the lower. They open in June. New Zealand.

violacea　✳
A 6 ft evergreen shrub with densely hairy branches bearing small deep green, simple leaves, with irregular marginal teeth and lobes. The loose terminal clusters of flowers are borne in July, the individual blooms being ½ in. across, pale yellow to lilac with violet spots. Chile. **305.**

Jupiter's Beard see **Anthyllis barba-jovis**

K

Kaffir Lily see **Clivia**
Kahikatea see **Podocarpus dacrydioides**
Kahili Ginger see **Hedychium gardnerianum**

KALANCHOE (CRASSULACEAE)
Popular leaf-succulents grown in some cases for their flowers and in other cases for their attractive leaves. They are closely allied to *Bryophyllum*, which is sometimes included in this genus. The main difference is that kalanchoes do not bear plantlets in the notches of the leaves, they mostly flower in winter, and require somewhat higher winter temperatures. Whatever the botanical position, therefore, there are sound practical reasons for treating them separately. Cultivation as for terrestrial succulents, remembering that the main growing period is often in winter. They should not however be wholly dry even in the resting period. Propagation is either by seed, or by stem cuttings in summer. Winter temperatures should be 50°F., but plants will survive 40°F., though winter flowers will be checked.

beharensis　🐦
The small, pink flowers appear in March and April, although they are seldom seen in cultivation, the plant being grown for its leaves. These are brown, triangular, 5–8 in. long and edged with a double row of teeth. They are covered in short brown fine hairs which give them the appearance and feel of velvet. The hairs gradually become white and disappear as the leaves age. Behara, Madagascar.

blossfeldiana　✳
A winter or spring flowering species grown for the 1–1½ in. long scarlet flowers which are borne in large branching heads. The leaves are dark green with a red edge, 3 in. long and 1½ in. wide, with a notched tip. Cuttings will root but propagation is best from seed sown in February. Madagascar. There are a number of forms and hybrids, popular as flowering pot plants.
'Emma Lord', with large heads of loosely held scarlet flowers. **306;**
'Morning Sun' is a yellow variety, **307.**
'Tom Thumb', a dwarf variety with scarlet flowers. **308.**

marmorata　🐦
The flowers, which occur from March to May, are white, 3 in. long but rarely produced in cultivation. The roundish leaves, up to 4 in. wide, are green with a waxy coating and large brown markings. Ethiopia, Eritrea.

millotii
A softly hairy branched plant having spoon shaped leaves which are fleshy and have wavy margins. They grow on 2–3 in. stems making a compact plant. Africa. **309.**

pumila　🐦
The leaves are completely covered with a white, pink-tinged meal; they are narrow, about 1 in. long and have coarse teeth. With its prostrate stems, this species is a good plant for a hanging basket. The flowers are pink to red-violet, 1 in. long. Madagascar. **310.**

tomentosa　🐦
Flowers are very rare in cultivation. The leaves are covered with short silvery hairs, becoming rust-red near the serrated tip. They are 1½ in. long, ¾ in. wide, and are borne in a loose rosette at the end of a stem which branches from the base. Madagascar.

verticillata see **Bryophyllum tubiflorum**
Kaleidoscope Flower, Orange see **Streptanthera cuprea**
Kaleidoscope Flower, White see **Streptanthera elegans**
Kangaroo Apple see **Solanum aviculare**
Kangaroo Paw see **Anigozanthos manglesii**
Kangaroo Thorn see **Acacia armata**
Kangaroo Vine see **Cissus antarctica**
Karo see **Pittosporum crassifolium**
Kashmir Cypress see **Cupressus cashmeriana**
Kentia see **Howea**
King of the Bromeliads see **Vriesea hieroglyphica**
King Protea see **Protea cynaroides**
Kleinia see **Senecio**
Knife Acacia see **Acacia cultriformis**

KOCHIA (CHENOPODIACEAE)

scoparia trichophylla Summer Cypress, Fire Bush
A 3 ft annual which forms a dense, cypress-like bush and makes a most colourful pot plant for the cool greenhouse. The very narrow, almost thread-like 2–3 in., pale-green leaves turn a deep bronze-red to crimson in autumn. Grow in a loam-based compost and propagate from seed in March. S. Europe, Asia.
'Childsii' is a neater, more compact cultivar.

KOHLERIA (GESNERIACEAE)

A genus of evergreen plants for the warm greenhouse. They have attractive, tubular, somewhat foxglove-like flowers which open at the mouth into slightly recurved lobes. Grow in pots in loam-based compost in a humid atmosphere, keeping moist while the plants are growing. Propagate by dividing the rhizomes in March, or by taking stem cuttings in summer.

amabilis
An erect, hairy plant reaching 2 ft in height. The ovate scalloped leaves are dark green with dark purple veins. The large, dark rose flowers are spotted and blotched with darker red-purple 1–2 in the axils and open singly from June to August. Colombia.

bogotensis syn. **Isoloma bogotensis**
An erect plant to 24 in. with hairy stems. The large, closely toothed leaves are ovate and conspicuously net-veined under a softly downy surface. They are dark green with whitish mottling, especially at the centre, and reddish beneath. The 1½ in. orange and yellow flowers are spotted with red, and are borne in the leaf axils on long stalks, opening from June to September. Colombia.

digitaliflorum syn. **Isoloma digitaliflorum**
A robust, erect, hairy plant, 12–18 in. high, with large ovate, pointed leaves and short, terminal clusters of big, foxglove-like flowers, the tube rose-purple above and white beneath, the lobes green with purple spots. They open from July to November. Colombia.

elegans
A softly hairy, somewhat reddish species with mid to deep green 6 in. oval leaves and orange-red flowers which grow in clusters of about 4 and are produced from July to September. Southern Mexico to Panama.

eriantha syn. **Isoloma eriantha**
A stout species which can reach 4 ft but will produce flowers when less than a foot in height. Reddish stems carry dark green, ovate-lanceolate leaves with red hairs along the margins. The woolly hairy, scarlet flowers are 1½–2 in. in length, the lower petals being yellow spotted. The flowers are borne in small clusters from June to September. Colombia. **311.**

tubiflorum syn. **Isoloma tubiflorum**
A 1½–2 ft hairy plant with large, ovate leaves having a corrugation of veins over the bronze-green upper surface, the underside being red. The small inflated orange flowers are softly hairy with yellow markings at the mouth. Colombia.

Kohuhu see **Pittosporum tenuifolium**
Kris Plant see **Alocasia sanderiana**

L

Lace Fern, Grotto see **Microlepia speluncae**
Lace Orchid see **Odontoglossum crispum**
Lace Trumpets see **Sarracenia drummondii**

LACHENALIA (LILIACEAE) Cape Cowslip

A genus of decorative bulbous plants which make good pot plants for winter and early spring flowering in the cool greenhouse. They also grow well in hanging baskets. Flowering specimens also make attractive short term house plants. They have soft, green strap-shaped leaves often attractively mottled and spikes of tubular flowers borne on erect, stems. Plant the bulbs in loam-based compost and water while the plants are making leaf and flowering. Keep dry after the leaves have died down. Propagate by separating bulbils when repotting.

aloides syn. **L. quadricolor, L. tricolor**
A multicoloured species having yellow pendulous flowers which shade to green and red and open from December to March on 9–12 in. purple mottled stems. The long leaves are similarly marked. S. Africa. **312.**
'Aurea', (syn. *L. aurea*) has bright, clear golden-yellow flowers on tall stems;
'Nelsonii' (syn. *L. nelsonii*) a hybrid with yellow and green flowers.

aurea see **L. aloides** 'Aurea'

bulbifera syn. **L. pendula**
The purple or red pendulous flowers are edged with green and carried in few-flowered heads on stout 10 in. stalks in January and February. S. Africa.

glaucina Opal Lachenalia
A low growing species with stems often not exceeding 6 in. The white to deep blue flowers are tinged with yellow or red and borne almost at right angles to the stem, in dense spikes at the top of the stout stalk. They are produced in February and March. S. Africa.

mutabilis syn. **L. orchioides** Fairy Lachenalia
The stubby violet blue flowers fade to yellow green and finally brownish as they age. They are borne in February on slender pale green stems. The leaves are usually spotted. S. Africa.

nelsonii see **L. aloides** 'Nelsonii'
orchioides see **L. mutabilis**

× **pearsonii**
A hybrid with brilliant orange flowers, red on the outside of the tube, and edged a deeper hue. They are borne from January to March on 18 in. mottled stems. The mid-green leaves are also purple marked. Garden origin.

pendula see **L. bulbifera**
quadricolor see **L. aloides**
tricolor see **L. aloides**

Lady's Slipper see **Paphiopedilum**

LAGERSTROEMIA (LYTHRACEAE)
indica Crape Myrtle
A handsome, deciduous shrub which makes a large plant for the cool greenhouse. It has 1–2½ in. elliptic leaves and 6–8 in. terminal clusters of pink to deep red flowers. Each blossom has 6 petals which appear as though stalked, being narrowed at the centre and opening out into a rounded, frilled lobe, crinkled like crepe paper. Grow in tubs or the greenhouse border, using a loam-based compost. Water freely in the growing season, sparingly in winter. Cut back the flowered shoots by at least a half each spring. Propagate by stem cuttings in spring or late summer. S. Asia.

LANTANA (VERBENACEAE)
A genus of showy evergreen shrubs, two of which make excellent plants for the cool greenhouse, growing well in pots, tubs or in the border. Plant in a loam-based compost, keep well watered in summer and give plenty of light and air. Propagate by sowing seeds in spring or taking stem cuttings from young shoots in late summer.

camara
A hairy, sometimes prickly shrub with spreading branches and shining,

dark green, ovate leaves. The small, compact flower heads change in colour as they age from white through yellow to brick-red. As the heads open outwards from the centre they show many variations in colour in one head. They are borne on stiff erect stalks from May to October. Tropical America. **313.**

'Cloth of Gold', has single coloured, yellow-gold flowers;
'Snow Queen' has snow white flowers.

montevidensis see **L. selloviana**

selloviana syn. **L. montevidensis**
A downy, procumbent shrub rarely exceeding 1 ft in height, but spreading to 3 ft or more horizontally. It has ovate leaves and clustered flattish heads of small, bright rosy-lilac flowers with a yellow eye. They are borne throughout the year but are at their best in summer. Uruguay. **315.**

LAPAGERIA (LILIACEAE)
rosea Chilean Bell Flower
A slender evergreen climber which needs a supporting frame of wires or trellis up which it can twine. It is best in the cool greenhouse border, though it will respond to pot culture. The chief feature of the plant is the beautiful, waxy rosy crimson, bell-shaped blooms which are borne on pendent stems and are 3 in. long. The petals are white spotted within and they open from July to October, contrasting well with the very deep green, oval leaves. Propagate by seeds in March or April or by layering shoots in spring or autumn. Chile. **314.**

Lasiandra macrantha see **Tibouchina semidecandra**
Latania borbonica see **Livistona chinensis**
Lavender, Sea see **Limonium**
Leadwort see **Plumbago**
Leaf Flower see **Breynia nivosa** 'Roseopicta'
Ledebouria socialis see **Scilla violacea**
Lemon see **Citrus limon**
Lemon-scented Gum see **Eucalyptus citriodora**
Lemon Verbena see **Lippia citriodora**
Lemon Vine see **Pereskia aculeata**

LEPTOSPERMUM (MYRTACEAE)
A genus of nearly hardy evergreen shrubs which make excellent plants for the cool greenhouse. They have very small, entire, dark-green leaves and open, 5-petalled flowers. Grow in the border or in tubs of loam-based compost. Propagate by stem cuttings taken in June or July.

cunninghamii
The small silvery-grey leaves and dark red stems make this a most attractive species. It bears white flowers in July and can reach an overall height of about 6 ft. Australia. **316.**

humifusum syn. **L. scoparium prostratum**
A prostrate shrub reaching 6 in. in height, with a spread of 3 ft. It has dark green, narrow, blunt leathery leaves and is covered with $\frac{3}{4}$ in., white flowers which open from May to June. Tasmania.

laevigatum Australian Tea Tree
A tall shrub or tree reaching 20 ft or more. It has narrow oblong, blunt leaves, 1 in. in length and is completely hairless. The white flowers have $\frac{1}{2}$ in. petals which open flat and are borne singly in the axils of the leaves. Australia.

myrtifolium
An 8-15 ft shrub with flexuous, silky shoots and small, oblong pointed leaves scarcely reaching $\frac{1}{2}$ in. in length. The white flowers are borne abundantly on solitary stalks in the leaf axils. Australia, Tasmania.

scoparium Manuka, Tea Tree
A small tree usually growing to 10 ft in cultivation, though reaching twice this height in the wild. The tiny leaves are fragrant when crushed, and the flat flowers can be white, pink or red, and open in May and June. New Zealand.

'Nanum' is a dwarf form with abundant rose-pink flowers, **317;**
'Red Damask' has fully double, deep red flowers.

scoparium prostratum see **L. humifusum**

LESCHENAULTIA (GOODENIACEAE)
biloba
A beautiful evergreen shrub of bushy habit up to 3 ft. It has narrow, heather-like leaves borne along the length of the stems, and 1-1¼ in. blue flowers growing stalkless in the leaf axils from June to August, forming a loose, leafy cluster. Grow in a well ventilated cool greenhouse in a peat compost, either in pots or the border. Propagate by seeds in spring or stem cuttings in late summer. West Australia.

LEUCADENDRON (PROTEACEAE)
argenteum Silver Tree
A very beautiful foliage tree for the large greenhouse, eventually reaching 10 ft or more. It has 2½-5 in. leaves, spear-shaped with a slender point, which are clothed on both surfaces with a dense covering of fine, silvery silky hairs. The small tight cone-like clusters of flowers are borne in 1 in. heads at the ends of the branches, but only on large mature specimens. Grow in the border of a light, well ventilated, cool greenhouse or in tubs and do not overwater. Use a loam-based or proprietary peat compost. Propagate by seeds in spring. S. Africa. **318.**

Leucophyta see **Calocephalus**
Levant Cotton see **Gossypium herbaceum**
Liberian Coffee see **Coffea liberica**
Libonia floribunda see **Jacobinia pauciflora**
Life Plant see **Bryophyllum**

LILIUM (LILIACEAE) Lily
A mainly hardy genus of bulbous plants with handsome waxy flowers. Certain tender species are very suitable for pot culture or for the greenhouse border. They have scaly bulbs and stout stems bearing lanceolate leaves. The flowers are large and either trumpet or turks-cap shaped. Plant in a loam-based compost or a peat mix and keep just moist until the shoots appear, then water freely, especially when in flower. Shade from hot sun and keep well ventilated in summer. Propagate by offsets at potting time or in autumn or by seed in spring.

auratum Gold-rayed Lily
The largest flowered most spectacular of the genus *Lilium* with 8-10 in. wide gold-rayed white flowers on 4-6 ft stems. The willowy leaves are rich dark green. There are forms with crimson rays to the petals which are quite often seen. Although a hardy species it responds well to culture in large pots in the cool conservatory or greenhouse. It has a heavy sweet fragrance and is suitable as a short term house plant when in bloom. Japan. **319.**

brownii
A beautiful species bearing large, trumpet-shaped blooms, 6 in. long, ivory-white with a deep chocolate brown flush on the outside of the petals. They are borne on a stiff, 3 or 4 ft stem in spikes of 2-5 flowers, and are produced in July. China.

formosanum
A stately species having 1-6 ft stems bearing trumpet-shaped flowers in August and September. They are waxy white, often marked on the outside with maroon or dark brown. The plant has many, narrow-pointed leaves and the stem is a deep purple-brown. Formosa.

longiflorum Easter or White Trumpet Lily
A beautiful pure white, fragrant species which makes an excellent pot plant. The 5-7 in. trumpet-shaped blooms have yellow anthers and are borne on 2-3 ft stiff stems which are clothed with 3-5 in. narrow pointed, upward arching leaves. The flowers are produced in July and August. Formosa.

nepalense
A bi-coloured species having fragrant, narrow, drooping flowers, greenish-yellow, flushed with deep maroon or purple in the throat, the outer petals recurved. They are borne on 2-3 ft purplish stems in June and July. The leaves are few and rather distant. Nepal.

Lily see **Lilium**
Lily, African see **Agapanthus**
Lily, Amazon see **Eucharis grandiflora**
Lily, Australian Sword see **Anigozanthos manglesii**
Lily, Aztec see **Sprekelia formosissima**

Lily, Belladonna see **Amaryllis belladonna**
Lily, Blood see **Haemanthus**
Lily, Boat see **Rhoeo spathacea**
Lily, Bow see **Cyrtanthus mackenii**
Lily, Butterfly see **Hedychium coronarium**
Lily, Corn see **Ixia**
Lily, Fire see **Cyrtanthus sanguineus**
Lily, Giant Spider see **Crinum giganteum**
Lily, Ginger see **Hedychium**
Lily, Glory see **Gloriosa**
Lily, Golden Spider see **Lycoris aurea**
Lily, Guernsey see **Nerine sarniensis**
Lily, Hidden see **Curcuma roscoana**
Lily, Ifafa see **Cyrtanthus mackenii**
Lily, Inanda see **Cyrtanthus sanguineus**
Lily, Jacobean see **Sprekelia formosissima**
Lily, Kaffir see **Clivia**
Lily-of-the-Nile see **Agapanthus africanus**
Lily-of-the valley see **Convallaria majalis**
Lily, Ox-tongue see **Haemanthus coccineus**
Lily, Pink Arum see **Zantedeschia rehmannii**
Lily, Red Ifafa see **Cyrtanthus o'brienii**
Lily, Rock see **Arthropodium cirrhatum**
Lily, Salmon Blood see **Haemanthus multiflorus**
Lily, Scarborough see **Vallota speciosa**
Lily, Scarlet Ginger see **Hedychium coccineum**
Lily, Sea see **Pancratium maritimum**
Lily, Siberian see **Ixiolirion montanum**
Lily, Spider see **Hymenocallis**
Lily, Swamp see **Crinum × powellii**
Lily, Triplet see **Brodiaea coronaria**
Lily Turf see **Ophiopogon**
Lily, White Arum see **Zantedeschia aethiopica**
Lily, Yellow Arum see **Zantedeschia pentlandii**
Lily, Zephyr see **Zephyranthes**

LIMONIUM (PLUMBAGINACEAE) Sea Lavender, Statice
A genus which includes the familiar sea lavenders. The two species described below are both treated as annuals in cultivation and make very attractive pot plants for the cool greenhouse. Propagate by seeds sown in a loam-based compost in autumn or spring.

bonduellii
This species as well as making an attractive pot plant is excellent for drying for flower decoration. It grows to 12 in. or more, and has a basal rosette of 3–5 in. deeply lobed, narrow light green leaves, and loose clusters of yellow flowers borne in much branched heads from July to September. Algeria.

suworowii syn. **Statice suworowii**
An 18 in. species with the same uses as *L. bonduellii*. The long undulate leaves are light green and are borne in a rosette, from which rise a number of stiff stalks bearing branched plume-like spikes of rose-pink flowers. They are produced from July to September. W. Turkestan. **320.**

Linden, Window see **Sparmannia africana**

LIPPIA (VERBENACEAE)
citriodora syn. **Aloysia triphylla** Lemon Verbena
A strongly lemon-scented shrub growing to 5 ft. It has long, narrow, yellowish-green leaves and panicles of very small, pale mauvish-white flowers. Nearly hardy it makes a very good plant for the greenhouse or conservatory border or for large pots, when it should be planted in a loam-based compost. Keep well watered and ventilated during the summer months and repot every other year in March. Propagate by cuttings of side shoots taken in July. Chile. **321.**

Lipstick Vine see **Aeschynanthus lobbianus**

LITHOPS (AIZOACEAE) Pebble Plants, Living Stones, Stoneface
Formerly included in *Mesembryanthemum*, they are so well camouflaged to resemble stones that in their native desert habitats it is difficult to distinguish them from stones of the same size. The plant body consists of a pair of immensely thick leaves, about 1 in. high, joined together to form what seems to be a single stem with a slit across the top. The stem, from which the leaves grow, is buried in the soil. They eventually form thickened clumps, spreading outwards, never upwards, but it may take many years for some extremely slow-growing species. The flowers, yellow or white, are about 1 in. across and usually appear in September. For culture see terrestrial succulents in the Introduction. Keep absolutely dry from October to April. Minimum winter temperature 40°F. Propagate by seed.

bella
The brownish-yellow leaves have darkish markings of blue, green or grey on the slightly concave upper surface, resemble the stones, usually granite, of their native surroundings. They eventually form clusters of 6–8 stems. The white flowers, 1 in. across, are borne freely in autumn. Namaqualand.

erniana
An attractive species with greyish leaves marked with reddish-brown reticulations, 1 in. high, producing white flowers in September.

lesliei
Up to 1¾ in. high, the upper reddish-brown surface intriguingly patterned with greenish-brown grooves. Yellow flowers, 1 in. across, form in September. E. S. Africa.

olivacea
The dark green leaves, ¾ in. high, have a deep cleft between them and bear yellow flowers in autumn. Cape Province.

optica
Forming clustered clumps, the greyish-green leaves are divided by a deep cleft. Among the few with leaf tips having 'windows' of translucent cells which admit light to the inner tissues. Small plants, barely ¾ in. high, bearing white flowers in autumn. Namaqualand.

pseudotruncatella
The leaves are generally grey-green in colour with darker striations. The yellow flowers are borne in September and October. S. W. Africa.
mundtii, with orange-yellow flowers, petals red tipped.

salicola
The 1–1½ in. ovoid plant bodies are cleft and flattened on top. They grow singly or in clumps. Their colour is grey with dark green, translucent mottling above, outlined with a somewhat whitish line. S. Africa. **322.**

turbiniformis
The brownish, warty leaves, ¾–1 in. high, are attractively marked with rusty veining. The flowers are yellow, 1½ in. across, and appear in September. Namaqualand.

Little Banana see **Chirita micromusa**

LITTONIA (LILIACEAE)
modesta
An unusual, but very attractive climbing species reaching 2–6 ft. It has long, narrow shining green leaves which are widely spaced along the unbranched stem, each leaf ending in a small tendril. The wide spreading, bell-shaped flowers are a rich orange, and are borne singly in the axils of the leaves. A plant for pots or the border in a cool greenhouse. Grow in a loam-based or a proprietary peat compost, and shade from the summer sun. Propagate by seed in spring or offset tubers when re-potting. S. Africa.
'Keitii', a more free-flowering, vigorous plant.

Living Stones see **Lithops**

LIVISTONA (PALMAE)
A species of tall palms which make good house plants when young, larger specimens being suitable for tubs. Grow in loam-based compost, keep a humid atmosphere in summer and shade from summer sun. Propagate by seed in spring.

australis Australian Fountain Palm
When fully mature, this palm can reach 80 ft, but it is extremely decorative when young. It has fan-like leaves, the segments narrow and

ribbon-like, dark glossy green with a yellow central nerve. When young the trunk is brown and fibrous, but it loses this as it ages. Australia.

chinensis miscalled **Latania borbonica** Chinese Fan Palm
A very attractive plant for decoration when young, having fan-like leaves divided half way to the centre into long, pointed segments, and borne on stiff stems which rise from the centre of the plant. As it matures the trunk grows and it can finally attain 30 ft with gigantic leaves 6 ft across. China.

LOBIVIA (CACTACEAE)

Almost spherical-stemmed small cacti with large spines and bristly hairs. Very attractive bell-shaped flowers of red or yellow are often freely borne. They open during the day and close again at night. The name is an anagram of Bolivia, where most of the plants grow. For culture see terrestrial cacti in the Introduction. Shading in hot weather is desirable. Offsets form easily from the base and are detached and rooted without difficulty. Minimum winter temperature 45°F.

allegraiana
Striking pink or red, broad funnel-shaped flowers, 2 in. long, form in summer on 6 in. high, rounded dark green stems which have 7–11 pronounced ribs, spiralled and tubercled. There are about 12 curved brownish spines, up to 1¼ in. long to each areole. Peru.

hertrichiana
The virtually globular dark green stems, rarely more than 4 in. in height, bear splendid scarlet flowers, about 2 in. in diameter and 2–3 in. long, in summer. Pale to dark yellow spines, 7 radials and a single longer central, 1 in. in length, grow on each areole. Peru.

jajoiana
The roughly cylindrical, 2 in. diameter stems are green and composed of 14–20 tubercled ribs. The areoles have ten pinkish radial spines and one extra large, black central. Brilliant claret blooms, 2 in. across, are borne in summer. Argentina.

pygmaea see **Rebutia pygmaea**

Lobster Claw see **Clianthus puniceus**
Lollipop Plant see **Pachystachys lutea**
Lomaria see **Blechnum**
Lophomyrtus bullata see **Myrtus bullata**
Lophomyrtus obcordata see **Myrtus obcordata**

LOTUS (LEGUMINOSAE)

A widespread genus of which the two species described are suitable for greenhouse culture. *L. bertholetii* makes a very good plant for a hanging basket while both are good pot plants. Propagate by seed, though *L. jacobaeus* can also be raised by stem cuttings in summer.

bertholetii Coral Gem
A silvery hairy perennial with straggling branches and leaves with fine, needle-like spreading segments. The vermilion pea flowers grow in clusters towards the ends of the branches in May. Canary Isles.

jacobaeus St James Trefoil
A sub-shrubby, grey-hairy perennial 1–3 ft in height. The leaflets are long, narrow and fine pointed. The pea-shaped flowers are a black-purple with a yellow standard and grow in clusters along the grey branches. Cape Verde Island.

Lotus of Egypt, Blue see **Nymphaea caerulea**
Lotus, Sacred Indian see **Nelumbo nucifera**

LUCULIA (RUBIACEAE)

A genus of evergreen shrubs with terminal clusters of fragrant, waxy, tubular flowers. They can be grown in pots or tubs in loam-based compost, but are best in the greenhouse border. They need to be kept moist through the growing season and should be repotted in spring every second or third year. Propagate by stem cuttings taken in May.

grandifolia
A large shrub or small tree reaching 10 ft. It has broadly oval, mid-green leaves which are rust coloured at the margins and can grow to 15 in. in

length. The fragrant white flowers have a 2–2½ in. tube opening into flat, star-like lobes at the mouth. They are borne in loose clusters at the ends of the branches in May and June. Bhutan.

gratissima
A 6 ft shrub with pairs of oval, entire, mid-green leaves which are smooth above and downy beneath. The mauve-pink flowers are borne in rounded clusters 4–9 in. across, at the ends of the branches. They open in winter. Himalayas, China.

pinceana
A somewhat similar shrub to *L. gratissima*, but having larger, creamy white flowers, flushed with pink which are borne from May to September. India.

LUFFA (CUCURBITACEAE)

cylindrica syn. **L. aegyptica** Vegetable Sponge
A fast growing tropical climber, holding on by means of tendrils. It has 5–7 lobed, rough hairy leaves like those of a cucumber, and 3 in. wide white or yellow flowers. These are followed by cylindrical fruits up to 2 ft long. They are edible when very young, but are grown commercially for the fibrous skeletal material of the dried fruit as abrasive bathroom 'sponges'. Grow in a warm or cool greenhouse, preferably in a border which has been enriched with well decayed farmyard manure. Alternatively, grow in large pots or tubs of a loam based compost or a proprietary peat mix, preferably with manure added. Provide a support of string or wires. Shade from the hottest sunshine and maintain a humid atmosphere until the fruits are forming. It may be necessary to artificially pollinate the flowers to obtain fruits. Female flowers can be recognized by the tiny immature luffa behind the petals. Propagate by seeds sown in spring. Tropical Asia and Africa.

LYCASTE (ORCHIDACEAE)

A genus of tropical, tree-dwelling (epiphytic) orchids with conical bulbs bearing tough deep green leaves. The waxy, showy flowers are very long lasting and usually fragrant; they comprise three large sepals and three smaller petals. Grow in the cool greenhouse in hanging pots or pans with a compost of equal parts loam, osmunda fibre, leaf mould and sphagnum moss. Keep shaded, but well ventilated during the summer, watering freely. During the winter period, or when they are resting keep just moist but maintain good ventilation. Propagate by division in spring. There are many hybrids between the species, among them the Auburn group with flowers in shades of pink to red, **324, 325.**

cruenta
An excellent house plant bearing, on 6 in. stems, spicily fragrant flowers. They have greenish-yellow sepals and golden-yellow petals 2–4 in. across, at their best in March and April, but flowering spasmodically over a long period. The leaves are 15–18 in. long, firm and a bright mid-green. Guatemala.

fimbriata
A winter and spring flowering species having large, white, fragrant flowers, tinted with yellow or green. The sepals are 2½ in. in length and wider than the 2 in. incurved petals. The lip is 3-lobed and fringed. Brazil.

macrophylla
Most attractive flowers with brownish-red, pale green backed sepals and white petals, both spotted and marked with pink. They are 4–5 in. across and are borne on stems the same height. They open in succession from July to November in many-flowered clusters. Peru, Bolivia.

schilleriana
A pretty species with 3 in. wide flowers comprising long, greenish-brown sepals spreading behind 3 smaller white petals which fold down to the pure white lip. The 2–3 leaves are up to 2 ft long and a deep green. NE. S. America.

skinneri see **L. virginalis**

virginalis syn. **L. skinneri**
A very beautiful and freely flowering species, preferring slightly warmer conditions than those described above. The 10 in. stems bear white, waxy blooms; the sepals and lip with rose-pink marking, the lip being more heavily marked, the petals pinkish or white. They are 4–6 in. across and appear at intervals throughout the year, contrasting with

the very dark green, strap-shaped leaves. Guatemala, Mexico.

'Alba', a pure white species with yellow markings on the lip.

Lycium japonicum see **Serissa foetida**

LYCORIS (AMARYLLIDACEAE)

An attractive group of bulbous plants for the cool greenhouse. They have funnel-shaped flowers with spreading petals and long, strap-shaped leaves which usually develop after flowering. Grow in pots in a loam-based compost and do not allow the bulbs to dry out. Propagate by bulb offsets or by seed in spring.

aurea Golden Spider Lily

A dainty species with golden-yellow flowers with a short tube opening into narrow segments, the spidery look being enhanced by the long yellow stamens which protrude beyond the mouth of the bloom and several are borne on each 12 in. stem. They open in August and September. Better planted in a border than in pots. China.

cinnabarina

A strikingly beautiful species with rich burnt-orange flowers to 3 in. across, borne in 4–6 flowered clusters on 18 in. stems. They open in July and August. E. Asia.

incarnata

A plant similar in form to *L. aurea* but with pale rose-coloured flowers, 3–4 in. across with smoother, straighter petals. 6–12 flowers are borne on the 18 in. stalk in August. Scented. China.

sanguinea

A species with the red flowers in umbels of 3–4 and bearing smooth petal-like lobes, not reflexed as is more usual in this genus. They are borne on 12–18 in. stems in July and August. Japan.

M

Mackaya bella see **Asystasia bella**
Madagascar Dragon Tree see **Dracaena marginata**
Madagascar Jasmine see **Stephanotis floribunda**
Madagascar Periwinkle see **Vinca rosea**
Maidenhair Fern see **Adiantum**
Mallow, False see **Malvastrum**
Mallow, Globe see **Sphaeralcea**
Mallow, Hairy see **Malvastrum scabrosum**

MALVASTRUM (MALVACEAE) False Mallow

A genus of perennial plants of which the following species are tender and need to be grown in cool conditions, either in a border or in pots. Plant in loam-based compost. Propagate by stem cuttings in late summer or seeds in spring.

campanulatum

A 12–18 in. plant, slightly hairy, with large leaves cut into 3–7 deeply toothed lobes. The mallow-like flowers appear in loose heads at the ends of the branches in summer, and the notched petals are a pale, rosy purple. Chile.

capense see **M. scabrosum**

scabrosum syn. **M. capense** Hairy Mallow

A shrubby, branched species bearing ovate leaves with 3-toothed lobes. Deep rose to purple flowers are borne singly or in pairs in the axils of the upper leaves and are produced in late summer. S. Africa.

MALVAVISCUS (MALVACEAE) Sleeping Hibiscus

A genus of shrubs and trees with red tubular flowers borne in the axils of the terminal leaves. They make good plants for the greenhouse or conservatory border or for tubs or large pots. Propagate by stem cuttings in summer.

arboreus

A 10–12 ft shrub with rich red flowers 1 in. across borne in autumn on 1–3 in. stalks in the axils of the leaves. The $2\frac{1}{2}$–$4\frac{1}{2}$ in. long leaves are broadly heart-shaped to elliptic, 3-lobed and rough above, shortly hairy beneath. Mexico. **352.**

mollis

Very similar to *M. arboreus* but the whole plant covered in soft, downy hairs. The 3-lobed leaves are 3–5 in. long. The rich red flowers are borne from August to October in the axils of leaves towards the ends of the branches. S. America.

MAMILLOPSIS (CACTACEAE)

senilis

Globular to cylindrical plants, $2\frac{1}{2}$ in. across and up to 4 in. high. The showy green tubercles give rise to woolly white areoles bearing about 40 short white radial bristles and 4–6 pale yellow central spines, the lowest of which is longest, $\frac{3}{4}$–1 in., and hooked at the tip. Wisps of woolly substance also form in the axils of the areoles, so that the plant appears to be covered with soft white hairs. Orange-yellow to violet flowers, $2\frac{1}{2}$ in. long, with greenish stigmas, appear from near the tubercles at almost any point on the stem. Forms clusters freely when old. For culture see under terrestrial cacti in the Introduction. Propagate by offsets. Minimum winter temperature 40°F. This genus differs from *Mammillaria* in having a long scaly flower tube and projecting stamens. Mexico.

MAMMILLARIA (CACTACEAE)

Sphere-shaped or columnar cacti with tubercles arranged in a spiral fashion and not in ribs as with many other cacti. The short bell-like flowers appear in a ring near the top of the plant, sometimes surrounded by a ring of the previous year's fruits. Generally plants bearing white or cream coloured flowers produce them at a younger stage than those bearing red flowers. Some species are grown purely for the effect of their handsome spines. Most species branch from the base; few plants have solitary stems. Offsets form readily and are easily rooted. For culture see terrestrial cacti in the Introduction. Minimum winter temperature 40°F.

bocasana Powder Puff

One of the easiest forms. Blue-green stems, around 6 in. high and 2 in. across, are massed with silvery white spines and hairs. Each areole has a pronounced yellow or red central spine, longer than the rest and hooked at the top. Small cream flowers are followed by purple fruits. Left undisturbed, clusters of stems will develop 6–8 in. across. Mexico. **326.**

densispina

Growing up to 12 in. high, the cylindrical stems, which do not normally branch, bear cone-shaped tubercles with 25 striking yellow radial spines and up to 6 long centrals, red turning to brown. In summer purplish flowers with yellow inner petals appear freely in a ring round the tips of the shoots. A slow growing species. Mexico.

echinaria see **M. gracilis**

elegans

A slow growing species to 6 in. high, 2–3 in. thick, single-stemmed when young but branching with age. The closely spaced tubercles bear areoles covered in a fuzz of 25–30 short white spines, like small umbrellas all over the stems. White, brown-tipped centrals, usually 2, form strikingly from the centre of the areole. Violet-red flowers form freely in July and August. Mexico.

elongata

Stems cylindrical, upright or spreading, form clusters up to 6 in. high. The attractive spines are yellowish, tipped brown. The flowers are white or yellowish with or without a darker band, about $\frac{1}{2}$ in. long. Keep very dry in autumn and winter. Mexico. **327.**

erythrosperma

Globular 2 in. stems bear areoles with 14–20 fine white radiating radial spines, $\frac{1}{3}$ in. long, and 3–4 central spines yellowish in colour; the longest is hooked. Pinkish blooms form freely in summer followed by carmine-red fruit. Easy in cultivation. Mexico.

gracilis syn. **M. echinaria**

Branching and producing offsets freely, this 4 in. high species has column-shaped stems, 2–$2\frac{1}{2}$ in. thick, vivid green in colour. A mass of small white to yellow radial spines are relieved, in mature plants, by larger brown-tipped centrals. In summer the white or yellow flowers are a distinctive feature. Offsets are easily detached and rooted. Mexico.

hahniana Old Lady Mammillaria
Silky white spines almost cover the clusters of flat topped globular stems, up to 4 in. in diameter. Small crimson flowers are freely borne in summer. Mexico. **328.**

plumosa Feather Cactus
The globular stems are 2–3 in. across and form clusters, almost hidden by a network of plume-like white spines. Needs full sunshine and tolerates lime well. Small white flowers are rarely produced in cultivation. Mexico.

umbrina
Flowering easily when young, this is an exception among the mammillarias. Growing to about 4 in. high and 2 in. thick, plants usually remain single bodied when young but can branch with age. The columnar stems have flattened, even concave tops. Areoles are borne on long sharply cone-shaped tubercles, and have 20–24 slender radial spines and usually 2 centrals, which are much thicker and a striking bright red hue when young, ultimately changing to grey. Carmine to purple blooms develop in early summer. Mexico.

zeilmanniana
Small spines cover the bright green stem, globular when young, becoming cylindrical and about 4 in. high. Often, when these are barely ¾ in. in diameter, they start to flower. The tips of the areoles are surrounded by about 16–19 radial spines, whitish and silvery, and 4 larger reddish-brown centrals, the longest being hooked. Mauve, pale yellow throated blooms ring the tips of the stems in summer. Produces offsets freely. Mexico.
'Alba', a white flowered form, **329.**

Mandarin see **Citrus reticulata**

MANDEVILLA (APOCYNACEAE)

splendens see **Dipladenia splendens**

suaveolens syn. **M. laxa** Chilean Jasmine
A climbing plant with ovate, heart shaped leaves tapering to a narrow tip, dark green with white hairs in vein axils beneath. The 2 in. white or creamy white flowers have a long tube opening out at the mouth to 5 oval petals, tapering and reflexed at the tip. They are very fragrant and are freely produced in summer. A handsome plant for the border, but rarely a successful pot plant, it grows well trained against a wall or posts. Propagate by stem cuttings from the short side shoots. Argentina, Bolivia. **330.**

MANETTIA (RUBIACEAE)
A genus of evergreen climbers with pairs of tapering, undivided leaves and tubular, sometimes somewhat inflated flowers. They are good plants for covering a trellis or pillar in the warm or cool greenhouse. Propagate by cuttings of young shoots in summer.

bicolor
A twining plant with long, narrow, pointed, somewhat blue-green leaves. The stalkless tubular, waxy flowers are a brilliant scarlet in the lower half and bright yellow in the upper half of the tube. These are produced from early summer to late autumn or later. Brazil.

inflata Firecracker Plant
A similar species to *M. bicolor* but generally more roughly hairy and with a mainly red tube to the flower. Like *M. bicolor* it can be grown as a pot plant for the house, and looks particularly attractive trained over a circular wire support. Paraguay, Uruguay.

Manuka see **Leptospermum scoparium**
Maple, Flowering see **Abutilon**
Maple-leaf Begonia, Miniature see **Begonia dregei**

MARANTA (MARANTACEAE)
A genus of evergreen plants grown for their decorative foliage. They make excellent house or warm greenhouse plants and should be grown in pots in loam-based or a proprietary peat compost. They grow rapidly and frequently need re-potting while small. Once established

repot each year in spring. Shade from the sun through the summer. Propagate by division of the rhizomes when repotting, or take cuttings of basal shoots with 2–3 leaves, in summer.

bicolor
The 4–6 in. leaves are elliptic, hairless and dark green on the upper surface having a light green central area with wavy edges and purple beneath. Brazil, Guiana.

leuconeura Prayer Plant, Rabbit's Tracks
The commonest species in cultivation, with elliptic leaves which lie almost horizontally by day, becoming more upright at night like hands in prayer. When young, the leaves are a light emerald-green with brown-purple patches either side of the veins. As they get older the brightness fades and the leaves become more dull.
'Erythrophylla'. Red Herring-bone Plant has leaves patterned with a network of deep crimson veins on a light yellow-green background at the margins, which darkens to a velvety deep green at the centre, **331**;
'Kerchoveana', like *M. leuconeura*, the leaves fold upwards from the centre in the evening. The coloration is a grey-green background with brighter veins and shading from the centre. There are also large blotches between the veins which start a rich chocolate and change to dark green as the leaves age. The underside of the leaf is purple, **332**;
'Massangeana', Rabbit's Foot, a smaller-leaved cultivar with pale green margins and a darker green centre, the whole overlaid by a feathery band of silvery white along the midrib and extending outwards along the lateral veins.

Marbleleaf see under **Peristrophe angustifolia**
Marmalade Bush see **Streptosolen jamesonii**
Martha Washington Pelargonium see **Pelargonium × domesticum**

MARTYNIA (MARTYNIACEAE)
louisiana syn. **Proboscidea jussieui** Unicorn Plant
A 2–3 ft annual plant with wavy, roundish to heart-shaped sticky leaves, 4–12 in. long on branched stems. The 1½–2 in. flowers are bell-shaped and have a yellowish tube marked with green and bright yellow marks and purple dots and lines. The petal lobes are similarly marked on a pale violet background. They are followed by unique horned seed pods. Grow in pots in a cool greenhouse in loam-based or a proprietary peat compost, and propagate by seeds in spring. USA. **333.**

MASDEVALLIA (ORCHIDACEAE)
A rather strange genus of tree-dwelling epiphytic orchids having large colourful sepals which in many species are prolonged into a 'tail' giving the flower a most exotic appearance. None of the species has bulbs. They make good plants for hanging pots or baskets, thriving in the cool greenhouse if kept well watered and shaded from direct sunshine. Propagate by division.

bella
A curiously beautiful species, the large dark yellow sepals are heavily blotched with a dark reddish-brown and taper to 4 in. tails. The lip is white and shell-shaped swings with every movement of the air. The leaves are dark green, 5–7 in. long, and the flowers are produced during winter and spring. Colombia.

coccinea syn. **M. harryana**
A most remarkable and showy orchid of a rich magenta or purple colour. The upper sepal is small, tapering into a 1½ in. tail, often hooked at the tip, while the side sepals are joined for a third of their length and claw-shaped, 1 in. wide and 1½–2 in. long. They have no tail. The small petals and lip are enclosed within the tube formed by the joined sepals. Colombia.

harryana see **M. coccinea**

MAURANDIA syn. ASARINA (SCROPHULARIACEAE)
Climbing perennials, which hold on by twisting the leaf stalks around the supports, with foxglove-like flowers. They are very good for trellis or a wire frame in the cool greenhouse and flower during winter. Propagate

by seeds in spring or by cuttings of young shoots taken in August.

barclaiana ✳ 🐛

A somewhat woody climber having angular lobed leaves on long stalks and $1\frac{1}{2}$–3 in. flowers, with white, rose or purple rounded lobes and a greenish tube, all downy on the outside. They are borne in summer. Mexico.

erubescens ✳ 🐛

The long tubular flowers are rosy-pink, opening to 3 in. across with notched lobes; the tubes are whitish. The flowers are borne in summer and autumn on long stalks in the axils of the angled to rounded, toothed, slightly hairy leaves. Mexico. **334.**

scandens ✳ 🐛

The $1\frac{1}{2}$ in. flowers are lilac, lavender or red, with a white throat. They are borne in summer. The long pointed leaves are spear-head shaped. Mexico. **335.**

Mask Flower see **Alonsoa**

MAXILLARIA (ORCHIDACEAE)

A genus of evergreen orchids with leaves arising simply from the top of the bulbs and solitary flowers carried on erect stems from the base. Grow in pots, pans or baskets in a mixture of 1 part sphagnum moss to 2 parts osmunda fibre. Repot every 2 or 3 years in spring. Shade from full sunlight and water freely in summer; in winter keep just moist. Propagate by division in spring.

nasuta ✳

The leaves are 10–12 in. long, and the solitary flowers, 1–$1\frac{1}{2}$ in. across, have pale yellow-green petals, flushed purple on the reverse, and a red-purple lip with a yellow, recurved tip. They are borne on erect 4–6 in. stems from March to September. This species is best in a warm greenhouse. Costa Rica.

nigrescens see M. rufescens

picta ✳

An attractive, somewhat bushy species with 2 in. bulbs from which rise 1 or 2 dark green, strap-shaped leaves about 12 in. in length. The 2 in. blooms are fragrant, yellow peppered with chocolate and purple markings inside and a white, purple-spotted lip. The petals are curved inwards, and each flower is carried singly on a 4 in. erect stem during winter. It will thrive in a cool greenhouse. Brazil.

rufescens syn. M. nigrescens ✳

A somewhat variable species with 4–5 in. stems bearing in winter and spring, $1\frac{1}{2}$ in. flowers with 3 outer petals, rust brown, 3 inner, smaller and yellow. The yellow, 3-lobed lip is covered with red spotting. Tropical America.

sanderiana ✳

A good cool greenhouse plant, often considered the best of the genus. It has fleshy flowers, 5–6 in. across, whitish with deep red markings at the centre of the triangular, pointed sepals, petals, and on the creamy lip. They are borne sometime between May and October, exact timing varying considerably between different plants. Best grown in a hanging basket. Ecuador, Peru. **336.**

tenuifolia ✳

The $1\frac{1}{2}$–2 in. blooms are yellow with heavy rust-red spots and bars and are borne in March on short, $1\frac{1}{2}$–2 in. stems. They are often almost concealed by the 1 ft leathery, dark green leaves but their value lies partly in the powerful fragrance which is produced by the long-lasting flowers. Mexico.

variabilis ✳

An elegant purplish-red flowered species with the blooms carried on 2 ft stems and abundantly borne. They open from spring to autumn. The leaves are short, rarely exceeding 4 in. Mexico to Panama.

May Apple see **Passiflora incarnata**
Maypop see **Passiflora incarnata**

MEDINILLA (MELASTOMATACEAE)

magnifica Rose Grape ✳ 🐛

A most attractive evergreen shrub, 3–5 ft high, suitable for the warm greenhouse where it will flower in late spring. The 8–10 in., broadly elliptic, shining, dark green leaves have prominent midribs and veins. The rosy-pink flowers, with conspicuous purple anthers are borne in pendent clusters often over a foot long, at the ends of the branches. Grow in large pots in loam-based compost or a proprietary peat mix, and maintain a humid atmosphere. Propagate by cuttings of semi-ripened shoots in early spring. Philippines. **337.**

Mediolobivia aureiflora see **Rebutia aureiflora**
Mediolobivia pygmaea see **Rebutia pygmaea**

MELIANTHUS (MELIANTHACEAE)

major Honey Bush ✳

A rather lax, sparsely branched evergreen shrub reaching 7 ft or more, with 9 or 11 elliptic, coarsely toothed, grey-green leaflets, each up to 5 in. in length; they have a rather unpleasant scent when bruised. The 1 in. long flowers are a reddish-brown and are borne in dense, erect clusters at the ends of the branches. A useful plant for the cool greenhouse border with the support of a wall or a pillar. It can also be grown in large pots or tubs. Use a loam-based compost or a peat mix. Propagate by stem cuttings in spring or late summer. South Africa.

Melon Pear see **Solanum muricatum**
Melon Tree see **Carica papaya**
Mescal Bean see **Sophora secundiflora**
Mesembryanthemum see under **Faucaria**
Mexican Bread Fruit see **Monstera deliciosa**
Mexican Foxglove see **Tetranema mexicanum**
Mexican Treefern see **Cibotium schiedei**

MICHELIA (MAGNOLIACEAE)

doltsopa ✳

A rather large, nearly hardy, semi-evergreen species which will thrive in a large tub, or planted in the large greenhouse border against a wall. It has long, narrow slender pointed leaves, up to 11 in. in length and deep cream fragrant flowers tinged green at the base, cup-shaped with 12–16 petals and sepals. Propagate by cuttings of half ripened shoots, taken in summer. E. Himalaya.

MICROLEPIA (POLYPODIACEAE)

A genus of ferns of which the three species described are suitable for the warm greenhouse or home. Grow in pots of a proprietary peat-based compost and keep shaded from direct light. Propagate by spores or division in spring.

pyramidata 🐛

A strong growing plant with fronds that can reach 3–6 ft. They are sub-divided deeply 3 or 4 times to give a light, feathery appearance. Tropical Asia, Hawaii.

  'Cristata' has crested fronds and a drooping habit.

speluncae Grotto Lace Fern 🐛

A fast growing plant with soft, light green 2 ft long fronds which are finely cut into lacy fronds, and are sparsely hairy. An attractive decorative species. Tropics.

strigosa 🐛

A similar but less vigorous species than *M. speluncae* with a woody rootstock and lacy fronds to $1\frac{1}{2}$ ft long. It will tolerate cool greenhouse conditions. Japan and Pacific Islands.

Mignonette Peperomia see **Peperomia resediflora**
Milkwort see **Polygala**

MILTONIA (ORCHIDACEAE) Pansy Orchid

A genus of attractively flowered orchids, the large flowers of which are flat and somewhat pansy-like, and borne on erect, arching stems. They have long, narrow leaves borne in groups of 1–3 on the bulbs. They require cool or warm greenhouse treatment and should be grown in pots or baskets in a compost made up of 2 parts osmunda fibre to 1 part sphagnum moss. Keep well ventilated and shade on bright sunny days in summer. Propagate by division every 2 or 3 years in late summer or spring. There are many hybrids between the species, mainly with large pansy-like flowers. Typical of this group is Everest in shades of yellow, suffused and blotched with purple, **338.**

candida
The 3 in. flowers have greenish-yellow petals, bearing red-brown markings, while the white lip is tinged with a rosy pink. They are borne in spikes of 3–6 on a 12 in. stem. The leaves are dark green, and the plant, which flowers in autumn, is a good strong growing species for the cool greenhouse. Brazil.

regnellii
The 3–5 flowers are 2–3 in. across, with white to pale rose-pink petals and a flat, almost round lip with deep violet markings and a yellow crest. They are borne on 18 in. stems from July to October. The 2 in. bulbs each carry two, dark green leaves, 10–15 in. in length. A cool greenhouse species. Brazil.

spectabilis
A solitary flowered species with large blooms 3–4 in. across. The petals are pure white tinged with rose-pink towards the base and the lip is rosy-purple with a white margin and may exceed 2 in. in width. The thin yellow-green leaves are borne on 2–3 in. bulb. The blooms open in autumn. Brazil.

'Moreliana', has deep purple flowers with a rose marked lip, and is more often seen in cultivation.

MIMOSA (LEGUMINOSAE)
pudica Sensitive Plant, Humble Plant
A curious sprawling perennial, usually grown as an annual. It has slightly spiny stems and wiry branches which bear the deeply cut, feathery leaves composed of many pairs of elliptic leaflets. If the leaves are touched during daylight they fold upwards along the midrib and the leaf stalks droop. They then recover slowly to their original position. The purple flowers are borne in ball-like clusters in the leaf axils in July and August. A fascinating warm greenhouse or house plant which is best grown in a loam-based compost. Give shade and provide humidity during the hottest months. Propagate by seed in spring. Tropical America.

Mimosa see **Acacia**
Mimosa, Pink see **Albizia julibrissin**
Mina lobata see **Quamoclit lobata**
Mind-your-own-business see **Soleirolia soleirolii**
Miniature Eyelash Begonia see **Begonia boweri**
Miniature Grape Ivy see **Cissus striata**
Miniature Maple-leaf Begonia see **Begonia dregei**
Mint, Australian see **Prostanthera**
Mint Bush, Snowy see **Prostanthera nivea**
Mist Flower see **Eupatorium**
Mistletoe Cactus see **Rhipsalis cassutha**
Mistletoe Fig see **Ficus diversifolia**

MITRARIA (GESNERIACEAE)
coccinea
An attractive, evergreen, climbing or sprawling shrub for the cool greenhouse. The small glossy, leathery leaves are oval and a good foil to the bright scarlet flowers. These are borne on long pendent stalks from May to autumn and have a 1½ in. somewhat inflated, hairy tube which opens at the mouth into 5 round lobes. A good plant for the cool greenhouse border where it must be kept shaded. Propagate by division in spring, or by stem cuttings in spring or summer. Chile. **339.**

MOMORDICA (CUCURBITACEAE)
A tropical genus of climbers, of which the species described are best treated as annuals, growing well in large pots or a border in the warm or cool greenhouse. They climb by means of tendrils and have lobed leaves and bell-shaped flowers followed by conspicuous lantern-like fruits.

balsamina Balsam Apple
The 5-lobed flowers are yellow with brown spotting and are borne on long stems in June, followed by oval, pointed, warty orange fruits. The

leaves are toothed and shining green. Australian, Asian and African Tropics.

charantia Balsam Pear
A larger plant than *M. balsamina* with rather more hairy leaves and yellow flowers enclosed by entire bracts and opening in June. The fruits are oblong, yellow or coppery and when they burst, the scarlet flesh around the seeds inside is very conspicuous. Tropical Africa, S.E. Asia. **340.**

Monarch of the East see **Sauromatum guttatum**
Monarch of the Veldt see **Venidium fastuosum**
Monkey-tail Fern see **Cyathea mexicana**

MONSTERA (ARACEAE) Ceriman
A genus of tropical, evergreen climbers with large leaves often irregularly cut or perforated, especially when adult. They should be planted in pots in a loam-based compost or a proprietary peat mix, and make decorative plants for the warm greenhouse. They are also favourite house plants. Propagate by removing the growing point of a stem with one leaf, in summer. This will root in a mixture of equal parts peat and sand. Leaf bud cuttings can also be taken.

deliciosa Mexican Bread Fruit
In the adult stage this plant will grow to 20 ft or more with dark green leaves up to 4 ft in length. It carries, when mature, 4–6 in. creamy arum-like spathes which are followed by greenish, cone-like, edible fruits. The leaves, especially when grown in warmth and good light, expand rapidly, with the pattern of perforation becoming more distinctive. It makes an excellent pot plant until too large. Mexico.

deliciosa 'Borsigiana' see **M. pertusa**

pertusa syn. **M. deliciosa** 'Borsigiana'
A smaller, more compact version of *M. deliciosa* which makes a neat pot plant. Tropical America. **341.**

Moonstones see **Pachyphytum oviferum**
Moonstones, Sticky see **Pachyphytum brevifolium**

MORAEA (IRIDACEAE)
A genus of graceful plants with clumps of stiff, narrow leaves and short-lived but brilliantly-coloured, sweet-scented, iris-like flowers. The following species make delightful pot plants for the cool greenhouse. Plants with rhizomes are put into the genus *Dietes* by some authorities. Propagate by division or separating the corms singly.

bicolor syn. **Dietes bicolor**
The yellow blooms have a blackish-brown blotch at the centre of the 3 outer petals, and are borne in a many-flowered loose cluster in summer. The pale green leaves are long and somewhat lax. The overall height of the plant is about 2 ft. S. Africa.

glaucopsis Peacock Iris
The wide outer petals are white with a glossy, blue-black spot near the base, rather like the 'eye' on a peacock's feather; they open in summer. The stems are 1½–2 ft long. S. Africa.

iridioides syn. **Dietes grandiflora** African Iris
The dark green leaves grow from the base in a fan-like cluster, while the white, iris-like flowers have yellow and brown spots. The yellow style has a blue crest. They are borne in July. S. Africa. **342.**

ramosa see **M. ramosissima**

ramosissima syn. **M. ramosa**
A branching species with 2–3 ft stems and abundantly borne, small, pale yellow blooms making a cluster somewhat like a branched candelabra. They open in May and June. S. Africa.

Morning Glory see **Ipomoea**

MOSCHOSMA (LABIATAE)
riparium syn. **Iboza riparia**
A stout, branched sub-shrub reaching 2–5 ft in height. It has oval, simple finely toothed leaves and long erect clusters of small, creamy-

white, often lilac-tinted flowers which appear from December to February. It makes a good large pot plant for the cool greenhouse, or can be planted in a border. Use a loam-based compost and propagate from soft stem cuttings in spring. If grown as a perennial, cut back hard after flowering each year. S. Africa.

Mother-in-law's Tongue see **Sansevieria trifasciata**
Mother of Thousands see **Saxifraga stolonifera**
Mother Spleenwort see **Asplenium bulbiferum**
Mountain Palm, Dwarf see **Chamaedorea elegans**
Mulberry, French see **Callicarpa americana**
Mule's Fern see **Phyllitis hemionitis**

MUSA (MUSACEAE)
This genus is best known for its banana-bearing members, though there are several species grown purely for ornamentation. They are large, evergreen, somewhat palm-like perennials with closely ensheathing leaf bases that form a false trunk or stem. They make impressive tub plants for warm greenhouses or may be planted in a border. Use a loam-based compost and grow in a humid atmosphere shaded from the hottest sunshine. Propagate by suckers, division, or seeds of the ornamental sorts, in spring.

acuminata Banana
A tall, tree-like species up to 10 ft with massive oblong leaves that may part into several unequal lobes. The tubular flowers are greenish, yellowish or purple tinged, enclosed in large boat-shaped reddish bracts on a pendulous stalk. As the flowers fade, the bracts drop away and the young fruits curve upwards. Ceylon to Malay Peninsula. Many cultivars and hybrids are known, several of which produce the banana of commerce. The best one for greenhouse culture is 'Dwarf Cavendish' (*M. cavendishii*), a dwarf mutant often known as the Canary Island Banana. This grows about 6 ft tall and fruits well in a large tub. **343.**

cavendishii see under **M. acuminata**

coccinea Scarlet Banana
A smaller, clump-forming species, 3–4 ft tall, with dark green oblong leaves. The yellow-green-tipped flowers are borne on an erect stem and enclosed in bright scarlet bracts. They are followed by orange-yellow oblong fruits. A most ornamental plant. Indochina.

velutina
A clump-forming plant similar to *M. coccinea*, having glossy 3 ft long leaves with a red midrib. The tubular flowers are orange to orange-yellow and enclosed within large pink bracts. The small hairy fruits are pink and split open when ripe. Assam.

MUTISIA (COMPOSITAE) Climbing Gazania
Unique climbing members of the daisy family with wiry stems and evergreen leaves often ending in a tendril. The somewhat daisy-like flowers range from creamy-yellow through pink and red to orange. Nearly completely hardy, they require well aerated cool greenhouse or conservatory conditions and are best grown over a shrub or on a trellis work in a border. Shade from strong sunlight and grow in a peat mix or a loam-based compost. Propagate by seeds in spring or cuttings of short lateral stems in spring or late summer.

clematis
A vigorous species having the leaves composed of several oblong leaflets, dark green above, white woolly beneath. The flower heads appear in summer and autumn. They are pendulous, 2–3 in. across, with bright orange petals. Colombia, Ecuador.

decurrens
This rare species tests the cultivator's skill, but when thriving happily it produces 4 in. wide brilliant orange flowers all summer. The stalkless leaves, borne on 6–8 ft stems, are narrowly oblong and dark green. Chile.

ilicifolia
A strong growing climber to 10 ft or more having dark green, oblong, stalkless leaves with prominent teeth. The 2–3 in. wide flowers are bright pink with a hint of purple and open during summer and early autumn. Chile.

latifolia
This distinctive species has broadly winged stems 8 ft or more tall and strongly toothed oblong leaves. The 3 in. wide pink daisy blossoms are borne in summer and autumn. Chile.

oligodon
A suckering climber to 4 ft which is happiest growing through a living shrub as support. Each oblong, coarsely toothed leaf has a winged base, in the axils of which are borne the 2–3 in. wide satin-pink flowers. These open in summer and continue into autumn. Chile. **344.**

MYRSINE (MYRSINACEAE)
africana African Boxwood
A small evergreen bushy shrub 2–4 ft high. The ½ in., rounded, dark green leaves are finely toothed and notched at the apex. They are borne on red, angular, downy stems. It makes an attractive foliage plant for the cool greenhouse and home. The small brown male and female flowers are borne on different plants, and only if the two are grown together do they produce the shiny, purplish blue berries. Grow in pots or small tubs of a proprietary peat compost and water freely in summer, less in winter. Ventilate on all warm days and provide light shade from the hottest sunshine. Propagate by cuttings of lateral shoots, preferably with a heel, in summer. Seeds, when available, may be sown in spring. Africa, Arabia to China.

Myrtle see **Myrtus**
Myrtle, Crape see **Lagerstroemia indica**

MYRTUS (MYRTACEAE) Myrtle
A genus of fragrant, evergreen shrubs which have saucer-shaped, white flowers with fine, brush-like masses of stamens. They thrive in the cool greenhouse border or in large pots. Plant in a loam-based compost and keep well ventilated in summer. Propagate by cuttings of lateral shoots with a heel, in June or July.

bullata syn. **Lophomyrtus bullata** Ramarama
A 10–15 ft shrub, smaller when grown as a pot plant, with downy shoots bearing oval, entire, wrinkled, stalkless leaves, purplish when young, becoming reddish-brown later. The ¾ in. flowers are borne singly in the axils of the leaves and grow from a purple calyx. They open in May and June. The edible berries are purple-black. New Zealand.

obcordata syn. **Lophomyrtus obcordata**
A 10–15 ft shrub making a densely branched plant. The inverted ovate leaves are notched at the tip and dark green, while the ¼ in. white flowers are carried on slender stalks in the leaf axils. The berry is round red-violet, and edible. New Zealand.

ugni syn. **Ugni molinae** Chilean Guava
The solitary white flowers of this species are tinged pink and followed by juicy, red-black, edible fruits. They are set off by the dark glossy green, entire, leathery leaves which are borne on downy shoots. The plant can reach 8 ft or more and the flowers open in May. Chile.

Mystacidium distichum see **Angraecum distichum**

N

Naegelia see **Smithiantha**
Namaqualand Daisy see **Venidium fastuosum**

NANDINA (BERBERIDACEAE)
domestica Heavenly Bamboo
An elegantly attractive evergreen shrub which can reach 6 ft or more. It is somewhat like bamboo in appearance having long, slender red-brown stems which carry branched leaves. Each branch has 3–10 narrow leaflets which taper to slender points; they are light green becoming bright crimson in autumn. In June and July long, branched clusters of small white, starry flowers are produced, followed by brilliant red berries. A white or ivory fruited cultivar is known. Grow in the cool or cold greenhouse border or in large pots or tubs of a loam based or proprietary peat compost. Small plants make good subjects for a cool room. Ventilate freely on all warm days and shade from direct sun-

shine. Propagate by division or seeds in spring or stem cuttings with a heel in late summer. China, Japan.

NARCISSUS (AMARYLLIDACEAE) Daffodil, Narcissus ❋

The botanical generic name *Narcissus* covers all the familiar sorts of daffodil and narcissi, most of which are popular hardy garden plants. They are also useful as short term pot plants, providing a welcome splash of colour in the home or cool conservatory. Pot the bulbs in September or October, using a loam or peat based compost and plunge in a bed of ashes, sand or peat. If this is not possible, place in a cool room or cellar and keep dark. When the shoots are about 2 in. long, place in a light place with an average temperature of 45–50°F. Make sure the compost is always just moist; if it dries out, even briefly, the flower buds may wither or fail to expand properly. Recommended cultivars suitable for pot work are as follows:
Trumpet narcissi or daffodils
  'Dutch Master' clear yellow self;
  'Queen of the Bicolors' white petals, canary-yellow trumpet;
  'Mount Hood' cream-white self.
Large-cupped narcissi
  'Carlton', soft yellow self with a frilled cup;
  'Fortune', yellow petals orange cup.
Small-cupped narcissi
  'La Riante' white petals, intense deep orange cup;
  'Snow Princess', snow-white petals, yellow cup edged orange.
Double-flowered narcissi
  'Double Event', white with pale orange centre, **345**;
  'Irene Copeland', yellow and white on strong stems;
  'Texas' yellow and brilliant orange.
Tazetta narcissi
  'Geranium', a bunch flowered sort each small flower having white petals and an orange red crown;
  'Paperwhite Grandiflora', a white self bunch-flowered cultivar, **346.**

Nasturtium see **Tropaeolum**
Natal Plum see **Carissa grandiflora**
Neanthe elegans see **Chamaedorea elegans**
Necklace Fern see **Asplenium flabelliforme**
Nelumbium see **Nelumbo**

NELUMBO syn. NELUMBIUM (NYMPHAEACEAE)

nucifera syn. **N. speciosa** Sacred Indian Lotus ❋ ✿

A beautiful aquatic plant, sacred to Buddhists, bearing 4–10 in. delicate pink, richly fragrant cup-shaped blooms which open by day and close each night, flowering in summer. The large shield-like leaves are 1–2 ft across and are borne on stiff stalks which can stand from 2–6 ft above the water. They need 6–10 in. of water to thrive, and are best grown by themselves in a tank. The rhizomes should be planted in 8–10 in. of rich soil. Propagate by division of rhizomes or seeds sown under water, in spring. S. Asia.

NEOREGELIA (BROMELIACEAE)

A genus of evergreen bromeliads which have rosettes of spiny, strap-shaped leaves with a tubular centre forming a water-holding reservoir. The numerous flowers grow at the centre of the plant and open throughout the year. Grow in pots in the cool greenhouse and keep in full sun. Water well when the plants are growing, keeping the central leaf cup full. Keep just moist through the winter. Propagate by removing rooted offsets in summer.

carolinae ❋ ✿

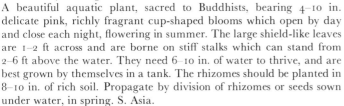

The leaves are shiny bright green with toothed margins and of a coppery sheen. At flowering time bright pomegranate-purple leaves are produced, surrounding the violet-purple clustered flower heads and folding back horizontally. Brazil.
  'Tricolor', the glossy green leaves have an ivory-white stripe running along the centre, the whole plant turning pink at flowering time, the central leaves being carmine-red, **347.**

spectabilis Fingernail Plant ❋ ✿

This species has long, leathery olive-green leaves with a red spot at the tip, undersides having grey-white bands. They are 12 in. long in a flattened rosette measuring 2 ft across. When the dense head of blue flowers is formed, the surrounding leaves turn rose-red. Brazil.

NEPENTHES (NEPENTHACEAE) Pitcher Plants

A species of curious, insectivorous plants including both climbers and low growing species. The leaf midribs are prolonged into tendrils, frequently with the brightly coloured pitcher at the end of it. They are pendulous, urn-shaped with a rolled back rim and angled lid, and contain pepsin liquid which digests the insects which are attracted into it by the honey glands near the mouth. For successful cultivation they need a warm, humid atmosphere and are best grown in baskets or hanging pots to allow the pitchers to show to best advantage. Plant in a compost of peat and sphagnum moss and keep well watered in summer once established. Keep shaded from the sun at all times. Propagate by cuttings from well-ripened shoots or by seeds. Several hybrids were raised at the end of the nineteenth century, among them 'F.W. Moore', **348.**

ampullaria ✿

A strong growing plant with pale green pitchers, sometimes red marked and growing from broad, oblong leaves. Malaya to New Guinea.

× **intermedia** (*N. gracilis* ? × *N. rafflesiana*) ✿

A plant of hybrid origin with 6 in. pitchers with a slight swelling at the centre bringing it to 2½ in. across and broad fringed wings. The leaves taper at both ends are dark green and leathery. Garden origin.

khasiana ✿

A strong growing climbing plant with long narrow leaves and 3–7 in. pitchers coloured green to reddish-green, tubular with narrow, fringed wings. The rim is a bright green, and the oval lid flushed red beneath. India.

NEPHROLEPIS (OLEANDRACEAE) Sword Fern

A genus of handsome, tropical ferns with once divided fronds rising at intervals from the wiry rhizomes. They make most decorative house plants but are shown to their best in hanging baskets and make excellent foliage plants for the warm greenhouse. Plant in a mixture of 3 parts peat, 2 parts loam and 1 part sharp sand, keep moist and away from draughts. Propagate by removing the young plants produced on the spreading runners.

acuminata ✿

An attractive species which grows in a fan-shaped form, the leaves arching from the central crown. The fronds are 1–2 ft long and are borne on 4–6 in. stalks, once divided, the segments being long ovate. Malaya.

cordifolia ✿

A 2–2½ ft evergreen fern with light green, once divided fronds on short stalks, the segments carried close together and often overlapping. Tropics.
  'Duffii', a very small, crowded species with fronds sometimes forked and always less than an inch wide;
  'Plumosa', a more feathery plant than the type. The segment tips of the stiff fronds almost completely divided and a rich, dark green.

exaltata ✿

One of the most attractive of ferns in some of the many cultivars which have been raised from it.
  'Elegantissima', with bright green compact fronds, **349;**
  'Hillii', a strongly growing plant with deeply lobed, crinkled, pale green fronds;
  'Marshalii', the pale green, broad fronds are densely crested. A very attractive form;
  'Rooseveltii', long, arching leathery fronds with light green wavy leaflets;
  'Todeoides', pale green, deeply divided feathery fronds.

NERINE (AMARYLLIDACEAE)

A genus of superb, autumn flowering bulbous plants with strap-shaped, or linear leaves, appearing after the long stalked clusters of vivid, shining flowers. They grow best in pots in the cool greenhouse, *N. bowdenii* being the only species to thrive in the cold greenhouse. Plant in loam-based compost leaving the tops of the bulb showing and water from the first appearance of the flowers until the leaves are fully grown. Propagate by bulb offsets removed when re-potting every 3 or 4 years. Seeds may be sown as soon as ripe.

bowdenii ❋

This fine species makes an excellent specimen plant. The rounded heads of several, wavy-petalled pink flowers 4–6 in. across are borne on 18 in. stems from September to November. S. Africa. **350.**

   'Fenwick's Variety', a larger and more vigorous plant with superb rich pink flowers.

crispa see **N. undulata**

filifolia

The 8–10, 1 in. rose-red flowers are carried in a loose head borne on a 1 ft stem. The slender rush-like leaves are shorter than the flower stem. S. Africa.

flexuosa

An unusual species in that some of the narrow, curved leaves are borne at the same time as the pink flowers which have crisped margins to the petals and are borne in loose clusters of up to 12 blooms. A robust plant reaching 3 ft in height. S. Africa.

   'Alba', a white-flowered form.

sarniensis Guernsey Lily

A species somewhat variable in colour with flowers ranging from pale pink to red and borne in 6 in. clusters on 2 ft stems. The mid-green leaves appear at the same time as the flowers. S. Africa.

   'Corusca Major', a cultivar with orange-scarlet flowers;
   'Miss E. Cator', a vigorous plant with deep red flowers, **351**;
   'Nicholas', white flowers with red stripes;
   'Sacred Heart', pure white flowers.

undulata syn. **N. crispa**

This species has white to flesh-pink flowers with crisped edges to the petals and is very free flowering. The narrow, pale green leaves usually appear before the flowers open. S. Africa.

NERIUM (APOCYNACEAE) Oleander

oleander

An erect evergreen shrub, 6 ft or more tall with leathery-textured, willow-shaped leaves. The large periwinkle-like flowers are borne in terminal clusters from June to October. Grow in the cool conservatory or greenhouse, minimum winter temperature 45°F., in large pots or tubs of a loam-based compost. Propagate by half ripe heel cuttings in July or August. Several colour forms ranging from white through pink to red, both single and double, are known. **352.**

   'Variegata', with leaves margined with creamy-yellow and bearing pink flowers. **353.**

Netleaf, Painted see **Fittonia verschaffeltii**
Netleaf, Silver see **Fittonia argyroneura**
Netted Vriesea see **Vriesea fenestralis**
Never-never Plant see **Ctenanthe oppenheimiana**
New Zealand Cabbage Tree see **Cordyline australis**
New Zealand White Pine see **Podocarpus dacrydioides**

NIDULARIUM (BROMELIACEAE)

Rosette forming plants with strap-shaped leaves which form water-holding reservoirs at the base. At flowering time the bases of the central leaves turn bright red. Grow in pots or pans of a proprietary peat compost, preferably mixed with an equal part of sphagnum moss. Grow in a warm greenhouse, keep moist from spring to autumn and make sure the reservoir is kept filled. Keep on the dry side in winter. Propagate by offsets removed in late spring or summer.

fulgens syn. **N. pictum**

The shiny, arching leaves are 12 in. long and the flowers comprise 3 violet blue petals surrounded by red bracts. Brazil.

innocentii

The finely toothed leaves are narrow and strap shaped, green with a purplish flush above and dark red beneath. The white flowers have orange bracts. Brazil. **354.**

pictum see **N. fulgens**

Nightshade see **Solanum**
Nikau Palm see **Rhopalostylis sapida**
Nodding Bells, Red see **Streptocarpus dunnii**
Nodding Bells, Royal see **Streptocarpus wendlandii**

NOPALXOCHIA (CACTACEAE)

ackermannii see **Epiphyllum ackermannii**

phyllanthoides

This species, the only one in the genus, closely resembles a small epiphyllum. It is very popular, producing a profusion of pink flowers, 3 in. long and 2 in. across, in May. These usually arise from the areoles towards the ends of the stems. It has a distinctly trailing habit, with flattened leafless stems, 8–12 in. long. A good plant for the hanging basket. There was a variety known as 'Deutsche Kaiserin', but plants now sold under that name appear to be the true species. It has been extensively hybridized. Culture as for *Epiphyllum*. Probably from Mexico and Colombia, but now known only in cultivation. **355.**

Norfolk Island Pine see **Araucaria excelsa**
Northern Pitcher Plant see **Sarracenia purpurea**
Nutmeg Geranium see **Pelargonium** × **fragrans**

NYMPHAEA (NYMPHAEACEAE) Water Lily

A large genus of water plants of which the species listed below are of tropical origin and only suitable for culture in a large tank in the warm greenhouse. Given the right conditions they are not difficult to grow. They have large decorative leaves, often fluted at the edges and mottled and are in flower from July to September. To grow successfully, a water temperature of 70°F. in summer and 50°F. in winter must be maintained. Propagate by removing offsets or sowing seeds under water in spring.

caerulea Blue Lotus of Egypt

A faintly scented day flowerer, the light blue flowers have 12–20 petals arranged in 3 rows. The oval leaves can measure 16 in. across and are slightly wavy at their bases. They have purple markings underneath. Africa.

capensis Cape Blue Water-lily

Somewhat similar to *N. caerulea*, with fragrant, brighter blue, larger flowers which stand 4 or 5 in. out of the water. The leaves have wavy, toothed margins. Africa, Madagascar.

   'Zanzibariensis Rosea', with flowers ranging from deep carmine to pink, Zanzibar. **356.**

stellata

The pale blue flowers are 3–7 in. across and are made up of 11–14 petals fading to creamy-white at the centre. The rounded leaves are violet beneath and green above. S.E. Asia.

   'Director G.T. Moore', a hybrid cultivar with blue-purple flowers having a yellow circle around the centre and a base of bright blue anthers, **358**;
   'Mrs G. H. Pring', creamy-white flowers splashed with maroon;
   'St Louis', pale lemon-yellow flowers with golden-yellow anthers.

O

Oak-leaved Geranium see **Pelargonium quercifolia**
Oak, Silk see **Grevillea robusta**

OCHNA (OCHNACEAE)

A genus of evergreen and deciduous trees and shrubs of which the two species described below make attractive plants for the warm greenhouse, the curious form and colour of the fruits being their most decorative feature. They make good pot or tub plants, and grow best in loam-based compost. Propagate by heel cuttings of half ripe shoots in summer.

atropurpurea Carnival Bush

A 4 ft shrub with tapering oblong, leathery, shining, distinctly toothed leaves. The solitary flowers are yellow and are borne within a dark purple calyx. S. Africa.

serrulata

The species most frequently seen in cultivation, it makes a 4–5 ft shrub with bright green, glossy, toothed leaves and long-stalked yellow flowers within a calyx of oval lobes, green at first, becoming red as the fruits ripen. These are glossy, black berries which are borne on the red, almost strawberry-like, swollen centre of the flower. The flowers open in spring, followed by the berries in summer. Natal.

× **ODONTIODA** (*Cochlioda* × *Odontoglossum*) (ORCHIDACEAE) ✳

A hybrid genus of orchids, somewhat similar to *Odontoglossum* in form, but with more colourful and longer lasting flowers. They will tolerate some heat, but cultivation is generally the same as that for *Odontoglossum*.

'Astomar' clear rosy-mauve petals with the broader petal-like sepals and lip purple blotched;
'Florence Stirling', white flowers marked with light purple to deep magenta;
'Mazurka', bright red blooms of good size and substance.

ODONTOGLOSSUM (ORCHIDACEAE)

A genus of tropical epiphytic orchids with long, arching sprays of flowers which have wide, flat petals and petal-like sepals. The long, strap-shaped leaves are mid-green and evergreen. Grow in pots or baskets in a compost of 2 parts osmunda fibre to 1 part sphagnum moss. Keep cool and moist, shading from summer sun. Propagate by division every 2 or 3 years in spring or late summer.

bictoniense ✳
The 2½ ft stems carry widely spaced blooms, each 1½ in. across with long, narrow, greenish sepals and petals bearing purple-brown markings. The large heart-shaped, pointed lip is pale pink and has white markings. They open from October to April. Very variable. Guatemala.
'Album' has similar coloured sepals and petals and a pure white lip;
'Sulphureum' has yellow sepals and petals and a white lip.

citrosmum syn. O. pendulum ✳
The 3–5 in. bulbs bear two broad, leathery leaves and the flower stalk, which is about 2 ft. in length, becomes arched over with the weight of 15–30 blooms it carries. Each flower is 2½–3 in. across with white, pink-flushed sepals and petals and a rose to deep rose lip, having a yellow crest. They open in May. Guatemala.
'Album', pure white flowers with a yellow crested lip;
'Sulphureum', yellow petals with a pink overlay.

crispum Lace Orchid ✳
Often considered one of the most beautiful of all orchids, it has 6–12 flowered, arched stems, reaching 2 ft in length, and bearing numerous blooms. The latter are 4 in. across with glistening white, crisped sepals and petals, slightly flushed with rose, the lip spotted with red and having a yellow crest towards the base. These are produced at all times of the year, but most freely from February to April. Very variable. Colombia. **357.**
'Lyoth Arctic', pure white, heavily crisped petals.

grande ✳
A very attractive orchid which is relatively easily grown and makes a successful pot plant for the home. The 12 in. flower spikes are borne from August to November with each bloom up to 7 in. across, the long, narrow, spreading petals being orange-yellow with brown bands across the basal half and the small lip creamy-yellow with red-brown markings and an orange crest. The dark green leaves are borne in pairs on each bulb. Guatemala. Some hybrids are:
× 'Alport', hybrid cultivar with about 15 white flowers per spike, each having white, wavy-edged petals bearing pink and crimson markings;
Edalva, a hybrid group with white flowers variously patterned with crimson;
Kopan 'Lyoth Aurea', golden-yellow with brown markings, **359;**
Stropheon 'Lyoth Galaxy', maroon, edged and banded pale rose.

nobile see O. pescatorei
pendulum see O. citrosmum

pescatorei syn. O. nobile ✳
A most striking species with 10–100 separate 3 in. blooms carried on the 1–2 ft stems which droop with their weight. The flowers are white, sometimes tinged with pink and marked with light brown blotches. The lip which is violin or moth-shaped, has purple markings and a yellow and crimson crest. The brown, speckled bulbs carry two 6–12 in. leaves. Colombia.

× **ODONTONIA** (*Miltonia* × *Odontoglossum*) (ORCHIDACEAE) ✳

A group of hybrid orchids which are very similar to *Odontoglossum*.
Andreana 'Stonehurst', white, finely freckled with pink dots, creating a rosy hue;
Atheror 'Lyoth Majesty', pale lilac petals blotched and marked with purple and maroon. The white lip is yellow flushed with a rich maroon centre, **360;**
Olga 'Icefall', a pure white cultivar, **361.**

Oil Cloth Flower see **Anthurium andreanum**
Old Lady Mammillaria see **Mammillaria hahniana**
Old Man Cactus see **Cephalocereus senilis**
Old Man's Beard see **Tillandsia usneoides**
Oliveranthus elegans see **Echeveria harmsii**

ONCIDIUM (ORCHIDACEAE)

A genus of evergreen orchids with variable leaf shape and petal form. They are not difficult to grow, thriving in a cool or warm greenhouse in pots or baskets containing a compost of 2 parts osmunda fibre to 1 part sphagnum moss. They need shade during the summer months and a humid atmosphere; water sparingly. Propagate by division when repotting, in March or April.

flexuosum Dancing Doll Orchid ✳
A charming species with 2–3 ft flexuous stems, branched towards the ends and carrying a profusion of 1 in. flowers with small golden-yellow petals and sepals, colour barred with dark brown and a broad, spreading notched lip, yellow with a few red dots. The whole flower fancifully resembles a full-skirted dancing figure. They are produced in late summer. One or two 6–8 in. strap-shaped leaves rise from each of the bulbs. A plant for the cool greenhouse. Brazil.

ornithorhynchum ✳
The 2 ft branched and pendulous stems carry dense clusters of sweet scented long lasting flowers. The sepals and petals are lilac-pink with a deeper rose-coloured lip, yellow crested at base. Flowers from October to December and grows well in the cool greenhouse. Mexico to Salvador.

papilio Butterfly Orchid ✳
A striking plant for the warm greenhouse with a single, 6–8 in. mottled, stiff leaf rising from each bulb, and 2–4 ft erect stems bearing a succession of blooms. The two deep red petals and one sepal are marked with yellow cross bands, spread outwards to reach 3–7 in. from tip to tip. The large, golden-yellow lip has a broad reddish, fluted margin and a central notch. It flowers spasmodically throughout the year. Trinidad, Venezuela, Peru, Brazil.

sarcodes ✳
A spring flowering species with dark green bulbs bearing 2 or 3 shining, dark, tapering leaves and arching stems of flowers, sometimes up to 5 ft in length. Each 2 in. glossy bloom has petals and sepals orange-yellow with chestnut spotting and blotching, and a wavy edged, bright yellow lip having a few red-brown spots. A good plant for the cool greenhouse. Brazil.

varicosum ✳
A beautiful species when in full flower, with grey green, pendulous stems up to 3 ft in length and bearing 80–90 separate blooms. These have small, yellow-green sepals and petals barred with dull brown, and a large deeply notched lip, slightly wavy and a bright golden-yellow, with a basal brown-red blotch. The flowering period is from September to November. This species thrives in a cool to warm greenhouse. Brazil.

Opal Lachenalia see **Lachenalia glaucina**

OPHIOPOGON (LILIACEAE) Lily Turf

A genus of tufted, narrow-leaved plants, almost grass-like, having dense spikes of flowers borne on stiff stems. They grow well in the cool or cold greenhouse and are useful for ground cover in the border. They also make durable pot plants for a cool or cold room. Grow in a proprietary peat compost, shade from direct sunshine and ventilate on all warm days. Propagate by division in spring.

jaburan White Lily Turf ✳ ◗
An evergreen species forming clumps of thick, dark green, ribbon-like leaves, sometimes variegated, curving over at the tips and up to 2 ft or

more in height. The drooping flowers are pale purple or white and are borne in a dense, one-sided spike, 3–6 in. long, on 6–18 in. stalks. They open in July. Japan.

'Variegatus' or 'Vittatus', the leaves are striped with creamy-white lines and the flowers are deep blue-purple, **362.**

japonicus Snake's Beard, Dwarf Lily Turf
A somewhat similar species to *O. jaburan*, but smaller, the very dark green, grassy leaves reaching only 6–10 in. It spreads by means of underground stems into large clumps or mats. The small spikes of flowers are pale lilac or white and are borne on a 2–4 in. stem. They are produced in June. Japan, Korea, China.

planiscapus
This species resembles *O. japonicus*, but is slower growing and has wider arching leaves. It is mainly represented in cultivation by the dark, purple-black leaved form 'Nigrescens'. Japan.

OPLISMENUS (GRAMINAE)

burmanii 'Albidulus'
Leaves white with pale green centre strip. India.

hirtellus Basket Grass
A slender creeping grass, rooting at the nodes, which has erect tufts of wavy leaves, 1½–5 in. long. It is an attractive hanging basket or ground cover plant for the cool or warm greenhouse. It is always represented in cultivation by variegated forms. Grow in a proprietary peat compost and shade from direct sunshine in summer. Propagate by division in spring, or rooted shoots severed and potted any time except winter. Tropical America, Africa, Polynesia.

'Albidus', white leaves with a green line along the midrib;

'Variegatus', the leaves pink and white striped. Popular in the W. Indies. **363.**

Opopanax see **Acacia farnesiana**

OPUNTIA (CACTACEAE) Prickly Pear

Ranging from plants of tree-like proportions to small specimens which will grow happily in a 4 in. pot, all species are characterized by having jointed stems. The joints are pad-like, cylindrical or globose. All species also have tufts of fine barbed bristles, called glochids, which break off and lodge in the skin and are difficult to extricate. Red or yellow bell-shaped flowers form from areoles situated on the edges of the stems and appear throughout June and July. A peculiar feature in some species is that new flowers may arise from old fruits. For culture see under terrestrial cacti in the Introduction. Minimum winter temperature 40°F. Propagate by seed or stem cuttings.

bergeriana
This species has widely spaced areoles with 3–5 spines and prominent yellow glochids. The pads are long and flat, freely bearing deep red flowers in summer. The red fruit is 2 in. long, pear-shaped. Not known in the wild but common on the Mediterranean coast where it forms thickets.

decumbens
A low shrub, the oval pads are dark green with a reddish flush around the areoles and yellowish glochids. The branches are somewhat drooping and the pale yellow flowers are 2 in. across, fading to red as they age. Central America. **364.**

engelmannii
Rounded flattened pale green pads bear distant areoles with white spines, dark red at the base, 3–4 in number, spreading. The larger spines are flattened and can be 2 in. long. The very large, yellow flowers, up to 4 in. across, appear in summer. The plants grow to 6 ft tall. New Mexico, Texas, Arizona.

furiosa see **O. tunicata**

humilis syn. **O. tuna**
The flat circular joints with large areoles form a shrub about 3 ft high. There are 2–6 yellow spines with yellowish glochids. The flowers are also yellow, but tinted scarlet, and 2 in. across. Jamaica.

microdasys Bunny Ears
Growing up to 3 ft, with closely jointed flattened-oblong pads, bright

green in colour, and yellowish-brown glochids filling the areoles. There are no spines. The flowers are usually yellow, sometimes tinted scarlet, 1½–2 in. across. Mexico.

'Albispina', has white glochids. **365.**

monacantha syn. **O. vulgaris**
Flattened, oblong pads, narrower at the base, form a 6 ft tall plant. The white woolly areoles have 1–3 long spines and brownish-yellow glochids. Golden-yellow or reddish flowers, 3 in. across, are borne in summer. Brazil, Uruguay, Argentina.

robusta
Edible fruits form on this sometimes tree-size opuntia, which in Britain usually only grows to 2 ft. The glaucous green pads with distant areoles and brownish glochids, often reach a width of 12 in. The flowers are yellow and about 3 in. across. Mexico.

salmiana
Normally growing to 18 in. high, with sausage-shaped stems which are ½ in. across, lax and sprawling, and needing stakes to keep them orderly. They are glaucous green, sometimes reddish or purplish. Small yellow spines and numerous glochids grow on the small areoles. The flowers, also small, 1–1½ in. across, and yellowish, are borne freely at the pad tips. They are followed by seedless red fruits, with few or no spines, that often drop off and root. Brazil, Paraguay, Argentina.

scheeri
Spreading 2–3 ft high plant with flattened joints, 6–8 in. long, blue-green in colour and covered with yellow spines and hairs. The large yellow flowers are not often produced in cultivation. Mexico.

sulphurea
A straggling plant, 18 in. high, with oblong flattish shoots, tuberculate. The small areoles have yellowish-red glochids and 2–8 thick, sometimes curved spines up to 4 in. long and often with reddish-brown markings. The flowers are about 2 in. long and sulphur yellow. Argentina.

tomentosa
A vigorous opuntia, often used as rootstocks for weaker species. The deep green joints are obovate, about 5 in. long, with distant areoles sometimes bearing a few small white spines or none. The fiery orange flowers are usually produced on old plants. C. Mexico.

tuna see **O. humilis**

tunicata syn. **O. furiosa**
A bushy plant about 18 in. high with cylindrical stems which are easily detached. The areoles are covered in whitish wool, and the yellow barbed spines are encased in papery white sheaths. Flowers are yellow, about 2 in. across. Mexico, Ecuador to Chile.

× verschaffeltii
An odd hybrid connecting two subgenera of *Opuntia*, *Tephrocactus* and *Cylindropuntia*. A low spreading plant, up to 12 in. high, with round to short cylindrical joints, becoming long and thin in cultivation. The glochids are sparse and white in colour; the flowers are orange to blood red. Bolivia.

vulgaris see **O. monacantha**

Orange, Calamondin see **Citrus mitis**
Orange Kaleidoscope Flower see **Streptanthera cuprea**
Orange, Seville see **Citrus aurantium**
Orange, Sweet see **Citrus sinensis**
Orchid Bush see **Bauhinia acuminata**
Orchid, Butterfly see **Oncidium papilio**
Orchid, Christmas see **Cattleya trianaei**
Orchid, Cockleshell see **Epidendrum cochleatum**
Orchid, Cocktail see **Cattleya intermedia**
Orchid, Dancing Doll see **Oncidium flexuosum**
Orchid, Easter see **Cattleya mossiae**
Orchid, Fox-tail see **Aerides**
Orchid, Lace see **Odontoglossum crispum**
Orchid, Pansy see **Miltonia**
Orchid, Poor Man's see **Schizanthus pinnatus**
Orchid, Rainbow see **Epidendrum prismatocarpum**
Orchid, Slipper see **Paphiopedilum**
Orchid, Star of Bethlehem see **Angraecum sesquipedale**

Orchid Tree, Purple see **Bauhinia variegata**

OREODOXA (PALMAE)
granatensis
A tall, slender-stemmed palm which makes a very good house plant in its juvenile stage. In its native country it will reach over 100 ft at maturity. It has gracefully arching leaves, deeply cut into long, narrow somewhat drooping segments and a dark glossy green. Grow in pots in loam-based compost watering most freely in summer. Propagate by sowing the seeds in February and March. Colombia.

Ornamental Yam see **Dioscorea discolor**

ORNITHOGALUM (LILIACEAE)
thyrsoides Chincherinchee
An attractive bulbous species for the house and cool greenhouse, the 6–18 in. stems carrying 20–30 white to golden-yellow starry flowers which open from May to July. The individual blooms are 6-petalled and star-like and are borne in a dense spike which opens upwards. Place the bulbs in pots of loam-based compost in autumn. Propagate by removing offset bulbs when re-potting or by seed in autumn. S. Africa. **366.**

OXALIS (OXALIDACEAE) Wood Sorrel
A large genus of mainly low growing, bright flowered plants which includes species with corms, tubers, rhizomes and fibrous roots. The leaves are clover-like and close in the dark, folding along the midrib of each leaflet. They make very good house and cool greenhouse plants needing a sunny position. Grow in pots in loam-based compost and repot in alternate years in autumn. Propagate by division of bulbous species after flowering and all other species in spring. Seeds may also be sown in spring.

bupleurifolia
A plant with linear leaf-like stalks, occasionally a few bearing 3 leaflets. Up to 3 in. stalks carry small branched clusters of 2–4 flowers which have small, yellow petals. A curious rather than lovely species. Brazil.

cernua syn. **O. pes-caprae** Bermuda Buttercup
Although a weed in mild regions, the delightful 1½ in. wide, buttercup yellow, bell-shaped flowers make this an attractive species for pot culture. The long stalked rather fleshy leaves have 3 leaflets, which are produced from April to September, are borne in clusters of 3 to 8 on long erect stalks. S. Africa.

dispar
A densely branching sub-shrub with small softly hairy, leaves divided into 3, narrow, pointed leaflets. The 1 in. yellow, 5-petalled flowers are thickly borne on long stalks and open off and on from spring to autumn. Guiana.

hirta
A bulbous species with an erect or creeping stem bearing divided, hairy leaves, having narrowly oblong leaflets. The glossy violet flowers, which have a yellow tube, are profusely borne along the tips of the shoots in the axils of the leaves. They open in autumn. S. Africa.

ortgiesii
A tall species sometimes reaching 18 in. in height, but more usually about 8 in. The unbranched, fleshy stem carries the stalkless leaves which are divided into three 2½ in. segments and are dull green above and purplish-red beneath. The small, lemon-yellow flowers have bright yellow veins. They are carried on long stalks in clusters of 5–10 blooms, and open in sun throughout the year. Peru.

pes-caprae see **O. cernua**

succulenta
A shrubby plant up to 1 ft or so tall, having small, notched grey-green leaflets on long, fleshy, cylindrical stalks. The small bronze-yellow flowers are borne in clusters on 3–4 in. long smooth stalks spasmodically from spring to autumn. The plant grown and described under this name is probably mis-identified. S. America.

Ox-tongue Lily see **Haemanthus coccineus**

P

PACHYPHYTUM (CRASSULACEAE)
A genus of striking succulent plants with open rosettes or spikes of very thick, fleshy leaves. The bell-shaped flowers are borne in a pendent cluster. Grow in a well ventilated, sunny, cool greenhouse. The compost should be well drained, preferably loam-based with added coarse sand. Water freely in summer but keep almost dry in winter. Propagate by stem or leaf cuttings in summer.

brevifolium Sticky Moonstones
The 10 in. stems bear thick, fleshy elliptic leaves, upturned and round ended with a small point. They are 1–1½ in. in length, blue, often with a reddish tinge, covered with a pearly bloom and the stems are slightly sticky between the young leaves. The bell-shaped flowers are dark carmine-red and are borne in short clusters. Mexico.

oviferum Moonstones
A very attractive species, the short stems and the 1½ in., egg-shaped leaves covered with a silvery-white bloom which makes them appear opaque, becoming pink and blue tinged in the summer. The flowers are deep red, bell-shaped, but almost completely covered by the white sepals. They are produced in May. Mexico.

PACHYSTACHYS (ACANTHACEAE)
coccinea see **Jacobinia coccinea**

lutea Lollipop Plant
An erect, branched, plant up to 18 in. tall, bearing elliptical, pointed, rich green leaves. Each stem terminates in a 4–6 in. cone-like cluster of rich yellow overlapping bracts, from which protrude white tubular flowers. Plants flower off and on most of the year. A striking plant, making an excellent pot plant for the home or a cool to warm greenhouse. Grow in loam-based compost or a proprietary peat mix, and shade from hottest sunshine. Propagate by stem cuttings, preferably young non-flowering shoots from cut back plants, in spring or summer. Brazil. **367.**

Painted Drop Tongue see **Aglaonema costatum** and **A. crispum**
Painted Fern, Japanese see **Athyrium goeringianum**
Painted Netleaf see **Fittonia verschaffeltii**
Painted Tongue see **Salpiglossis sinuata**
Painter's Palette see **Anthurium andreanum**
Palm, Areca see **Chrysalidocarpus lutescens**
Palm, Australian Fountain see **Livistona australis**
Palm, Cabbage see **Cordyline**
Palm, Canary Island see **Phoenix canariensis**
Palm, Chinese Fan see **Livistona chinensis**
Palm, Curly Sentry see **Howea belmoreana**
Palm, Date see **Phoenix dactylifera**
Palm, Dwarf Mountain see **Chamaedorea elegans**
Palm, European Fan see **Chamaerops humilis**
Palm, Feather Duster see **Rhopalostylis sapida**
Palm, Fern see **Cycas circinalis**
Palm, Grass see **Cordyline australis**
Palm, Kentia see **Howea forsteriana**
Palm-leaf Begonia see **Begonia luxurians**
Palm, Nikau see **Rhopalostylis sapida**
Palm, Paradise see **Howea fosteriana**
Palm, Parlor see **Chamaedorea elegans**
Palm, Peaberry see **Thrinax**
Palm, Pygmy Date see **Phoenix roebelinii**
Palm, Sago see **Cycas revoluta**
Palm, Shaving-brush see **Rhopalostylis sapida**
Palm, Silver see **Thrinax argentea**

PAMIANTHE (AMARYLLIDACEAE)
peruviana Peruvian Daffodil
A beautiful lily-like plant with long, strap-shaped evergreen leaves which form a stem-like, tubular sheath as they rise from the bulb. The flowers are borne on short, angled stems and have a long, 4½ in. deep green tube which opens into 6, spreading outer white petals ending in a short point, the outer 3 with a central green stripe. It has an inner crown about 3 in. long, similarly coloured and bell-shaped. Flowering season is February and March. Grow in the warm greenhouse in a humid

atmosphere in pots using loam-based compost. It also makes an attractive house plant if the temperature is reasonably constant. Propagate by division of bulbs or by seed sown as soon as it is ripe. Peru. **368.**

PANCRATIUM (AMARYLLIDACEAE)
A genus of large, white-flowered, bulbous plants which make attractive specimens for the cool greenhouse. They have grey-green, strap-shaped leaves. Grow in loam-based compost in pots and water sparingly except during the growing season. Repot every 2 or 3 years in autumn. Propagate by removing bulb offsets when re-potting or by seed sown in March.

canariense ✺
The white blooms are 3 in. across having a short tube opening to narrow, slender spreading lobes, and a central crown of 12 short segments. The long, drooping leaves are blunt-tipped and borne in pairs. Canary Isles.

illyricum ✺
An 18 in. high species with clusters of up to 12 blooms at the top of the stem. The tube is pale green and only half the length of the narrow petals which spread to give a starry appearance to the flowers. The central white crown is short. They are borne in May and June. S. Europe.

maritimum Sea Daffodil, Sea Lily ✺
A somewhat similar species to *P. illyricum* having a longer tube and narrow leaves which can persist through the winter. The fragrant flowers have a prominent cup-like crown and open from July to September. S. Europe.

Panamiga see **Pilea involucrata**
Panamiga, Black Leaf see **Pilea repens**

PANDOREA (BIGNONIACEAE)
A genus of evergreen climbers with divided leaves and clusters of long, bell-shaped flowers. They make attractive cool to warm greenhouse and conservatory plants needing a sunny position, and should be grown in a border with some form of support up which they can twine. Propagate by stem cuttings in summer or by seed.

jasminoides Bower Plant ✺ ☙
The drooping clusters of flowers are 1½–2 in. long, white, with a pink flush in the throat, and open into a flat bell-shape at the mouth. They are borne at the ends of branches or in the axils of the lower leaves, and open in summer. The leaves are divided into 5–9 slender pointed, oval leaflets. Australia.

pandorana Wonga-wonga Vine ✺ ☙
A small-flowered species with yellow or pinkish white blooms opening to 5 small lobes and spotted violet in the throat. The divided leaves have slender pointed oval leaflets somewhat broader than those of *P. jasminoides*. Australia, New Guinea.

Pansy Orchid see **Miltonia**
Paper Flower see **Bougainvillea glabra**

PAPHIOPEDILUM (ORCHIDACEAE) Slipper Orchids, Lady's Slipper
A genus of most attractive slipper-flowered orchids, often still called *Cypripedium*. They are tufted plants having strap-shaped, leathery leaves and 2–5 in. wide flowers comprising a large upright petal (really a sepal) at the top, 2 narrow wing petals and a slipper-shaped lip. They are not difficult to grow, most requiring a humid atmosphere and should be grown in pots in a compost of equal parts osmunda fibre, sphagnum moss and loam. Water frequently and repot every 2 to 3 years in spring. Propagate by dividing congested plants when repotting. All are warm greenhouse species unless stated.

callosum ✺
The blue-green leaves of this species are marbled with light and dark patches. The 4 in. flowers are carried on a 12 in. stem; the large upright petal is white with maroon and green veining and the wings are green-striped with shining red warts on the margin. The lip forms a deep

red-brown slipper. They are produced from January to June. Cochin China, Thailand.

fairieanum ✺
A dwarf species only 8–10 in. in height with mid-green leaves. The creamy white petals are sickle-shaped and crimson striped, while the pouch is green, marked with red-brown and crimson. All the petals have wavy margins, and are borne from August to October. This is an excellent species for the cool greenhouse. Assam, Himalayas.

hirsutissimum ✺
The solitary flowers are often up to 6 in. across and have green sepals which are shaded and dotted with rose purple, the petals are magenta-purple with green at the base. The lip is spotted with brown-red. They are produced from March to May. The pale green leaves are about 10 in. long. N.E. India.

insigne ✺
A vigorous species with broad pale green strap-shaped leaves. The solitary flowers, up to 5 in. across, have the broad upper petal bright yellow-green blotched with purple-brown, and tipped white; the helmet-shaped lip is tawny gold. A regular flowerer from early winter to spring. Nepal, Assam. **369.**

× **maudiae** ✺
A handsome hybrid with white petals striped rich olive green, and a helmet-shaped lip also olive green in colour. **370.**

purpuratum ✺
A dwarf species with mottled leaves. The large upright sepal is white with green shading towards the base and is marked with brown-purple stripes. The petals are purplish red with purple veining, while the lip is a brownish-purple. Hong Kong.

rothschildianum ✺
A strong growing 3 ft species, bearing in May and June 24 in. spikes with up to 5, 6–8 in. blooms. They have long, narrowly pointed petals, light green with distinctive longitudinal dark purple striping, and a red-brown pouch which is yellow above. The leaves are leathery and a glossy dark green. E. Indies.

venustum ✺
A delicately coloured species having marbled bluish and light green leaves and solitary 3 in. flowers which have white sepals striped with green, the large wings flushed with rosy-purple at the tips and bearing blackish warts. The yellow-green pouch is marbled with rose and veined a darker green. Suitable for the cool greenhouse. Nepal.

Papyrus see **Cyperus papyrus**
Paradise Palm see **Howea fosteriana**

PARKINSONIA (LEGUMINOSAE)
aculeata Jerusalem Thorn ✺ ☙
An elegant 8–10 ft evergreen species with long streamer like leaves borne on tiny and spiny stalks. The tiny oval leaflets are very widely spaced on long midribs. In spring and summer clusters of golden yellow flowers appear, each blossom having one petal spotted or suffused red. Grow in tubs or the border in a cool greenhouse well ventilated in summer. Use a loam-based compost. Propagate by seeds in spring. Mexico, S.W. USA.

Parlor Palm see **Chamaedorea elegans**
Parlour Ivy see **Philodendron scandens**

PARODIA (CACTACEAE)
A group of cacti with small plant bodies which may be globular or somewhat elongated, very spiny and usually solitary, though some form groups. For cultivation see under terrestrial cacti in the Introduction.

chrysacanthion ✺ ☙
The commonest species in cultivation with a globular to shortly columnar plant body, up to 2½ in. tall, sometimes with subsidiary stems at the base. The flowers are borne at the top of the plant, and are funnel shaped, golden yellow and up to 1 in. long. Argentina. **371.**

Parrot Leaf see **Alternanthera amoena**
Parrot's Bill see **Clianthus puniceus**
Partridge-breasted Aloe see **Aloe variegata**

PASSIFLORA (PASSIFLORACEAE) Passion Flower
A genus of evergreen, tendril-climbing vines with showy flowers comprising a number of regular petals making a star or bowl-shaped flower with a central crown bearing outward radiating fringe of thread-like filaments around the stalk supporting the ovary and stamens. They are best planted in the cool or warm greenhouse border, but can be grown in pots or tubs in loam-based compost. They need training up light supports. Propagate by cuttings of stem sections in July or August, or by seed.

× **allardii** (*P. caerulea* × *P. quadrangularis*)
The 3 in. flowers have white petals flushed with pink, and blue filaments, and are produced from June to October. The mid-green leaves are 3–5 lobed and the plant can reach a height of 20 ft. Garden origin. **372.**

caerulea Common or Blue Passion Flower
This will grow in mild regions, but thrives best in a cool greenhouse or when young as a house plant. It has 5–7 lobed leaves, bright green and up to 7 in. across, and solitary, slightly fragrant flowers which are produced from June to September. The petals and the central ovary and stamens are pure white, while the filaments are a contrasting deep blue fading to white towards the centre, but with deep violet at the base. The plant sometimes produces ovoid pale orange-yellow fruits 1–1¼ in. long. Brazil and S.S. America.

× **caponii** 'John Innes' (*P. quadrangularis* × *P. racemosa*)
A hybrid rather similar to *P. quadrangularis* but with 3-lobed leaves and deep rose petals inside, greenish on the reverse, with blue and white banded filaments. Garden origin.

coccinea Scarlet Passion Flower
A species having striking scarlet petals, yellowish on the reverse, with filaments white at the base, shading through pink to purple at the tips. The oval, toothed leaves are undivided and borne on somewhat purplish stems. Tropical S. America.

edulis Granadilla
A species cultivated in warm countries for its delicious, 2 in. diameter fruits. Each 2½ in. wide, white flower has white and purple banded filaments and opens in summer. The egg-shaped fruits may be purple or yellow. The 4–6 in. leaves are deeply 3-lobed and have wavy edges. Tropical S. America. **373.**

incarnata May Apple, Maypop
The popular names for this species are derived from the oval yellow fruits, about the size of a hen's egg. The flowers are 2 in. across, the petals pale lavender or white with a hard, horn-like point and the filaments are purple. A summer to winter flowering species, depending on climate, with large, 3-lobed leaves, S.E. USA.

laurifolia Jamaica Honeysuckle, Water Lemon, Yellow Granadilla
The 3–5 in. long unlobed leaves are oval, leathery and shining. The fragrant flowers are 2–3 in. across with petals green on the reverse and red inside. The filaments are purple, banded with white, blue and red. They are produced in June and July and are followed by yellow, ovoid fruits, shaped rather like a lemon and 2–3 in. long. They are edible. Tropical America.

manicata
A strong climbing species with deeply 3-lobed, leathery leaves having oval, toothed lobes. The 4 in. flowers have vivid scarlet petals. A plant for the warm greenhouse. Venezuela to Peru.

mixta
A brightly coloured species bearing flowers 3½ in. across, the petals pink to orange-red with a reduced lavender or purple-rimmed crown. They are produced from July to September. The leaves are 3-lobed with pointed, toothed lobes and are smooth above and velvety hairy below. Tropical S. America.

mollissima
A softly downy species with wide, deeply 3-lobed leaves and 3 in. pink, long-tubed flowers bearing an inconspicuous crown reduced to a somewhat warty rim. They are produced from June to October and are sometimes followed by yellow, 3 in. ovoid fruits. Tropical S. America.

quadrangularis Giant Granadilla
A free flowering species having a very exotic appearance. The petals are white, flushed deep pink to purple on the inside and the crown is of up to 4 in. wavy filaments banded with purple, white and blue. They are borne from July to September. The oblong yellow fruits are 8–12 in. long but rarely or erratically produced in a greenhouse. The leaves are ovate to elliptic, 4–8 in. long and the whole plant is hairless. Tropical America. **374.**

racemosa Red or Red Cluster Passion Flower
A species with variable wavy leaves, sometimes entire and oval, though more often 3-lobed. The rose-crimson flowers are 4–5 in. across and have a crown of short filaments, the outer purple with white tips, the inner red and short. They are produced in autumn, and are borne in clusters of 8–13 blooms on the tips of long, pendulous stems. Brazil.

Passion Flower see **Passiflora**

PAVONIA (MALVACEAE)
multiflora
A tropical evergreen shrub usually with long, undivided stems and narrowly oblong leaves to 10 in. in length and tapering to a slender point. The curious flowers are borne singly in the axils of the leaves at the top of long stems forming a leafy rounded cluster. Each flower has a whorl of long, narrow, hairy bracts which are red and exceed the similar whorl of purple petal-like sepals. The stamens protrude beyond both and have blue anthers. An interesting autumn flowering species for the warm greenhouse. Grow in pots of loam-based compost or a proprietary peat mix. Maintain a humid atmosphere and shade from the hottest sunshine. Propagate by cuttings from young lateral shoots in late spring. Brazil.

Pawpaw see **Carica papaya**
Peaberry Palm see **Thrinax**
Pea, Butterfly see **Clitoria ternatea**
Peacock Iris see **Moraea glaucopsis**
Peacock Plant see **Calathea makoyana**
Peacock Tiger Flower see **Tigridia pavonia**
Pea, Flame see **Chorizema**
Pea, Glory see **Clianthus formosus**
Pea, Holly-leaved Glory see **Chorizema ilicifolium**
Peanut Cactus see **Chamaecereus silvestrii**
Pear, Balsam see **Momordica charantia**
Pearl Acacia see **Acacia podalyriifolia**
Pear, Prickly see **Opuntia**
Pebble Plant see **Lithops**

PEDILANTHUS (EUPHORBIACEAE)
tithymaloides Ribbon Cactus, Redbird Cactus
A branching, succulent bush up to 3 ft high, having cylindrical, fleshy, grey-green stems which grow in a zig-zag line, bearing a leaf at each bend. These are 2–3 in. long, oval and green in the wild species. The red flower head is spurred, and resembles a bird's head. Grow in a proprietary peat compost preferably mixed with coarse sand. Ventilate on warm days. Propagate by stem tip cuttings in summer which have been allowed to dry off for several hours before insertion. W. Indies.
  'Variegata', the leaves variegated, edged with white and faintly red-tinted.

Peepul see **Ficus religiosa**

PELARGONIUM (GERANIACEAE) Storksbill, Geranium
A genus of tender sub-shrubs which make excellent pot plants for house or greenhouse. Grow in loam-based compost, keep just moist in winter and water freely during the growing period. Shade from hottest summer sun. Propagate by stem tip cuttings in late summer or spring. Repot annually.

crispum
A 2 ft erect, densely branched shrub with mid-green, fan-shaped,

coarsely-toothed, curled leaves, having a strong fragrance of balm. The clusters of 2 or 3 flowers are carried on stalks in the axils of the upper leaves from May to October. They are pale pink or lavender, 1 in. across with narrow petals. S. Africa.

'Variegatum', distinctive for its creamy white leaf markings, **375.**

cucullatum
A densely hairy shrub, densely branched, sometimes exceeding 3 ft in height. The kidney-shaped, toothed leaves are up to 3 in. in length and the many flowered clusters of flowers are borne at the ends of the branches. The large petals are red with darker veins and the flowers are produced in September. S. Africa.

denticulatum
A densely leafy species, not truly shrubby, with slender branches bearing 1½–3 in. leaves which are deeply cut into narrow lobes. The almost stalkless flowers are carried in clusters of 1–3 at the ends of the branches in summer. They are lilac to rose-purple with dark blotches on the two upper petals. S. Africa.

× **domesticum** Regal Pelargonium, Martha Washington Pelargonium
A group of hybrids with 1½–2 in. flowers borne in rounded clusters in the axils of the leaves towards the ends of the branches. They are in all shades from pink to purple and are variously marked with darker veining or spotting, and are borne abundantly from late spring to autumn. Many cultivars have been produced.
'Aztec', bright red flowers veined red purple with white margins;
'Doris Frith', a fine white-flowered variety with waved petals bearing small purple feathering at the base, **376;**
'Grand Slam', rose red flowers shading to violet red, **377;**
'Kingston Beauty', a vigorous cultivar with large frilled cherry red blooms, white in the centre, **378;**
'May Magic', large frilled orange flowers with pale centre and edges.

× **fragrans** Nutmeg Geranium
A much branched, leafy sub-shrub with hairy, 3-lobed, heart-shaped leaves smelling strongly of nutmeg. The small, white petals have red veins and the flowers are borne in clusters of 4–8 blooms throughout summer.

fulgidum
A compact shrubby species with 3-lobed silvery hairy leaves and long stalks bearing 5–12 fiery red flowers with darker veining. This is one parent of the Regal group. Summer flowering. S. Africa.

graveolens Rose Geranium
A spreading species reaching 3 ft in height with 5–7 lobed, hairy fragrant leaves and 3 in. stems carrying 5–10 flowered clusters of rose to purple blooms marked with a dark spot. They are borne from June to October. S. Africa.

× **hortorum** Common or Fish Geranium
A name for a large group of hybrids largely derived from *P. zonale*. They are tall, reaching to 6 ft and have distinctively rounded leaves with brown or mauve zoned markings.
'Distinction', neat rounded foliage with narrow purple-brown zone close to the margin; flowers crimson, **379;**
'Fiat', semi double coral flowers, **380;**
'Gazelle', compact habit, lobed leaves with a purple-brown zone close to the centre; flowers bright salmon pink in profusion, **381;**
'Irene' group. This covers a new race of American cultivars which produces compact, well branched plants and a long succession of large flower heads. In a sunny window or conservatory they flower well in the depth of winter. A variety of colours is obtainable, among the best being:
'Fire Brand', poppy red, very free flowering;
'Modesty', pure white, occasionally touched with pink;
'Lollipop', brilliant orange-scarlet;
'Party Dress', delicate salmon pink flowers borne in profusion;
'Mr Henry Cox', rose coloured, notched petals, yellow edged leaves with pink and green markings partly superimposed, **382;**
'Mrs Pollock', vermilion flowered, the leaves having creamy margins, a pale centre and dark red and orange irregularly marked between;
'Spitfire', single red flowers with strongly contrasting green and white foliage, **383;**

miniatures
'Pink Harry Hieover', glossy yellow green leaves with a chestnut brown band; pink with darker veins, **384;**
'Red Black Vesuvius', almost black foliage with single large, red flowers;
'Sprite', dark green leaves with an ivory white border and a pink flush. Salmon pink, single flowers.

odoratissimum Apple Geranium
A dwarf shrubby species not exceeding 6 in. in height, with velvety, ruffled, ovate to kidney-shaped light green leaves pleasantly apple-scented. 5–10 flowers are borne in each cluster, the upper white petals spotted and veined red. S. Africa.

peltatum Ivy-leaved Geranium
A trailing or mat-forming species with fleshy, ivy-like leaves. The flowers vary from white and pale pink to crimson, often with deeper veined petals. Several distinctive cultivars are grown.
'L'Elegante' has pink and cream variegated leaves and pink flowers;
'Claret Crousse' or 'Mexican Beauty' is a vigorous grower with claret-red flowers;
'Sussex Lace' bears lilac-pink blossoms and leaves handsomely veined with ivory, **385.**

quercifolia Oak-leaved Geranium
A freely branched shrub with oak-shaped, dark green leaves marked brown along the veins, and with a pungent scent. The 3–7 flowered clusters are borne on short stalks, the individual blossoms being pinkish-mauve with purple marked upper petals; they open in May. S. Africa.

radula syn. **P. radens**
A 3 ft grey-green much-branched shrub with an aromatic scent like that of balsam. The rose-coloured petals have dark red central marks on the upper 2 and are borne in 5-flowered clusters in June. S. Africa.

tetragonum
An erect, densely branched, succulent stemmed species bearing small dull green, hairy leaves with a central dark blotch. The 1–3 rose and purple flowers with darker markings are carried on short stalks and open in June. S. Africa.

tomentosum Peppermint Geranium
A sprawling or semi-climbing shrub with softly hairy, mid-green shallowly lobed leaves which smell strongly of peppermint. The small white flowers have reddish veining and are borne from May to the first frosts.

triste
Nocturnally sweet scented with yellow-margined, brown-purple flowers borne in clusters on long stalks in July. The large leaves are deeply cut and toothed at the margins. S. Africa.

zonale Zonal or Horseshoe Geranium
A sub-shrub, woody below and somewhat fleshy stemmed above. The rounded, heart-shaped, wavy-edged leaves have a faint horseshoe mark on the upper surface. The flowers are borne in clusters and have narrow petals usually pinkish-purple fading to a white centre, but also can be white, pink or red. They are produced in summer. See also *P.* × *hortorum*. S. Africa.

PELLAEA (SINOPTERIDACEAE) Cliff Brake
rotundifolia Button Fern
A most attractive small fern, making good ground cover and an attractive pot plant for the cool greenhouse. It has 12 in. fronds which arch downwards to the ground and are divided to the midrib into 20–30 waxy and somewhat leathery textured segments, almost round when young, but becoming oblong in shape when mature. Grow in a peat compost and keep shaded from direct sunlight. Propagate by division of rhizomes in March or April or from spores sown in spring. New Zealand. **386.**

PELLIONIA (URTICACAE)
A genus of plants cultivated for their ornamental foliage. They are low growing and make fine plants either trailing from a basket, or growing over supports in pots. They need warmth and are best in the warm greenhouse though they tolerate cooler conditions and can be grown as house plants. Grow in a proprietary peat mix or loam-based compost. Propagate by division or by stem-tip cuttings in spring.

daveauana see **P. repens**

pulchra
The oval, light green leaves are marked with a network of dull, black-purple veins on the upper side of the leaf, and are pale grey beneath with purple veining. They are borne on creeping, succulent, pinkish-purple stems. Cochin China. **387.**

repens syn. **P. daveauana**
A creeping plant with succulent stems bearing thin, fleshy leaves, roundish when young, becoming long-oval up to 2¼ in. when mature. They are dark bronzy green variegated with a paler green centre. The flowers are greenish and inconspicuous. S. Vietnam, Burma, Malaya.

Pentapterygium serpens see **Agapetes serpens**

PENTAS (RUBIACEAE)
lanceolata syn. **P. carnea** Egyptian Star Cluster
An 18 in. sub-shrubby perennial, somewhat inclined to be straggling unless the growing shoots are pinched out when young. The downy branches bear pairs of bright green, oval, hairy leaves which taper to a point. Each stem terminates in a roundish cluster of 1¼ in. tubular flowers spreading open at the throat to appear starry; mainly pale purple, though may vary from white through pink to a deep rose-red. They open in summer. The plants are good for the cool greenhouse, or a sunny window sill and should be grown in pots in loam-based compost. Propagate by stem cuttings of young non-flowering shoots in spring. Tropical Africa. **388.**
'Quartiniana', has more abundantly borne, bright rose-pink flowers.

PEPEROMIA
A genus of tropical, largely succulent plants, many of which have attractively marked foliage and make good house plants. They mainly have narrow spikes of insignificant yellow or white flowers like mouse-tails, but a few have decorative blossoms. Grow in loam-based or a proprietary peat compost. Allow to become almost dry in winter, but keep moist at other times. Maintain a humid atmosphere and shade from direct sun in summer. Repot annually and propagate by stem-tip cuttings taken in late spring or summer except where stated differently.

argyreia syn. **P. sandersii** Watermelon Peperomia, Rugby Football Plant
The broadly ovate leaves are smooth and fleshy with bright green, feathery-edged veins on a silvery-white background. They are borne on stiff red stems and the plant grows to 8–10 in. in height. Propagate by leaf cuttings from spring to autumn. Brazil. **389.**

caperata 'Emerald Ripple'
The pale pink stems carry numerous 1¼ in. oval to heart-shaped leaves, a deep velvety green with a silvery-grey sheen between the veins. These are deeply sunken and create a quilted surface. The greenish-white flowering 'tails' are borne on purplish-red stalks flecked with a deeper red. They are produced from April to December. Brazil. **390.**

fraseri see **P. resediflora**

glabella Wax Privet
The small, waxy green leaves are shaped like those of privet and are borne on red stems which make a spreading, branching plant. Central America.
'Variegata', a dainty plant with the leaves light green, bordered and variegated milky white.

griseo-argentea see **P. hederifolia**

hederifolia syn. **P. griseo-argentea** Ivy-leaved Peperomia
A somewhat similar plant to P. caperata but with larger, more rounded leaves up to 2½ in. in length. They are a duller silvery green and the corrugation is flatter. Brazil. **391.**

maculosa Radiator Plant
A plant with ovate, pendent fleshy leaves up to some 7 in. long. They have a waxy texture and are blue-green with silvery ribs and are borne on red-marked stalks. The tail-like flower spikes are green and up to 1 ft in length. W. Indies.

magnoliifolia syn. **P. tithymaloides** Desert Privet
A much branched, shrubby species with 4–5 in. oval to elliptical, fresh green, glossy leaves borne on brown-purple stems. The type is seldom grown, most cultivated plants being of the variegated forms. W. Indies.
'Variegata', the young leaves are almost completely creamy white, changing gradually to a pale green as the plant matures. The leaf stalks are at first red and later green with red markings, **392.**

obtusifolia Baby Rubber Plant
The ovate to round, fleshy leaves are dark green and purple edged. They grow on maroon stems, the whole plant becoming well branched as it matures. The white flower spikes are 2 in. long and appear from June to September. Florida, W. Indies.

resediflora syn. **P. fraseri** Mignonette Peperomia
A small, branched species forming rosettes of heart-shaped, quilted, dark green finely hairy leaves with an almost frosted appearance. They are paler green beneath with outstanding, red veins. The flowers are white and showy, somewhat like mignonette and borne on long red stems. Propagate by leaf cuttings in spring or summer. Colombia, Ecuador.

sandersii see **P. argyreia**

scandens syn. **P. serpens**
'Variegata' is the form met with in cultivation. A climbing or trailing plant with fleshy, reddish stems which can be trained up a support. The 2 in. leaves are pointed, heart-shaped, creamy white at first, later becoming light green, but keeping the creamy coloured margins. Vigorous, best in a basket where the long shoots can hang down. Peru.

serpens see **P. scandens**
tithymaloides see **P. magnoliifolia**

Pepino see **Solanum muricatum**
Pepper, Chilli see **Capsicum annuum**
Peppermint Geranium see **Pelargonium tomentosum**
Pepper, Red see **Capsicum**

PERESKIA (CACTACEAE)
aculeata Barbados Gooseberry, Lemon Vine
The most common pereskia, semi-evergreen, with shrubby branching stems 6 ft or more in height, and areoles forming in the leaf axils. On young shoots these bear 3 hooked spines enabling them to scramble among other plants. Ageing branches have straight dark brown spines about 1 in. long. Saucer-shaped white, pale yellow or pink, scented flowers, 1½ in. wide, open in October. The mid-green leaves form in spring and usually drop in autumn. An interesting genus, being a primitive type of cactus that still bears leaves. For culture see under terrestrial cacti in the Introduction. Minimum winter temperature 40°F. Propagate by cuttings or seed. Tropical America.

Perilepta dyerana see **Strobilantes dyerianus**

PERISTROPHE (ACANTHACEAE)
A genus of perennials and sub-shrubs the following species of which make ornamental flowering and foliage pot plants for the cool or warm greenhouse. They are also suitable as short term plants for the home. Grow in loam-based compost. Propagate by stem cuttings, preferably of basal shoots from cut-back plants in spring or summer. Pinch the young plants to promote a well branched habit.

angustifolia syn. **P. salicifolia**
A low growing plant with horizontal branches clad in slender pointed, lance-shaped leaves. The slender 2-lipped flowers are rose-pink and borne in small terminal clusters during winter. It is mainly represented in cultivation by the variegated form 'Aurea-variegata', Marble-Leaf, which has a large, feathered, yellow splash on each leaf. It is best in a warm greenhouse. Java. **393.**

salicifolia see **P. angustifolia**

speciosa
This handsome species forms slender-branched bushes up to 3 ft or more tall, though usually less when grown as a pot plant. It has oval, long-pointed rich green leaves and terminal leafy clusters of 2 in. long flowers. These are a glowing rose-purple with two prominent tongue-like lobes the upper one reflexed back. It makes an excellent winter flowering pot plant for the warm or cool greenhouse. India.

Periwinkle see **Vinca**
Persian Shield see **Strobilanthes dyerianus**
Persian Violet see **Exacum affine**
Peruvian Daffodil see **Pamianthe peruviana**

PETREA (VERBENACEAE)
volubilis Purple or Queen's Wreath
A beautiful tropical climbing shrub, reaching 20 ft or more. The short-stalked, elliptic leaves are rough and rather brittle, from 1–8 in. in length. The star-like lilac and violet-blue flowers are borne in showy, pendent clusters up to 12 in. long, opening mainly in spring, with odd flushes through the summer. The plant needs full light, good ventilation and a rich soil to thrive. It is best in the warm greenhouse border where it can grow against a wall and under the glass at the top. Propagate by lateral stem cuttings in spring or summer. Mexico, W. Indies.

Pharbitis purpurea see **Ipomoea purpurea**

PHASEOLUS (LEGUMINOSAE) Bean
caracalla Snail Flower
A twining perennial, which can be grown as an annual, with leaves divided into 3 ovate, pointed leaflets. The fragrant, purple and yellow flowers are of a most curious shape, having a twisted upper petal and the wing petals and lip spirally coiled so that they resemble a snail shell. They are carried in long pendent clusters. A plant for the warm or cool greenhouse. Grow in pots in loam-based compost or in the border and propagate from seed. Tropical S. America.

Pheasant Leaf see **Cryptanthus fosterianus**

PHILESIA (LILIACEAE)
buxifolia syn. **P. magellanica**
A 2 ft evergreen shrub having narrow, leathery, dark and glossy green leaves with the margins inrolled. The flowers are borne singly, or in clusters of 2 or 3, slender bell-shaped, 2 in. in length, pink or red and waxy in texture. They are produced in May and June. A plant for the cool or sheltered cold greenhouse, growing well in pots in loam-based compost, preferably without lime, or a proprietary peat mixture. Propagate by separating basal suckers or by cuttings of young shoots with a heel in July. Chile. **394.**

PHILODENDRON (ARACEAE)
A genus of handsome foliage plants having large, leathery leaves. They make very decorative pot plants when young, and can be allowed to reach full size in the greenhouse border. Flowers are seldom produced in cultivation. Grow in a loam-based compost or a proprietary peat compost and keep well watered, especially during the summer months. The climbing species need the provision of some form of support. Propagate non-climbing species by basal shoots taken as cuttings and the climbers by tip cuttings, both during the summer. Both types will also grow from seed sown in spring.

andreanum syn. **P. melanochryson** Velour Philodendron
A climbing species, reaching 6 ft when grown in pots but capable of far exceeding this. The velvety, heart to arrow-shaped, pendent leaves reach 2 ft in length and are dark olive in colour with a coppery sheen and ivory-white veins. While young they are purple-pink on the under-surface. The smaller juvenile form is known as *P. melanochryson*. Colombia, Costa Rica. **395.**

bipinnatifidum Tree Philodendron
A compact, non-climbing species which forms a tree when mature. The juvenile leaves, which it bears for 2 years, are heart-shaped, but after this the plant produces deeply divided, dark green leaves which have up to 20 narrow, wavy-edged lobes, the whole leaf reaching 2–3 ft in length. They are borne on long, upright stems. Brazil.

domesticum see **P. hastatum**

erubescens Blushing Philodendron
When the leaves of this species first emerge, they are a delicate rose-pink, soon changing to a deep glossy green with a bronze sheen and pinky-red edges. The undersides deepen to a maroon-red and the leaf

stalks are the same colour. These arrow-shaped leaves grow to 10 in. in length and are carried on vigorous climbing stems which root at each joint. Colombia.

hastatum syn. **P. domesticum** Elephant's Ear
A strong-growing climber reaching 5 ft. The fleshy, arrow-shaped leaves can grow to 1 ft in length; they are mid-green and have paler veins and lengthen with age. Brazil. **396.**

laciniatum
A climbing species with deeply lobed leaves having narrow segments, the upper 2 sub-divided and somewhat reflexed. They have pale central shading on the dark green shining leaves. Brazil.

melanochryson see **P. andreanum**

micans Velvet-leaf Vine
An elegant, small-leafed plant which some consider to be a juvenile form of *P. scandens*. The heart-shaped leaves taper to a slender point having a silky bronze sheen above and reddish coloration beneath. Dominica, Tobago.

oxycardium syn. **P. scandens**

panduriforme Fiddle Leaf, Horse's Head
A handsome climbing plant having 3–5 lobed or waisted leaves, the lowest lobe large and ovate the upper heart-shaped at the top. They are a dull mid-green and tough and leathery in texture. Brazil.

sagittifolium
A climbing species suitable for the home. The arrow-shaped leaves and stems are mid-green without any red or purple coloration. Mexico.

scandens syn. **P. oxycardium** Parlour Ivy, Heart-leaf Philodendron

The most popular member of this genus for pot culture in the home. It has glossy green, heart-shaped leaves which taper to a fine point. They are 4–6 in. long at first, reaching 12 in. at maturity. It is remarkably tolerant of poor light and a polluted atmosphere. Central America, W. Indies. **397.**

selloum
A non-climbing, tree-like species with glossy dark green leaves up to 3 ft in length and deeply dissected to within 2 in. of the mid-rib, the segments narrow and toothed. They are borne on long, slender stalks. A most ornamental species best as a solitary specimen in a large space or in the greenhouse. Rather too large for the average home. Brazil.

PHOENIX (PALMAE)
A genus of palms including the date palms. They have feathery leaves and many will reach 100 ft at maturity. In their juvenile stage they make very decorative pot plants. Grow in large pots or containers in loam-based compost and when young provide some shade from summer sun. Propagate by seed sown in February and March, or from suckers when available.

canariensis Canary Isles Palm
A decorative species, the leaves growing while young from ground level, the trunk not produced until the tree is several years old. The bright green arching fronds are deeply dissected into long, sharp-pointed strap-like segments which are held stiffly from the mid-rib. A species for the cool greenhouse. Canary Isles.

dactylifera Date Palm
The commercial date palm, this species has bluish-green, arching fronds similarly divided to those of *P. canariensis*, but the segments are fewer, more pendulous and wider spaced along the mid-rib giving a more sparse appearance. Will grow in a warm or cool, well ventilated greenhouse. S.E. Asia.

roebelinii Pygmy Date Palm
A graceful, almost stemless palm when young, slender feathery fronds divided into narrow, somewhat pendent segments. An excellent species for ornamentation especially in a large room or warm greenhouse. S.E. Asia. **398.**

PHYLLITIS (ASPLENIACEAE)
A genus of ferns with simple, strap-shaped fronds, occasionally forked but never divided into segments. The 2 species described below are good pot plants for cool or warm greenhouse culture. Grow in a proprietary peat compost, maintain a humid atmosphere during the

hottest days, and shade from direct sunlight. Propagate by division or spores in spring.

brasiliensis
The entire, 6–12 in., fronds are 1–1½ in. wide, leathery and tapering towards the ends. They have an arching habit and are an attractive deep green. Brazil.

hemionitis Mule's Fern
The 4–6 in. fronds are long spear-shaped, bluntly pointed at the end but heart-shaped where they join the 4–6 in. slender stalk, with almost pointed lobes. S. Europe.

Phyllocactus see under **Epiphyllum**
Piaranthus pullus see **Caralluma mammillaris**

PILEA (URTICACEAE)
A genus of evergreen perennials which are grown for their decorative foliage. They make excellent plants for the house and warm greenhouse. Grow in pots of loam-based or a proprietary peat compost. Shade from sun and water freely from April to September, keeping just moist for the rest of the year. Propagate by stem cuttings taken in spring or summer.

cadierei Aluminium Plant
An erect, branched species, somewhat succulent when young, with thin, fleshy, oval leaves about 3 in. in length. They are a dark bluish-green with a silvery sheen and a quilted surface. A rapid growing plant, inclined to become straggly with age. Indo China. **399.**
 'Nana', a compact, dwarf form without the faults of the type. It has
 silvery patches on the leaves.

involucrata syn. **P. spruceana** Panamiga, Friendship Plant
A dwarf plant with oval, deep bronze-green, quilted leaves on short purplish stems, and crowded clusters of small greenish-white flowers borne in the axils of the leaves. Peru.

microphylla see **P. muscosa**

muscosa syn. **P. microphylla** Artillery Plant
The leaves of this species are tiny, mid-green, giving a mossy appearance. The whole plant is somewhat succulent and fleshy. The popular name derives from the fact that the inconspicuous flowers discharge small puffs of pollen when ripe, during May and September. Tropical America. **400.**

repens Black Leaf Panamiga
A species with richly coloured foliage and a useful dwarf, spreading habit. The small, round, quilted leaves are a glossy bronze above, purple and hairy below, and are borne on purplish-brown branches. It produces small greenish-white flowers on long stalks in summer. Mexico.

spruceana see **P. involucrata**

Pilosocereus chrysacanthus see **cephalocereus chrysacanthus**

PIMELEA (THYMELAEACEAE) Rice Flower
A genus of compact, free flowering shrubs with very small, almost stalkless, evergreen leaves. The small clusters of tubular flowers are carried at the ends of the branches. They grow well in the cool greenhouse border, or in pots in loam-based or a proprietary peat compost. Shade from the hottest sun. Propagate by cuttings of young shoots taken in late summer.

ferruginea
An erect, densely branched shrub growing 1½–2 ft tall. The round heads of flowers are 1–1½ in. across, each rose-pink bloom has a ½ in. tube and small spreading lobes, downy on the outside. They are produced in spring. W. Australia.

longiflora
A white flowering species with a silky tube and narrow lobes. They are borne on slender, hairy shoots which carry narrow hairy leaves. The overall height of the plant is 4 ft. It flowers in June. W. Australia.

spectabilis
A large-flowered species, 3–4 ft high with hairless shoots and leaves.

Flowers are white to rich pink with hairy tube and lobes about ½ in. across, clustered into heads 2–3 in. across beneath which grow 6 large oval green leaf-like bracts. W. Australia.

Pincushion Cactus, Desert see **Coryphantha deserti**
Pincushion Flower see **Hakea laurina**
Pine, African Fern see **Podocarpus gracilior**
Pineapple see **Ananas comosus**
Pineapple Flower see **Eucomis**
Pineapple Lily see **Eucomis zambesiaca**
Pineapple Scented Sage see **Salvia rutilans**
Pineapple, Variegated Wild see **Ananas bracteata** 'Striatus'
Pine, New Zealand White see **Podocarpus dacrydioides**
Pine, Norfolk Island see **Araucaria excelsa**

PINGUICULA (LENTIBULARIACEAE) Butterwort
A genus of insectivorous perennials with attractive snap-dragon-like spurred flowers borne on long stalks. The pale green fleshy leaves are covered with a sticky, digestive fluid which traps insects and gradually absorbs them. Plant in a compost of equal parts of peat and sphagnum moss, and stand the pots or pans in a tray of water. Shade from sun and keep well ventilated. Propagate by sowing seeds in autumn or early spring in a similar compost.

bakerana see **P. macrophylla**
caudata see **P. macrophylla**

grandiflora Greater Butterwort
The flat, light green, oval leaves grow in flat rosettes. From them rise long stalks each bearing in summer a single violet-blue flower, 1 in. across. W. Europe.

gypsicola
A species distinguished by its habit of producing a different form of leaf in summer and winter. The winter leaves are very small, up to ⅓ in. in length, borne in a tight rosette, while the summer leaves are long and narrow, reaching 2¼ in. and covered with glandular hairs. They are held upright, and from the base grow the 3 in. stalks which bear in summer, purple flowers with a short white tube and a long, purplish spur. Mexico.

macrophylla syn. **P. bakerana, P. caudata**
The rosettes of fleshy leaves are dense and pale-green when young, becoming larger and darker as they age. Single beautiful carmine flowers, each 1 in. across are borne at the ends of long stalks rising from the rosettes. They are produced in autumn. Mexico.

Pink see **Dianthus**
Pink Arum Lily see **Zantedeschia rehmannii**
Pink Calla see **Zantedeschia rehmannii**
Pink, Indian see **Quamoclit pennata**
Pink Mimosa see **Albizia julibrissin**
Pink Quill see **Tillandsia cyanea**
Pink Tips see **Callistemon speciosus**
Pitcher Plant see **Nepenthes** and **Sarracenia**
Pitcher Plant, California see **Darlingtonia californica**

PITTOSPORUM (PITTOSPORACEAE)
A genus of evergreen flowering shrubs and trees with glossy foliage and tubular flowers opening flat at the mouth. They make excellent large pot or tub plants for the cool or cold greenhouse. Grow in loam-based compost and propagate by seeds in March or by stem cuttings of side shoots taken with a heel in July.

crassifolium Karo
A 6 ft shrub hardy in the mild areas, but needing protection elsewhere. It has oblong, leathery leaves, dark green and shining above, shortly hairy, creamy or rusty beneath. The red-purple flowers are borne in April and May in 2 in. clusters at the ends of the shoots and are followed by hard white fruits. New Zealand.

dallii
An 8–10 ft tree with long, pointed leathery leaves borne on shoots which

are red and shining when young. The flowers, which are produced in July, are white and carried in clusters up to 1½ in. wide. New Zealand.

daphniphylloides
A 6–10 ft shrub with clusters of small, greenish-yellow scented flowers which are borne in May and June. These are often followed in August and September by round, red berries. China, Formosa.

tenuifolium Kohuhu
This species, when fully grown, makes a shapely tree up to 15 ft or more in height. The leaves are pale green, wavy-edged and borne on black stems. Several variegated forms are known. The small clusters of fragrant dark purplish-brown flowers are borne in the axils of the leaves in May, and are followed by round, red fruits. New Zealand.
 'Garnettii', leaves flushed white and pink;
 'Silver Queen', leaves suffused silver-grey.

tobira Japanese Pittosporum
A shrub with beautifully glossy, dark green oval leaves and beautifully fragrant clusters of creamy yellow flowers which are borne at the ends of the leafy stems. China. **402.**
 'Variegatum', an attractive form with silvery, variegated leaves. Japan.

PLATYCERIUM (POLYPODIACEAE) Stag's-horn Fern
A unique and handsome group of large ferns for the warm greenhouse or home. They have 2 distinct types of foliage, the barren fronds or mantle leaves, which are often shield-shaped, and the fertile fronds, which are tall and forked in the manner of a stag's antlers. In the wild these ferns grow on tree trunks or branches and in cultivation they are best grown hanging up attached to pieces of bark or in hanging baskets. A suitable compost can be made by mixing equal quantities of a proprietary peat mix with sphagnum moss. If grown on bark wrap a ball of compost or leaf mould around the roots and secure with soft wire. Maintain a humid atmosphere during the warmest months and shade from direct sunlight. Propagate by detaching the small plantlets that arise on the roots of mature specimens.

alcicorne see P. bifurcatum

bifurcatum syn. **P. alcicorne** Common Stag's-horn Fern
This is the most commonly met with species and the best kind for a house plant. Although best in warmth it will tolerate a cool greenhouse. It has erect or spreading fertile fronds which are 2–3 ft long and forked 2 or 3 times. The barren fronds are shield-like, rounded and convex, hugging the support. It produces several offset plants each year which, if grown on a tree trunk or in a basket, gradually form a large globose clump. Australia, E. Indies, New Caledonia. **401.**

grande Regal Elk-horn Fern
One of the finest species with great triangular fertile fronds 4 ft or more long, each lobed and forked along the top. They are rich glossy green. The sterile fronds are somewhat shield-shaped, but lobed and crinkled along the margins. E. Australia to Philippines.

PLECTRANTHUS (LABIATAE)
A genus of evergreen plants of which the species described are suitable for cultivation in the greenhouse or home, making very attractive foliage plants with spikes of pretty flowers. Grow in pots in loam-based compost, water freely and give some shading in summer; keep just moist in winter. Propagate by stem-tip cuttings in spring, or by detaching rooted portions, or division when re-potting in April.

coleoides Candle Plant
A low, bushy plant with erect stems, covered with hairy, oval, dark-green leaves which have scalloped margins. The white and purple flowers are borne on erect stems. It is mainly represented in cultivation by the variegated form. India.
 'Marginatus', a variegated form with the wavy margins of the leaves creamy white. A very attractive plant, **403.**

oertendahlii Prostrate Coleus, Swedish Ivy
A prostrate plant with creeping, reddish stems bearing bronze-green, almost circular leaves with silver along the veins, and purple coloration beneath. The 2-lipped, tubular flowers are pink and are borne in loose erect clusters 4–6 in. in length. It makes an excellent plant for a hanging basket. Natal. **404.**

PLEIONE (ORCHIDACEAE)
A genus of free flowering orchids which are suitable for growing in the cool greenhouse or in the home. The flowers which have spreading, pointed petals and a fringed, trumpet shaped lip appear before the long, ovate leaves. Plant in a proprietary peat mix with added sphagnum moss in spring, keep out of direct sunlight in summer and keep well ventilated. Water freely while in full growth, but dry off when leaves turn yellow and store dry in a frost free place until the spring. Propagate by removing offsets in spring when re-potting.

bulbocodioides syn. **P. formosana**
A variable species with petals ranging from white, through deep pink to mauve. The paler lip is marked with brick red to magenta blotches. It flowers from February to June. China, Formosa, Tibet.
 limprichtii, a rich reddish coloured form.

forrestii
An attractive species with creamy-yellow to bright orange flowers having reddish-brown blotches on the lip. They open in May and June. S.E. Asia. **405.**

formosana see **P. bulbocodioides**

praecox
The deep rose-pink petals are 3 in. across, and the pale pink lip is yellow marked. They are borne on 2–4 in. stems from November to January. India, China.

Pleomele see **Dracaena**

PLUMBAGO (PLUMBAGINACEAE) Leadwort
Two members of this genus are in general cultivation and make excellent pot plants for the cool or warm greenhouse. Grow in a loam-based compost and water freely in the summer. Propagate *P. capensis* by cuttings with a heel from non-flowering shoots in June and July, and *P. indica* by basal shoot cuttings from cut back plants in spring.

auriculata see **P. capensis**

capensis syn. **P. auriculata** Blue Cape Plumbago
A climbing plant having 9–12 in. clusters of light blue flowers with a long tube opening to a saucer shape 1 in. across. The leaves are mid-green and oval. Best grown in the indoor border with some support, it may also be grown as a short term pot plant. The flowers are produced from April to November. Cool greenhouse. S. Africa. **406.**

indica syn. **P. rosea** Scarlet Leadwort
A shrubby perennial with scarlet to purplish flowers borne in 6–9 in. clusters from June to August. The 4 in. elliptic leaves are borne on wiry stems and the plant reaches 2–3 ft in height. It is less hardy than *P. capensis* and does best in a warm greenhouse. E. Indies.

rosea see **P. indica**

PLUMERIA (APOCYNACEAE)
rubra Frangipani, Temple Tree
A magnificent shrub or small tree 12 ft or more in height suitable for the border in a large, warm greenhouse, or for large pots and tubs. Stout fleshy twigs bear long, narrow, somewhat fleshy leaves and large waxy, very fragrant flowers 2 in. across, rose-pink or carmine with a yellow eye. They are borne in crowded clusters at the ends of the shoots from June to September. Grow in a loam-based compost and keep well watered and in good light and air during the summer growing period. In winter when the plant is dormant allow to become almost dry. W. Indies, Mexico to Ecuador.

Plum, Natal see **Carissa grandiflora**

PODALYRIA (LEGUMINOSAE)
A genus of evergreen shrubs with undivided leaves and large, pea-like flowers. They grow best in the greenhouse border, but can be accommodated in large pots or tubs. Grow in a cool, light greenhouse with plenty of ventilation. If grown in containers use a loam-based compost or a proprietary peat mix. Propagate by seeds sown in spring or short lateral stem cuttings with a heel in summer.

argentea

A 1–2 ft shrub with variably shaped, silky leaves. The white flowers are in ones or twos on a stout 1½ in. stalk in the axils of the leaves, and open in June. S. Africa.

calyptrata

A 3–6 ft shrub, densely branched, with thinly hairy shoots. Elliptic leaves are 1-2 in. long, and the pale rose flowers are borne singly towards the end of stems in May and June. S. Africa.

PODOCARPUS (PODOCARPACEAE)

A genus of coniferous trees which in the wild make superb specimens up to 150 ft in height, but which in the juvenile stage make most attractive ornamental foliage plants. Grow in a loam-based compost or a proprietary peat mixture in large pots and keep moist. Propagate by seed or by stem cuttings taken with a heel in late summer.

dacrydioides Kahikatea, New Zealand White Pine

When mature, this large timber tree has stiff, scale-like leaves, but while at the juvenile stage, the leaves are soft and needle like. They are borne on pendulous stems giving a willowy appearance to the plant. New Zealand.

gracilior African Fern Pine

A valuable timber tree, this, like *P. dacrydioides* has distinctive and decorative juvenile foliage. The branches are somewhat pendulous in habit and on older plants carry deep bluish-green leaves, up to 2 in. long, and arranged irregularly on the branches. On young plants the leaves are glossy, dark green up to 4 in. long. At this stage it makes a most attractive pot plant. Kenya, Uganda, Ethiopia.

Poinciana see **Caesalpinia**
Poinsettia see **Euphorbia pulcherrima**

POLIANTHES (AGAVACEAE)

tuberosa Tuberose

A distinctive, tuberous rooted perennial with mid-green, strap-shaped leaves and heavily fragrant pure white flowers. These are funnel shaped, opening to 6 waxy petals, 1 in. across, and are borne in erect spikes on long, stiff stems. They open in late summer and make very attractive plants for the cool greenhouse or a well-lit room. Grow in loam-based compost and keep in a light place. Propagation is difficult, for although offsets are freely produced, they do not usually ripen properly. Mexico. **407.**

POLYGALA (POLYGALACEAE) Milkwort

A large genus, of which the species described below make good indoor plants. Grow in a loam-based or a proprietary peat compost, watering freely and shading from the hottest sun in summer. In winter keep just moist. Propagate by taking heel cuttings of lateral shoots in spring, preferably from cut back plants.

grandifolia

An erect, unbranched, 1 ft shrub with oval, pointed leaves 4–5 in. in length, and large, pea-like flowers, the lateral petals white, rose tipped and the three inner sepals tinged with green and black-purple. They are borne in 6–10 flowered custers in spring. Brazil.

myrtifolia grandiflora

A 4 ft, evergreen shrub having oblong, pointed leaves and rich purple flowers, 1–1½ in. long, which are carried in small clusters at the ends of the branches from May to October. S. Africa.

POLYPODIUM (POLYPODIACEAE) Polypody

A genus of low growing ferns with wiry stems rising from the rhizomes and bearing leathery fronds, entire or variously dissected. The following species make good house and greenhouse plants. Grow in a loam-based compost or a proprietary peat mixture. Propagate by division of the rhizomes, or by spores in spring.

aureum Hare's-foot Fern

A decorative fern with large, deeply cut leaves up to 4 ft or more in length and 9–18 in. across the 4 or 6 long, strap-shaped, wavy edged segments. The rhizomes are covered with rusty-brown scales like little furry feet. Tropical America. **408.**

'Glaucum', a blue-grey form which is more often seen in cultivation than the type.

lucidum

The 2–4 ft fronds are divided almost to the mid-rib into simple segments, 6–12 in. long. The lowest are borne on short stalks and have finely pointed tips. They grow on a long stem from the thick, scaly rhizomes. India, N. Vietnam.

Polypody see **Polypodium**

POMADERRIS (RHAMNACEAE)

A genus of evergreen shrubs and small trees the leaves having a dense covering of whitish or rusty hairs. The small flowers are in clusters. Grow in the cool greenhouse border or large tubs. If in containers plant in a loam-based compost. Propagate by cuttings of semi-ripened shoots, or by seed in spring.

betulina

A small, slender shrub or tree reaching 15 ft or more. The 1 in. oval leaves are borne on rusty-hairy twigs and the pale yellow flowers appear in April, carried in tight, globular clusters towards the ends of the leafy shoots. S.E. Australia.

elliptica

A 4–8 ft shrub with larger leaves than *P. betulina*, 2–4 in. long, downy beneath, but hairless and shining above. The pale yellow flowers are borne in flat clusters 3–5 in. across in May and June. Tasmania.

Pomegranate see **Punica granatum**
Ponga Fern see **Cyathea dealbata**
Poor Man's Orchid see **Schizanthus pinnatus**
Popinac see **Acacia farnesiana**
Poppy, Water see **Hydrocleys commersonii**
Poroporo see **Solanum aviculare**
Potato Tree see **Solanum maeranthum**
Potato Vine see **Solanum jasminoides**
Potato Vine, Giant see **Solanum wendlandii**
Powder Puff see **Mammillaria bocasana**
Prayer Plant see **Maranta leuconeura**
Prickly Pear see **Opuntia**
Primrose see **Primula**
Primrose, Cape see **Streptocarpus**
Primrose Jasmine see **Jasminum mesnyi**

PRIMULA (PRIMULACEAE) Primrose

A large genus of perennial species of which the following are particularly good subjects for the home or the cool greenhouse. They are best grown in pots in a loam-based compost or a proprietary peat mix, and need to be kept moist throughout the year. Propagate by seeds, sowing them as soon as they are ripe or in spring.

bracteata

A softly glandular-hairy species bearing deep golden-yellow flowers with a long tube opening to 5 large lobes at the mouth. They are borne in an 8-flowered, branched cluster on short stalks and open in summer. The narrow leaves taper into the winged stem. China.

× **kewensis** (*P. floribunda* × *P. verticillata*)

A hybrid species with pale green leaves covered with a white, waxy bloom, and clusters of fragrant yellow flowers borne on the long, leafy stems from December to April. Garden origin (Kew). **409.**

malacoides Fairy or Baby Primrose

Although a perennial, this species is best renewed annually. It has many pale green, oval, toothed leaves and slender stems carrying from December to April, long-lasting whorls of star-like flowers ½ in. across. A wide variety of colours is produced and many named cultivars are grown. China. **410.**

'Fire Chief', brick-red flowers, large;
'Lilac Queen', lilac-mauve flowers;
'Snow Storm', pure white, double flowers.

obconica

A winter blooming primrose with broad, heart-shaped fresh green leaves having a pungent scent and a covering of short glandular hairs to which some people are allergic. The flowers occur in a great range of colours from pale pink to blue-purple and are 1–1½ in. across. They are borne in clusters on long stalks from December to May. Many cultivars are grown. China. **411.**

'Caerulea', blue-purple flowers;
'Giant White', pure white flowers;
'Wyaston Wonder', a deep, crimson red.

sinensis Chinese Primrose ❋
The mid-green, somewhat erect leaves of this species are lobed and toothed. The flowers are carried in 2 or 3 whorls on a stout stem which lengthens as the flowers mature. Each bloom is 1–2 in. across, frequently mauve with a yellow eye, but also occurring in reds, pinks and white. They open from December to March.
'Dazzler', brilliant vermilion flowers, **412;**
'Royal Blue', a dark bluish-purple.

Privet, Desert see **Peperomia magnoliifolia**
Privet, Wax see **Peperomia glabella**
Proboscidea jussieui see **Martynia louisiana**

PROSTANTHERA (LABIATAE) Australian Mint
A genus of small to medium sized shrubs, usually strongly aromatically fragrant. Good plants for a light airy cool greenhouse where they should be planted in the border or in large pots or tubs in a loam-based compost. Propagate by cuttings of lateral shoots with a heel, in summer.

cuneata ❋ ❧
A 2–3 ft spreading shrub with very small, orbicular, leathery leaves. The flowers, borne in clusters in the axils of the leaves towards the tips of the shoots, are 2-lipped and white with purple spots. They are produced in June. Australia.

melissifolia ❋ ❧
A strongly aromatic, slender shrub having coarsely toothed, ovate leaves up to 2 in. in length, and an abundance of mauve to violet flowers borne in loose, leafless clusters in June. Australia.

nivea Snowy Mint Bush ❋ ❧
A 3–6 ft shrub, almost completely hairless with long, narrow leaves having inrolled margins. The pure white flowers have a faint blue tinge and are borne singly in all the axils of the upper leaves making a leafy cluster 3–6 in. in length. They are produced, usually in abundance, in May. Australia.

ovalifolia ❋ ❧
A strongly fragrant, hairy shrub with oval, leathery leaves and purple to lilac-mauve flowers borne in short spikes at the ends of the branches. They are produced in June. Australia. **413.**

Prostrate Coleus see **Plectranthus oertendahlii**

PROTEA (PROTEACEAE)
A remarkable genus of evergreen shrubs with spectacular flower clusters comprising a large number of tubular flowers packed together within a protecting sheath of brightly coloured, silky hairy, petal-like bracts. Grow in pots, tubs or, preferably, the cool greenhouse border and keep as well ventilated as possible and in full light. Avoid root disturbance as much as possible. Propagate by seed sown in spring.

cynaroides King Protea, Honeypot Sugarbush ❋ ❧
A spectacular shrub 2–6 ft high having thick, leathery leaves 2–5 in. in length borne on red stems. The flowers are white or pink, silky hairy forming a rounded, fluffy centre 8–12 in. across and surrounded by a series white to pink, stiff bracts in overlapping rows like the head of an artichoke. Flowers are produced in May and June. S. Africa. **414.**

eximia syn. **P. latifolia** ❋ ❧
In this species the central mass of flowers is carmine red, or occasionally deep pink or green, as are the 9–12 rows of bracts. They open from June to August. The shrub itself grows to 5 ft or more, and the downy shoots carry crowded, oval, blunt leaves, 3–4 in. in length with slightly woolly margins. S. Africa.

grandiceps ❋ ❧
A 4–5 ft shrub bearing flower heads 4–6 in. across, having white, silky flowers in the centre and a surrounding series of pink to red-purple over-

lapping bracts, increasing in size towards the centre. The stemless leaves are oval, somewhat fleshy with red, finely hairy margins. S. Africa.

latifolia see **P. eximia**
mellifera see **P. repens**

nana syn. **P. rosacea** ❋
A 2–3 ft, hairless shrub with long, needle-like, spine-tipped leaves and pendulous heads of flowers. These are made up of a central mass with a fringe of red hairs, and 3 or 4 rows of bright red bracts. An attractive dwarf species flowering in May. S. Africa.

repens syn. **P. mellifera** ❋ ❧
A beautiful 6–8 ft shrub or small tree, having 3–5 in. long, ovate grey-green leaves and cup-shaped heads of flowers 3 in. wide, surrounded by 14–18 rows of red to palest pink bracts, opening in September. S. Africa.

rosacea see **P. nana**

speciosa ❋ ❧
The 9–11 rows of silvery pink or yellow bracts surround the 5 in. flower heads which open in April. The 3–5½ in. leaves are thick in texture, wavy and softly hairy at the base and are borne on the 3–6 ft tall shrub. S. Africa.

PSEUDERANTHEMUM (ACANTHACEAE)
A genus of tropical shrubs many of which have ornamental foliage as well as decorative flowers. Grow in the warm greenhouse in pots, planting in a loam-based compost. Shade from the hottest sunshine in summer and maintain a humid atmosphere. The plants can be brought into the home for flowering for a short while. Propagate by cuttings of lateral shoots, preferably from cut back plants, in spring. Keep the leading growths pinched out to promote bushy growth.

kewense syn. **P. atropurpureum, Eranthemum atropurpureum**
❋ ❧
The very dark coloured foliage of this species – the 4–6 in. leaves are blackish purple – make it a very striking pot plant. The white tubular flowers opening to 2 lips, are red spotted and make a good contrast. They are borne in spring in 8 in. erect spikes at the ends of the branches. Pacific Islands.

reticulatum ❋ ❧
A good foliage plant with the long spear-shaped leaves green with a network of golden-yellow veins. The white, red-spotted flowers are tubular with 5 lobes, opening flat, starlike at the mouth. They are borne in spring in terminal clusters. New Hebrides.

PTERIS (PTERIDACEAE) Brake
The species described below are evergreen ferns which make good greenhouse and house plants. Grow in pots in a proprietary peat compost, water freely during the growing season and shade from the hottest sun. Propagate by sowing spores or by division of congested plants in spring.

argyraea see **P. quadriaurita**

cretica Ribbon Fern ❧
A 12–18 in. plant with deeply divided fronds, the segments light green and strap shaped. They are borne on upright stems which arch over at the tips. Many cultivars are grown with different leaf coloration and shape. Temperate and Tropical regions.

ensiformis Sword Brake ❧
A rather similar species to *P. cretica*, but with darker green fronds, and longer, narrower segments. S.E. Asia to Australia and Samoa.
'Victoriae', Silver Table Fern, a graceful cultivar, the leaflets of the fronds banded with white; more dwarf habit than the type.

quadriaurita ❧
The species is hardly seen in cultivation, the form grown being known as *P. q. argyraea* though this is now considered to be a separate species, *P. argyraea*. It is a robust fern with 2–3 ft fronds divided into lobed segments borne in pairs along the mid-rib. They are a light green in colour with a creamy-white band along the centre of each segment. India.

tremula Trembling Bracken ❧
A robust species with large fronds three or four times divided to make

light graceful foliage. They are borne on erect, bright chestnut stalks, and the fronds can reach 3 ft or more. New Zealand, Australia.

Pudding Pipe Tree see **Cassia fistula**

PUNICA (PUNICACEAE)
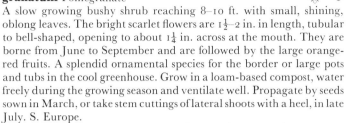
granatum Pomegranate ✳ ●
A slow growing bushy shrub reaching 8–10 ft. with small, shining, oblong leaves. The bright scarlet flowers are $1\frac{1}{2}$–2 in. in length, tubular to bell-shaped, opening to about $1\frac{1}{4}$ in. across at the mouth. They are borne from June to September and are followed by the large orange-red fruits. A splendid ornamental species for the border or large pots and tubs in the cool greenhouse. Grow in a loam-based compost, water freely during the growing season and ventilate well. Propagate by seeds sown in March, or take stem cuttings of lateral shoots with a heel, in late July. S. Europe.
> 'Flore Pleno', fully double pompon flowers of orange-red, **415**;
> 'Nana', a hardier, dwarf form, smaller in all its parts. A very good pot plant for the house or greenhouse, **416**.

Purple Bell-vine see **Rhodochiton volubile**
Purple Heart see **Setcreasea purpurea**
Purple Orchid Tree see **Bauhinia variegata**
Purple Wreath see **Petrea volubilis**
Purslane, Rock see **Calandrinia umbellata**
Pussy-ears see **Cyanotis somaliensis**
Pygmy Date Palm see **Phoenix roebelinii**

Q

QUAMOCLIT (CONVOLVULACEAE) Star Glory
A genus of twining climbers with showy long-tubed flowers related to Morning Glory, (*Ipomoea*). Grow in the greenhouse border or in pots in a loam-based compost and give some form of support. Water well during the summer. Propagate by seeds sown in spring.

coccinea Star Ipomoea ✳
The entire slender-pointed leaves are arrow-shaped at the base and grow on stems which can reach 8 ft in height. The scarlet flowers are fragrant with a $\frac{3}{4}$–$1\frac{1}{2}$ in. tube opening at the yellow throat to 5 shallow lobes. They are borne in late summer in the axils of the upper leaves. Mexico, Arizona.

lobata syn. **Mina lobata** ✳
A vigorous climber with 3-lobed leaves which are heart-shaped at the base. The inflated tube opens to 5 tiny lobes at the mouth and is bright red, paling through orange to yellow, the stamens long projecting. The flowers are borne in curving clusters from June to September. Mexico.

pennata Indian Pink, Cypress Vine ✳
A brightly coloured species with a vivid orange-scarlet flower with a narrow tube opening to 5 flat lobes. They are borne in summer on few flowered, long stalks in the axils of the leaves. The leaves are deeply divided into narrow almost thread-like segments giving them a feathery appearance. They grow on smooth slender stems which twine to 6 or 8 ft. Peru.

Queen Cattleya see **Cattleya dowiana**
Queensland Umbrella Tree see **Schefflera actinophylla**
Queen's Wreath see **Petrea volubilis**
Queen's Tears see **Billbergia**

QUISQUALIS (COMBRETACEAE)
indica Rangoon Creeper ✳ 🐦
A beautiful, but very vigorous climbing shrub with slender stems and soft, oval, pale green leaves, 5 in. in length. The fragrant flowers are borne in drooping clusters in the axils of the leaves. They change in colour as they open, from pink to white, then darken to red. The flowering period extends from May to August. It is best grown in a large tub in the warm greenhouse where it can be kept to a manageable size by pruning. Use a loam based compost for preference or a proprietary peat mix. Shade lightly from the hottest sunshine and maintain a humid atmosphere. Propagate by lateral stem cuttings, preferably with a heel, in summer. Tropical Asia.

R

Rabbit's Foot see **Maranta leuconeura** 'Massangeana'
Rabbit's Tracks see **Maranta leuconeura**
Radiator Plant see **Peperomia maculosa**
Rainbow Orchid see **Epidendrum prismatocarpum**
Rainbow Star see **Cryptanthus bromelioides**
Raintree, White see **Brunfelsia undulata**
Ramarama see **Myrtus bullata**
Rangoon Creeper see **Quisqualis indica**
Rat's-tail Cactus see **Aporocactus flagelliformis**
Rattle-box see **Crotalaria**
Rattlesnake Plant see **Calathea insignis**

REBUTIA (CACTACEAE)
Profusely flowering, globular cacti which develop their flowers from areoles almost in a ring, often round the base of the plant. The funnel-shaped flowers are of many different colours, according to species, and remain for about a week, opening during the day and closing at night. The green stems have spirally arranged tubercles rather than ribs. For culture see under terrestrial cacti in the Introduction. Minimum winter temperature 40°F. Propagate by offsets, freely produced round the base, or by seed. Mixed species with *R. xanthocarpa* in the centre are shown on plate **417**.

aureiflora syn. **Mediolobivia aureiflora** ✳ 🐦
The spherical, 2 in. high stems are dark green, with a reddish tinge, and grow in clusters. The spines, 15–20 radials and 3–4 longer centrals to each areoles, are yellow-white in colour. The yellow, white-throated flowers, almost 2 in. across, are borne freely in spring. Argentina.

deminuta syn. **Aylostera deminuta** ✳ 🐦
The 2–4 in. high, slightly flattened spherical stems branch freely around the base and have 11–13 rows of tubercles. Each areoles has 10–12 spines, white, tipped brown, or completely brown. Bright orange, funnel-shaped flowers are produced from May to July. Argentina.

kupperiana syn. **Aylostera kupperiana** ✳ 🐦
Globe-shaped reddish-green stems, 2–4 in. high, with areoles bearing 12–20 small white spines with copper tips. Red flowers form from May to June. Bolivia.

marsoneri ✳ 🐦
Ball-shaped stems, 2 in. high, slightly concave at the crown, with round tuberculate areoles bearing 20–35 very small spines, the upper ones whitish, the lower ones brownish-red. The $1\frac{1}{2}$ in. wide, golden flowers are borne in April and May. Argentina.

minuscula syn. **Echinocactus minuscula** ✳ 🐦
1–$1\frac{1}{2}$ in. high and about 2 in. across, the flattened globular stems are pale green and, even on one year plants, bear bright red flowers freely around the base and sides in summer. The areoles have 20–25 very short, whitish spines. Argentina. **418**.

pseudodeminuta syn. **Aylostera pseudodeminuta** ✳ 🐦
The clump-forming spherical stems are 2–$2\frac{1}{2}$ in. high and broad, slightly depressed at the top. Tiny areoles appear on raised tubercles, with 11 radial spines and 2–3 centrals; all the spines are white with brown tips. Bright yellow-gold flowers, about 1 in. across, form in May and June. Argentina.

pygmaea syn. **Lobivia pygmaea, Mediolobivia pygmaea** ✳ 🐦
Very small ovoid stems, less than 1 in. in height, develop from a stout thick rootstock and bear tubercles with 9–12 small whitish spines. The 1 in. long, salmon to rose-purple flowers develop in May and June. Bolivia, Argentina.

senilis ✳ 🐦
The flattened spherical stems, about 3 in. high, are clump forming with spirally arranged tubercles set with 25–40 bristly spines, almost obscuring the stems. The flowers, about 2 in. long and $1\frac{1}{2}$ in. wide, are bright red and appear from April to July. Argentina.

spegazziniana syn. **Aylostera spegazziniana**
The cylindrical stems, 4 in. high and 1½ in. across, are light green in colour and form clumps readily. The tubercles are spirally arranged, with areoles that bear 14 white radial spines recurved against the stem, and 2 yellow, brown-tipped, very short centrals. Deep red flowers form in May and June around the base. Argentina.

violaciflora
Flattened spheres of olive-green stems grow 1½ in. high and 3 in. across, in groups. Tubercles are arranged spirally and bear woolly, yellow-grey areoles. These have 15 or more yellowish-white radial spines and about 5–10 longer, thickened central spines, white at first, turning to yellow. The lilac-rose flowers, about 2½ in. long, are borne freely in June. Argentina.

xanthocarpa
Clump-forming 2 in. high pale green stems form clusters 4 in. across and covered with very short, thin white spines. Reddish flowers, ¾ in. wide and long appear from May to July. Argentina.
    salmonea has pale brick-red flowers, central plant plate **417.**

RECHSTEINERIA (GESNERIACEAE)
A genus of tuberous rooted perennials with showy tubular flowers which make most attractive pot plants for the home and cool greenhouse. Grow in pots of loam-based compost or a proprietary peat mixture, water and feed during the summer keeping shaded from the brightest sun. When the plant finishes flowering and the leaves wither, gradually dry off and store in a frost proof place until spring. Propagate by division of tubers or by basal cuttings with a small piece of tuber attached, taken in spring, or by seed. Renew plants after about 3 years. This genus is now included in *Sinningia*.

cardinalis Cardinal Flower
A stout plant growing to 9–18 in., the stems covered with white hairs and broad soft, emerald-green velvety leaves, 3–6 in. long. The brilliant scarlet flowers are 2 in. long and tubular, opening to 2 lips, with paler markings in the throat. They are carried on short stalks in clusters grouped in the axils of the leaves towards the ends of the stems, and are produced from June to August. Brazil. **419.**
    'George Kalmbacher', a seed-sport with upright flowers with ends star-shaped instead of 2-lipped.

cooperi
A tall, erect species with downy stems reaching 2 ft or more and broad, bright green undivided leaves with a softly hairy surface. The scarlet flowers are 3 in. in length and the long tubes have an inflated, yellow base. They are borne in large clusters towards the ends of the branches, opening in summer. Brazil.

cyclophylla see **R. macropoda**

leucotricha Brazilian Edelweiss
A very decorative species with silvery-grey, elliptic leaves covered as are the stems, with fine silvery-white hairs. The clusters of bright coral-red, tubular slightly pendent flowers make a striking contrast to the soft leaf colour, each bloom being 1½ in. long and opening from August to October. Brazil. **421.**

Red Alder, African see **Cunonia capensis**
Redbird Cactus see **Pedilanthus tithymaloides**
Red Cluster Passion Flower see **Passiflora racemosa**
Red Gum see **Eucalyptus ficifolia**
Red Hairy Heath see **Erica cerinthoides**
Red Herringbone Plant see **Maranta leuconeura** 'Erythrophylla'
Red-hot Catstail see **Acalypha hispida**
Red Ifafa Lily see **Cyranthus mackenii**
Red Nodding Bells see **Streptocarpus dunnii**
Red Passion Flower see **Passiflora racemosa**
Red Pepper see **Capsicum**
Red Signal Heath see **Erica mammosa**
Regal Elk-horn Fern see **Platycerium grande**
Regal Pelargonium see **Pelargonium** × **domesticum**

REINWARDTIA (LINACEAE)
A genus of only two species, both colourful winter flowering shrubs for the warm or cool conservatory or greenhouse. Grow either in the border or in pots of loam-based or a proprietary peat compost, in a light position and ventilate freely, keeping well watered during the growing season. Pinch out growths of young plants to keep them compact and propagate in April or May by cuttings of young, preferably basal shoots taken with a heel.

indica see **R. trigyna**

tetragyna
A 2–4 ft shrub with 4–6 in. long oval leaves. The bright yellow flowers open flat and are borne in terminal clusters from autumn to spring. N. India.

trigyna syn. **R. indica** Yellow Flax
A handsome shrubby plant with wiry branches up to 3–4 ft in height and tapered, oval dark green leaves, 3 in. long. From October to March it bears a profusion of funnel-shaped bright yellow flowers which open to 2 in. across. India. **420.**

Resurrection Plant see **Selaginella lepidophylla**
Rex Begonia Vine see **Cissus discolor**

RHIPSALIDOPSIS (CACTACEAE)
This is a genus of what are popularly called 'link-leaf' cacti, because the leaf-like stems branch dichotomously, that is to say, normally 2 new stems branch out of a long areole at the end of the stem, but anything from 1–4 stems may be produced. The flowers are produced from the areoles on the new stems. The species described are easily grown and flower profusely making them very popular. Stem growth takes place in summer. Culture as for epiphytic cacti, see Introduction. Great care must be taken to avoid alkalinity in the soil. Minimum winter temperature 40°F.

gaertneri syn. **Schlumbergera gaertneri**
The stems are 2–3 in. long, green often with a reddish tinge. The scarlet tubular flowers open to about 2 in. across and are very freely produced in May, even on young plants. The resting period is from November onwards, but the plants should not get dry at any time. Brazil. **422.**

rosea
This species has 1–2 in. long stems, oval in cross-section; they are green with a red margin. The rose-pink, tubular flowers open to about 1 in. across, being very freely produced on older plants in May. The resting period is as for *S. gaertneri*. Brazil. **423.**

RHIPSALIS (CACTACEAE)
Grown for its unusual stems, the flowers of this genus are usually small and uninteresting, though sometimes they are followed by brightly coloured fruit. An unusual feature is that, whereas cacti are normally found wild only on the American continent, some species grow in an apparently wild state in Ceylon and tropical Africa. It is thought that they must have been introduced by some means in prehistoric time. Culture as for epiphytic cacti, see Introduction. Minimum winter temperature 50°F.

baccifera see **R. cassutha**

cassutha syn. **R. baccifera** Mistletoe Cactus
The small, cream coloured flowers appear in summer. The cylindrical stems, each about 4–5 in. long, hang in large branching clusters up to 18 in. long. The areoles bear a few bristles. Florida, Mexico, Central America to Peru; also Africa, Ceylon.

crispata
This species has wide, flat, jointed stems, about 12 in. long, with a crenate margin, and cream or pale yellow flowers in summer. Brazil.

paradoxa
The short, 3-angled stems, 3–4 in. long, fork freely to form branches 15 in. long, with each segment set at a slightly different angle giving an unusual appearance. The areoles are very woolly, particularly in young plants. Large white flowers grow at the end of the stems in summer. Suitable species for a hanging basket. Brazil.

pentaptera
The creamy flowers are borne irregularly along the branching stems in summer. The stems themselves have about 6 ribs with broad bracts at the areoles, which sometimes bear bristles. Brazil, Uruguay.

prismatica

The white flowers appear in summer. The prostrate cylindrical stems branch freely, often to a length of 18 in. and the areoles usually bear bristles. Brazil.

RHODOCHITON (SCROPHULARIACEAE)
volubile syn. **R. atrosanguineum** Purple Bell-vine

A showy 10 ft climber holding on by means of the leaf and flower stalks which twist around any support as they grow. The leaves are heart-shaped at the base and taper to a slender point. They are lightly hairy and have a few pointed teeth. The blood-red, tubular flowers are large and irregularly 5-lobed, being enclosed in a 5-toothed, widely bell-shaped pink calyx. They are borne in June. Although a perennial species it is best treated as an annual, propagated each year from seed. Grow in the cool greenhouse border, or in large pots or tubs in a loam-based compost. Shade from direct summer sun and keep well ventilated in summer. Mexico.

RHODODENDRON (ERICACEAE)

A large genus which includes those formerly classified under the now obsolete genus *Azalea*. Mainly evergreen shrubs with attractive, open funnel-shaped flowers. Grow in the cool or cold greenhouse border or in tubs in a lime free peat-based compost. Keep well ventilated and shade from the sun from spring to autumn. Propagate by seeds, layering or by stem cuttings taken with a heel in summer or early autumn.

bullatum

A very beautiful species making an 8 ft bush having long ovate, dark green, wrinkled leaves. The large flowers are white, tinged with pink and are borne in small clusters from April to June; they are sweetly scented. China. **424.**

ciliicalyx

A large evergreen shrub to 10 ft, with long, narrow, pointed leaves 2½–4½ in. long, borne on bristly stalks. The sweet scented flowers are 4 in. across, pure white to pink with a yellow blotch. The stamens are long and protrude from the mouth of the flower. The flowers open in March and April. China.

edgeworthii

A 6–10 ft, somewhat straggling shrub with felted stems bearing oval leaves 2–4½ in. long, wrinkled above and also brown-felted below. The richly fragrant flowers are borne in clusters of 2–4, they are a waxy white, tinged with pink and up to 4½ in. in width. They open in April and May. Himalayas.

griffithianum

A large shrub which can reach 20 ft, the oblong leaves are dull green above, bluish beneath and grow to 12 in. in length. This is the largest flowering species with white to pink widely bell-shaped blooms each 5–6 in. across. They are fragrant and are borne in clusters of 3–6 in May. A magnificent plant and one frequently used in hybridization. Himalayas.

indicum see under **R. simsii**

johnstonianum

A pale yellow to white flowered species with 2–2½ in. blooms having a deep yellow patch and red spotting inside. The fragrant flowers are borne in clusters of up to 4 in May, contrasting with the dark green, 2–4 in. oval leaves. The overall height of the shrub is eventually about 6 ft. India.

kaempferi

This azalea-type shrub is almost deciduous and grows to 8 ft. It has dark green, oval leaves and orange to brick-red, funnel-shaped flowers 1½–2 in. wide and spotted with darker markings. They are borne in clusters of 2–4 and open in May. Japan.

lindleyi

The white, waxy flowers are strongly fragrant and are carried on clusters of 2–4 blooms in April. The shrub is 2–4 ft in height and has long, hairless leaves up to 6 in. in length. Himalayas.

nuttallii

A strong growing, stout-stemmed plant, a good specimen reaching 12 ft or more in height. It has long oval leaves 2–12 in. long, which are strongly veined, and 3–6 fragrant flowers in each cluster, borne in April-May. The blooms are white to creamy-yellow and large, being

4–5 in. across the lobes. Probably the best of the tender yellow species. India.

simsii Indian Azalea

This plant is often confused with *R. indicum*. It is a delightful plant for pots, with long, pointed, dark green evergreen leaves and terminal clusters of brightly coloured flowers varying from white through all shades of pink and red to crimson. The 2–3 in. flowers can be single or double and are borne in May. China. Many hybrids are available of which the following is only a selection.

‘Hexe’ syn. ‘Firefly’, glowing crimson, semi-double;
‘Perle de Noisy’, pink, flushed white, **425**;
‘Purple Queen’, fuchsia purple with frilled margins to the petals, semi-double;
‘Satsuki’, pink with darker central blotch, single;
‘Vervaeneana’, double pink, like a small camelia, **426.**

taggianum

A particularly fragrant species growing to 6 or 7 ft. The elliptic leaves are 3–6 in. in length, hairless and smooth above, somewhat scaly beneath. 3 to 4 flowers are borne in each cluster, the white, funnel-shaped blooms having a yellow blotch on the back petal and growing to 3–4 in. in length. Burma. **427.**

RHOEO (COMMELINACEAE)
spathacea syn. **R. discolor** Boat Lily

An attractive foliage plant with lance-shaped stiff, fleshy leaves, 8–12 in. in length, a deep shining green above and purplish beneath. They are borne in crowded rosettes which also carry clusters of very small white or bluish flowers lying within large, boat-shaped, purple bracts. Grow in pots in the warm or cool greenhouse or the home in a loam-based or a proprietary peat compost. Shade from direct sun and keep humid in summer. Propagate by cuttings of basal shoots or by seeds in spring. Mexico.

RHOICISSUS (VITIDACEAE)

A genus of evergreen, climbing plants of which 2 species described below are grown for their ornamental foliage. Plant in the cool greenhouse border, or in pots of loam-based compost and keep well ventilated in the summer. They also make very durable house plants. Repot annually. Propagate by cuttings of lateral shoots in April and May.

capensis syn. **Cissus capensis** Cape Grape

A strong growing vine with woody stems and rusty hairy leaves. These are leathery and glossy and are shallowly lobed or angled. The flowers are inconspicuous, but are followed by deep red glossy fruit. S. Africa.

rhomboidea Grape Ivy

A very popular evergreen climber reaching 4–6 ft when pot grown, but up to 20 ft when not restricted. It climbs by means of tendrils. The leaves are divided into three rhomboidal leaflets, each glossy green and toothed. Natal. **428.**

RHOPALOSTYLIS (PALMAE)
sapida Nikau, Shaving-brush or Feather Duster Palm

A graceful palm for the cool greenhouse, eventually reaching a maximum of 30 ft, but taking many years to do so. In its juvenile stage it makes a good pot plant for a large room. The deeply dissected leaves have strap-shaped segments giving them a feathery appearance, and they grow upwards from the top of the main stem without the arching habit normally associated with palms. Grow in large pots or tubs in a loam-based compost or a proprietary peat mixture. Propagate by seed in Spring. New Zealand, Norfolk Is.

Ribbon Aglaonema see **Aglaonema treubii**
Ribbon Cactus see **Pedilanthus tithymaloides**
Ribbon Plant see **Dracaena sanderiana**
Rib Fern see **Blechnum brasiliense**
Rice Flower see **Pimelea**

RICINUS (EUPHORBIACEAE)
communis Castor Oil Plant

A shrubby species usually grown as an annual when it will reach about 4 ft. Grown as a shrub or tree it can attain 8–15 ft. It has mid-green leaves which are divided almost to a centre point into 5–7 leaflets. Spike of insignificant flowers are produced, followed by green or reddish spiny seed pods. Grow in pots in loam-based compost in a cool greenhouse. Propagate by seed in early spring. Probably Tropical Africa.

'Gibsonii' has the leaves and stems flushed a deep reddish, **429;**
'Zanzibarensis', 10 in. long leaves with a pale stripe along the mid-rib.

River Rose see **Bauera rubioides**

RIVINA (PHYTOLACCACEAE)
humilis Rouge Plant, Baby Pepper ●
An attractive plant grown chiefly for the pendent clusters of bright-crimson glossy berries which are at their best in winter. The leaves are oval with tapering points, rather thick and slightly hairy, borne on spreading branches making an 18–24 in. plant. Long clusters of white or rosy flowers are produced from January to October. Grow in pots of loam-based compost in the cool or warm greenhouse. Shade from the hottest sunshine and water freely when in full growth. Propagate by seeds in spring. S. USA to S. America.

ROCHEA (CRASSULACEAE)
Tender succulents represented by one species in cultivation. For culture see under terrestrial succulents in the Introduction. Minimum winter temperature 40°F.

coccinea ✳ 🦋
Growing to about 15 in. high and spreading from 8–12 in., the stems are massed with mid-green leaves set in 4 close ranks. Terminal clusters of flowers, 3–5 in. across, are composed of carmine-red blooms, each with a short tube about 1 in. long. The petals resemble a cross. Propagate by seed. Various cultivated forms are grown. S. Africa. **430.**

falcata see **Crassula falcata**

Rock Lily see **Arthropodium cirrhatum**
Rock Purslane see **Calandrinia umbellata**

RONDELETIA (RUBIACEAE)
A genus of colourful, evergreen shrubs of tropical origin. They have leathery, oval leaves and stalked clusters of small, tubular flowers which open out flat at the mouths. They are borne on long stalks in the axils of the leaves and at the ends of the branches. Although best grown in the cool or warm greenhouse border, they may also be accommodated in large pots or tubs of a loam based or proprietary peat compost. Shade lightly from the hottest summer sun and maintain a humid atmosphere. Ventilate on warm days. Propagate by lateral stem cuttings, preferably with a heel, in summer.

amoena ✳ 🦋
A 4 ft shrub bearing 2–5 in. leaves which taper to a slender point. The flowers are pink with golden-yellow inside the throat, which also has a ring of hairs. They are borne in June. Guatemala.

odorata ✳ 🦋
A somewhat lax shrub with downy shoots reaching 3 ft in height. The ovate leaves are wavy and with very short stalks while the brilliant orange-scarlet, fragrant flowers, which are yellow in the throat, are borne in 3-branched clusters. They open in November. Cuba.

roezlii ✳ 🦋
A slender shrub with 1–4 in. leaves tapering to a narrow point. The flowers are rose-purple with a yellow eye, the tube widening gradually to the flat petals. Guatemala. **431.**

Rose, Cotton see **Hibiscus mutabilis**
Rose Geranium see **Pelargonium graveolens**
Rose Grape see **Medinilla magnifica**
Rose Heath see **Erica gracilis**
Roseleaf Sage see **Salvia involucrata**
Rose-mallow see **Hibiscus**
Rose of China see **Hibiscus rosa-sinensis**
Rose, River see **Bauera rubioides**
Rooting Fig see **Ficus radicans**
Rouge Plant see **Rivina humilis**
Royal Red Bugler see **Aeschynanthus pulcher**
Royal Nodding Bells see **Streptocarpus wendlandii**

Rubber Plant see **Ficus elastica**
Rubber Plant, Baby see **Peperomia obtusifolia**

RUELLIA (ACANTHACEAE)
A genus of evergreen perennials which have decorative foliage and showy trumpet-shaped flowers. They make most attractive plants for the warm greenhouse. Grow in pots in loam-based compost and preferably replace every second year with young plants which will flower more freely. Propagate by cuttings of basal shoots taken in April or May.

devosiana ✳ 🦋
A purple-stemmed sub-shrub with long, narrow, toothed deep green leaves with pale to whitish marked veins above, and purplish beneath. The rose-tinted, white flowers have a long tube which is bent in the centre, opening to 5 deeply cut lobes. They are produced in early spring. Brazil.

macrantha Christmas Pride ✳ 🦋
A 3 ft shrub with 6 in. dark green, narrow leaves. The rose-pink flowers have a $3\frac{1}{2}$ in. tube, opening gradually to the throat, which is streaked with darker red, and the rounded lobes at the mouth. They are borne in clusters in the axils of the leaves at the ends of the shoots, and open from winter to spring. Brazil. **432.**

portellae ✳ 🦋
A much smaller species than the other two described, reaching only 9 in. or so. It makes a neat, rounded plant with 2–3 in. narrowly ovate, pointed leaves which are dark green with a bronzy sheen, silvery veined above and purplish beneath. The solitary flowers are rose-purple with a $1\frac{1}{2}$ in. tube, opening to 1 in. at the mouth. They are produced in winter. Brazil.

Rugby Football Plant see **Peperomia argyreia**

RUSSELIA (SCROPHULARIACEAE) Coral Blow
A genus of evergreen shrubby plants with showy, scarlet cylindrical flowers. They make excellent hanging basket plants for the greenhouse or can be grown in pots and pans. Plant in a loam-based compost, maintain humidity in summer and shade from the hottest sun. Propagate by cuttings of lateral or basal stems in spring, or by division at the same time.

equisetiformis see **R. juncea**

juncea syn. **R. equisetiformis** Coral Plant ✳
A 3–4 ft shrub with small, narrow leaves, reduced on the rush-like branches to minute scales. The 1 in. scarlet flowers are borne in loose, long-stalked, drooping clusters and open in summer. Suitable for the cool greenhouse. Mexico.

sarmentosa ✳
A 4 ft or clambering shrub having whorls of ovate to triangular leaves and clusters of scarlet flowers, with up to 30–40 blooms on each stem. They are produced in July. Best in a warm greenhouse. Mexico.

S

Sacred Bo-tree see **Ficus religiosa**
Sacred Indian Lotus see **Nelumbo nucifera**
Saffron Spike see **Aphelandra squarrosa**
Sage see **Salvia**
Sage, Blue see **Eranthemum pulchellum**
Sago Fern see **Cyathea medullaris**
Sago Palm see **Cycas revoluta**
St James Trefoil see **Lotus jacobaeus**

SAINTPAULIA (GESNERIACEAE)
ionantha African Violet ✳ 🦋
A very popular house or warm greenhouse plant needing a steady temperature of 60°F. minimum. For preference water should not be below that when watering. The dark velvety leaves are round and heart-shaped at the base making a broad tuft or rosette of leaves at ground level. From them rise the stalked clusters of $\frac{3}{4}$–$1\frac{1}{2}$ in. flowers which are similar in shape to those of a broad-petalled violet, but are

flatter and larger, with an 'eye' of golden stamens. Named cultivars are grown in shades of pink to deep purple or white; double flowered ones are also grown and new varieties are developed every year. The blooms are produced most freely in summer, but some occur throughout the year. Modern cultivars are more resistant to changes of temperature and humidity in the home. They are therefore more reliable as house plants and the flowers persist for a long time. Grow in pots in a peat based compost and keep moist, but never allow to become soaked. Keep in a light place but away from direct sun. Propagate by seeds in March and April, or by leaf cuttings, taken with a small piece of stem attached in summer. E. Tropical Africa.

'Blue Fairy Tale', deep blue single flowers;
'Calypso', single purple with a white edge;
'Diana Blue', bright purple-blue flowers, **433**;
'Diana Double Pink', semi-double, rose-purple;
'Grandiflora Pink', single rose-pink;
'Icefloe', double flowered white;
'Red Spark', semi-double red;
'Rhapsodie', a good modern strain with a wide range of self colours and bicolours, **434–437**.

Salmon Blood Lily see **Haemanthus multiflorus**

SALPIGLOSSIS (SOLANACEAE)
sinuata Painted Tongue
An annual plant which makes an attractive specimen for the cool greenhouse. It has slender stems reaching 24 in. in height, bearing pale-green, wavy-edged narrow leaves. The flowers are velvety, funnel-shaped opening to 2 in. across the lobes at the mouth. They occur in shades from yellow through orange to reds and purples and are often veined in a darker colour. They are produced from June to October. Grow in pots in loam-based compost and propagate by seed. Chile.
'Superbissima', very large flowers with golden veins, **438**.

SALVIA (LABIATAE) Sage
A large genus of annual and perennial species of which the following members are decorative greenhouse plants, mostly shrubby and perennial. Grow in a cool greenhouse border or in pots in a loam-based compost. Ventilate freely and water regularly while in full growth, less in winter. Propagate the herbaceous species by seed sown in April and the shrubby species by cuttings taken from non-flowering lateral or basal shoots in April and May, or September.

ambigens syn. **S. caerulea**
Now correctly known as *S. guarantica*, this species makes a shrubby perennial to 5 ft in height when grown in the greenhouse border, much less in a pot. It has oval, wavy-margined leaves tapering to a point, but heart-shaped at the base. The 2 in. dark blue flowers are tubular, opening to 2 lips and enclosed in a ½ in. violet-blue calyx. They are produced in late summer. Brazil.

caerulea see **S. ambigens**

greggii Autumn Sage
A 3 ft shrub with small, narrowly oblong, undivided leaves growing on stems which are often arching when young. The 1–1½ in. carmine-red flowers are borne in pairs in the axils of the leaves opening from August to October. Texas, Mexico.

guarantica see **S. ambigens**

involucrata Roseleaf Sage
Herbaceous and woody at the base, usually growing to 4 ft in height. The long pointed oval leaves have a toothed margin and reach 4 in. in length. The flowers are pink or red, the tube in in. long and enclosed by a short pink calyx; they open from August to October. Beneath the flowers are large pinky-red leaves (bracts) which fall as the flowers open. Mexico, Guatemala.

microphylla see **S. neurepia**

neurepia syn. **S. microphylla**
A rich red flowering species with 1 in. blooms enclosed by purplish bracts and opening from July to October. The leaves are elliptic and pale green and have an aromatic fragrance when crushed. Mexico.

patens Gentian Sage
The bright clear blue flowers of this species are 2 in. or more in length and appear from August to September. The perennial stems reach

2–3 ft, and bear broadly oval leaves, slightly toothed and hairy, making a bushy, softly hairy plant. Mexico.

rutilans Pineapple Scented Sage
The leaves of this species have a fragrance not unlike that of pineapple, when crushed. They are oval and pointed, light green and shortly hairy. The flowers are deep pink and grow from bell-shaped bracts; they open in winter. The origin of this 1½–3 ft shrub is not known.

SALVINIA (SALVINIACEAE)
auriculata Floating Fern
A tiny aquatic fern having oval, yellow-green leaves less than 1¾ in. in length and borne on very fine stem-like rhizomes. The whole plant floats on the surface of the water and is most attractive in aquaria or pools in the greenhouse. It requires warmth and when happy will multiply rapidly by division. Cuba to Paraguay. **439**.

SANCHEZIA (ACANTHACEAE)
nobilis
A handsome tropical shrub with long, oval leaves, tapering gradually to the stalk and 2 in. yellow, tubular flowers borne in clusters of 8–10 within each pair of bright red bracts. The bracts and flower clusters grow on long stems grouped in fives or sixes at the ends of the shoots. They are held upright. This is a striking plant for the warm, humid, greenhouse. Grow in a loam-based or a proprietary peat compost and shade from the hottest sunshine. Propagate by stem cuttings in summer. Ecuador. **440**.
'Glaucophylla', an excellent variegated plant with the grey-green leaves striped white and yellow.

SANDERSONIA (LILIACEAE)
aurantiaca Chinese Lanterns
A delightful 18 in. tuberous plant with stalkless, spear-shaped leaves tapering to a fine point and borne up the slender stem in decreasing size. The showy orange flowers are lantern-shaped and borne on long pendent stalks from the axils of the leaves on the upper half of the main stem. Grow in pots in a loam based or proprietary peat compost and provide twiggy supports. Pot the tubers in spring and water sparingly until growth commences, then more freely. Dry off when the foliage begins to yellow and store in a frost free place. Ventilate on warm days and provide light shade from direct sunlight. Propagate by seeds sown in spring or offset tubers separated at potting time. Natal.

SANSEVIERIA (LILIACEAE) Bowstring Hemp
A genus of evergreen perennials with decorative erect, sword-shaped leaves. They make good ornamental foliage plants for the home or greenhouse. Grow in a loam-based or a proprietary peat compost and allow to become dry between waterings throughout the year. Propagate by suckers from the underground roots or by leaf cuttings in summer.

cylindrica
The rigid leaves grow up to 5 ft in length and 1¼ in. thick, being round in cross-section. They arch slightly and taper to a point. While young they are dark green with paler greyish cross-bands, and have noticeable grooves running the length of the leaves. Tropical Africa, Natal.

grandis
A species with 3–4 ft colourful leaves, 1–2 ft broad which are banded with dark and mid shades of green. Some plants have reddish-brown leaf margins. Tropical Africa.

hahnii syn. **S. trifasciata** 'Hahnii'
A species with a different appearance from the other members of the genus described here. It has oval to triangular leaves about 4 in. long and 2½ in. wide, with sharp-pointed apices, and forms spreading rosettes. The leaves are dark green and yellow banded. Tropical West Africa.

trifasciata Mother-in-law's Tongue, Snake Plant
The commonest species in cultivation with stiff, straight leaves tapering to a sharp point and 12–18 in. high. They are cross banded on both sides with shades of dark and yellow or greyish-green. Tropical West Africa. **441**.
'Hahnii' see *S. hahnii*
'Laurentii', a variety with creamy-yellow margins to the leaves, **442**.

SARRACENIA (SARRACENIACEAE) Pitcher Plant

A genus of strange, insectivorous perennials with hollow leaves. These hold a digestive liquid at the bottom, neatly protected by a fold at the top like a lid. The insides of the leaf tube have downward pointing hairs and a sugary secretion which attracts flies, beetles and other small insects. Once in the tube, the insects are unable to escape because of the hairs, and eventually fall into the bottom of the leaf – or pitcher – where they are ingested. The plants produce colourful flowers and make curiously interesting subjects for the cool greenhouse. Plant in pans of equal parts of peat and chopped sphagnum moss, and spread a layer of live sphagnum on the surface. Keep this moist all the time, and maintain a humid atmosphere in summer. Propagate by seed in March.

drummondii syn. **S. leucophylla** Lace Trumpets, Fiddler's Trumpet
A most colourful species with the pitchers tall and fluted, 18–30 in. in height, green with purple veining, especially towards the top where the background colour pales to a creamy-white, especially the lid. The 2–4 in. nodding flowers are a greenish-purple with yellow shading and are borne on long stalks. They open during April and May. N. America.

flava Yellow Pitcher Plant, Trumpets
The tall, slender tubes are a bright yellow-green with crimson veining in the throat. The large flowers are 3–5 in. across, yellow and drooping. They have an unpleasant pungent smell. S.E. U.S.A.

leucophylla see **S. drummondii**

purpurea Northern Pitcher Plant
The pitchers of this species are usually semi-prostrate or reclining, arranged in rosettes. They are purple and green, having a markedly swollen area in the middle, with rich red veining in the throat and on the lid. The greenish-purple to purple, nodding flowers are borne in April and May. N.E. U.S.A. to Canada. **443-4.**

SAUROMATUM (ARACEAE)

guttatum Monarch of the East
A tropical plant with large tubers producing thick 18 in. stalks on which grow the deeply and irregularly dissected leaves, the segments oval, tapering to a point and up to 10 in. in length. The flowers are rather like those of an arum having a hood 12–25 in. long, purple inside with black-purple spots, shading to green above and on the outside, and a 2–4 in. spathe within. They are produced in May. A variable species which can be grown in a warm or cool greenhouse. Plant the tubers in large pots of loam-based compost in autumn, water freely until the leaves turn yellow, then dry off until growth begins again the following spring. Keep shaded from hot sun and maintain a humid atmosphere in summer. Propagate by offsets from the tubers when repotting. Sub tropical Asia to Tropical Africa.

SAXIFRAGA (SAXIFRAGACEAE)

stolonifera syn. **S. sarmentosa** Mother of Thousands, Strawberry Geranium
A tufted species with many strawberry-like branching red runners upon which numerous new plants are formed. It is grown chiefly for its decorative foliage, the rounded leaves being green above with pale or silvery veins and suffused red or pink beneath. It also bears loose clusters of starry white flowers with petals of irregular size. They are carried on long stalks and open in July and August. It makes an attractive plant for the cool greenhouse or home, especially when grown in a hanging basket, and should be planted in a loam-based compost. Propagate by detaching the young plants from the runners and potting separately. Several cultivars with different foliage colour are grown. China. **445.**
    'Tricolor' has leaves splashed with cream and pink.

Scarborough Lily see **Vallota speciosa**
Scarlet Banana see **Musa coccinea**
Scarlet Flowering Gum see **Eucalyptus ficifolia**
Scarlet Ginger Lily see **Hedychium coccineum**
Scarlet Leadwort see **Plumbago indica**
Scarlet Passion Flower see **Passiflora coccinea**
Scarlet Plume see **Euphorbia fulgens**
Scarlet Trompetilla see **Bouvardia triphylla**

SCHEFFLERA (ARALIACEAE)

A genus of ornamental evergreen trees and shrubs of which the species described below make good foliage plants for the cool greenhouse or for the home. Grow in pots of loam-based compost and shade in summer. Keep moist and in a humid atmosphere. Propagate by seeds sown in spring.

actinophylla syn. **Brassaia actinophylla** Queensland Umbrella Tree
A slow growing shrub reaching 6–8 ft or more, with glossy green leaves divided into 3–5 narrow, long oval, pointed leaflets, borne on the erect branches which rise from a single stem. A good plant for a decorative effect, being suited to the large warm office or greenhouse. Polynesia, Australia.

digitata Seven Fingers
A bush or small tree, 10 ft or more when adult, with thin, leathery glossy leaves divided into 7–10 leaflets, radiating from a central point at the end of the stalk. Each leaflet is up to 7 in. in length, a deep matt green above and light green and shiny beneath, the margin wavy. Best grown in the cool greenhouse as it is not happy in a warm, dry atmosphere. New Zealand.

SCHIZANTHUS (SOLANACEAE)

pinnatus Butterfly Flower, Poor Man's Orchid
A very attractive annual plant, about 2 ft high, with erect, brittle, somewhat sticky stems carrying pale green, deeply divided, fern-like leaves and an abundance of showy, orchid-like flowers. These are pale lilac with deep rose and purple markings, and a large yellow central patch. They open from June to October, and grow best in pots in a loam-based compost. Pinch out leading shoots when small to maintain bushy growth. Propagate by seed sown in August and September for growth in pots. Many hybrids and cultivars are grown. Chile. **446.**
    'Crimson Cardinal', deep red flowers with a darker blotch;
    'Dwarf Bouquet', a dwarf form producing an abundance of flowers in a great range of colours;
    'Pansy Flowered', a very free flowering strain with large flowers.

SCHIZOCENTRON (MELASTOMATACEAE)

elegans syn. **Heeria elegans**
A charming trailing or carpeting plant suitable as ground cover in the cool greenhouse border or for hanging baskets. The bright green leaves are oval and slender pointed, making a pleasing foil for the 1 in. diameter, wide open 4-petalled flowers of rich rose-purple. Grow in pans or baskets of a proprietary peat compost and water freely during the spring to autumn period; less in winter. Shade from hottest sunlight and ventilate on all sunny days. Propagate by separating rooted shoots or by division. Mexico.

SCHLUMBERGERA (CACTACEAE)

According to modern classification, there is now only one species in this genus, but there are a number of hybrids. Culture is the same as for *Rhipsalidopsis*. Flowering is from October to February, the resting period being after flowering. Minimum winter temperature 55°F. for flowering, 35°F. for survival. Often grafted on *Pereskia* and *Hylocereus undatus*.

gaertneri see **Rhipsalidopsis gaertneri**

truncata syn. **Zygocactus truncatus, Epiphyllum truncatum** Crab Cactus
The stems are 1½–2 in. long, branching dichotomously (in pairs). They are green and have curved projections at the end, resembling crabs' claws, thus the common name. The red flowers are 2 in. long and ½ in. wide. Brazil. This species is no longer found wild, and it is doubtful if the true species is now in cultivation. It was the original Christmas Cactus and is a parent of the Buckley hybrids, the current Christmas Cacti, see below.
Many hybrids and cultivars are grown.
    × *buckleyi*, Christmas Cactus, has mauvish-pink flowers, produced around Christmas time, but later if the temperature is low, **447;**
    'Frankenstolz', with carmine flowers;
    'Königers Weihnachtsfreude', 'Christmas Joy', has scarlet flowers in November and December, **448;**
    'Noris', with rose-pink flowers at almost any time, usually around Christmas;
    'Wintermärchen', 'Winter Tales', bears white flowers, flushed carmine, around Christmas, **449.**

SCILLA (LILIACEAE) Squill

A genus of small bulbous plants with strap-shaped leaves and clusters of small starry flowers borne on long stalks. Grow in the cool greenhouse or house, in pots of loam-based compost, pot in autumn and keep well ventilated. Water sparingly at all times. Propagate by removal of offsets from the bulbs in autumn. These are attractive house plants.

adlamii

The fleshy, narrow, somewhat pleated leaves grow singly from each bulb, and reach 8–9 in. in length. The starry, mauve-purple blooms are borne in a short, dense cluster on 3–4 in. stems and open in April. S. Africa.

violacea syn. Ledebouria socialis Silver Squill

A delightful plant with 3–5 in., fleshy leaves olive-green mottled with silvery markings above and a glossy red-purple beneath. They are borne on short stems and lie almost at right angles to the stem. The small green flowers with violet stamens open in winter and several at a time are carried above the leaves on stiff, erect stems. S. Africa.

SCINDAPSUS (ARACEAE) Ivy Arum

A genus of tropical climbers with decorative, often variegated foliage. While young, the leaves are up to 8 in. in length and they make excellent pot plants, especially for rooms with central heating. As they age, the leaves increase in size and the plants must be replaced. Grow in pots in a warm greenhouse in a proprietary peat compost, keep moist during the summer and shade from the hottest sun. Propagate by stem tip cuttings with one leaf, or leaf-bud cuttings, in spring.

aureus Devil's Ivy, Golden Pothos

A tall, fleshy vine, the pointed, oval leaves reaching 2 ft in length when mature, but 3–5 in. in the juvenile stage. They are waxy in texture and are a bright, rather dark green, variegated with spots, lines and splashes of yellow-gold. Solomon Is.

'Marble Queen', the variegation on the leaves is white and covers more of the surface than in the type, **450**;

'Tricolor', the green leaves are marked with shades of pale green, deep yellow and creamy-white.

pictus Silver Vine

A similar plant to *S. aureus* in growth form, having silvery marbling on the thick dark green, leathery leaves. These have the pointed tips curved to one side, and the basal lobes heart-shaped. E. Indies, Philippines.

Sea Daffodil see **Pancratium maritimum**
Seaside Grape see **Coccoloba uvifera**
Sea Lavender see **Limonium**
Sea Lily see **Pancratium maritimum**
Sea Onion see **Urginea maritima**
Sea Squill see **Urginea maritima**
Sea Urchin see **Hakea laurina**
Sea Urchin Cactus see **Echinopsis**
Sedge see **Carex**

SEDUM (CRASSULACEAE) Stonecrop

Colourful yellow, pink or white, star-shaped flowers grow in terminal panicles, frequently flattened like an umbel. The leaves are fleshy and attractive. For culture see terrestrial succulents in the Introduction. Minimum winter temperature 40°F. Propagate by stem cuttings, or seed.

allantoides

Evergreen, blue-green leaved sub-shrub growing to around 12 in. high. The leaves are alternate, thickest near the tip. Greeny-white flowers form in loose clusters, 4–5 in. long, in June to July. Mexico.

bellum

The unbranched leafy stems, to 6 in. long, bear blue-green spoon-shaped leaves, 1 in. in length, and the whole plant is coated with meal. The white flowers, $\frac{1}{2}$ in. across, are produced in flat cymes from April to May. Mexico.

brevifolium

The small 1–2 in. long stems spread to form 12 in. wide clumps. The pinkish leaves, densely coated with downy white meal are very small, ovate in shape and spaced closely round the stems. The white flowers are borne in sparse clusters in July. S.W. Europe, Morocco.

lineare

Prostrate species 1 in. high and about 12 in. across, with pale green strap-shaped leaves arranged in 3's around the creeping stems. The yellow flower clusters develop in May and continue to July. Japan.

morganianum Burro's Tail

Stems of thick fleshy incurving leaves form drooping cylinders 1–2 ft long. Flowers are borne in pale pink clusters, up to $1\frac{1}{2}$ in. across, at the stem tips throughout the summer. Ideal for a hanging basket. Mexico.

oaxacanum

The spreading 6 in. stems root wherever they meet the soil and have very short overlapping leaves, blunt and mid-green in colour. 1–3 yellow flowers, about $\frac{1}{3}$ in. long, are borne at the tips of the shoots in summer. Mexico.

pachyphyllum

A low-growing succulent shrub up to 10 in. high and across. Branching from the base, the stems are clad with club-shaped leaves, glaucous-blue in colour, with red tips. Yellow flower clusters, 2 in. across, are produced in spring. Mexico.

rubrotinctum Christmas Cheer, Jelly Beans

Cylindrical showy green, red-brown tipped, leaves grow thickly on 8 in. stems which branch freely from the base. A shrubby species which rarely produces flowers in Britain. Mexico.

'Aurora', with attractive glaucous-blue leaves, tinged red, **451**.

sieboldii

The arching, 9 in. long purplish stems are set with spirally arranged leaves in whorls of 3, the leaves being roundish, blue-green in colour with wavy margins. The small pinkish flowers are borne in much branched umbels at the top of the plant in October. Japan.

'Medio-variegatum', leaves marked with creamy blotches, **452**.

treleasei

About 12 in. high, this sprawling evergreen has stems set with club-shaped leaves $1\frac{1}{4}$ in. long and $\frac{1}{2}$ in. thick. Bright yellow flowers, $\frac{1}{2}$ in. across, appear in tight branched clusters in spring. Mexico. **453.**

Seersucker Plant see **Geogenanthus**

SELAGINELLA (SELAGINELLACEAE)

A genus of flowerless plants, akin to ferns, with small scale-like leaves. Some species make low growing, creeping plants, others are climbers growing more upright. Grow in a cool greenhouse, unless otherwise stated, in a humid, draught-free atmosphere shaded from the sun. Plant in pans in a peat-based compost and keep moist. Propagate by division or cuttings of small leafy shoots in spring.

apoda see S. apus

apus syn. S. apoda

A densely matted plant forming a rounded hummock with deeply dissected, moss like foliage borne on 1–4 in. stems. It is a good plant for a shallow pan. N. America.

braunii

An erect plant with 1–$1\frac{1}{2}$ ft pale straw-brown stems, branched in an intricate way and clad in small triangular leaves. The overall effect is that of a rather mossy fern, each branch appearing like an individual frond. W. China.

caulescens see S. involvens

grandis

This robust and decorative species bears frond-like stems, bare at the base, much branched above and clad with small, overlapping, oval leaves. Each branch is flattened and roughly triangular in outline, resembling a fern frond. A warm greenhouse plant. Borneo.

involvens syn. S. caulescens

A much branched erect species up to 1 ft tall, somewhat resembling a small bushy cypress with its closely overlapping, scale-like leaves. Japan, China, Malaysia.

argentea has a silvery sheen on the undersurface of the leaves. **454.**

kraussiana

A prostrate, mat-forming plant with stems up to 1 ft or so long. The branchlets are much divided and flattened, bearing oval, pointed, bright green leaves with a few long hairs. This species is very shade tolerant and will thrive even under cold greenhouse benching. S. Africa.

lepidophylla Resurrection Plant, Club Moss

The frond-like, leafy branches of this species form a flattened rosette radiating from a central woody stem. When dry it rolls up into a tight brownish ball and is thus able to withstand the drought conditions that often prevail in its homeland. In this dried state it is often sold as a curiosity, for, when wetted it opens out dramatically revealing a revived green, fern-like appearance. Texas, south to Peru.

martensii

A trailing species bearing 6–12 in. tall, erect, flattened branches that resemble fern fronds. The tiny oval leaves are lop-sided, over-lapping and bright green. Suitable for a large hanging basket. Mexico.

vogelii

A tall slender species with fern-leaf like branches of bright green leaves borne on pinkish stalks. Well grown plants can attain 2 ft in height, but pot specimens rarely exceed 1 ft. W. Africa. **455.**

SELAGO (SCROPHULARIACEAE)

A genus chiefly comprising evergreen shrubs or sub-shrubs bearing clusters of tubular flowers opening to 5 irregularly sized lobes. They thrive best in the cool greenhouse border though they will grow in large pots or tubs. Keep well ventilated and with plenty of light. Plant in loam-based compost. Propagate by cuttings of lateral stems taken with a heel in summer.

fruticosa

A 1–1½ ft, well-branched sub-shrub with downy shoots bearing small, narrow leaves. The purple or white flowers are borne in dense spikes, 1–1¼ in. long at the ends of the branches. They open in April. S. Africa.

serrata

An attractive hairless undershrub; 1–2 ft in height with strongly toothed, dark green oval leaves. The fragrant flowers are funnel-shaped with a whitish tube and mauve petals. They are borne in dense rounded clusters 2–4 in. across in July. S. Africa.

SENECIO (COMPOSITAE)

An enormous genus containing well over a thousand species of worldwide distribution, mainly in temperate and mountainous places. They are either annuals or perennials, and many of them are hardy. The tender species are noted for their unusual leaves or stems, the daisy-like flowers usually being unimportant. For culture see under terrestrial succulents in the Introduction. Minimum winter temperature normally 40°F. Propagate by seed, or stem cuttings. Many species were once included in *Kleinia* but are now more usually in this genus.

articulatus syn. **Kleinia articulata** Candle Plant

Bluish-grey jointed stems, each joint 6–8 in. long, form a plant to 2 ft high; when young they are patterned with 3 dark green lines. The deeply divided leaves are blue-green in colour and borne at the top of the stems. The flowers are yellowish-white, on long stems in summer. S. Africa.

cinerascens see **S. haworthii**

citriformis

Spreading 4 in. high stems branch from a central rootstock and have spirally arranged lemon-shaped leaves, glaucous-blue and patterned with many vertical translucent lines; they are covered with a waxy coating or farina. Yellow daisy flowers appear in December and January. S. Africa. **456.**

cruentus see **Cineraria cruenta**

grandifolius

A fine, winter flowering shrub for the conservatory or large room, 5–15 ft tall, with one or more purplish stems. The leaves are large, 6–18 in. long, oval to oblong in shape, dark green on top and slightly downy beneath. The yellow flowers are produced in large terminal clusters 12–18 in. across. Mexico. **457.**

haworthii syn. **S. cinerascens, Kleinia tomentosa**

Growing 1–2 in. high, the stems are single and woody at first but

branching later. Tubular fleshy leaves taper at the ends and, in keeping with the stems, are coated with silky woolly white hairs. Orange-yellow flowers develop in July. S. Africa.

herreianus syn. **Kleinia herreiana**

Prostrate 2 in. high stems mass over 24 in. Grape-like leaves form at intervals along the stems and are marked with dark green lines. A very fleshy plant with creeping habit. The flowers are seldom seen in cultivation. S. Africa.

petasites California Geranium

Branching shrub 3–4 ft or more high with leaves 6–12 in. long and across, wavy-edged and downy beneath, with stalks as long as the leaves. The flowers are 1¼ in. across, bright yellow and arranged in large terminal panicles. They appear from December to February. Mexico.

radicans syn. **Kleinia radicans**

The creeping 3–4 in. high stems spread over 24 in. Round to cylindrical leaves form in great numbers on the stems, greyish-green with a dark green central stripe. Pale creamy-white flowers appear in December but this is unusual. S. Africa.

rowleyanus String of Beads

Forming a mat of beaded stems with globular, pointed-tipped leaves patterned with a vertical translucent band. The single flower heads, on 2 in. stalks, are produced from September to November, the white florets contrasting with the purple stigmas; sweetly scented. Ideal for hanging baskets or attractive floral carpets, spreading 2–3 ft. S. Africa.

serpens syn. **Kleinia repens**

The 8–12 in. long stems form 24 in. wide mats of strap-shaped fleshy leaves, blue-green in colour with a white waxy sheen. The leaves are grooved above and grow as rosettes round the stem tips. White flowers form in summer. S. Africa. **458.**

Senna see **Cassia**
Sensitive Plant see **Mimosa pudica**

SERISSA (RUBIACEAE)

foetida syn. **S. japonica, Lycium japonicum**

This charming 2 ft tall twiggy evergreen shrub makes a good plant for the cool greenhouse or home. The rather leathery small leaves are oval, dark green and slender-pointed. In their axils are borne starry white blossoms in summer and autumn, often in abundance. They are followed by small fleshy fruits. There is a form with golden margined leaves. Grow in pots of a proprietary peat compost. Shade from hottest sunshine and ventilate on warm sunny days. Propagate by lateral stem cuttings, preferably with a heel in summer. Japan, China.

'Plena', the commonest form in cultivation, with double flowers like tiny white roses.

SESBANIA (LEGUMINOSAE)

punicea syn. **Daubentonia punicea**

A 3 ft shrub with long pendent leaves divided into 10–20 pairs of oval blunt-ended leaflets. The bright scarlet, pea-like flowers are borne on ½ in. stalks to form a long, drooping cluster. They are produced in July and are followed by stout pods, 2–4 in. long with leathery segments. A very attractive shrub for the warm greenhouse border or pots. Grow in loam-based compost, keep humid and shade from the hottest sun in summer. Propagate by cuttings of lateral shoots in summer with a heel, or by seed in spring. Brazil.

SETCREASEA (COMMELINACEAE)

A genus of perennial plants with decorative foliage. The following species make good ornamental plants for the house or cool greenhouse. Grow in loam-based compost or a proprietary peat mixture. In summer keep well watered but slightly shaded if they are standing in full sunlight. In winter keep just moist. Repot annually in April. Propagate by basal cuttings taken from May–August.

purpurea Purple Heart

A good house plant with striking purple leaves which deepen in colour with good light. They are strap shaped, up to 6 in. in length and have a sparse coating of woolly hairs especially along the margins. The long, purple flowering stems bear, from May to December, 3-petalled, deep rose-pink flowers, in dense clusters, which open singly in succession. They grow within a bract-like leaf which partly encloses them. Mexico.

striata syn. **Callisia elegans** Striped Inch Plant
A decorative spreading plant very like *Tradescantia* in appearance. The ovate-triangular leaves are dark green with ivory white veins running longitudinally, and purple beneath. They are stalkless and clasp the stem, forming a dense mat of foliage. The 3-petalled flowers are white, but small and insignificant. They are borne from May to October. Mexico.

Seven Fingers see **Schefflera digitata**
Seville Orange see **Citrus aurantium**
Shaving-brush Palm see **Rhopalostylis sapida**
Shrimp Plant see **Beloperone guttata**
Siberian Lily see **Ixiolirion montanum**
Silk Oak see **Grevillea robusta**
Silk Tree see **Albizia julibrissin**
Silver Chirita see **Chirita sinensis**
Silver King Fern see **Cyathea dealbata**
Silver Netleaf see **Fittonia argyroneura**
Silver Palm see **Thrinax argentea**
Silver Squill see **Scilla violacea**
Silver Table Fern see **Pteris ensiformis** 'Victoriae'
Silver Thatch see **Thrinax argentea**
Silver Tree see **Leucadendron argenteum**
Silver Vine see **Scindapsus pictus**
Silver Wattle see **Acacia dealbata**

SINNINGIA (GESNERIACEAE) Gloxinia
Handsome tuberous rooted perennials with velvety textured foliage and colourful trumpet flowers. The species and hybrid cultivars described here are better known under the popular name 'gloxinia'. They make excellent pot plants for the warm conservatory, greenhouse or home and will tolerate cooler conditions for short periods. Grow in a proprietary peat compost and shade from direct hot sunshine. Propagate from seeds sown in spring or summer, or from cuttings taken from newly started tubers (corms). Flowering sized tubers can be purchased and should be potted so that the upper surface is just level with the compost surface. See also *Rechsteineria*.

regina
The 2 in. violet, tubular flowers are borne on long stalks and carried above the long ovate leaves. They open from May to July. The leaves are velvety green above with ivory white veins and deep red beneath. Brazil. **459.**

speciosa
A rosette-forming plant with large oval leaves and a central cluster of large, fleshy textured, velvety purple foxglove-like flowers. The many cultivars are mainly of hybrid origin and are often grouped under the names Gigantea, or Fyfiana see plate **460.** They bear flowers of mixed colours, including tricoloured forms, in white, red, pink and purple. Mixed seed strains and the following cultivars are available. Brazil.
'Blanche de Meru', pale pink with a white margin;
'Defiance', bright red;
'Emperor Frederick', red edged white;
'Mont Blanc', pure white;
'Prince Albert', violet-blue;
'Reine Wilhelmine', deep rich pink;
'Rose Bells', rose-pink with narrow smaller blooms than the foregoing. This hybrid between *S. eumorpha* and *Rechsteineria macropoda* is now known as *Sinningia* × *rosea* 'Rose Bells'.

tubiflora
A taller branched plant, up to 3 ft, with fragrant, waxy white bells and smaller hairy green leaves. Argentina.

Sleeping Hibiscus see **Malvaviscus**
Slipper Orchid see **Paphiopedilum**
Slipperwort see **Calceolaria**

SMILAX (LILIACEAE) Greenbrier
A genus of climbing species with stems often spiny or bristly, grown for their ornamental foliage. They are best grown in the cool greenhouse border or tubs. Propagate by seed or division in spring.

asparagoides see **Asparagus medeoloides**

aspera
An evergreen climber with zig-zag, spiny stems and oval leathery leaves, heart-shaped at the base, tapering to a slender point. They have prickly margins and are often mottled with white. The small pale green flowers are borne in clusters in the axils of the leaves in August and September, followed by red berries. S. Europe.

excelsa
A thorny deciduous climber with ovate leaves similar in shape though not texture to those of *S. aspera*. The small green flowers are borne in clusters of 5–10 in June and the red berries ripen in autumn. S. Asia.

rotundifolia Horse or Cat Brier
A vigorous deciduous climbing species with very spiny stems. The greenish-yellow flowers in May to June are followed by black berries. E. U.S.A. and Canada.

Smilax see **Asparagus medeoloides**
Smilax, Baby see **Asparagus medeoloides** 'Myrtifolius'

SMITHIANTHA syn. **NAEGELIA** (GESNERIACEAE)
A genus of herbaceous plants with toothed, softly hairy leaves and erect clusters of colourful, foxglove-like flowers with a long flowering season. Grow in pots in a loam-based compost or a proprietary peat mixture in a cool greenhouse and keep moist while flowering and shade from summer sun. They make excellent house plants if brought indoors on the point of flowering. Allow to dry off when the leaves begin to yellow and store in a frost proof place until growth starts in the spring. Propagate by division of rhizomes in spring, or by leaf cuttings in summer.

cinnabarina Temple Bells
The dark green, velvety leaves are suffused with red. They make a splendid foil to the spikes of strikingly coloured, vermilion flowers which are borne on short pendulous stalks on strong upright branches to 2 ft in height. The blooms, which are abundantly produced from June to December, are orange-yellow inside the mouth with red spotting. Mexico.

multiflora
A most attractive species with pendent white flowers, flushed with pale yellow at the throat and borne, from June to October, on long erect stems, to 3 ft in height. The heart-shaped leaves are velvety and deep green, mottled with brown, paler beneath with long, soft hairs. Mexico.

zebrina
A 2–3 ft species with dark green, silky hairy leaves, having red-brown patterning. The slender, light hairy stems carry 1½ in. long pendent blooms, brilliant scarlet on the outside and yellow in the throat with red spotting. They are borne on long, erect spikes from June to October. Mexico.
'Elke', golden-orange flowers, yellow within and olive-green foliage with an orange sheen, **461**;
'Firebird', bright carmine-scarlet flowers with a yellow throat, spotted scarlet;
'Orange King', rich orange flowers with bronze foliage;
'Pink Domino', rose-pink flowers with a red-marked, white throat, **462**;
'Rose Queen', deep rose-pink flowers marked with purple inside;
'White Pyramid', creamish-white flowers opening from greenish-white buds. Foliage suffused with purple.

Snail Flower see **Phaseolus caracalla**
Snake Plant see **Sanseviera trifasciata**
Snake's Beard see **Ophiopogon japonicus**
Snake Vine see **Hibbertia scandens**
Snow Bush see **Breynia nivosa**
Snowy Mint Bush see **Prostanthera nivea**

SOLANUM (SOLANACEAE) Nightshade
A large genus of annuals, perennials and shrubs, which includes some attractive ornamental plants particularly valued for their berries.

Grow in the cool greenhouse in pots, or with the larger and climbing species, in the border. Use a loam-based compost and keep moist during the growing season. Propagate the annuals by seeds, and take cuttings of side shoots in the case of the perennial and climbing species.

aviculare Kangaroo Apple, Poroporo ❋ ●
A 6 ft shrub for the cool greenhouse having narrow deeply divided leaves, 6–10 in. long, becoming less dissected as the plant ages. The violet flowers open at the mouth to $\frac{3}{4}$–1 in. across and are borne in summer, in loose clusters towards the ends of the young stems. The berries are greenish or yellow, Australia, New Zealand.

capsicastrum Winter Cherry, False Jerusalem Cherry ●
A popular house plant, grown for its round fruits which change from green, through yellow to brilliant scarlet as they ripen. The plant is a bushy sub-shrub with downy shoots, usually grown afresh each year. It has uneven pairs of dark green leaves, narrowly oval and slightly wavy at the margins and small white star-like flowers in June and July. Brazil, **463.**
    'Cherry Ripe', a free fruiting form with bright red berries.

cornutum ❋ ☙
An annual species, having unevenly lobed leaves with deeply wavy margins, borne on prickly stems reaching 4 ft in height. The yellow flowers are 1–1$\frac{1}{4}$ in. across the star-shaped lobes and are borne in small, terminal clusters. The fruit is small and spiny. Mexico.

jasminoides Potato Vine ❋ ☙
A handsome, shrubby evergreen climber with slender stems 8–10 ft long bearing deeply lobed, pale green glossy leaves. The showy flowers are white, blue tinged, $\frac{3}{4}$ in. across and star-shaped. They are borne in branched clusters from July to October. Brazil.

macranthum Potato Tree ❋ ☙
A large prickly shrub exceeding 6 ft in height and suitable for the greenhouse border. The narrowly ovate leaves are 10–15 in. in length, and shallowly lobed. The bluish-violet flowers are 1$\frac{1}{2}$–2$\frac{1}{2}$ in. across at the mouth, with 5 roundish lobes. They are borne in summer on long clusters in the axils of the leaves. Brazil.

melongena Egg Plant, Aubergine ❋ ●
An annual species grown chiefly for its fruits which are edible and vary in size and shape in a number of cultivars from the round, white fruits of *S. m. ovigerum* to the long narrow ones of *S. m. serpentinum* which curl up at the ends. The plant reaches 2–6 ft in height, or more, and has wavy edged, lobed leaves, woolly and prickly below. The flowers, which open in summer, are blue, 1–2 in. across and borne in small clusters at the ends of the side branches. Ethiopia.

muricatum Melon Pear, Pepino ●
A spiny species making an erect, shrubby plant. The oval leaves have wavy margins and the small blue flowers are followed by 4–6 in. fruits. These are yellow with purple markings and have yellow, juicy, fragrant flesh. Peru.

pseudocapsicum Christmas or Jerusalem Cherry ●
A plant somewhat similar to *S. capsicastrum* but more robust, with hairless stems. The 2–2$\frac{1}{2}$ in. leaves are velvety above, smooth beneath and a bright green, and the small, white, star-like flowers open in summer. These are followed by the lustrous fruits, at first yellow, but soon becoming orange and finally scarlet. They are at their best in December and make a popular Christmas pot plant. Madeira.

seaforthianum Brazilian Nightshade ❋ ☙ ●
A trailing species with deeply dissected, 4–8 in. leaves and pink or lilac flowers in spreading clusters. They are followed by round, yellowish-red fruits. A plant for the warm greenhouse. S. America.

wendlandii Costa Rican Nightshade, Giant Potato Vine ❋ ☙
A strong growing prickly climber which can reach 15 ft or more in favourable conditions. The bright green leaves are very variable in size and degree of dissection, while the large, 2$\frac{1}{2}$ in. bluish-mauve flowers are borne in 6 in. trusses at the ends of the drooping branches. They are produced in August. Costa Rica. **464.**

SOLEIROLIA (URTICACEAE)
soleirolii syn. **Helxine soleirolii** Mind-your-own-business, Baby's Tears ☙
Well known under its old name of *Helxine*, this is a prostrate creeping plant, rooting as it spreads. Ideal for ground cover in the greenhouse, conservatory or for growing in pots in a position where the tiny round leaves, set on pink stems can cascade downwards. There is a more attractive golden-leaved form. For pot culture grow in a loam-based compost and shade in summer. Propagate by detaching small rooted portions in early summer. Corsica.

SOLLYA (PITTOSPORACEAE)
fusiformis syn. **S. heterophylla** Australian Bluebell Creeper ❋
A twining species which will climb up supports in the cool greenhouse. It has slender pointed, oval leaves which taper into the stem, and branched clusters of 4–12 blue, cup-shaped flowers which are produced in July. Grow in the greenhouse border, or in pots in loam-based compost or a proprietary peat mix. Keep well ventilated and shaded on hot summer days. Propagate by seeds in spring. Australia. **465.**

SONERILA (MELASTOMATACEAE)
A genus of tropical flowering plants of which the following species are suitable for house or warm greenhouse cultivation. Grow in a proprietary peat compost, maintain humid conditions and shade from the hottest sun. Propagate by seeds sown in April, or by basal cuttings between April and June.

margaritacea ❋ ☙
A procumbent plant with red creeping stems bearing long oval, slender pointed leaves. These are dark green with silvery-white spots between the veins on the upper surface, and pink with purplish veins on the lower surface. The 3-petalled rose-coloured blooms are borne in 8–10 flowered clusters from May to September. Java. **466.**

orientalis ❋ ☙
The decorative leaves are broad with a pointed tip, and heart-shaped at the base. They are a reddish-purple with white markings, either a single band with feathered edges, or small spots on a light or dark green band. The 3-petalled pink or purple flowers open in summer. Burma.

SOPHORA (LEGUMINOSAE)
secundiflora Mescal Bean ❋ ☙
An evergreen tree which, when full grown, can exceed 20 ft. It makes a delightfully fragrant species for the greenhouse border where it is at its best against a wall. The 4–6 in. leaves are divided into 7–9 oval leaflets and the 1 in. violet-blue pea-like flowers, which have a violet scent, are borne in long pendent clusters at the end of the branches. Texas to Mexico.

SOPHRONITIS (ORCHIDACEAE)
coccinea syn. **S. grandiflora** ❋
A charming dwarf orchid suitable for the cool greenhouse. It forms small clumps of ovoid to globose bulbs, each bearing one oblong or lance-shaped, rigid, somewhat fleshy, dark green leaf. The flowers are borne 1 or 2 to a slender stem and vary from cinnabar-red or scarlet to orange-red, carmine-purple and pink. The invididual blossoms range from 1$\frac{1}{2}$–3 in. across and resemble a pansy, but with a narrow upper sepal and a pointed lip. They open during the winter months. Grow in small pans of equal parts osmunda fibre and sphagnum moss, preferably suspended from the greenhouse roof. Water freely in summer, less in winter. Lightly shade from the hottest sunshine and maintain a humid atmosphere during the warmest months. Propagate by division in late spring or just as the young growth is visible. Brazil.

Sorrel, Wood see **Oxalis**
Spanish Moss see **Tillandsia usneoides**

SPARAXIS (IRIDACEAE) Wand Flower
A small genus of attractive plants growing from corms. They have flat, sword shaped leaves tapering to a point and showy flowers. Grow in the cool greenhouse in loam-based compost. Water after planting, then only again when the leaves are showing. Keep well watered until the leaves begin to yellow, then allow to dry off. Propagate by offsets from the corms, or by seed.

grandiflora ❋
A very attractive species with 2 in. blooms, each with the 6 purple or

white marked petals opening wide, star-wise. They are borne in spikes of 3–5 flowers on a 1–2 ft leafy stem, and open in April. A very variable species from which many cultivars have arisen. S. Africa.

tricolor Velvet Flower ✳
The 12 in. strap-shaped leaves are borne in clusters, sheathing the 12–18 in. stems upon which are borne spikes of open, 6-petalled flowers, 1½–2 in. across. They are produced in a wide variety of colours including white, yellow, orange, red and purple, both self- and multi-coloured. They open in May and June. S. Africa.

SPARMANNIA (TILIACEAE)
africana African Hemp, Window Linden ✳ 🐛
An evergreen shrub which is often grown as a pot plant. In this state it will reach 2–3 ft, but if planted in the cool greenhouse border it can exceed 8 ft. The 1–1¼ in. white flowers have a conspicuous centre of purple tipped, yellow stamens and are borne in clusters in May and June. The heart-shaped leaves are bright green, toothed and somewhat hairy on both sides. Grow in loam-based compost or the greenhouse border, keep well watered and shaded during the summer and ventilate freely. Propagate by cuttings of young shoots in April. S. Africa. **467.**

SPATHIPHYLLUM (ARACEAE)
A genus of evergreen plants with typical arum flowers and entire, dark green, glossy leaves. Grow in a loam-based or a proprietary peat compost. Provide a humid atmosphere and plenty of warmth especially through the summer. Propagate when re-potting in April by dividing the plants.

cannifolium ✳ 🐛
The 12–20 in. leathery, ovate leaves are shining green above and matt below. They are borne on 12–16 in. stalks and provide a foil for the spathe which is green outside but shining white within. It is 5–8 in. long and surrounds the short cream spadix. N.W. South America.

cochlearispathum ✳ 🐛
A very large plant which can, when well grown exceed 5 ft in height. It has large, broadly oblong, corrugated leaves and a large, yellow-green spathe, darkening with age, enclosing the yellowish spadix which looks remarkably similar to a small spike of sweet corn. Mexico, Guatemala.

wallisii White Sails ✳ 🐛
A smaller species than those described above, the plant reaching 9–12 in. It has bright green, spear-shaped leaves on erect and pendent stems, and the yellow spadix of flowers lies within a pure white oval spathe, produced from May to August. Colombia, Venezuela. **468.**
 'Mauna Loa', an attractive hybrid with the low form of *S. wallisii*, but with larger spathes. When kept in warm conditions it can produce flowers throughout the year.

Speedy Jenny see **Tradescantia fluminensis**

SPHAERALCEA (MALVACEAE) Globe Mallow
A genus of perennial plants very similar in appearance to the mallows. The flowers have 5 petals and are usually reddish in colour. Grow in the cool or warm greenhouse, preferably in the border. *S. abutiloides* and *S. umbellata* also make good tub plants. Use a loam-based compost and shade lightly from the strongest sunshine. Make sure the plants are regularly watered in summer. Propagate by seeds sown in spring or lateral stem cuttings, preferably with a heel, in summer.

abutiloides Bahaman Globe Mallow ✳
A 4 ft shrub with roundish leaves, irregularly lobed. The rose-pink flowers are carried within a green calyx, half as long as the petals, and are borne in August in 1–5 flowered clusters in the axils of the leaves. Bahamas.

elegans ✳
A sub-shrub which makes a semi-prostrate mat with the stems spreading to form a bush 4 ft or more across. The 3-lobed leaves are wavy edged and covered in hairs. Pale pink flowers, marked with purple veining, are carried singly in the axils of the leaves towards the ends of the branches. They open in July. S. Africa.

umbellata ✳
An upright shrub with branches reaching 10 ft. The leaves are long stalked and 5–7 lobed and the brilliant scarlet or violet flowers are

borne in long-stalked clusters, or sometimes singly, in the axils of the leaves. They are produced from January to April. A very attractive species for the warm greenhouse. Mexico. **469.**

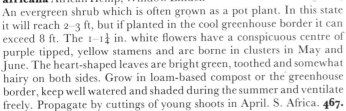

Spider Lily see **Hymenocallis**
Spider Lily, Giant see **Crinum giganteum**
Spider Lily, Golden see **Lycoris aurea**
Spider Plant see **Chlorophytum elatum**
Spiderwort see **Tradescantia**
Spiked Cabbage Tree see **Cussonia spicata**
Spiral Flag see **Costus sanguineus**
Spiral Ginger see **Costus speciosus**
Spleenwort see **Asplenium**
Sponge, Vegetable see **Luffa cylindrica**
Spotted Calla see **Zantedeschia albomaculata**
Spotted Flowering Maple see **Abutilon striatum** 'Thomsonii'

SPREKELIA (AMARYLLIDACEAE)
formosissima Jacobean or Aztec Lily ✳
A strikingly beautiful bulbous plant having long, strap-shaped leaves which develop after the flowers. These are borne singly and are a deep crimson-red, 4 in. across, and comprise 6 petals, 3 together forming a lip, 2 curled back at the sides and the sixth held upright at the top of the bloom. They open in June and July. Grow in a loam-based compost, leaving the neck of the bulb visible. Water well while the flowers and leaves are growing, then allow to become dry. Propagate by removing offsets when re-potting.

Spurge see **Euphorbia**
Spring Cattleya see **Cattleya mossiae**
Squill see **Scilla**
Stag's-horn Fern see **Platycerium**

STAPELIA (ASCLEPIADACEAE) Carrion Flower
These plants are grown for their unusual flowers, often very large and showy and always interesting. They are stem succulents which are not easy to grow, since too little water will cause them to shrivel, and too much leads to bloated plants, and often a black rot at the base of the stems; if this occurs the top can be cut off and rooted as a cutting. The stems are mostly 4-angled, branching freely from the base. There are usually spines on the ridges. The leaves are rudimentary and soon drop off. The flowers are usually star-shaped with 5 petals and of strange colours, often with 5 hairs which move at the slightest breeze. In many cases there is a smell of rotting meat or fish. The explanation of the unusual flowers is that they are pollinated by flies, particularly blowflies. Cultivation is as for terrestrial succulents, paying particular attention to good drainage and not too much water in winter, though they should not get completely dry. Slight shading should be given in very hot weather, but otherwise full light is needed. Propagation is by cuttings of the stems, taken from June to August, which should be dried off for a day or two before potting, but they must not be left long enough to shrivel. Often the clumps can be split up. Seed germinates very quickly at 65–70°F., sometimes in 24 hours, but seed from mixed collections is likely to be hybridized. To avoid rotting, winter minimum temperature should be 50°F., but plants will usually survive at 40°F.

gigantea see **S. nobilis**

hirsuta ✳ 🐛
The flowers are yellow or cream, with purple-brown markings and open in August. They are 2½–5 in. across and covered with fine, sometimes long, hairs which may be brown, white or purple. The stems are bronze-green to green, about 8 in. long and have fine short hairs. A very variable plant. S. Africa.

nobilis syn. **S. gigantea** ✳ 🐛
This species flowers during the summer. The flowers are large, 10 in. across, with long, slender lobes and bell-shaped centre. They are a pale buff colour, marked with fine purple lines and covered with thin purple hairs. The stems are upright and velvety-green. S. Africa.

pillansii ✳ 🐛
Another summer-flowering species with purple-brown, almost black unpleasant smelling flowers, about 5 in. across with lobes extended into

long tails which are covered with dark hairs. The square, upright stems are green. They have velvety hairs and conspicuous teeth. S. Africa.

variegata ✳ 🐛
The hairless, grey-green stems are mottled with purple, grow to 6 in. long and have spreading teeth. The pale yellow flowers are 2–3 in. across and have purple spots. They lack the hairs of the previous species but they too have a disagreeable smell. They open in August and are very variable, 80 forms having been given names but they are so inconsistent that separate names are hardly justified. S. Africa. **470.**

Star Acacia see **Acacia verticillata**
Star Anise see **Illicium anisatum**
Star Cluster, Egyptian see **Pentas lanceolata**
Star Glory see **Quamoclit**
Star Ipomoea see **Quamoclit coccinea**
Star of Bethlehem Orchid see **Angraecum sesquipedale**
Statice see **Limonium**

STENOCARPUS (PROTEACEAE)
sinuatus Fire-wheel Tree 🐛
Although in its native habitat, it is a 100 ft tree, this species makes an excellent foliage plant for pots and tubs when young. The leaves are cut into 2–8 oblong lobes which are glossy and leathery and a bright mid-green. With maturity the amount of lobing decreases. Well established plants will produce 2–3 in. scarlet and yellow flowers. These grow in a wheel-like cluster radiating from a central point and open from August to November. Grow in a loam-based compost and shade from hottest sunlight. Propagate by seed in spring. Australia.

STEPHANOTIS (ASCLEPIADACEAE)
floribunda Madagascar Jasmine ✳ 🐛
A delightfully fragrant twining shrub which makes a superb specimen trained on supports on the wall of a warm greenhouse where it will reach 10 ft. The dark green, leathery leaves are oval and evergreen, while the 1½ in. tubular flowers with spreading lobes are waxy white. They are borne from May to October. Grow in a loam-based or a proprietary peat compost either in large pots or tubs or preferably in the greenhouse border. Provide shade and water freely in summer. Propagate by cuttings from non-flowering lateral shoots from April to June. Madagascar. **471.**

Sticky Moonstones see **Pachyphytum brevifolium**
Stonecrop see **Sedum**
Stoneface see **Lithops**
Storksbill see **Pelargonium**
Strawberry Geranium see **Saxifraga stolonifera**

STRELITZIA (MUSACEAE)
A genus of evergreen perennials with most remarkably shaped and coloured flower clusters, like the crested head of a bird. For cultivation notes see under the species described.

augusta Great White Strelitzia ✳
A most distinctive plant, but only suitable for the large greenhouse as it does not flower until approaching maturity. When adult the trunk can exceed 20 ft in height, and carries 4–6 ft shining green, erect, leathery leaves, the stem bases closely overlapping along the trunk. The flowers, which open in March, are pure white and are borne within a stiff purplish spathe-like bract. A very striking plant. Grow in the warm greenhouse, either in a border or in tubs of loam-based compost. Shade from hottest sunshine and provide humidity during the summer. Propagate by seeds or suckers in spring. S. Africa.

reginae Bird of Paradise Flower ✳
A compact, slow growing plant 3–5 ft high. The 18 in. grey-green leathery leaves are narrowly oval and borne in fan-shaped rosettes. In April and May the exotic flowers are produced. Each 3½ ft flowering stem has a large green, red-edged boat-shaped bract from which emerge the erect, crest-like orange and blue blooms which have long narrow petals, and open in succession for several weeks. Grow in pots in loam-based compost or preferably in the greenhouse border. Water freely and shade in summer, allowing to become nearly dry through the winter. Propagate by division, or by separating rooted suckers when repotting

in spring. Seeds can also be sown in spring but are a very slow method of increase. S. Africa. **472.**

STREPTANTHERA (IRIDACEAE)
This genus contains two species only; both are dwarf, bulbous plants about 9 in. high with fan-shaped tufts of pointed, sword shaped leaves. The flowers, borne on slender stalks, grow 2–3 to the scape. They are attractive cool greenhouse plants. Grow in pots in loam-based compost keeping moist during the growing season and keep cool and fairly dry during the winter. Propagate by offsets when repotting in November.

cuprea Orange Kaleidoscope Flower ✳
The attractive flowers are 1½ in. across with 6 golden yellow petals, the centre deep purple with pale yellow spots. They open quite flat and are borne on slender stalks in May and June. S. Africa.
   'Coccinea', the bright orange petals have an almost black centre. Very striking.

elegans White Kaleidoscope Flower ✳
The white petals are flushed with pale pink and have a black circle marked with bright yellow spots around the bright violet-purple centre. S. Africa.

STREPTOCARPUS (GESNERIACEAE) Cape Primrose
A handsome genus of plants with attractive flowers and foliage. It is unusual in that some of its members have the unique habit of producing only one leaf in their lives. They are interesting plants for the cool greenhouse, flowering in May and June. Grow in pots in a loam-based or a proprietary peat compost. Propagate by seed, or in the case of tufted species, by division in spring, or leaf cuttings in summer.

dunnii Red Nodding Bells ✳ 🐛
A remarkable plant bearing a single, oblong to oval, silvery-hairy leaf which curves downwards reaching as much as 3 ft in length and has strong wrinkled folds. It bears rounded clusters of 1½ in. funnel-shaped brick-red flowers opening to 5 lobes at the mouth. S. Africa.

holstii ✳ 🐛
An erect branching plant reaching 18 in. in height, with fleshy stems, swollen at the joints. The 1½–2 in., oval, entire, dark green leaves are hairy, especially on the veins beneath, and wrinkled. The 1–1¼ in. purple flowers have a white throat and are borne on 2–6 flowered, slender stems. E. Tropical Africa.

× hybridus ✳
A group of hybrids, many derived from S. rexii are included under this name. They have mid- to light green, strap-shaped, somewhat wrinkled leaves growing from a tufted base, and the large flowers, 1½–2½ in. across vary in colour from white through pinks and reds to purple. They are produced from May to October.
   'Constant Nymph', blue-purple flowers with a bright sheen and darker veining in the throat. **473;**
   'Peed's Superb', a giant flowered strain in a wide range of colours.

rexii ✳
A small tufted plant with stemless, narrowly oval, wrinkled leaves which are a very dark green. From the centre rise 9–12 in. stalks bearing 1½–2 in. trumpet-like flowers which are blue or mauve and have purplish markings on the petals. They are borne in May and June. This species has been largely replaced in cultivation by S. × hybridus. S. Africa.

saxorum False African Violet ✳ 🐛
A charming, semi shrubby species which has branches spreading along the ground, and thick fleshy, mid-green elliptical leaves crowded on the stems. The flowers are most attractive having the white tube contrasting with the lilac-mauve, violet-like lobes. They are produced continuously from April to August. E. Tropical Africa.

wendlandii Royal Nodding Bells ✳ 🐛
Perhaps the most remarkable species, with a huge, solitary leaf which can reach 3–4 ft in length and 2 ft across. It has an olive green, hairy, deeply corrugated upper surface and is purple beneath, hanging downwards from the base of the plant. The blue-purple and white, violet-like flowers are borne in clusters of up to 30 blooms on the 1 ft stems. They open in May and June. S. Africa.

STREPTOSOLEN (SOLANACEAE)

jamesonii Marmalade Bush
A beautiful and unusual shrub for the cool greenhouse having dense rounded clusters of bright orange flowers, each tubular, opening to $\frac{3}{4}$ in. at the mouth. It has $1\frac{1}{2}$ in. oval, wrinkled and softly hairy leaves which are borne on long, arching branches, 4–6 ft in length which appear to best effect when trained against a wall or some other support. The flowers are produced from May to July. Grow in the greenhouse border or in large pots of loam-based compost and tie to supports. Keep well ventilated and pot on annually in spring. Propagate by cuttings of non-flowering side shoots taken with a heel, in spring. Colombia, Ecuador. **474.**

String of Beads see **Senecio rowleyanus**
String of Hearts see **Ceropegia woodii**
Striped Inch Plant see **Setcreasea striata**

STROBILANTHES (ACANTHACEAE)

A large genus of shrubby plants with attractive foliage and flowers. The species described below is a good subject for the warm or cool greenhouse. Grow in a proprietary peat mix or loam-based compost. Shade in summer and maintain a humid atmosphere. Propagate by lateral basal or stem cuttings, preferably with a heel, in spring and summer.

dyerianus syn. **Perilepta dyerana** Persian Shield
A beautiful foliage plant, having magnificent, 6 in. leaves, dark green with a remarkable silvery purple iridescence on the upper surface. The flowers are $1\frac{1}{2}$ in. long, tubular opening to $\frac{1}{2}$ in. at the mouth, and pale blue. They are borne in small spikes in the axils of the leaves. As the leaf effect is at its best in young plants, it is best to renew frequently. Malaya. **475.**

STYLIDIUM (STYLIDIACEAE)

graminifolium Trigger Plant
A beautiful perennial plant with large tufts of deep green, stiff, grass-like leaves, 2–9 in. in length. The flower spikes are borne on long stems growing from the base of the plant. They are up to 18 in. high and carry a cylindrical head of small, stalkless magenta-pink flowers which open in summer. Each has a sensitive curved 'trigger', composed of the fused style and stamens, which springs up when visited by insect pollinators. Grow in pots in the cool greenhouse in loam-based compost or a proprietary peat mix. Ventilate freely and make sure it does not dry out during the summer. Propagate by division or seeds in spring. Australia.

Sugarbush, Honeypot see **Protea cynaroides**
Summer Cypress see **Kochia scoparia trichophylla**
Summer Torch see **Billbergia pyramidalis**
Sun Cactus see **Heliocereus speciosus**
Sundew see **Drosera**
Sunn Hemp see **Crotalaria juncea**

SUTHERLANDIA (LEGUMINOSAE)

frutescens syn. **S. tomentosa**
A 5–15 ft shrub for the cool greenhouse, it has $2\frac{1}{2}$–$3\frac{1}{2}$ in. leaves divided into 13–21 long oval leaflets. The rich scarlet flowers are pea-like and borne in pendent 6–10 flowered clusters from the axils of the leaves. They are produced in June and are followed by a 2 in. inflated pod. Grow in the greenhouse border, or in large pots or tubs in loam-based compost. Ventilate freely in summer. Propagate by seeds in spring or by lateral stem cuttings with a heel in summer. S. Africa.

SWAINSONA (LEGUMINOSAE)

galegifolia
A very decorative plant with erect, flexible branches 1 ft or more in length. The leaves are divided into 11–21 oblong, blunt-ended and notched leaflets and the pea-like flowers open in July. These are usually orange-red, but also occur in shades from mauve through reds, browns and oranges to yellow. There is also a white variety. Grow in a proprietary peat mix in pots and place in a cool, well ventilated greenhouse. Propagate by seeds in spring. Queensland.

Swamp Lily see **Crinum × powellii**
Swedish Ivy see **Plectranthus oertendahlii**
Sweet Bouvardia see **Bouvardia longiflora**
Sweet Orange see **Citrus sinensis**
Sweet Potato Vine see **Ipomoea batatas**
Sword Brake see **Pteris ensiformis**
Sword Fern see **Nephrolepis**
Sword Lily, Australian see **Anigozanthos manglesii**
Sydney Golden Wattle see **Acacia longifolia**

SYNGONIUM (ARACEAE)

A genus of climbing plants akin to *Philodendron* with attractive leaves which are very decorative in the juvenile stage when they often have a lighter patterning. This fades as the plants mature. They make good plants for the house or for the warm greenhouse. Plant in pots of loam-based compost and keep well watered and in a humid atmosphere. Shade from direct sunlight, particularly in summer. Propagate by stem-tip or leaf-bud cuttings in summer.

auritum Five Fingers
The mid-green, glossy leaves are divided into 5 irregular sized lobes, all radiating out from the top of the shoots upon which they grow. They have a long terminal lobe, up to 10 in. long, smaller segments at the side, and 2 very small leaflets, often not exceeding an inch, next to the stem. Jamaica, Haiti, Mexico.

podophyllum African Evergreen
This species is an excellent pot plant in its juvenile stage, when it has dark, shining green, arrow-shaped leaves held erect on rigid stems. Many variegated forms are grown. When mature, this plant grows lobed leaves and makes a large, heavy leaved climbing plant. Mexico to Costa Rica.
'Albo-virens', the young leaves are shaded ivory white except for a green margin;
'Emerald Gem', the dark green leaves are glossier and more exactly arrow-shaped than the type, shorter stemmed and more compact.

vellozianum
A slender plant with arrow-shaped young leaves, becoming 5-lobed when adult. It is very similar to *S. podophyllum* in its young stage. Brazil.

Syzygium cuminii see **Eugenia jambolana**

T

TACCA (TACCACEAE)

A genus of curious, tropical evergreen perennials with terminal clusters of flowers which have conspicuous, leaf-like bracts, and long trailing 'tails' which can reach 1 ft in length. Grow in a proprietary peat compost and maintain warmth and humidity. Shade from direct sunshine. Keep well watered while growing and flowering, but allow to become almost dry during the resting period.

aspera
A $1\frac{1}{2}$–2 ft shrub with long stalked, broadly spear-shaped leaves and dense clusters of dull purple cup-shaped flowers. Beneath these grow 4 purple, leaf-like bracts and the long thread-like tails which give the plant such an unusual appearance. They are produced in summer. S.E. Asia.

chantrieri Cat's Whiskers, Devil Flower
The olive green, oval leaves rise on long stalks from the base of the plant, as do the curious brownish-purple flowers which have large, wing-like, very dark purple bracts and long thread-like filaments, almost whisker-like and 2 ft long. They are produced in early spring. Malaya.

leontopetaloides
The leaves of this species are divided into 3 leaflets, each of which is deeply cut and lobed. The clusters of purplish, funnel-shaped flowers have 4 large bracts and long filaments. They open in June. Tropics.

Tail Flower see **Anthurium andreanum**

TALINUM (PORTULACACEAE) Fame Flower

A genus of pretty, succulent plants with flat, rather fleshy leaves and clusters of 5-petalled flowers. Grow in a cool, airy greenhouse, using a compost of 2 parts loam-based compost and one part coarse sand. Water very sparingly in winter. Propagate by seeds in spring and by cuttings of lateral shoots in summer.

caffrum

A prostrate species with long narrow, fleshy leaves 1–1½ in. long and ¼–½ in. wide. The lemon yellow flowers are borne in small clusters of 1–3 on short stems carried in the axils of the upper leaves. S. & Tropical Africa.

guadalupense

A curious succulent species with thick, fleshy swellings above the ground from which an 8–15 in. branched stem, up to 1 in. thick, rises. It bears clusters of fleshy, spathulate leaves which are blue-green edged with red. Stalkless pink, starry flowers with conspicuous reddish stamens appear in summer. Mexico.

portulacifolium

An erect shrub to 18 in. in height, bearing ovate-triangular leaves, round-ended with a short point. The reddish-purple flowers are borne in a cluster at the ends of the branches and are produced in July and August. India.

Tangerine see **Citrus reticulata**
Tea Tree see **Leptospermum scoparium**
Tea Tree, Australian see **Leptospermum laevigatum**
Tea Tree, Botany Bay see **Correa alba**

TECOMA (BIGNONIACEAE)
stans syn. **Stenolobium stans** Yellow Elder, Yellow Bells

A 12 ft tropical evergreen flowering shrub with slender stems rising from the base and arching at the tips. It has light green leaves 6 in. long and divided into 5–11 narrow, toothed and slender pointed leaflets. At the ends of the branches are 6–9 in. pendulous clusters of bright yellow funnel-shaped flowers, 1½ in. across. They are produced from June to August. Grow in large pots or tubs of loam-based compost or in the cool greenhouse border. Water freely during the growing season and give good ventilation. Propagate by cuttings of lateral, non-flowering shoots with a heel, taken in late spring. W. Indies.

TECOMARIA (BIGNONIACEAE)
capensis Cape Honeysuckle

A 6–8 ft evergreen, semi-climbing shrub which is best trained against a wall in the cool greenhouse. It has long shining green leaves divided into 4 pairs of toothed leaflets each up to 2 in. in length. The 2 in. vermilion flowers have long stamens which protrude beyond the mouth of the curved funnel-shaped blooms. They are borne in dense clusters which open from May to September. S. Africa. **476.**

Teddy-bear Vine see **Cyanotis kewensis**
Telegraph Plant see **Desmodium gyrans**

TELOPEA (PROTEACEAE)

A genus of showy evergreen trees and shrubs of which the three described below make splendid plants for the cool or warm greenhouse. Grow in a border or tubs of a proprietary peat compost. Ventilate freely on warm days. Propagate by seeds in spring.

oreades Gippsland Waratah

A small tree or shrub with entire, narrow to oblong, deep green leaves, 6–8 in. long. It carries dense, roundish, terminal heads of very showy deep crimson flowers about 3–4 in. across. Each bloom has a 1 in. curving tube, split open along one side, with the long style protruding from it and curled over at the tip. The easiest of the 3 species to cultivate. Australia.

speciosissima Waratah

A magnificent shrub with 3–4 in. round heads of deep coral flowers with dark red bracts 1½–3 in. long. The 5–9 in. leaves are narrowly oval, coarsely toothed but not divided. Although growing easily to 5 or 6 ft in a warm greenhouse this is not an easy plant to flower. New South Wales. **477.**

truncata

A small evergreen shrub for the cool greenhouse with 2–5 in., slender,

lobed or toothed leaves. The 1 in. long flowers are a rich crimson and are tubular with a long, protruding style. They are produced in June in crowded terminal clusters 2–3 in. across. Tasmania.

Temple Bells see **Smithiantha cinnabarina**
Temple Tree see **Plumeria rubra**

TEPHROSIA (LEGUMINOSAE)
grandiflora

A 1–2 ft erect shrub with long leaves divided into 5–7 pairs of narrow to oblong leaflets. The pea-like flowers are red-brown on the outside and red inside. They are borne in long clusters opposite the leaves on the side branches, and in a close mass of clusters at the top of the stem. Grow in pots of loam-based compost or a proprietary peat mix. Ventilate freely on warm days. Propagate by seeds sown in spring or lateral stem cuttings with a heel in summer. S. Africa.

Testudinaria see **Dioscorea**

TETRANEMA (SCROPHULARIACEAE)
mexicanum syn. **Allophyton mexicanum** Mexican Foxglove

An upright, short stemmed perennial species which makes an attractive pot plant for the warm greenhouse or home. The small foxglove-like flowers are purplish violet with paler markings and they are borne in spikes at the end of the 6–8 in. slender purple stems. They are produced chiefly in summer but can bloom throughout almost the whole year. Plant in pots of loam-based compost, keep moist and the atmosphere humid. Shade on warm sunny days. Propagate by seeds or by division in spring. Mexico.

TETRASTIGMA (VITIDACEAE)

A genus of deciduous or evergreen climbing plants allied to *Cissus* with leaves divided into 3 or 5 lobes. Plant in loam or peat-based compost in pots or tubs in a warm room or greenhouse; minimum winter temperature 50–55°F.

voinieriana syn. **Vitis voinieriana**

A vigorous climbing plant with somewhat fleshy stems and trifoliate toothed leaves up to 5 in. long; they are glossy green above and hairy beneath. The tiny greenish flowers are rarely produced on small plants. Indo China. **478.**

Thistle, Torch see **Cereus**
Thorn, Kangaroo see **Acacia armata**
Thread Agave see **Agave filifera**

THRINAX (PALMAE) Peaberry Palm

A genus of slow growing palms, several of which are used as container plants for room decoration in their juvenile state. They have very ornamental foliage, the fronds growing in a fan-like semi-circle on a long arching stem. When mature they can exceed 15 ft so are only suitable for the largest greenhouse except when young. Grow in loam-based compost in a cool greenhouse, ventilating well in summer. Shade lightly during the hottest months. Water freely during the summer and keep just moist during winter. Propagate by seeds sown in spring.

argentea Silver Thatch, Silver Palm

This species is now correctly known as *Coccothrinax argentea*. The delicately arching fronds have long, sword shaped segments, tapering to points and silvery grey beneath. The segments are joined at the base of the fan-shaped leaf. At maturity the stem will reach 12 ft or more, but it is a slow growing and a beautifully decorative species. W. Indies.

THUNBERGIA (ACANTHACEAE) Clock Vine

A genus of annual and perennial climbers also including a few erect, perennials of which one, *T. natalensis* is described below. They have long tubular flowers opening at the mouth to 5 saucer-shaped lobes. All the species will grow best in the greenhouse border, though the smaller ones also make good pot plants in loam-based compost. The climbing species need wire or string supports. Keep just moist in winter, but water well in summer and shade from the hottest sun.

Propagate the woody species by stem cuttings taken in April or May, and the others by seeds sown in spring.

alata Black-eyed Susan
An annual twining plant which can reach 10 ft in its one season's growth. The leaves are ovate and mid-green and the flowers are borne singly in the axils from June to September. The individual blooms have flat orange yellow lobes with a chocolate-brown eye, and a deep purple tube; they are 2 in. across. S. Africa. **479.**

coccinea
A large, climbing species with branches exceeding 15 ft. The oval leaves are 5–8 in. long with a heart-shaped base, and the 1 in. flowers are red and borne in long, 6–18 in. pendulous clusters. They open in spring. India to Malaya.

fragrans
A climbing perennial with 2–3 in. oval, toothed leaves, the base with narrowly heart-shaped lobes. The 1¼ in. flowers are white and sometimes very fragrant, but not always; they are borne on 2–3 in. pedicels in the axils of the leaves in summer. India.

gibbsonii see under **T. gregorii**

grandiflora
A beautiful evergreen climber with 2–3 in., pale blue flowers borne in clusters from June to September. The leaves are up to 6 in. long, oval with a heart-shaped base, dark green and shining. A superb plant for a large greenhouse. India.

gregorii
Sometimes known as *gibbsonii* which is an allied species not generally in cultivation. A perennial climber having dark green, triangular leaves and 1½ in. waxy, orange flowers borne singly on long stalks from the axils of the leaves. They are produced from June to September. E. and S. Africa. **480.**

mysorensis
A 15 ft climber having 4–6 in. long pointed elliptical leaves. The funnel-shaped flowers have a 1½ in. purple tube, and yellow lobes, 2 in. across. A spring flowering species. India.

natalensis
A 2 ft erect sub-shrub, the flowers with a yellow tube curved upwards in bud, and opening to show blue, flat lobes. They are produced in July. The stalkless leaves are mid-green and narrowly oval. S. Africa. **481.**

TIBOUCHINA (MELASTOMATACEAE)
semidecandra syn. **T. urvilleana, Lasiandra macrantha**
The shrub usually grown under this name is *T. urvilleana*. It can reach 15 ft, and has deep green, oval leaves with a soft velvety texture which sometimes turn red as they fade. The 3–5 in. flowers are a rich glowing purple with a satin sheen and are borne almost throughout the year, though at their best from July to November. Grow preferably in the greenhouse borders, but pot or tub culture is also successful. Use a loam-based compost and grow in a warm greenhouse. Give some support and water well during the growing season. Propagate by cuttings with a heel, taken from non-flowering lateral shoots in spring or late summer. S. Brazil. **482.**

Tick Trefoil see **Desmodium**
Tiger Flower and **Peacock Tiger Flower** see **Tigridia pavonia**
Tiger-nut see **Cyperus esculentus**
Tiger's Jaws see **Faucaria**

TIGRIDIA (IRIDACEAE)
Intriguing bulbous plants with narrow, often pleated, leaves and curiously shaped and spotted flowers that seem to blend the characters of tulip and iris. They can be easily grown in pots or borders in a well ventilated cool greenhouse. Pot the bulbs 2 in. deep in spring, using a loam-based compost. Water sparingly until the shoots appear, then more freely. Keep dry when the foliage fades and repot annually. Propagate by seeds in spring or bulblets removed at potting time.

pavonia Tiger or Peacock Tiger Flower
A showy plant having yellow flowers with 3 large unmarked petals and

3 smaller which are red-brown spotted. Many named cultivars are grown. Mexico. **483.**
　'Alba', white petals with carmine spots;
　'Lutea', yellow, **484;**
　'Rubra', orange-red.

violacea
The bell-shaped flowers are violet, marked with white and rose purple and borne in spikes of 3–4 flowers enclosed at first by long, leafy bracts. The leaves all grow from the base of the plant and are 8–14 in. long. The flowers are produced in May. Mexico.

TILLANDSIA (BROMELIACEAE)
A genus of evergreen perennials, most of which grow on tree branches in the wild. These make interesting plants for pots or hanging baskets, needing a very warm, humid atmosphere to thrive. *T. usneoides* will grow attached to wires or twigs, but the other species require pots and grow best in a compost made up of equal parts of peat, sand and osmunda fibre. Water freely during the summer and keep in a warm greenhouse. Propagate by removing well developed offsets from the plants in summer.

cyanea Pink Quill
A rosette forming epiphytic species having long, grass-like leaves, grooved and lined with red-brown. From the centre rises the 2 in. flower head comprising overlapping ranks of green tinged pink bracts, from which the 2 in., 3-petalled violet-blue flowers protrude. Ecuador.

distachya
The 1 ft long narrow leaves are borne in a rosette and are pale green. The green bracts are borne on a 6 in. stem and form an overlapping spike from which the 1½ in. white, 3-petalled flowers emerge. British Honduras.

lindenii see **T. lindeniana**

lindeniana syn. **T. lindenii** Blue-flowered Torch
A showy species, the 15 in. long leaves being green above, purplish beneath and borne in a rosette. The 4–8 in. blade-like spike of flowers borne on a 6–12 in. stem is made up of deep rose-pink bracts and deep blue flowers with white markings in the throat; they are produced in the summer. Peru, Ecuador. **485.**

pulchella syn. **T. tenuifolia**
A small, tufted species with 4–6 in. leaves, narrow and fine pointed, with a thin covering of white hair. The overlapping bracts are dark red, forming a 4–6 in. spike, and almost concealing the white, blue or rose flowers. W. Indies, Brazil.

tenuifolia see **T. pulchella**

usneoides Spanish Moss, Old Man's Beard
A pendulous epiphyte with wiry stems and grey, thread-like leaves, 1–3 in. long giving the plant a mossy appearance. The small yellow-green flowers are sparingly produced throughout the summer. Tropical America. **486.**

Torch Thistle see **Cereus**

TORENIA (SCROPHULARIACEAE)
fournieri Wishbone Flower
An attractive annual species which makes an attractive pot plant with flowers abundantly produced from July to September. It is a bushy plant with narrow, finely toothed, pale green leaves and lilac-blue tubular flowers the large reflexed petals having deep purple, velvety blotches and a yellow mark on the bottom lip. Grow in pots in loam-based compost. Keep shaded from the hottest sun and give some twiggy support to the growing plants. Propagate by seed sown in March. Indochina. **487.**
　'Alba', a white flowered form;
　'Grandiflora', a large flowered strain.

Tortoise Plant see **Dioscorea elephantipes**
Touch-me-not see **Impatiens**

TRADESCANTIA (COMMELINACEAE) Spiderwort
A genus of perennial species of which the following are very popular

foliage plants for the house or greenhouse. The flowers are 3-petalled. Grow as pot plants or in hanging baskets in loam-based compost. Water well in summer and shade from direct sunshine. Repot each year in spring preferably, replace with spring rooted cuttings. Propagate by tip cuttings taken from spring to autumn.

albiflora Wandering Jew, Inch Plant

A low growing species with long stems which make it an ideal subject for the hanging basket. The plants in cultivation are almost all variegated cultivars, the type being green leaved. S. America.

'Albo-vittata', a large plant with bluish-green leaves 3–4 in. in length, banded and margined with white;

'Tricolor', the green leaves banded with white and purplish-pink stripes.

blossfeldiana Flowering Inch Plant

A robust, hairy, semi-erect species with waxy, dark green leaves, purple beneath. The pink-purple flowers have white centres and are freely produced from March to August or later. Argentina.

'Variegata' has the leaves creamy-white striped.

fluminensis Speedy Jenny

A sturdy trailing plant having green or purplish, wiry stems bearing bright green, oval leaves, often pale purple beneath. S. America.

'Aurea', green leaves with yellow variegation;

'Quicksilver', narrow lines of silvery-white variegation. **488;**

'Variegata', broader stripes of creamy-white variegation.

sillamontana White Velvet

A stiffer stemmed species densely covered with soft, fluffy white hairs, the leaves purple-tinted beneath, 1½–3 in. long and clasping the stem. The flowers are a rich carmine, opening in succession from early summer to late autumn. If allowed to become too cold or dry in winter this plant will die back to ground level, but will grow again in spring. A very attractive species. Mexico.

Transvaal Daisy see **Gerbera jamesonii**
Tree Cotton see **Gossypium arboreum**
Treefern see **Cibotium** and **Cyathea**
Treefern, Golden see **Dicksonia fibrosa**
Treefern, Woolly see **Dicksonia antarctica**
Tree Philodendron see **Philodendron bipinnatifidum**
Trefoil, St James see **Lotus jacobaeus**
Trefoil, Tick see **Desmodium**
Trembling Bracken see **Pteris tremula**

TRICHOCEREUS (CACTACEAE)

A distinctive genus with characteristic hairy flowering areoles. Column-shaped plants usually with many ribs, bearing night-flowering blooms, usually white and scented. The flower tubes are scaly and hairy, like *Echinopsis*. Sun lovers which prefer fairly high temperatures. For culture see under terrestrial cacti in the Introduction. Minimum winter temperature 40°F. Propagate by seed or cuttings.

candicans

Robust stems with 9–11 ribs, up to 3 ft high and 2–7 in. thick, freely branching from the base. The large areoles have yellowish spines, the 10–14 radials fanning out, and 1–4 thicker centrals, up to 4 in. long. The large, sweetly scented flowers are white, about 10 in. long and produced in summer. Argentina. **489.**

chiloensis

Tall but slow-growing species with dull green stems, 2–4 in. thick, sometimes branching from the base. There are 10–17 ribs bearing white woolly areoles with stout radial spines and 1–4 stronger centrals, sometimes 5 in. long. The large flowers, 6 in. long, are white with green, reddish rimmed outer petals, and open in summer. Chile.

coquimbanus

The stems grow to 3 ft high, and about 3 in. thick. They are light green with 12–13 ribs and brownish areoles bearing numerous curved radial spines and about 4 centrals, one being 3 in. long. The flowers, borne in summer, have pointed white inner petals contrasting with black hairs on the outers, are about 5 in. long. Chile.

schickendantzii

The erect dark green stem, 10 in.–2 ft tall and 1–2 in. thick, has about 16

ribs and branches from the base. The spines, about 10 radials and 1–4 thicker centrals, are short and yellow, turning to yellowish-brown then grey. The strongly scented flowers are large, 9 in. long, and white with black hairs on the tube side. A fast growing species, easily propagated by cuttings and much used as a grafting stock. Argentina.

spachianus

The stems, branched at the base, grow to about 4 ft high. It is light green with 10–15 ribs. Bristley yellow to brown spines grow from the curly white, softly woolly areoles. The large white flowers, to 8 in. long, are freely formed on ageing plants in summer. Also sometimes used as a stock for grafting weaker varieties. Avoid too much lime in the soil. Argentina.

TRICHOPILIA (ORCHIDACEAE)

An attractive genus of tree-dwelling (epiphytic) orchids with very showy flowers borne on leafless stems. The bulbs each bear one, rather leathery, erect leaf. They make excellent subjects for hanging pans or baskets growing in a compost of 2 parts osmunda fibre to 1 part sphagnum moss. Keep in the warm greenhouse, shaded from the hottest summer sunshine but in light, airy conditions. Propagate by division of large plants in summer after flowering.

coccinea

An early summer flowering species having large flowers with 2½ in. twisted, brownish petals and sepals with a deep red bell-shaped lip, white outside and on the margins. The central lobe is a deep pink with darker red streaks. One flower is borne on each of the 3–5 in. wiry stems from April to June. The leaves are 6–9 in., narrow and dark green. Costa Rica.

suavis

A beautiful plant with a hawthorn-like fragrance. The flowers are 4 in. across, creamy white, having a large, white-frilled lip spotted with red-purple and a yellow patch in the throat. They are produced in March and April, the flowers being very long-lasting and borne in clusters of 3–4. The large, broad leaves can reach 12 in. in length. Costa Rica.

tortilis

A species with most attractive flowers; the 2½ in. yellow-green petals and sepals are purple along the centre and are spirally twisted with 2 or 3 turns. The bell-like lip has an undulate edge and is white outside and yellowish white within, bearing red and yellow markings. The 5–7 in. leaves are dark green and somewhat wavy. Mexico.

Trichosporum see **Aeschynanthus**
Trigger Plant see **Stylidium graminifolium**
Triplet Lily see **Brodiaea coronaria**
Triteleia laxa see **Brodiaea laxa**
Trompetilla, Scarlet see **Bouvardia triphylla**

TROPAEOLUM (TROPAEOLACEAE) Nasturtium

A genus of annual and perennial species of which the 2 described are tuberous rooted perennials suitable for an airy, cool greenhouse. Grow in pots of loam-based compost and provide a support of twiggy sticks or wires. Pot the tubers in summer and water very sparingly until growth appears. Water more freely when in full growth, but always with care. Overwatering is a frequent cause of rotting or death. Ventilate freely on sunny days. When the foliage starts to yellow, dry off completely. Repot annually. Propagate by seeds when ripe or by dividing the tubers at potting time.

azureum

A fragile-stemmed species, rarely more than 2 ft long in cultivation, bearing small, somewhat greyish leaves, divided into 5 narrow, pointed lobes. The rounded flowers, up to 1 in. wide, are a deep velvety violet-blue with a whitish eye and a short brownish spur. They appear in autumn. This is a difficult species to maintain long in cultivation, needing careful watering and a dry, airy atmosphere. Chile.

tricolorum

This slender stemmed climber can reach 3 ft or more long. The small, neat leaves are divided into 5 or 6 oval leaflets and make a pleasing foil to the quaint, but showy, hooded flowers. These have large, curved, red or orange spurs, maroon-tipped sepals and small lemon yellow petals. They open between March and May. Chile, Bolivia. **490.**

Trumpet, Fiddler's see **Sarracenia drummondii**
Trumpet Lily, White see **Lilium longiflorum**
Trumpets see **Sarracenia flava**
Tuberose see **Polianthes tuberosa**

TULIPA (LILIACEAE) Tulip ✳

All the *Tulipa* species and hybrid cultivars are hardy and mainly used for display in the open garden. However, they respond well to pot culture and make a colourful display in the home and conservatory early in the year. Pot the bulbs in October or November, using any proprietary compost and plunge in a bed of sand, ashes or peat. Alternatively place in a cool room or cellar. When the shoots are an inch or so tall bring into the light and a temperature of 50–55°F. Make sure that the compost does not dry out when buds are visible or they may abort or fail to open properly. The following cultivars are recommended for pot culture:

Single early-flowered
   'Brilliant Star' scarlet, **491**;
   'Diana' white;
   'Keizerskroon' yellow striped red.
Double early
   'Murillo' pink and white;
   'Electra' mauve-pink;
   'Marechal Niel' glossy yellow.
Darwin (May flowering)
   'Queen of the Bartigons' clear pink and white;
   'Bartigon' geranium red;
   'Sunkist' brilliant gold.

Tulip Cattleya see **Cattleya citrina**

TWEEDIA (ASCLEPIADACEAE)
coerulea syn. **Amblyopetalum caeruleum** ✳

A twining sub-shrub remarkable for its flowers which have 5 narrow petals. These open pale blue with a green tinge and change first to purple and finally to lilac. They are open in July. The hairy leaves are spear-shaped, rounded at base and tip but ending with a short point. A beautiful climbing plant when the flowers are open in all their shades and colours. Grow in the greenhouse border or in pots of loam-based compost and provide support. Ventilate freely on warm days. Propagate by seeds or cuttings of basal shoots in spring. Argentina.

U

Ugni molinae see **Myrtus ugni**
Umbrella Grass see **Cyperus alternifolius**
Umbrella Tree, Queensland see **Schefflera actinophylla**
Unicorn Plant see **Martynia louisiana**

URCEOLINA (AMARYLLIDACEAE)
peruviana ✳

A beautiful bulbous species having 6–8 in. long pointed, spear-shaped leaves clearly marked with ridged veins. The brilliant red tubular flowers are borne in clusters of 2–6, each 1½ in. long and having oval petal-like lobes. They are carried on 8–14 in. stems in September. Pot the bulbs in summer, with the upper half above the soil surface. Use a loam-based compost and keep well ventilated. Propagate by removing offset bulbs when repotting, or by seed sown in spring. Peru.

URGINEA (LILIACEAE)
maritima Sea Onion, Sea Squill ✳

A remarkable plant which has a large onion-like bulb. In the spring it bears 10–20, fleshy, grey-green, strap-shaped leaves 12–18 in. long. These die off during the summer, and the autumn produced flowers grow in a long spike on 3 ft reddish stalks. They are ¼–½ in. across, whitish with green markings and are carried in dense cylindrical spikes up to 12 in. in length. Plant in summer in large pots of loam-based compost in the cool greenhouse, leaving half the bulb above the level of the compost. Water freely while in leaf and once the flowering spikes have emerged. During the summer resting period allow to become dry and store in a warm sunny place. Propagate by offsets when re-potting or by seeds sown in autumn. Mediterranean.

Urn Plant see **Aechmea fasciata**

V

VALLOTA (AMARYLLIDACEAE)
speciosa syn. **V. purpurea** Scarborough Lily ✳

A delightful bulbous plant with 18–24 in., strap-shaped, bright green evergreen leaves. It has a cluster of up to 10 3–4 in. bright scarlet funnel-shaped flowers which are held stiffly erect on the 2–3 ft fleshy, hollow stem. They are produced from June to September. Plant in pots of loam-based compost in spring, allowing the tips of the bulbs to remain above the surface. Keep watered throughout the year as the plant is continuously replacing old leaves. Propagate by removing offsets when potting. A good plant for the cool greenhouse or home. S. Africa. **492.**

VANDA (ORCHIDACEAE)

A genus of tropical, evergreen orchids with colourful, showy flowers, most species needing warm greenhouse treatment. Grow in pans or baskets in a hanging position, in a compost of 2 parts osmunda fibre to 1 part sphagnum moss. Keep well watered from March to October and sparingly the rest of the year. Ventilate well and shade from hot sun in summer. Propagate by removing side shoots in March and April.

caerulea ✳

A delightful species with 2½–4 in. wide light blue flowers, sometimes having darker blue markings, and bearing a deep purple-blue lip. They are borne in clusters of 8–20 from August to November on strong stems 2 or 3 ft in height. The 5–12 in. leathery, strap-shaped leaves are deeply grooved and are borne in 2 overlapping rows up the length of the flowering stem. Many named cultivars are grown. Assam.

parishii ✳

The 2 in. flowers are strongly scented and have yellow-green petals dotted with reddish-brown. The lip has a red-purple central lobe, edged with white. The blooms open during summer, being borne on an erect leafy stem. Each leaf is 6–9 in. in length, fleshy and bright green. Burma.

roxburghii syn. **V. tessellata** ✳

An often fragrant plant with clusters of 6–12 flowers, each 2 in. across. The petals are light green with brown markings and white on the reverse. The violet-purple lip has white sides, while the short spur is pink. They are borne on erect, stems which carry 5–9 in. long narrow overlapping leaves. S.E. Asia.

teres ✳

A 2–5 flowered species with long stems which can reach 6 ft or more and need support. The sepals are creamy white, those at the sides being flushed with pink and twisted; the petals are deeper pink. The lip tip is a magenta-red and the throat orange or yellow with red markings. They are borne from June to August. The leaves and stem are dark green. Burma.

tessellata see **V. roxburghii**

tricolor ✳

A robust species with stems up to 7 ft with thick, strap-shaped leaves borne along it. The clusters of fragrant flowers are borne from October to February and bear pale creamy-pink petals which have brown spotting within and white on the reverse. The 3-lobed lip is deep pink, the middle lobe darker than the outer. One of the easiest vandas for the amateur to try. Java.

Variegated Wild Pineapple see **Ananas bracteatus** 'Striatus'
Vegetable Sponge see **Luffa cylindrica**
Velour Philodendron see **Philodendron andreanum**

VELTHEIMIA (LILIACEAE)
capensis see under **V. viridifolia**

viridifolia Forest Lily ✳ 🍂

A handsome bulbous plant having a rosette of 8–12 broad, strap-shaped leaves with strongly undulate margins. They are a bright intense green and are shiny, almost as if they had been varnished. From the rosette rises, in spring, a red spotted, fleshy stem 1–1½ ft long, which carries a spike of up to 60 tubular, nodding flowers. These are 1½ in. long, yellow to pink or red, and green-tipped. The form commonly met with in cultivation has pink flowers. Grow in pots of a proprietary peat mix or loam-based compost and place in a cold greenhouse or in the home. Shade from direct sun in summer. Water sparingly when first potted in late summer then more freely when in full growth. Dry off when the leaves begin to yellow. The plant often cultivated as *V. capensis* probably belongs to this species, the true *V. capensis* being a different species. S. Africa. **493.**

Velvet Alloplectus see **Alloplectus capitatus**
Velvet Flower see **Sparaxis tricolor**
Velvet-leaf Vine see **Philodendron micans**
Velvet Plant see **Gynura aurantiaca**

× VENIDIO-ARCTOTIS

Venidium fastuosum has been hybridized with *Arctotis grandis* and *A. breviscapa* to produce this showy race of hybrid cultivars. They resemble *Venidium fastuosum* in general habit, but with arctotis-shaped flowers in shades of crimson, orange, purple and ivory white. **494.**

VENIDIUM (COMPOSITAE)

A group of handsome annuals and perennials bearing large daisy flowers having contrastingly coloured centres. Grow in the cool greenhouse border or in pots of loam-based compost. Ventilate freely on warm days. Propagate by basal or lateral stem cutting in summer or spring or by seeds sown in spring.

decurrens
A sparingly branched plant up to 1½ ft tall. The leaves are roughly lyre-shaped, covered with white cobwebby hairs, particularly when young. From July to October are borne a succession of bright yellow daisies, 2 in. across, with a dark brown or almost black central disk. S. Africa. **495.**

fastuosum Monarch of the Veldt, Namaqualand Daisy
This species is somewhat more robust than *V. decurrens*, having similar leaves but with several basal lobes, grey-hairy on both surfaces. The daisy flowers are most handsome, 5 in. across and rich golden yellow marked purple at the base. The disk is brown-purple or black. Unfortunately the flowers remain closed in dull weather. S. Africa. **496.**

Venus's Fly Trap see **Dionaea muscipula**
Verbena, Lemon see **Lippia citriodora**

VINCA (APOCYNACEAE) Periwinkle
rosea syn. **Catharanthus roseus** Madagascar Periwinkle
An erect evergreen perennial plant, in fact a shrub, but usually grown as an annual pot plant for the greenhouse. *Catharanthus* is now considered to be its correct name. It has mid to deep green shining leaves and 1–1½ in. rosy-pink flowers with a darker eye which are produced from April to October. Grow in pots of a proprietary peat compost, keep well ventilated and watered throughout the summer. Propagate by seeds in spring or by stem cuttings in summer. Many named cultivars are grown. Tropics. **497.**

Vine, Bleeding Heart see **Clerodendrum speciosissimum**
Vine, Coral see **Antigonon leptopus**
Vine, Cypress see **Quamoclit pennata**
Vine, Giant Potato see **Solanum wendlandii**
Vine, Goldfish see **Columnea microphylla**
Vine, Kangaroo see **Cissus antarctica**
Vine, Lipstick see **Aeschynanthus lobbianus**
Vine, Rex Begonia see **Cissus discolor**
Vine, Silver see **Scindapsus pictus**
Vine, Snake see **Hibbertia scandens**
Vine, Sweet Potato see **Ipomoea batatas**
Vine, Teddy-bear see **Cyanotis kewensis**
Vine, Velvet-leaf see **Philodendron micans**
Vine, Wonga-wonga see **Pandorea pandorana**
Vine, Zebra Basket see **Aeschynanthus marmoratus**
Violet, African see **Saintpaulia ionantha**
Violet Mist Flower see **Eupatorium ianthinum**

Violet, Persian see **Exacum affine**
Viper's Bugloss see **Echium**
Vitis voinieriana see **Tetrastigma voinieriana**
Voodoo Plant see **Amorphophallus rivieri**

VRIESEA (BROMELIACEAE)

A genus of very ornamental plants grown both for their curiously marked and coloured evergreen leaves, and for their flower spikes of which the conspicuous part comprises large, colourful bracts. They make good, decorative plants for the home and for the warm greenhouse. Grow in pots in a compost of equal parts sand, peat and sphagnum moss and maintain warmth and humidity. Shade from direct sun in summer. Water freely during the summer months. Propagation by seed is possible, but it takes a long time to produce flowering plants and it is best to remove rooted offsets in spring or summer.

fenestralis Netted Vriesea
This species is grown for its rosette of recurved yellow-green leaves which are covered with a close network of green veins and cross lines and have purplish circles beneath. The fragrant, sulphur-yellow, tubular flowers are borne in a loose spike at the end of the 18 in. stems and open in summer. They are not however as attractive a feature as the decorative leaves. Brazil. **498.**

heiroglyphica King of the Bromeliads
A superb species having a large rosette of yellow-green leaves reaching 18 in. in length and 4 in. in breadth. They are marked with a deep green to purplish-brown patterning, forming irregular bands like hieroglyphics, the colour deepening towards the centre of the rosette. The flowers are yellow and tubular, 2½ in. long and are carried in a long spike on a 2½ ft stalk. They open in spring but are not regularly produced. Brazil.

psittacina Dwarf Painted Feather
A smaller plant than the preceding species, the thin, yellowish-green leaves reaching only 8 in. in length. They are borne in a rosette, from which rises the 10–12 in. flowering stem. This bears a long flower head made up of overlapping, red fleshy bracts with yellow margins from which the small yellow, green-tipped flowers just protrude. Brazil, Paraguay.

regina
A magnificent plant for the greenhouse. The broad green leaves are 7 in. across and 4 ft in length with recurved ends, and grow in a dense rosette. The flowering stem can reach 7 ft, bearing a branched head of jasmine-scented flowers. These are white, fading to dull yellow and are borne within overlapping, deep pink bracts in summer. Brazil.

speciosa see **V. splendens**

splendens syn. **V. speciosa** Flaming Sword
A good foliage plant, the large leaves being 15 in. in length and 2½ in. across, dark green with dark purple transverse bands. They are borne in an elegant, flared rosette. From it rises the 18 in. flowering stem which bears a blade-like spike of brilliant red bracts, closely overlapping in 2 rows, and small yellow flowers almost concealed within them. The overall length of the spike can be as much as 15 in. Trinidad, N.E. South America. **499.**

× VUYLSTEKEARA

A complex hybrid group involving species of *Cochlioda*, *Miltonia* and *Odontoglossum*. In general habit and flower form they tend to resemble the *Odontoglossum* parent. **500.**

W

Wandering Jew see **Tradescantia albiflora**
Wandering Jew see **Zebrina pendula**
Wand Flower see **Sparaxis**
Waratah see **Telopea speciosissima**
Waratah, Gippsland see **Telopea oreades**
Water Hyacinth, Floating see **Eichhornea speciosa**

WATSONIA (IRIDACEAE)

A genus of handsome bulbous plants in appearance midway between gladiolus and montbretia. The leaves are long and sword-like, and the tubular to trumpet shaped flowers are borne within enfolding bracts in stiffly held spikes. Grow in a loam based or proprietary peat compost with coarse sand added. Pot the corms in autumn and ventilate the cool greenhouse on all sunny days. Water freely when in full leaf, less at other times of the year. Propagate by seeds or by offset corms at potting time.

beatricis

The $1\frac{1}{2}$–$2\frac{1}{2}$ ft green leaves have a thickened, yellowish border. The showy flowers are large, up to 3 in. in length, deep orange red, with the long tube opening to 6 spreading and recurved lobes. They are produced from July to September, several individual blooms being open at the same time. S. Africa.

coccinea

The large, bright crimson flowers have a curved tube, 2–$2\frac{1}{2}$ in. long and 1 in. spreading lobes. They are borne in a loose spike on a 1 ft unbranched stem opening in June and July. The narrow, basal leaves are 6–9 in. in length. S. Africa.

fourcadei

A 3 ft species with 1–2 ft basal leaves and a long, loose cluster of large coral-red flowers. Each blossom has a tube 2 in. in length and spreading petals 1 in. across. They are borne in June. S. Africa.

'Maculata', a variety with larger flowers having purple blotches at the mouth of the tube.

tabularis

A tall species which can reach 5–6 ft. The leaves are 2–$3\frac{1}{2}$ ft in length and the flowering spike is branched. The blooms have a bright coral-red tube, and are the same colour on the outside of the outer 3 petals. The inside of the open flower is yellow to a pale rose pink. A delightful species. S. Africa.

Wax Plant see **Hoya carnosa**
Wax Privet see **Peperomia glabella**
Water Lemon see **Passiflora laurifolia**
Water-lily see **Nymphaea**
Watermelon Peperomia see **Peperomia argyreia**
Water Poppy see **Hydrocleys commersonii**
Wattle, Cootamunda see **Acacia baileyana**
Wattle, Silver see **Acacia dealbata**
Wattle, Sydney Golden see **Acacia longifolia**
Weeping Fig see **Ficus benjamina**

WESTRINGIA (LABIATAE)
rosmariniformis

A small, neat shrub 2–3 ft high which has 1 in. long, narrow leathery leaves, very much like those of rosemary, green and shining above and silvery beneath. The pale blue flowers are borne in leafy spikes at the ends of the branches, the blooms having a short tube opening to 2 lips, the upper large and 2-lobed, the lower 3-lobed and somewhat spreading. It is a good plant for the cool greenhouse. Grow in large pots of a proprietary peat compost with coarse sand added. Ventilate freely on all sunny days. Propagate by lateral stem cuttings, preferably with a heel. Pinch out the growing tip of young plants to encourage bushy growth. Australia.

White Arum Lily see **Zantedeschia aethiopica**
White Kaleidoscope Flower see **Streptanthera cuprea**
White Lily Turf see **Ophiopogon jaburan**
White Paint Brush see **Haemanthus albiflos**
White Pine, New Zealand see **Podocarpus dacrydioides**
White Raintree see **Brunfelsia undulata**
White Sails see **Spathiphyllum wallisii**
White Trumpet Lily see **Lilium longiflorum**
White Velvet see **Tradescantia sillamontana**
Wild Pineapple, Variegated see **Ananas bracteatus** 'Striatus'

× WILSONARA (ORCHIDACEAE)

A group of hybrids between 3 genera of orchids, *Cochlioda*, *Odontoglossum* and *Oncidium*. They are generally similar in form to *Odontoglossum* species and flower from November to May. Grow in perforated

pots or baskets in a compost of 2 parts osmunda fibre to 1 part sphagnum moss. Keep the greenhouse well ventilated and the plants moist, shading from hot sun in summer. Propagate by division when repotting in spring or early autumn. Many cultivars exist, typified by such groups as Lyoth, **501.**

Lyoth 'Gold', dark red to orange flowers;
Lyoth 'Ruby', has many flowered spikes of scarlet-red blooms;
'Tangerine', orange-yellow flowers.

Window Linden see **Sparmannia africana**
Winter Cattleya see **Cattleya trianaei**
Winter Cherry see **Solanum capsicastrum**
Winter-sweet see **Acokanthera spectabilis**
Wishbone Flower see **Torenia fournieri**
Wonga-wonga Vine see **Pandorea pandorana**
Wood Sorrel see **Oxalis**
Woolly Treefern see **Dicksonia antarctica**

Y

Yam see **Dioscorea**
Yatay Palm see **Butia**
Yellow Arum Lily see **Zantedeschia pentlandii**
Yellow Bells see **Tecoma stans**
Yellow Calico Plant see **Alternanthera bettzickiana** 'Aurea Nana'
Yellow Elder see **Tecoma stans**
Yellow Flax see **Reinwardtia trigyna**
Yellow Ginger see **Hedychium flavum**
Yellow Granadilla see **Passiflora laurifolia**
Yellow Pitcher Plant see **Sarracenia flava**
Yesterday, Today and Tomorrow see **Brunfelsia calycina**

Z

ZANTEDESCHIA (ARACEAE) Calla

A genus of attractive spring and summer flowering plants for the cool greenhouse. They have dark green, fleshy arrow-shaped leaves and striking arum-like flowers. Grow in large pots in a proprietary peat compost and keep the pots just moist until the first shoots appear. Water freely until the flowers fade. Shade from the hottest sunshine. Propagate by removing offsets or by dividing the tuber-like rhizomes when repotting in January and February. The exception to this is *Z. aethiopica* which should be repotted in late autumn.

aethiopica White Arum Lily, Common Calla

The tuft of mid to dark green leaves is 2–3 ft high, and the flowering stems which rise from it can reach 5 ft. These carry a single waxy white spathe, 5–9 in. long which surrounds a conspicuous yellow spadix. They are produced from March to June. S. Africa. **502.**

albomaculata Spotted Calla

A slender plant having tufts of 1–2 ft, arrow-shaped leaves which are marked with whitish, semi-opaque spots. The creamy white trumpet shaped spathe is 4–5 in. long and blotched with crimson at the base. S. Africa.

elliottiana Golden Calla

The 12 in. leaves are oval, heart-shaped at the base and dark green, with transparent spots which appear white. The bell-shaped spathe is a rich yellow, greenish at its base and opening to a wide mouth. It is borne on a $1\frac{1}{2}$–2 ft stalk in June. **503.**

melanoleuca Black-throated Calla

The arrow-shaped leaves are 6–12 in. long and are marked with transparent spots. The small, wide spreading spathe is pale yellow with a black patch at the base and is borne on a slender stem in summer. Natal.

pentlandii Yellow Arum Lily

A 2 ft high species having mid green, arrow-shaped leaves and tall stems bearing single flowers. These have a wide, deep golden yellow spathe, 6 in. in length, with purple blotches at the base. They are produced in June. S. Africa.

rehmannii Pink Arum Lily or Calla

A distinctive species having slender, tapering leaves with transparent streaks, appearing white against the bright green surface. The spathes are widely flaring at the mouth and vary from cream to rose-pink to purple-red inside and are produced from April to June. S. Africa. **504.**

Zebra Basket Vine see **Aeschynanthus marmoratus**
Zebra Plant see **Aphelandra squarrosa, Calathea zebrina** and **Cryptanthus zonatus**

ZEBRINA (COMMELINACEAE)
A genus with 2 species which are attractive foliage plants for the house or greenhouse. They are trailing perennials which are good for hanging baskets as well as pots, or for ground cover. Grow in a loam-based or proprietary peat compost. Keep well ventilated but lightly shaded during summer. Propagate by stem-tip cuttings taken from May to August.

pendula Wandering Jew
A fleshy trailing plant having $2\frac{1}{2}$ in. ovate leaves purple beneath, and green to purple above with 2 silvery bands. 3-petalled, purple-pink flowers, $\frac{1}{2}$ in. across are borne within leaf-like bracts from June to September. Mexico. **505.**
   'Quadricolor', a very colourful form with rose-purple and white leaves, suffused with purple beneath.

purpusii
A strong growing plant, its $2-2\frac{1}{2}$ in. ovate leaves green with a purple flush above, and a shining, bright purple beneath. The 3-petalled flowers are lavender and are produced in autumn. Mexico.

ZEPHYRANTHES (AMARYLLIDACEAE) Zephyr Lily
A genus of attractive bulbous plants with narrow strap-shaped leaves and solitary flowers borne on a hollow stem. These are tunnel-shaped, opening outwards to show 6 spreading or incurved petals. An attractive genus for the cool greenhouse. Grow in a proprietary peat compost, watering well while growing, and allowing to become almost dry when dormant. Repot every 3 or 4 years and propagate by offset bulbs at repotting time or by seeds sown in spring.

candida Flower of the Western Wind
A subtropical evergreen species with dark green, fleshy leaves. The 4-8 in. stem bears white blooms, sometimes with a faint pink flush. They are crocus-like and up to 2 in. long, appearing in September and October. Argentine, Uruguay. **506.**

citrina
The 8-14 in. narrow strap-shaped leaves appear at the same time as the golden yellow flowers. These are borne on a 5-10 in. stem and have a green tube and spreading tips to the petals. They are produced from June to September. British Guiana.

grandiflora
A most attractive plant with 1 ft narrow, almost grass-like basal leaves and solitary rose-pink flowers, funnel shaped, the long tube opening to 3-4 in. across the spreading petals at the mouth. They are borne on the 5-8 in. stems in June and July. Central America, W. Indies.

rosea
The 8 in. narrow, strap-shaped leaves curve downwards, almost to the ground, exposing the $3\frac{1}{2}-7$ in. stem which bears the solitary pink flowers. These are $1-1\frac{1}{2}$ in. long, and $\frac{1}{2}$ in. across at the mouth. They are borne from July to December. Guatemala, W. Indies.

Zephyr Lily see **Zephyranthes**
Zonal Geranium see **Pelargonium zonale**

ZYGOCACTUS (CACTACEAE)
In Britain and the United States, this genus is considered now to be included in *Schlumbergera*, but it seems that this is not recognized in some countries, and plants are still sold under the old name. To add to the confusion, plants are still sometimes sold under the even older name of *Epiphyllum*. It is possible that further clarification of the position may take place, but the classification adopted here is that current at the time of printing.

truncatus see **Schlumbergera truncata**

ZYGOPETALUM (ORCHIDACEAE)
mackayi
A striking orchid, the mid-green leaves 8-10 in. in length, curving over as they lengthen. The 12-24 in. flowering stem bears 5-7 flowers. These are fragrant and have narrow, wavy green and brown blotched sepals and petals, 2 in. across, and a full, rounded lip, slightly undulate, white with pinky spots and streaks. They are produced from November to February. Grow in the cool greenhouse in baskets or pans in a compost of 2 parts peat, 2 parts loam and one part sphagnum moss. Shade and maintain humidity in summer. Ventilate on all warm sunny days and water freely throughout the year. Propagate by division when re-potting in spring. Brazil.